Lecture Notes in Computer S

Edited by G. Goos, J. Hartmanis, and J.

Springer
Berlin
Heidelberg
New York
Barcelona
Hong Kong
London
Milan
Paris
Tokyo

Michael J. Wooldridge   Gerhard Weiß
Paolo Ciancarini (Eds.)

Agent-Oriented Software Engineering II

Second International Workshop, AOSE 2001
Montreal, Canada, May 29, 2001
Revised Papers and Invited Contributions

Springer

Series Editors

Gerhard Goos, Karlsruhe University, Germany
Juris Hartmanis, Cornell University, NY, USA
Jan van Leeuwen, Utrecht University, The Netherlands

Volume Editors

Michael J. Wooldridge
The University of Liverpool. Department of Computer Science
Chadwick Building, Peach Street, Liverpool L69 7ZF, UK
E-mail: M.J.Wooldridge@csc.liv.ac.uk

Gerhard Weiß
Technische Universität München, Institut für Informatik
80290 München, Germany
E-mail: weissg@informatik.tu-muenchen.de

Paolo Ciancarini
University of Bologna, Dipartimento di Scienze dell'Informazione
Mura Anteo Zamboni 7, 40127 Bologna, Italy
E-mail: ciancarini@cs.unibo.it

Cataloging-in-Publication Data applied for

Die Deutsche Bibliothek - CIP-Einheitsaufnahme

Agent oriented software engineering II : second international workshop ;
revised paper and invited contributions / AOSE 2001, Montreal, Canada, May
29, 2001. Michael J. Wooldridge ... (ed.). - Berlin ; Heidelberg ; New York ;
Barcelona ; Hong Kong ; London ; Milan ; Paris ; Tokyo : Springer, 2002
  (Lecture notes in computer science ; Vol. 2222)
  ISBN 3-540-43282-5

CR Subject Classification (1998): D.2, I.2.11, F.3, D.1, C.2.4

ISSN 0302-9743
ISBN 3-540-43282-5 Springer-Verlag Berlin Heidelberg New York

Springer-Verlag Berlin Heidelberg New York
a member of BertelsmannSpringer Science+Business Media GmbH

http://www.springer.de

© Springer-Verlag Berlin Heidelberg 2002
Printed in Germany

Typesetting: Camera-ready by author, data conversion by PTP-Berlin, Stefan Sossna
Printed on acid-free paper   SPIN: 10840931   06/3142   5 4 3 2 1 0

Preface

Over the past three decades, software engineers have derived a progressively better understanding of the characteristics of complexity in software. It is now widely recognized that *interaction* is probably the most important single characteristic of complex software. Software architectures that contain many dynamically interacting components, each with their own thread of control, and engaging in complex coordination protocols, are typically orders of magnitude more complex to correctly and efficiently engineer than those that simply compute a function of some input through a single thread of control.

Unfortunately, it turns out that many (if not most) real-world applications have precisely these characteristics. As a consequence, a major research topic in computer science over at least the past two decades has been the development of tools and techniques to model, understand, and implement systems in which interaction is the norm. Indeed, many researchers now believe that in future, computation itself will be understood chiefly as a process of interaction.

Since the 1980s, software agents and multi-agent systems have grown into what is now one of the most active areas of research and development activity in computing generally. There are many reasons for the current intensity of interest, but certainly one of the most important is that the concept of an agent as an autonomous system, capable of interacting with other agents in order to satisfy its design objectives, is a natural one for software designers. Just as we can understand many systems as being composed of essentially passive objects, which have state, and upon which we can perform operations, so we can understand many others as being made up of interacting, semi-autonomous agents.

This recognition has led to the growth of interest in agents as a new paradigm for software engineering. The AOSE 2001 workshop sought to examine the credentials of agent-based approaches as a software engineering paradigm, and to gain an insight into what agent-oriented software engineering will look like. AOSE 2001, building on the success of AOSE 2000 (Lecture Notes in Computer Science, Volume 1957, Springer-Verlag), was held at the Autonomous Agents conference in Montreal, Canada, in May 2001. Some 33 papers were submitted to AOSE 2001, following a call for papers on all aspects of agent oriented software engineering, and particularly the following:

- Methodologies for agent-oriented analysis and design
- Relationship of AOSE to other SE paradigms (e.g., OO)
- UML and agent systems
- Agent-oriented requirements analysis and specification
- Refinement and synthesis techniques for agent-based specifications
- Verification and validation techniques for agent-based systems
- Software development environments and CASE tools for AOSE
- Standard APIs for agent programming
- Formal methods for agent-oriented systems, including specification and verification logics

- Engineering large-scale agent systems
- Experiences with field-tested agent systems
- Best practice in agent-oriented development
- Market and other economic models in agent systems engineering
- Practical coordination and cooperation frameworks for agent systems

The present volume contains revised versions of the 14 papers presented at AOSE 2001, together with 5 invited contributions, by Federico Bergenti et al., Jürgen Lind, Morris Sloman, Wamberto Vasconcelos et al., and Eric Yu. It is structured into five parts, reflecting the main issues that arose at the event. We believe this volume reflects the state of the art in the field very well, and hope it will stimulate further exciting development.

Acknowledgments. Thanks to Alfred Hofmann at Springer for his continued support, and for giving us the wonderful volume number (2222!). Thanks also to Adele Howe, the Autonomous Agents 2001 workshops chair, for her excellent technical support. Last – but not least – we would like to gratefully acknowledge all the contributions to the workshop: by the authors, the participants, and the reviewers.

November 2001   M.J. Wooldridge
                                                                      G. Weiß
                                                                   P. Ciancarini

Organizing Committee

Michael Wooldridge (chair)
    University of Liverpool, UK
    email: M.J.Wooldridge@csc.liv.ac.uk

Paolo Ciancarini (co-chair)
    University of Bologna, Italy
    email: ciancarini@cs.unibo.it

Gerhard Weiss (co-chair)
    Technical University of Munich, Germany
    email: weissg@in.tum.de

Program Committee

Bernard Bauer (Germany)

Federico Bergenti (Italy)

Stefan Bussmann (Germany)

Chris Hankin (UK)

Michael Huhns (USA)

Carlos Iglesias (Spain)

Nicholas Jennings (UK)

Liz Kendall (Australia)

David Kinny (Australia)

Joost Kok (The Netherlands)

Yannis Labrou (USA)

Alex van Lamsweerde (France)

Jaeho Lee (Korea)

Jürgen Lind (Germany)

Jörg Müller (Germany)

James Odell (USA)

Andrea Omicini (Italy)

Van Parunak (USA)

Robert Tolksdorf (Germany)

Jan Treur (The Netherlands)

Leon Sterling (Australia)

Franco Zambonelli (Italy)

Table of Contents

Part IV: Agent-Oriented Requirements Capture & Specification

Part V: Analysis and Design

Representing Social Structures in UML

H. Van Dyke Parunak[1] and James J. Odell[2]

[1] ERIM, PO Box 13400 1, Ann Arbor,
MI 48113-4001 USA
vparunak@erim.org
http://www.erim.org/~vparunak/

[2] James Odell Associates, 3646 West Huron River Drive, Ann Arbor
MI 48103-9489 USA
jodell@compuserve.com
http://www.jamesodell.com

Abstract. From a software engineering perspective, agent systems are a specialization of object-oriented (OO) systems, in which individual objects have
their own threads of control and their own goals or sense of purpose. Engineering such systems is most naturally approached as an extension of object-oriented
systems engineering. In particular, the Unified Modeling Language (UML) can
be naturally extended to support the distinctive requirements of multi-agent
systems. One such requirement results from the increasing emphasis on the correspondence between multi-agent systems and social systems. Sociological
analogies are proving fruitful models for agent-oriented constructions, while so-
ciologists increasingly use agents as a modeling tool for studying social systems. We combine several existing organizational models for agents, including
AALAADIN, dependency theory, interaction protocols, and holonics, in a general
theoretical framework, and show how UML can be applied and extended to
capture constructions in that framework.

1 Introduction

From a software engineering perspective, agent systems are a specialization of object-
based systems, in which individual objects have their own threads of control and their
own goals or sense of purpose. Elsewhere we have defined agents as objects that can
say „go" (reflecting their separate threads of control and the resulting ability to execute without being externally invoked) and „no" (reflecting the priority of their internal goals over external direction) [23]. Engineering such systems is most naturally
approached as an extension of object-oriented systems engineering. In particular, the
Unified Modeling Language (UML), a product of the OO community, is a natural
starting point for developing requirements and designs for agent-based systems. It is
widely known, and supported by a number of computer-aided software engineering
platforms.

M.J. Wooldridge, G. Weiß, and P. Ciancarini (Eds.): AOSE 2001, LNCS 2222, pp. 1-16, 2002.
© Springer-Verlag Berlin Heidelberg 2002

Some researchers have already called the attention to the potential of UML, in its unmodified form, for addressing many aspects of agent-based systems [3, 33]. As valuable as these efforts are, they cannot accommodate the additional functionality of agents over objects. Earlier work addressed one such area, the definition of interaction protocols between autonomous processes, and suggested constructs and conventions for Agent UML (AUML) [24, 25].

This paper addresses another area of agent functionality that goes beyond the capabilities of current UML. Sociological concepts have always been a source of inspiration for multi-agent research, and recently the agent community has been returning the favor by exploring the potential of agent-based models for studying sociological phenomena (e.g.,[6, 11, 21, 32]). The result of this interaction has been the formalization of a number of sociological and psychological concepts with important applications in engineering agent systems, concepts that are not directly supported in UML.

This paper brings together a number of these concepts, including „group,“ „role,“ „dependency,“ and „speech acts,“ into a coherent syntax for describing organizational structures, and proposes UML conventions and AUML extensions to support their use in the analysis, specification, and design of multi-agent systems. Our approach is distinct from some other approaches to roles in that it is behavioristic rather than mentalistic. We define roles in terms of features that are accessible to an outside observer, rather than those available only to introspection by the agent.

Section 2 outlines the syntax of group structure on which our representation is based. Section 3 describes a simple scenario and illustrates the use of the proposed UML constructs to model it. Section 4 summarizes our contribution.

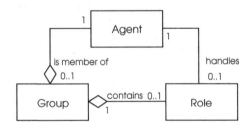

Fig. 1. AALAADIN architecture expressed as a UML class diagram.

2 A Group Syntax

We begin with the AALAADIN architecture proposed by Ferber and Gutknecht [13]. Their model, expressed as a UML class diagram in Fig. 1, involves three elements:
- An *agent* is an active communicating entity.
- A *group* is a set of agents.
- A *role* is an abstract representation of an agent's function, service, or identification within a group.

(The one-to-one mappings in this diagram reflect the original AALAADIN model, not the one we propose in this paper.) A fundamental insight of AALAADIN is that groups interact only through shared agents. An agent can be a member in several different groups at the same time, perhaps playing a different role (or roles) in each of them, and can move from one group to another dynamically. From a classical OO point of view, this multiple and dynamic role capability distinguishes the agent-based from the OO approach. An OO class can be defined by extension as a role, the set of all instances that belong to the class, or role; but simulaneous membership in multiple classes is the exception rather than the rule, and dynamic change of class membership is even rarer. (Although, UML now supports multiple and dynamic classification of objects.)

AALAADIN's notion of a group is naturally extended to organizations. We understand „group" as the generic term for a set of agents related through their roles. The term „organization" refers to groups distinguished by formality and stability, but the underlying model and formalisms are the same.

AALAADIN offers an attractive combination of parsimony and expressiveness. It is a straightforward basis for developing representational mechanisms for organizational concepts. We refine AALAADIN in three ways. First, we suggest that the notion of „role" can be defined in terms of two other notions current in the agent community, dependencies and action templates. Second, the ontology should be extended with the concept of an environment through which agents interact. Third, we confront the issue of aggregation as developed in the holonic model and its apparent tension with AALAADIN's flat network of groups.

2.1   Looking Behind Roles

AALAADIN defines a group as a set of agents. An agent's role mediates between it and the group. That is, it participates in the group not in its own right, but as an incumbent of a particular role, and the nature of the group is defined by the set of roles that it includes and their relations to one another. This observation encourages us to seek a more fundamental way to define roles, one that makes explicit their relations with one another. Two concepts from the theory of multi-agent systems contribute to this refined definition: dependency theory and speech acts. Both of these concepts define structured relations among interacting agents. Our insight is that a role is just a labeling of a recurring pattern of dependencies and (speech and other) interactions.

Dependency theory (e.g., [7, 8, 34], to cite only a few classic references) is based on the idea that interactions among agents result from an incompatibility between a single agent's goals and its resources and capabilities. Typically, an agent does not control all the resources or have the ability to execute all the actions required to achieve its objectives, so it must interact with other agents who do control those resources or who can perform those actions. For expository simplicity, we consider only action dependencies (since a dependency on an agent for a resource may be represented as depending on that agent to perform the action of providing the resource), and define a dependency as a three-tuple *<Dependent, Provider, Action>*. The literature on dependency theory works out many additional details that might be included in a dependency, including the specific goal that leads to the dependency, the specific plan leading to that goal that requires the specified resource or action, and which of the agents involved in the dependency recognizes its existence. Such details can readily be incorporated in our approach.

A pattern of dependencies is an important component of a role. For example, if agent A is a customer, there must be some agent B on whom A depends for goods and services, while B depends on A for money. However, dependencies alone leave many details of the role ambiguous. From dependencies alone, A and B might be thieves preying on one another. We can refine the definition of a role by incorporating more dynamic information, based on speech act theory.

Speech-act theory originates in the observation of [2] that utterances are not simply propositions that are true or false, but attempts on the part of the speaker that succeed or fail. The theory has become ubiquitous in the development of agent communication protocols such as KQML [15] and the FIPA Agent Communication Language [16]. Isolated utterances do little to characterize the relationships among interacting agents. However, the „speech-act" nature of utterances permits the definition of a set of relations that can obtain among successive utterances in a conversation [28]. For example, utterance B „responds" to utterance A if A caused B; it „replies" to A if it responds and in addition is addressed to the agent who uttered A, it „resolves" A if it replies and in addition causes A to succeed, and it „completes" A if it fulfills an earlier commitment. These relations may be extended to non-speech actions. For example, a request to close the door may be resolved by the physical action of closing the door. A formal construction based on these relations, the Dooley Graph [10, 28], consists of nodes corresponding to agents, with directed edges corresponding to utterances and other actions issued by the source of the edge and received by its sink. Each node in a Dooley Graph corresponds to a single agent, but an agent may occupy several different nodes. The significance of a single node is that it terminates speech acts associated with a single function of the agent. By a thespian analogy, this function has been called a „character" [28], but bears clear relationship to the notion of a role in AALAADIN. The characters disclosed through Dooley analysis are useful in engineering agent code, since they define reusable behavioral templates (cf. the modules in BRIC [12], AARIA's Actions [31], Contexts in Gensym's Agent Development Environment [29], and Singh's agent templates [35]). Such a template implements a particular protocol, defining an interrelated set of speech or other actions that an agent may undertake.

Table 1. A simple protocol characterizes the „customer" role.

Utterance #	Speaker	Utterance
1	B	Advertisement: Offers goods in exchange for money
2	A	Sends an order to B for the goods, accompanied by the payment
3	B	Sends the goods to A

From the point of view of a protocol, A is a customer of B if the two participate in the pattern of actions outlined in Table 1. This pattern is not the only protocol that would be appropriate for a customer and supplier. For example, a customer might initiate the exchange with a request for quotation. The point is that a protocol can capture part of the semantics of a role. As with dependencies, however, the semantics are incomplete. The same protocol would be appropriate between two actors in a play, neither of whom depends on the other for either money or goods. Adding the dependency information provides a clearer and more robust picture of the roles of customer and supplier than either offers by itself. Such a protocol can be represented in UML at various levels of abstractions. Previous work [24, 25].

From the point of view of system analysis, both dependency theory and interactions are attractive because they can be analyzed (at least at the level necessary for our purposes) without access to the internal state of the agents. Empirically, an agent's function in a group is defined by the network of dependencies and actions in which it is embedded. When a particular pattern of dependencies and protocols recurs, it is useful to summarize it as a role. However, the role is not primitive, but built up from dependencies and interactions. The dependencies and actions are what really matter. The role is simply a label that we attach to a recurring pattern to enable us to manipulate it with greater efficiency. This viewpoint implies (contrary to the original AALAADIN model exemplified in Fig. 1) that the same role can appear in multiple groups, if they embody the same pattern of dependencies and interactions (Fig. 2).

If an agent in a group holds multiple roles concurrently, it may sometimes be useful to define a higher-level role that is composed of some of those more elementary roles. For example, consider the three roles Customer, Vendor, and Employee, all within the group Market Economy. An end-user in such an economy is an agent who earns money in a job and uses that money to purchase goods. Thus the End User role is the composition of Customer and Employee roles. A supply chain link in such an economy is an agent who buys goods, transforms them into other goods, and then sells them. Thus Supply Chain Link is the composition of Customer and Vendor roles. Fig. 2 expresses this composition of roles by the composition association loop at the top of the Role class.

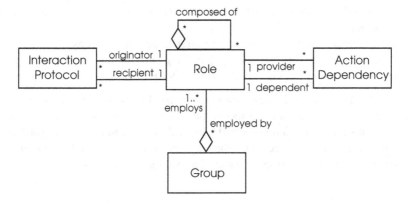

Fig. 2. UML Class Diagram expressing the role associations described in Section 2.1.

Our view of a role as a recurring pattern of dependencies and actions is deliberately behavioristic rather than mentalistic. Other researchers define roles in terms of mentalistic qualities, such as obligations, permissions, and rights, that require a detailed knowledge of the agents' internal structure [1, 9, 27]. One prominent definition even disavows behavioral considerations: „A role is here conceived as *a system of prescribed mental attitudes*, rather than a system of prescribed behaviour" [27]. The mentalistic approach is extremely useful theoretically, as an extension of the BDI model that can both inform the further development of that model and permit application of its formal mechanisms to role analysis. It is less useful to a systems analyst confronted with a heterogeneous system whose elements are often opaque. Examples of such systems might be a network of trading partners in a B2B ecommerce scenario, or a terrorist network in a military intelligence application. In such cases, internal beliefs, desires, and intentions are closely held secrets, and those who would model the system from the outside must rely on externally observable behaviors. The intended users of our extensions to UML must often cope with just such situations. An important question, which we do not engage here, is developing correlations between the two classes (mentalistic and behavioristic) of role models.

2.2 The Importance of the Environment

Agents cannot be considered independently of the environment in which they exist and through which they interact [14, 22]. This insight is often ignored in work on computational multi-agent systems, where researchers consider the environment as a passive communications framework and everything of interest is relegated to one or another of the agents. Even such purely electronic environments often prove embarrassingly active when an application is scaled up for real-world use, and those engineering agents for non-electronic domains (such as factory automation) must consider the environment explicitly.

Consider, for example, the active role of the environment in pheromone models of coordination [4, 30]. In natural insect societies and engineered systems inspired by them, the environment actively provides three information processing functions.
1. It *fuses* information from different agents passing over the same location at different times.
2. It *distributes* information from one location to nearby locations.
3. It provides *truth maintenance* by forgetting information that is not continually refreshed, thereby getting rid of obsolete information.

In modeling groups, it is important to recognize the role of the environment in supporting the dependencies and protocols that define the participants' roles. The exact form that this representation takes will vary widely, depending on the group in question. However, we should recognize that environment, along with the network of roles that it supports, is a defining component of a social group (Fig. 3).

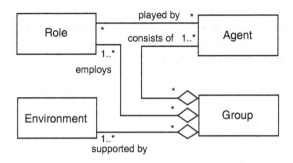

Fig. 3. The environment and its involvement with groups, agents, and roles.

2.3 Groups as Agents

At first glance, AALAADIN contrasts strongly with the holonic view of agent organization. A holon is an agent that may be made up of smaller holons and that may join
together with other holons to form higher-level holons [5, 17, 19, 20]. Thus the
holonic model explicitly permits groups to be members of other groups. The resulting
lattice of holons is called a holarchy, and is the dominant organizational metaphor in
holonic systems [36]. In AALAADIN, groups are related only through shared members,
and there is no provision for one group as a group to be a member of another.

Both models have their own attractions. The holonic model recognizes the need for
some form of hierarchical aggregation in real-world systems, which must remain
understandable while spanning a wide range of temporal and spatial scales. A modern
automotive factory incorporates hundreds of thousands of individual mechanisms
(each a candidate for agent-hood) in hundreds of machines that are grouped into a
dozen or so lines. Engineers can design, construct, and operate such complexes only
by shifting the focus from mechanism to machine or line, depending on the problem at
hand, and recognizing the higher-level agents are aggregates of lower-level ones.
Similarly, in e-commerce applications, a corporation is a legal entity that is independent of the individual people who make up its employees and directors. Conversely,
AALAADIN recognizes that when two groups (at any level) interact, they do so through
the interactions of their components. Negotiations between two companies take place
through individual people with the roles of representing their groups in the negotiation.
Two machines in a factory interact by virtue of a process involving the sensors of one
and the actuators of another.

As practicing engineers of agent-based systems, we recognize the need for both
perspectives, and resolve the tension pragmatically. When we begin to analyze a group
A, we identify the agents $\{a_1, a_2, ..., a_n\}$ occupying its roles. Those agents may be
individual persons, robots, or computer systems (atomic agents). They may also be
other groups, $a_i = B$, which we treat as black boxes. We take this „holonic" perspective as long as our analysis can ignore the internal structure of the member groups (Fig.

4a). However, subsequent analysis often requires us to open such a black box and look inside at its roles and their incumbent agents, analyzing $B = \{b_1, b_2, ..., b_m\}$. At that point, we insist on identifying which of B's member agents is actually responsible for filling B's role in A, thus adhering to the discipline of AALAADIN (Fig. 4b). Fig. 4c is thus the consolidated model for our approach.

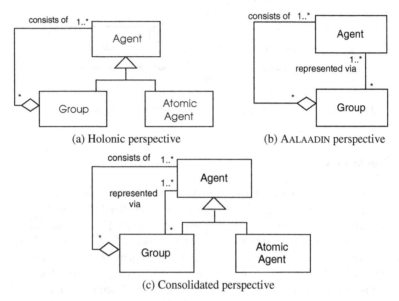

(a) Holonic perspective   (b) AALAADIN perspective

(c) Consolidated perspective

Fig. 4. Three perspectives on the relation between Groups and Agents.

2.4 Summary

In sum, our model is based on AALAADIN, but with three extensions:
- Roles are not ontologically primitive, but are defined as recurring patterns of dependencies and actions.
- The definition of a group includes not just a set of agents occupying roles, but also the environment through which they interact.
- AALAADIN's requirement that groups interact only through identified members is relaxed in the case of unanalyzed groups, which are permitted to occupy roles in higher-level groups following the holonic model.

Figure 5 consolidates the class views described in this section.

3   An Example

We illustrate the theory and its UML instantiation by modeling a simple example, a terrorist organization.

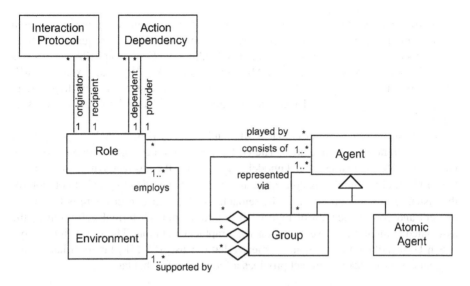

Fig. 5. Consolidated ontology.

3.1 A Terrorist Organization

A national security organization might construct an agent-based model of terrorism, for use in contingency planning and modeling emerging threats. In this particular model, we envision interactions among three groups with associated roles. Individual agent *A* occupies roles in all three groups:

- The terrorist organization (TO) has roles
  o   *Operative*, who actually deploys and operates the instrument of terrorism (e.g., plants and detonates the bomb, or shoots the gun) (= *A*)
  o   *Ringleader*, who sets the vision for the organization and may bankroll it personally
- The weapons cartel (WC) has roles
  o   *Customer*, who wishes to procure arms (= *A*)
  o   *Supplier*, who delivers arms to the customer
  o   *Negotiator*, who negotiates the deal with the customer and receives payment.
- Western society (WS) has roles
  o   *Citizen*, whom the terrorist operative wishes to target
  o   *Student*, a convenient cover for a foreign national (= *A*).

Informally, individual *A* procures financing and a mission from TO, while feeding back information that permits TO to expand its activities. *A* uses funds from TO to purchase weapons from WC, and then occupies a role in WS to deploy the weapons against citizens.

3.2 Its AUML Model

The OMG's Unified Modeling Language (UML) version 1.3 already provides a wealth of diagramming elements [18]. However, extensions to UML are required to effectively model agents and agent-based systems. Within both OMG and FIPA, an effort is currently underway to define a UML for agents (AUML) that extends UML (http://www.auml.org). This section proposes usages of and extensions to UML to represent groups, agents, and roles, as illustrated in the Terrorist Organization scenario, above.

A common misconception is that UML (and by extension, AUML) is a graphical notation with no formal semantics. The UML specification consists of two interrelated parts: the *UML Semantics* (a metamodel that specifies the abstract syntax and semantics of UML object modeling concepts), and the *UML Notation* (a graphic notation for the visual representation of the UML semantics) [26]. Our concern here is the development and communication of high-level intuitions, not the formal definition of the associated semantics, so we focus on the graphical notation. The close linkage between UML notation and semantics means that our use of UML, far from hampering subsequent formalization, in fact provides a foundation for that task.

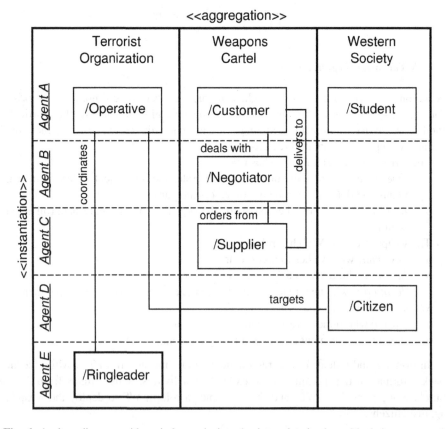

Fig. 6. A class diagram with swimlanes depicts the interrelated roles with their agents and groups.

3.3 Swimlanes as Groups

The scenario described in 3.1 involve three groups, each employing defined roles. Fig. 6 illustrates these groups and roles using two UML techniques: the class diagram and swimlane. The class diagram here models the various terrorist roles and their relationships. (The slash in front of each name indicates that the name is a role name, rather than a class name.)

In UML, swimlanes graphically organize responsibility of activities within an activity graph. However, AUML proposes that the same device be used for *any* kind of UML diagram—in the case of Fig. 6, a class diagram. For example, Fig. 6 indicates that the Terrorist Organization involves two roles, Operative and Ringleader, where the Ringleader agent coordinates Operative agents. Fig. 6 also depicts a second kind of swimlane based on agent instance. For example, agent *A* plays the roles of Operative, Customer, and Student. Multidimensional swimlanes are highly uncommon in the UML community, but are supported by UML version 1.3.

The UML 1.3 swimlane is only „syntactic sugar," a graphical packaging technique. It cannot specify a swimlane's underlying semantics. Understanding swimlanes like those in Fig. 6 could cause difficulty because vertical swimlanes specify group aggre-

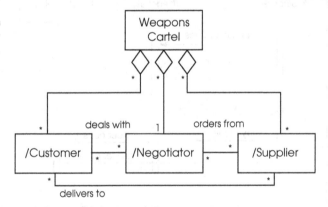

Fig. 7. A class diagram depicting that Terrorist Organizations consist of agents playing several distinct roles.

gation, while the horizontal swimlanes specify role instantiation. We propose that UML be extended to specify the swimlane's underlying relationship. In Fig. 6, the vertical swimlanes are indicated as <<aggregation>> and the horizontal as <<instantiation>>.

3.4 Class Diagrams to Define Roles

As mentioned above, the vertical swimlanes define an aggregation relationship between groups and the roles that comprise the group. Another way to express these relationships within a group is to use a class diagram as depicted in Fig. 7.

The class diagram in Fig. 7 and the Weapons Cartel swimlane in Fig. 6 are basically equivalent. They both show that each Weapons Cartel group consists of agents playing the roles of Customer, Negotiator, and Supplier. Additionally, they both depict relationships among the roles. The only difference is that Fig. 7 expresses the relationship cardinality constraints (multiplicity) between the Weapons Cartel and the various roles, while Fig. 6 does not. For example, Fig. 7 indicates that while each Weapons Cartel group may have multiple customers and suppliers, it may only have one negotiator. These constraints cannot be expressed by UML swimlanes.

3.5 Sequence Diagrams to Show Roles as Patterns of Interactions

Class diagrams model the kinds of entities that exist in a system along with their relationships. Modeling the interactions that may occur among these entities can be repre-

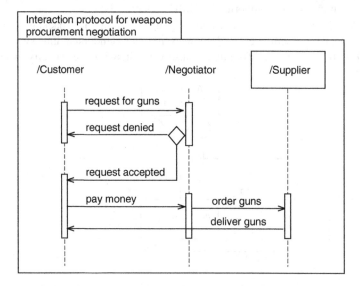

Fig. 8. Sequence diagram depicting an interaction protocol for buying guns from a terrorist operation agent.

sented using a UML sequence diagram. For example, Fig. 8 depicts the permitted interactions that may occur among Customer, Negotiator, and Supplier agents for a weapons procurement negotiation. The tabbed folder encompassing the sequence diagram indicates that the interaction can be viewed as a unit called a *package*.

The only extension to UML is the addition of the diamond-shaped decision symbol. While branching decisions can be expressed in UML 1.3 using guard conditions, we recommend using the same symbol employed for the same purpose in activity graphs—the diamond. (For more AUML extensions to the sequence diagram, see [24, 25].)

3.6 Activity Graphs to Show Groups as Patterns of Dependencies

The object-flow activity graph represents activities and the kinds of objects that they produce or consume. The weapons procurement in Fig. 9 states that a Terrorist Organization procures guns (and not butter) from a Weapons Cartel to which it pays money. Instead of representing the way in which roles relate or interact among groups (Fig. 6,

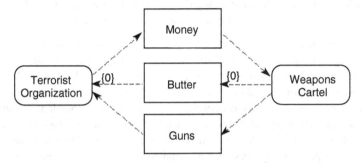

Fig. 9. An object-flow activity graph specifies roles as patterns of activities along with the products that are produced and consumed by each activity.

Fig. 7, Fig. 8), this diagram models *groups* as processing entities in their own right. For example, Fig. 9 depicts two groups and their dependencies, without regard to the underlying roles. In other words, it expresses the pattern of dependencies between a Terrorist Organization and a Weapons Cartel.

Object-flow activity graphs, then, provide a way to model a system by removing some of the detail, providing a "higher-level" view of the system components. Fig. 4c expresses the fact that all groups are agents; but until this point, the only agents we were modeling were as role-playing elements of a group. The activity graph allows us to model groups of agents as agents. In this way, we can express the kinds of dependencies that are best represented at a group level. When a more detailed view of the underlying interactions is required, a sequence diagram (e.g., Fig. 8) can be used.

Such an approach requires a UML extension. UML requires all activities terminate in order to produce their output. However, agent groups such as terrorist organizations or order processing departments are typically thought of as continuous activities, not as processes with definable starts and completions. This proposed extension is important when modeling long-lived groups that produce output many things during their lifetime.

4 Summary

Engineering of agent-based systems requires the availability of common languages for requirements analysis, specification, and design. The Unified Modeling Language (UML) has gained wide acceptance in the Object-Oriented community, and is supported by a number of computer-aided software engineering tools. The close relation between objects and agents has led numerous researchers to seek to apply it to agents. Carrying out this agenda requires that we identify the distinctive constructions required in designing agent-oriented systems and develop conventions for using and extending UML to accommodate them.

In the case of social structures, insights from AALAADIN, dependency theory, and holonics can be fused into a single metamodel of groups as composed of agents occupying roles (defined as patterns of dependency and interaction) in an environment. Various UML constructs, including swimlanes, class diagrams, activity diagrams, and sequence charts, can capture the crucial distinctions in such a model.

Acknowledgements. When the first author presented an invited talk on applications of UML to agents at MAAMAW'99, several participants, including Cristiano Castelfranchi and Yves Demazeau, raised the question of how a wide range of organizational structures could be captured in UML. Their challenge was the germ for this paper. Some of the ideas concerning the relation of dependencies and action relations to the definition of roles were stimulated by discussions with Catholijn Jonker, Gabriela Lindemann, and others at the MASHO'00 workshop, and by comments on a preliminary version with John Sauter, Mitch Fleischer, and others at ERIM.

References

[1]   A. Artikis and J. Pitt. A Formal Model of Open Agent Societies. In *Proceedings of Fifth International Conference on Autonomous Agents (Agents 2001)*, 2001.

[2]   J. L. Austin. *How to Do Things with Words*. Oxford University Press, 1962.

[3]   F. Bergenti and A. Poggi. Exploiting UML in the Design of Multi-Agent Systems. In *Proceedings of Engineering Societies in the Agents' World*, pages 96-103, 2000.

[4]   S. Brueckner. *Return from the Ant: Synthetic Ecosystems for Manufacturing Control*. Thesis at Humboldt University Berlin, Department of Computer Science, 2000.

[5]   H.-J. Bürckert, K. Fischer, and G. Vierke. Teletruck: A holonic fleet management system. In *Proceedings of 14th European Meeting on Cybernetics and Systems Research*, pages 695-700, 1998.

[6]   K. Carley and M. Prietula, Editors. *Computational Organization Theory*. Lawrence Erlbaum Associates, 1994.

[7]   C. Castelfranchi. Founding Agent's 'Autonomy' on Dependence Theory. In *Proceedings of 14th European Conference on Artificial Intelligence*, pages 353-357, IOS Press, 2000.

[8]   C. Castelfranchi, M. Miceli, and A. Cesta. Dependence Relations among Autonomous Agents. In Y. Demazeau and E. Werner, Editors, *Decentralized AI 3 (Proceedings of the Third European Workshop on Modeling Autonomous Agents in a Multi-Agent World)*, Elsevier, 1992.

[9]   L. Cavedon and L. Sonenberg. On Social Commitment, Roles and Preferred Goals. In *Proceedings of International Conference on Multi-Agent Systems (ICMAS'98)*, pages 80-87, IEEE, 1998.

[10]   R. A. Dooley. Appendix B: Repartee as a Graph. In R. E. Longacre, Editor, *An Anatomy of Speech Notions*, pages 348-58. Peter de Ridder, Lisse, 1976.

[11]   M. E. Epstein and R. Axtell. *Growing Artificial Societies: Social Science from the Ground Up*. Boston, MA, MIT Press, 1996.

[12] J. Ferber. *Multi-Agent Systems: An Introduction to Distributed Artificial Intelligence.* Harlow, UK, Addison Wesley Longman, 1999.

[13] J. Ferber and O. Gutknecht. A meta-model for the analysis and design of organizations in multi-agent systems. In *Proceedings of Third International Conference on Multi-Agent Systems (ICMAS'98)*, pages 128-135, IEEE Computer Society, 1998.

[14] J. Ferber and J.-P. Müller. Influences and Reactions: a Model of Situated Multiagent Systems. In *Proceedings of Second International Conference on Multi-Agent Systems (ICMAS-96)*, pages 72-79, 1996.

[15] T. Finin, J. Weber, G. Wiederhold, M. Genesereth, R. Fritzson, D. McKay, J. McGuire, R. Pelavin, S. Shapiro, and C. Beck. DRAFT Specification of the KQML Agent-Communication Language. 1993. Postscript, http://www.cs.umbc.edu/kqml/kqmlspec/spec.html.

[16] FIPA. FIPA Agent Communication Language Specifications. 2000. HTML, http://www.fipa.org/repository/aclspecs.html.

[17] K. Fischer. Agent-based design of holonic manufacturing systems. *Robotics and Autonomous Systems*, 27(1-2):3-13, 1999.

[18] M. Fowler and K. Scott. *UML Distilled: Applying the Standard Object Modeling Language.* Reading, MA, Addison-Wesley, 1997.

[19] C. Gerber, J. Siekmann, and G. Vierke. Flexible autonomy in holonic multi-agent systems. In *Proceedings of AAAI Spring Symposium on Agents with Adjustable Autonomy*, 1999.

[20] C. Gerber, J. Siekmann, and G. Vierke. Holonic Multi-Agent Systems. RR-99-03, DFKI, Kaiserslautern, Germany, 1999. URL ftp://ftp.dfki.uni-kl.de/pub/Publications/ResearchReports/1999/RR-99-03.ps.gz.

[21] G. N. D. Gilbert, J. *Simulating Societies: the computer simulation of social processes.* London, UCL Press, 1993.

[22] J. P. Müller. *The Design of Intelligent Agents.* Berlin, Springer, 1996.

[23] J. Odell. Agents: Technology and Usage (Part 1). *Distributed Computing Architecture/E-Business Advisory Service*, 3(4):1-29, 2000.

[24] J. Odell, H. V. D. Parunak, and B. Bauer. Extending UML for Agents. In *Proceedings of Agent-Oriented Information Systems Workshop*, pages 3-17, 2000.

[25] J. Odell, H. V. D. Parunak, and B. Bauer. Representing Agent Interaction Protocols in UML. In *Proceedings of Agent-Oriented Software Engineering*, pages 121-140, Springer, 2000.

[26] OMG. OMG Unified Modeling Language Specification. 1999. PDF File, http://www.rational.com/media/uml/post.pdf.

[27] P. Panzarasa, T. J. Norman, and N. R. Jennings. Modeling Sociality in the BDI Framework. In *Proceedings of First Asia-Pacific Conference on Intelligent Agent Technology (IAT'99)*, pages 202-206, 1999.

[28] H. V. D. Parunak. Visualizing Agent Conversations: Using Enhanced Dooley Graphs for Agent Design and Analysis. In *Proceedings of Second International Conference on Multi-Agent Systems (ICMAS'96)*, pages 275-282, 1996.

[29] H. V. D. Parunak. Workshop Report: Implementing Manufacturing Agents. Industrial Technology Institute, 1996. URL http://www.erim.org/~vparunak/paamncms.pdf.

[30] H. V. D. Parunak. 'Go to the Ant': Engineering Principles from Natural Agent Systems. *Annals of Operations Research*, 75:69-101, 1997.

[31] H. V. D. Parunak, A. D. Baker, and S. J. Clark. The AARIA Agent Architecture: From Manufacturing Requirements to Agent-Based System Design. *Integrated Computer-Aided Engineering*, 8(1):45-58, 2001.

[32] M. J. Prietula, K. M. Carley, and L. e. Gasser. *Simulating Organizations: Computational Models of Institutions and Groups.* Menlo Park, CA, AAAI Press, 1998.

[33] G. Satapathy and S. R. T. Kumara. Object Oriented Design based Agent Modeling. In *Proceedings of The Fourth International Conference on the Practical Application of Intelligent Agents and Multi-Agent Technology*, pages 143-162, The Practical Applications Company, 1999.

[34] J. S. Sichman, Y. Demazeau, R. Conte, and C. Castelfranchi. A Social Reasoning Mechanism Based on Dependence Networks. In *Proceedings of 11th European Conference on Artificial Intelligence*, pages 416-420, John Wiley and Sons, 1994.

[35] M. P. Singh. Developing Formal Specifications to Coordinate Heterogeneous Autonomous Agents. In *Proceedings of Third International Conference on Multi-Agent Systems (ICMAS'98)*, pages 261-268, IEEE Computer Society, 1998.

[36] University of Hannover. Holonic Manufacturing Systems. 2000. Web Page, http://hms.ifw.uni-hannover.de/.

Diagnosis of the Dynamics within an Organization by Trace Checking of Behavioural Requirements

Catholijn Jonker[1], Ioan Alfred Letia[2], and Jan Treur[1]

[1]Vrije Universiteit Amsterdam, Department of Artificial Intelligence
De Boelelaan 1081a, 1081 HV Amsterdam, The Netherlands
{jonker,treur}@cs.vu.nl

[2]Technical University, Department of Computer Science
Baritiu 28, RO-3400 Cluj-Napoca Romenia
letia@cs-gw.utcluj.ro

Abstract. The main question addressed in this paper is how requirements on the dynamics within an organization model can be specified and how the dynamics within such an organization can be formally analysed. A specification language is proposed, and a number of different types of requirements for dynamics at different levels in the organization are identified. Based on a logical analysis and a software environment to check requirements against traces of the dynamics, a diagnostic method is proposed to analyse the malfunctioning of an organization, and pinpoint causes of malfunctioning.

1 Introduction

Organization modelling aims at abstracting from agents and their interaction within a complex multi-agent system using notions such as role, interaction and group structure (cf. [8], [9]). The notion of role, for example, is independent of any particular agent fulfilling this role. Role interactions define the relationships between roles. A group structure is a set of roles and interactions between them. The advantage of organization modelling is to deal more adequately with complexity of multi-agent dynamics, in particular for multi-agent systems with nontrivial global behaviour.

In recent years Requirements Engineering for distributed and agent systems has been studied, e.g., [3], [4], [11]. At the level of the multi-agent system, requirements concern the dynamics of interaction and cooperation patterns. At the level of individual agents, requirements concern agent behaviour. Due to dynamic complexity, specification and analysis of such requirements is a difficult process. The importance of using more abstract and intuitive notions in requirements specification, as opposed to more directly formulated behaviour constraints, is emphasised in, e.g., [3]. Below, organizational concepts are used to serve this purpose. Because of their intuitive meaning and conciseness, such notions are easy to understand.

For description of multi-agent systems from the organizational point of view, the *Agent/Group/Role* (AGR) model, adopted from [8], is used (formerly called

M.J. Wooldridge, G. Weiß, and P. Ciancarini (Eds.): AOSE 2001, LNCS 2222, pp. 17-32, 2002.

Aalaadin). An organization is based on a definition of groups, roles and their relationships within the organization. In relation to an organization model four different types of requirements are distinguished (Section 2), varying from global requirements for the organization as a whole, to requirements for specific roles and for interactions between them. Section 3 briefly describes the example application used in the paper: a (simulated) organization model for work flow related to a Call Center and a bank. In Section 4 a temporal trace language to formally specify behavioural requirements is briefly introduced. Using this language, in Section 5 a number of requirement specifications for the example organization are presented.

For all different types of requirements discussed in this paper, for a given set of finite traces representing dynamics within the organization, the requirements can be verified automatically. By specifying the refinement of a global requirement for the overall organization in terms of more local requirements, in Section 6 it is discussed how it is possible to perform diagnosis of malfunctioning of the organization. If the overall requirement fails on a given trace, then subsequently, all refined requirements for the parts of the organization can be verified against that trace: the cause of the malfunctioning can be attributed to the part(s) of the organization for which the refined requirement(s) fail(s). This diagnostic method is applicable both to data on the dynamics of simulated organizations and empirical data on the dynamics of real organizations. Section 7 is a discussion.

2 Types of Requirements

Based on an organizational structure, the following types of requirements are distinguished: single role behaviour requirements, intragroup interaction requirements, intragroup transfer requirements, intergroup interaction requirements. To be able to specify ongoing interaction between two roles for which multiple appearances exist, the notion of *role instance* is used. This notion abstracts from the agent realising the role as actor, but enables to distinguish between appearances of roles.

For a given role within a group, *role behaviour requirements* specify the dynamics of the role within the group. They are typically expressed in terms of temporal relationships between the *input* and *output* of a role instance. *Intragroup role interaction requirements* specify the temporal constraints on the dynamics of the interaction protocol between two roles within a group. Intragroup role interaction requirements between two roles instances in one group instance are typically expressed in terms of the *output* of both role instances. Intragroup role interaction requires *communication* within the group. Therefore, in order to function properly, requirements are needed that communications are successful: *transfer requirements*. These requirements relate *output* of one role instance to *input* of another role instance in the same group.

Intergroup role interaction requirements specify the temporal constraints on the dynamics of the interaction protocol between two role instances within two different group instances. They are typically expressed in terms of the *input* of one of the role instances in one group instance and the *output* of the other role instance in the other group instance.

3 The Example Organization Model

The example organization model was inspired by the application addressed in [1]. The organization consists of a Call Center together with a (large) number of local banks. For simulating this organization and visualizing the experiments Swarm[1], an agent-based simulator [17], was used. A basic agent model has been developed with the core functionality required for the organization; see Figure 1 for an overview. This agent model has then been specialized in a bank employee (BE agent), a bank distributor (BD agent) and the Call Center distributor (CD agent). The organizational structure of the bank and call center is hierarchical with communication between Call Center Distributor (CD) and bank distributors (BD_i) and between bank distributors (BD_i) and bank employees (BE_{ij}).

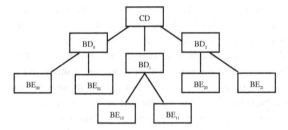

Fig. 1. Call Center distributor (CD), bank distributors (BD_i) and bank employees (BE_{ij}).

In the experiments each local bank had nine employees. The tasks come from the Clients to the Call Center Distributor. The Call Center Distributor allocates the tasks for the three banks according to its policy and the three queues below are the ones sent to the Bank Distributors. The same procedure is repeated by the Bank Distributor for the Bank Employees that have to process the tasks.

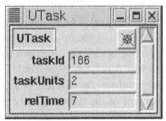

Fig. 2. Task probe

A task within this organization (shown as UTask in Figure 2) has an identifier (taskId), number of time units needed for its processing (taskUnits) and a relative time (relTime) specifying the time moment when the task has been promised to be processed. We can vary the policy used by distributors in the allocation of tasks for their subordinates. The availability of employees can also be varied with some degree of

---

[1] Swarm home page http://www.santafe.edu/projects/swarm/

absenteeism. The distributors can all use the same policy for scheduling the tasks to their subordinates or can use different policies. The kind of exceptions that can be currently injected in the dynamics of the organization are: (i) agent unavailable, (ii) task misrouted, and (iii) task delayed [6]. Currently the communication of tasks can be logged in both directions, to subordinates and to superiors. When the employees finish processing a task, they communicate it at the end of that particular time interval to their superior and from there it is communicated to the center distributor, also at the end of the same time interval. There is no time lag between accepting a task and its being sent to the bank which should process it, and similarly for acknowledging its finish back to the center distributor.

For tracing the communication of tasks between the Call Center Distributor and the Bank Distributors we have log files for the input and output of each of the role instances. These log files are used to generate the traces that are analysed by the checking software.

By testing for various situations, the designer of the multi-agent system can thoroughly check the requirements for interactions, actually see how well the organization is able to manage exceptions that can occur during the enactment of a process [6], and uncover agents that do not comply with coordination protocols [19]. Unreliable coordination between agents and the effect of various decisionmaking policies on the behavior of the organization as a whole is done by creating specific circumstances (e.g., exceptions) and observing behavior of the organization under these circumstances. The tools presented in this paper provide support for such an analysis.

4 A Temporal Trace Language

To specify requirements on the dynamics within the organization, the temporal trace language used in [11], [12] is adopted. An ontology is a specification (in order-sorted logic) of a vocabulary, i.e., a signature. A state for ontology Ont is an assignment of truth values {true, false} to the set of ground atoms At(Ont). The *set of all possible states* for ontology Ont is denoted by STATES(Ont). The standard satisfaction relation $\models$ between states and state properties is used: S $\models$ p means that property p holds in state S. To describe behaviour, explicit reference is made to time in a formal manner.

A *time frame* T is assumed which is linearly ordered. Depending on the application, it may be dense (e.g., the real numbers), or discrete (e.g., the set of integers or natural numbers or a finite initial segment of the natural numbers), or any other form, as long as it has a linear ordering.

A *trace* $\mathcal{M}$ over an ontology Ont and time frame T is a mapping $\mathcal{M} : T \rightarrow$ STATES(Ont), i.e, a sequence of states $\mathcal{M}_t$ (t $\in$ T) in STATES(Ont). The set of all traces over ontology Ont is denoted by TRACES(Ont) , i.e., TRACES(Ont) = STATES(Ont)^T.

Comparable to the approach in situation calculus, the sorted predicate logic temporal trace language TTL is built on atoms referring to, e.g., traces, time and state properties, such as

$$\text{state}(\mathcal{M}, t, \text{output}) \models p$$

which denotes that state property $p \in$ SPROP(InOnt) is true in the state of $\mathcal{M}$ at time point t. Here $\models$ is a predicate symbol in the language, comparable to the Holds-predicate in situation calculus. Temporal formulae are built using the usual logical connectives and quantification (for example, over traces, time and state properties). The set TFOR(Ont) is the set of all *temporal formulae* that only make use of ontology Ont. We allow additional language elements as abbreviations of formulae of the temporal trace language.

Ontologies can be specific for a role. In Section 5, for simplicity explicit reference to the specific ontologies per role are omitted; the ontology elements used can be read from the requirements themselves.

5 Example Requirements

In this section behavioural requirements related to the example are fomalised using the temporal trace language introduced in Section 4. Within these requirements specifications universal and existential quantification over role instances can occur. Role instances are denoted by I:R where R is a role. To be able to specify requirements for the example organization, first the following terms are introduced. The organization model used for the bank and Call Center consists of two groups: DISTRIBUTION, OPEN_GROUP. For the group OPEN_GROUP only one instance exists, open_group, standing for the Call Center. For the group DISTRIBUTION the following instances exist, cc, lb1, ..., lbn, standing for the cooperation between Call Center and local bank managers (cc), and for each of the local banks and their employees (lbi). Within the group DISTRIBUTION two roles exist: DISTRIBUTOR, PARTICIPANT. For these roles the following instances are distinguished: d: cc (distributor role instance within group instance cc), pcc1, ..., pccn : cc (n participant role instances within group instance cc), d: lb1 (distributor role instance within group instance lb1), ..., d: lbn, p11: lb1 (first participant role instance of group instance lb1), ..., p1m: lb1 (m-th participant role instance of group instance lbn), ..., pn1: lbn, ..., pnm: lbn. Within the group OPEN_GROUP, the following roles exist: RECEPTIONIST, CLIENT. Finally, the following role instances are distinguished: cl: open_group (client role instance within group instance open_group), and rec: open_group (receptionist role instance within group instance open_group).

Variable introduction at the beginning of a formula is done as ∀ v: s, or ∃ v: s, where s is the sort of the variable, and v is the variable name. Introducing several variables of the same sort can be done like: ∀ v1, v2, ..., vn: s. Variables used in the article are:

- GI: GROUP is a variable ranging over all possible group instances of group GROUP. Examples: GI: DISTRIBUTION, GI: OPEN_GROUP.
- RI: ROLE: gi is a variable ranging over all possible role instances of role ROLE within group instance gi. Examples: P: PARTICIPANT: cc, P: PARTICIPANT: GI: DISTRIBUTION.
- t: T is a variable ranging over time.
- $\mathcal{M}$: TRACES is a variable ranging over traces.
- id : TaskId is a variable ranging over task identifiers.

When used within a formula, with the exception of the introduction of the variable, only the variable name of the variable is used. Example:

$\forall \mathcal{M}: \text{TRACES}, \forall t : T \ nr\_of\_finished(\mathcal{M}, t, t) = 0$

It is assumed that job names are unique. One job is presented to the organization at a time. The requirements are specified below in a form that is specific for the application. However, it is not difficult to reuse them over different applications of the same type of organization.

5.1 Global Requirements

At the level of the organization as a whole the following requirements can be identified:

- Every request is answered (either by rejecting or by accepting and finishing it)
- No accepted jobs are lost: for every accepted job there is a time that that job is finished.
- The ratio of accepted jobs over requested jobs is at least r.
- The average delay of jobs is at most m.

These global requirements can be formalised as follows.

The first requirement specifies that at any point in time, if a client communicates a request to the receptionist, then at some later time point the receptionist will communicate either a rejection of the request or a notification that it was finished to that client.

GR1 All Requests Answered

$\forall \mathcal{M}: \text{TRACES} \ \forall tid : \text{TaskId} \ \forall t1, tf : T \ \forall C: \text{CLIENT:open\_group} \ \forall R: \text{RECEPTIONIST: open\_group}$
$[\ state(\mathcal{M}, t1, output(C)) \models comm\_from\_to(requested(tid, tf), C, R)$
$\Rightarrow \ \exists t2 : T \ [\ t2 \geq t1 \ \& \ [\ state(\mathcal{M}, t2, input(C)) \models comm\_from\_to(rejected(tid), R, C)$
$\vee \ state(\mathcal{M}, t2, input(C)) \models comm\_from\_to(finished(tid), R, C) \ ] \ ]$

The next requirement expresses that if at any point in time the receptionist communicates to a client that a request was accepted, then at some later time point the receptionist communicates to the same client that the task was finished.

GR2 No Lost Jobs

$\forall \mathcal{M}: \text{TRACES} \ \forall id : \text{TaskId} \ \forall t, t1 : T \ \forall C: \text{CLIENT: open\_group} \ \forall R: \text{RECEPTIONIST: open\_group}$
$[\ state(\mathcal{M}, t1, input(C)) \models comm\_from\_to(accepted(id, t), R, C)$
$\Rightarrow \ \exists t2 : T \ [\ t2 > t1 \ \& \ state(\mathcal{M}, t2, input(C)) \models comm\_from\_to(finished(id), R, C) \ ] \ ]$

For the next two requirements additional specifications are needed to define the frequency functions used. For shortness' sake these are left out; see, however, the Appendix. The first one, G3, can be viewed as a liveness property: it indicates that at least a certain amount of 'good events' in the sense of request acceptances must happen.

GR3 Acceptable ratio of Accepted Jobs over [t1, t2]

$\forall \mathcal{M}: \text{TRACES} \quad nr\_of\_accepted(\mathcal{M}, t1, t2) \ / \ nr\_of\_requested(\mathcal{M}, t1, t2) \ \geq r$

Requirement G4 below can be viewed as a safety requirement: it indicates that only limited 'bad events' in the sense of delays can happen.

GR4 Acceptable Average Delay of Accepted Jobs over [t1, t2]

∀℘: TRACES   average_delay(℘, t1, t2) ≤ m

In the next four subsections the different requirements on parts of the organization are identified. In Figure 3 below an overview can be found. In this figure three group instances are depicted, together with two role instances in each of them. Requirements of different types are depicted by arrows. The position from which an arrow starts indicates the role instance to which the *if*-part of the requirement refers. Whether the *if*-part refers to input or output is indicated by the start position of the arrow (resp. at the left hand side of the role instance or at the right hand side). In a similar manner the end point of an arrow indicates to which role instance the *then*-part of the requirement refers. The requirements distinghuished in Figure 3 and specified in detail below are selected in order to be able to derive global requirement GR1 from them. In Section 6.1 this will be addressed in more detail.

5.2 Intragroup Role Interaction Requirements

Intragroup role interaction requirements specify the cooperation within a group. Within each group instance at least one intragroup role Interaction requirements is specified. The first one specifies that within the open group proper interaction takes place: if a client communicates a request, then some time later, either the request will be rejected, or finished.

IaRI1 Client-Receptionist Intragroup Interaction

∀℘: TRACES ∀ tid : TaskId ∀ t1, tf : T ∀ C: CLIENT: open_group ∀ R: RECEPTIONIST: open_group
[state(℘, t1, output(C)) ⊨ comm_from_to(requested(tid, tf), C, R)
         ⇒ ∃ t2 : T [t2 ≥ t1 & [state(℘, t2, output(R)) ⊨ comm_from_to(rejected(tid), R, C)
                                 ∨ state(℘, t2, output(R)) ⊨ comm_from_to(finished(tid), R, C)]]]

The next requirement expresses that within the distribution groups proper interaction takes place: if a request is communicated to a participant (by a distributor), then the participant will respond (eventually) by rejecting it or having it finished.

IaRI2/IaRI3 Distributor-Participant Intragroup Interaction

∀℘: TRACES ∀ tid : TaskId ∀ t1, tf : T ∀ GI: DISTRIBUTION ∀ D: DISTRIBUTOR: GI: DISTRIBUTION
∀ P: PARTICIPANT: GI: DISTRIBUTION
[state(℘, t1, output(D)) ⊨ comm_from_to(requested(tid,tf), D, P)
         ⇒ ∃ t2 : T [t2 ≥ t1 & [state(℘, t2, output(P)) ⊨ comm_from_to(rejected(tid), P, D)
                                 ∨ state(℘, t2, output(P)) ⊨ comm_from_to(finished(tid), P, D)]]]

5.3 Intergroup Role Interaction Requirements

Intergroup role interaction requirements specify connectivity between the groups. This is achieved by an association between a role instance of one group and a role instance in another group, specified by the relation intergroup_role_relation(R, D). The first intergroup role interaction requirement specifies that an intergroup role relation between role instances of RECEPTIONIST and DISTRIBUTOR in open_group and cc exists, and, in particular that every request received by the role instance of RECEPTIONIST within open_group leads to a similar request of the role instance DISTRIBUTOR within cc.

IrRI1 Receptionist-Distributor Intergroup Interaction

∀ 𝔐: TRACES ∀ tid : TaskId ∀ t1, tf : T ∀ R: RECEPTIONIST: open_group ∀ C: CLIENT: open_group
∀ D: DISTRIBUTOR: cc ∀ P: PARTICIPANT: cc
[[intergroup_role_relation(R, D)
   & state(𝔐, t1, input(R)) |= comm_from_to(requested(tid, tf), C, R)]
        ⇒ ∃ t2 : T [t2 ≥ t1 & state(𝔐, t2, output(D)) |= comm_from_to(requested(tid, tf), D, P)]]

The next intergroup role interaction requirement specifies that also the return path from group instance cc to group instance open_group is guaranteed. This is achieved by an intergroup role relation from the distributor instance to the receptionist instance. The explanation of this requirement is as follows. If within the distribution group instance cc the distributor role instance gets information communicated by a participant, then within the open group instance the related receptionist role instance will communicate this information to the client. In this requirement (and other requirements) info ranges over { finished(tid), rejected(tid), accepted(tid) }.

IrRI2 Distributor-Receptionist Intergroup Interaction

∀ 𝔐: TRACES ∀ tid : TaskId ∀ t1, tf : T ∀ D: DISTRIBUTOR: cc ∀ P: PARTICIPANT: cc
∀ R: RECEPTIONIST: open_group ∀ C: CLIENT: open_group
[[state(𝔐, t1, input(D)) |= comm_from_to(info, P, D)
   & intergroup_role_relation(D, R)]
        ⇒ ∃ t2 : T [t2 ≥ t1 & state(𝔐, t2, output(R)) |= comm_from_to(info, R, C)]]

Similarly intergroup relations between the local bank group instances and the distributor group instance cc are specified:

IrRI3 Participant-Distributor Intergroup Interaction

∀ 𝔐: TRACES ∀ tid : TaskId ∀ t1, tf : T ∀ D1: DISTRIBUTOR: cc ∀ P1: PARTICIPANT: cc
∀ GI: DISTRIBUTION ∀ D2: DISTRIBUTOR: GI: DISTRIBUTION ∀ P1: PARTICIPANT: GI: DISTRIBUTION
[[state(𝔐, t1, input(P1)) |= comm_from_to(requested(tid, tf), D1, P1)
   & intergroup_role_relation(P1, D2)]
        ⇒ ∃ t2 : T [t2 ≥ t1 & state(𝔐,t2,output(D2)) |= comm_from_to(requested(tid,tf),D2,P2)]]

IrRI4 Distributor-Participant Intergroup Interaction

∀ 𝔐: TRACES ∀ tid : TaskId ∀ t1, tf : T ∀ D1: DISTRIBUTOR: cc ∀ P1: PARTICIPANT: cc
∀ GI: DISTRIBUTION ∀ D2: DISTRIBUTOR: GI: DISTRIBUTION ∀ P1: PARTICIPANT: GI: DISTRIBUTION
[[state(𝔐, t1, input(D2)) |= comm_from_to(info, P2, D2)
   & intergroup_role_relation(D2, P1)]
        ⇒ ∃ t2 : T[t2 ≥ t1 & state(𝔐,t2,output(P1)) |= comm_from_to(info,P1,D1)]]

5.4 Transfer Requirements

Successful cooperation within a group requires that communication takes place when needed. In particular this means that the two cooperating roles within the open group instance have to communicate successfully about requests, i.e., if a request is communicated by a client to the receptionist, this request will be received by the receptionist.

TR1 Client-Receptionist communication

$\forall \mathcal{M}$: TRACES $\forall$ tid : TaskId $\forall$ t1, tf : T $\forall$ C: CLIENT: open_group, $\forall$ R: RECEPTIONIST: open_group
[state($\mathcal{M}$, t1, output(C)) |= comm_from_to(requested(tid), tf), C, R)
        $\Rightarrow$ $\exists$ t2 : T [t2 $\geq$ t1 & state($\mathcal{M}$,t2, input(R)) |= comm_from_to(requested(tid), tf), C, R)]]

Moreover, they also communicate about acceptance, rejectance or finishing of tasks:

TR2 Client-Receptionist communication

$\forall \mathcal{M}$: TRACES $\forall$ tid : TaskId $\forall$ t1: T $\forall$ C: CLIENT: open_group $\forall$ R: RECEPTIONIST: open_group
[state($\mathcal{M}$, t1, output(R)) |= comm_from_to(info, R, C)
        $\Rightarrow$ $\exists$ t2 : T [t2 $\geq$ t1 & state($\mathcal{M}$,t2, input(C)) |= comm_from_to(info, R, C)]]

Similarly within the distribution groups proper communication has to take place about requests and what comes back for them:

TR3/TR5 Distributor-Participant Communication

$\forall \mathcal{M}$: TRACES $\forall$ tid : TaskId $\forall$ t1, tf : T $\forall$ GI: DISTRIBUTION $\forall$ D: DISTRIBUTOR: GI: DISTRIBUTION
$\forall$ P: PARTICIPANT: GI: DISTRIBUTION
[state($\mathcal{M}$, t1, output(D)) |= comm_from_to(requested(tid), tf), D, P)
        $\Rightarrow$ $\exists$ t2 : T [t2 $\geq$ t1 & state($\mathcal{M}$,t2, input(P)) |= comm_from_to(requested(tid), tf), D, P)]]

TR4/TR6 Distributor-Participant Communication

$\forall \mathcal{M}$: TRACES $\forall$ tid : TaskId $\forall$ t1: T $\forall$ GI: DISTRIBUTION $\forall$ D: DISTRIBUTOR: GI: DISTRIBUTION
$\forall$ P: PARTICIPANT: GI: DISTRIBUTION
[state($\mathcal{M}$, t1, output(P)) |= comm_from_to(info, P, D)
        $\Rightarrow$ $\exists$ t2 : T [t2 $\geq$ t1 & state($\mathcal{M}$,t2, input(D)) |= comm_from_to(info, P, D)]]

5.5 Single Role Behaviour Requirements

In this organization model many of the roles just earn their money communicating. But at least at some place in the organization the real work has to be done. This is performed by the participant roles in the local banks. If they do not reject a task, they have to finish it, as is expressed below:

PB1 Participant Behaviour

$\forall \mathcal{M}$: TRACES $\forall$ tid : TaskId $\forall$ t1, tf : T $\forall$ GI: DISTRIBUTION $\forall$ D: DISTRIBUTOR: GI: DISTRIBUTION
$\forall$ P: PARTICIPANT: GI: DISTRIBUTION
[state($\mathcal{M}$, t1, input(P)) |= comm_from_to(requested(tid), tf), D, P)
        $\Rightarrow$ $\exists$ t2 : T [t2 $\geq$ t1 & [state($\mathcal{M}$, t2, output(P)) |= comm_from_to(rejected(tid), P, D)
                          $\vee$ state($\mathcal{M}$, t2, output(P)) |= comm_from_to(finished(tid), P, D)]]]

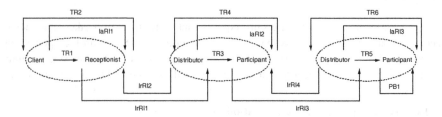

Fig. 3. Overview of non-global properties

6 Diagnosis of an Organization

In this section it will be shown how the palette of requirements of different types identified in Section 4 can be used to perform diagnosis of the dynamics within an organization. Before such a diagnostic process can be started, first a logical analysis is made of the relationships between global requirements and more local requirements for the organization (Section 6.1). Next a software environment to check behavioural requirements against traces is briefly discussed (Section 6.2). Finally, in Section 6.3 it is discussed how the logical analysis and the checking software environment can be used within a systematic diagnostic process.

6.1 Logical Relationships between the Requirements

Figure 3 shows possible logical relationships between different types of requirements. For example, within the rightmost group instance, the arrows for transfer requirement TR5 and role behaviour requirement PB1 'chain' in an appropriate manner to intragroup interation requirement IaRl3. Indeed, logically the latter requirement can be derived from the former two. This obtains a proof pattern

> TR5 & PB1 $\Rightarrow$ IaRl3

In a similar manner other proof patterns have been identified and actually proven for the intragroup interaction requirements IaRl1 and IaRl2, making use of inter group interaction requirements, transfer requirements, and (other) intragroup requirements:

> TR3 & IrRl3 &
> IaRl3 &
> TR6 & IrRl4 $\Rightarrow$ IaRl2

> TR1 & IrRl1 &
> IaRl2 &
> TR4 & IrRl2 $\Rightarrow$ IaRl1

Finally, the global requirement GR1 can be derived from IaRl1 and TR2.

> IaRl1 & TR2 $\Rightarrow$ GR1

These proof patterns, depicted in Figure 4 as an AND-tree, can be very useful in the analysis of malfunctioning of the organization in the following manner. For example, if for a given trace of the organization the global requirement GR1 is not satisfied, then, given the last proof pattern, by a refutation process it can be concluded that either transfer does not function properly or IaRI1 does not hold. If IaRI1 does not hold, then by one of the other proof patterns either IaRI2 does not hold, or one of the intergroup interaction requirements IrRI1 or IrRI2 does not hold, (or transfer fails). If the intragroup requirement IaRI2 does not hold, then either either IrRI3, IrRI4 or IaRI3 does not hold (or transfer fails). Finally, if IaRI3 does not hold, then by the first proof pattern either role behaviour requirement PB1 does not hold or transfer is not properly functioning. By this refutation analysis it follows that if GR1 does not hold for a given trace, then, skipping the intermediate requirements, the cause of this malfunctioning can be found in the set (the leaves of the tree in Figure 4):

{IrRI1, IrRI2, IrRI3, IrRI14} ∪ {PB1} ∪ {TR1, .., TR6}.

The logical analysis by itself does not pinpoint which one of these leaves actually is refuted. However, it shows a set of candidates that can be examined in more detail.

6.2 Checking the Temporal Trace Formulae

To check whether a given behavioural requirement is fulfilled in a given trace or set of traces, a Prolog programme has been developed. The temporal formulae are represented by nested term structures based on the logical connectives. For example, requirement GR1 from Section 4 is represented by

```
forall(M, T1, C:CLIENT, R:RECEPTIONIST, TID, TF,
    imp(holds(state(M, T1, output(C:CLIENT)),
                    communication_from_to(requested(TID, TF),
                              C:CLIENT, R:RECEPTIONIST), true),
    ex(T2=T1,
        or(holds(state(M, T2, input(C:CLIENT)),
                    communication_from_to(finished(TID),
                              R:RECEPTIONIST, C:CLIENT), true),
            holds(state(M, T2, input(C:CLIENT)),
                    communication_from_to(rejected(TID),
                              R:RECEPTIONIST, C:CLIENT), true)
        ))))
```

Traces are represented by sets of Prolog facts of the form

```
holds(state(m1, t(2), input(role)), a)), true).
```

where m1 is the trace name, t(2) time point 2, and a is a state formula in the ontology of the role's input. It is indicated that state formula a is true in the role's input state within the organization at time point 2. The Prolog programme for temporal formula checking uses Prolog rules such as

```
sat(and(F,G)) :- sat(F), sat(G).
```

that reduce the satisfaction of the temporal formula finally to the satisfaction of atomic state formulae at certain time points, which can be read from the trace.

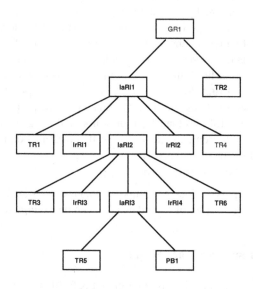

Fig. 4. AND-tree of requirements of different types

6.3 Diagnostic Method

Returning to the verification of the global organization property GR1, if the check shows that it is not satisfied, then subsequently, the candidate set of causes {IrRI1, IrRI2, IrRI3, IrRI14} ∪ {PB1} ∪ {TR1, .., TR6} generated from the logical analysis in Section 6.1 can be checked. Due to the logical relationships given by the proof patterns, at least one of them must be not satisfied. After having them checked it will be found which one is the culprit. Since the set only contains specific requirements which refer to local situations within the organization, this localises the problem. Thus this approach provides a method of diagnosing malfunctioning in an organization. In a more efficient, hierarchical, manner, based on the tree in Figure 4 (obtained from the logical analysis resulting in the proof patterns in Section 6.1), this method for diagnosis of malfunctioning in an organization runs as follows (according to a specific diagnostic method, sometimes called *hierarchical classification*):

1. First check the global properties
       (the top of the tree in Figure 4)
2. Focus the subsequent checking process on only those more local properties that in view of the logical dependencies relate to a more global property that has turned out to be false
       (the branches in the tree under a failed node)

3. Repeat this procedure with the focused more local properties as top-node
4. The most local properties that fail point at where the cause of malfunctioning can be found
    (one or more of the leaves of the tree)

Note that in step 2 all local properties that do not relate to a failing global property can be left out of consideration, which may obtain an advantage in the number of properties to be checked, compared to simply checking all properties, of n over 2^n (if the property refinement graph would have the structure of a binary tree with all branches of depth n).

This method has been used to analyse the organization simulation model presented in Section 3. In the simulation software environment log files containing the traces were automatically created that were saved at a place where the checking software environment can automatically read in the files and perform the checking process. Thus an overall software environment was created that is an adequate tool to diagnose the dynamics within the organization simulation model. In particular, the tool can be used for debugging of the simulation model.

7 Discussion

This paper contributes a framework to analyse the dynamics within an organization. One part of the framework is a temporal trace language to formally specify behavioural requirements of different types within the organization. Between different behavioural requirements specified in this language, logical relationships can be identified. A second part is a software environment to check behavioural requirements against a (set of) trace(s). The framework was tested by linking it to an organization simulation model implemented in Swarm. Traces generated by the simulation model were automatically checked by the checking software. The interface between the two parts of the software is defined on the basis of the log files created within the simulation model of the states of the different parts of the organization (i.e., input and output of the different role instances) over time. Since this is a very general notion, the approach can easily be applied using other simulation software. Another application is to use empirical traces of a real organization. Because it is not easy to obtain such empirical data about the dynamics, this application has not been performed yet.

By a systematic use of the framework a diagnostic method can be followed that is based on:
- logical relationships between global behavioural properties and local behavioural properties; i.e., a dependency tree such as the one depicted in Figure 4, obtained from a logical analysis of the requirements
- top down checking of behavioural requirements against traces

This diagnostic method for a malfunctioning organization first checks the global properties, next focuses the subsequent checking process on only these more local properties that in view of the logical analysis relate to a global property that has turned out false, and finally identifies the most local properties that fail; they point at where the cause of malfunctioning can be found.

This method obtains its efficiency from the fact that all more refined properties that (within the tree) are not a refinement of a failing more global property can be left out of consideration. Depending on the shape of the tree, and assuming that only one failure arises (single fault hypothesis), this may obtain a linear versus exponential advantage in the number of properties to be checked, compared to simply checking all properties.

The experiments carried out so far have already shown the advantage of the rapid prototyping in analysing processes at various levels of abstraction [16]. It enables the modeller to better understand the dynamic impact of organizational rules, organizational structures, and organizational   patterns [20]. Having an abstract prototype at hand is of great help for communication between modellers.

Compared to [2] our work allows for more expressive specification for dynamic properties; in [2] sequence diagrams are used for specification of interaction protocols, which is a more restricted format. Therefore dynamics that can be specified is of a simpler kind. Moreover, in [2] no specification language to analyse dynamic organization properties, checking software or diagnostic method is offered. In [7] a number of standard organization models are distinguished. Specification of dynamics within these organization models is not addressed. An interesting continuation would be to use the approach introduced in the current paper to add more detail about the intended dynamics within these organization models.

A similarity of our work to [18] is that in both cases Aalaadin (i.e., the AGR-model) is used as a point of departure. Moreover both papers emphasize a behaviouristic perspective on roles (in contrast to a mentalistic view which would commit to certain internal structures of an agent fulfilling a role; e.g., based on beliefs, desires and intentions). However, in [18] specification of dynamics is more restrictive than in our case: an extension of sequence diagrams is used that allows to express time durations between stimulus and response. Our temporal trace language is much more expressive. The idea of (dependency) relations between groups as put forward in [18] would be an interesting issue for further research in relation to our approach.

Monitoring of the multi-agent system is currently done within the environment of the simulated system. The next phase of our project will include monitoring agents (exception handling agents) for performing instrumentation, diagnosis and resolution tasks [5], [14] on the line of socially-attentive monitoring of failures in the social relationships between agents [13].

Future research will aim at building a library of different reusable organization models together with associated sets of behavioural requirements at different organizational levels (and their logical relationships). Moreover, in addition to the specification language used in this paper to analyse dynamics within an organization, a second language is planned to be developed: an executable temporal language for simulation of dynamics within an organization. For this second language also a software environment to support simulation will be developed.

References

1. Brazier, F. M. T., Jonker, C. M., Jungen, F. J., and Treur, J., Distributed Scheduling to Support a Call Centre: a Co-operative Multi-Agent Approach. In: *Applied Artificial Intelligence Journal*, vol. 13, 1999, pp. 65-90. H. S. Nwana and D. T. Ndumu (eds.), Special Issue on Multi-Agent Systems.
2. Caire, G., Garijo, F., Gomez, J., Pavon, J., Leal, F., Chainho, P., Kearney, P., Stark, J., Evans, R., and Massonet, P., Agent Oriented Analysis Using MESSGE/UML. In: M. Wooldridge, G. Weiss, and P. Ciancarini (eds.), Proc. of the Second International Workshop on Agent-Oriented Software Engineering, AOSE'01. Lecture Notes in CS, Springer Verlag. This volume.
3. Dardenne, A., Lamsweerde, A. van, and Fickas, S. (1993). Goal-directed Requirements Acquisition. *Science in Computer Programming*, vol. 20, pp. 3-50.
4. Darimont, R., and Lamsweerde, A. van (1996). Formal Refinement Patterns for Goal-Driven Requirements Elaboration. In: *Proc. of the Fourth ACM Symposium on the Foundation of Software Engineering (FSE4)*, pp. 179-190.
5. Dellarocas, C. and M. Klein. An experimental evaluation of domain-independent fault handling services in open multi-agent systems. In: *Proceedings of the 4th International Conference on Multi-Agent Systems (ICMAS-2000)*, Boston, MA, 2000.
6. Dellarocas, C., and M. Klein. A knowledge-based approach for handling exceptions in business processes. *Information Technology and Management* , 1:155--169, 2000.
7. Dignum, V., Weigand, H., and Xu, L., Agent Societies: Towards Frameworks-based Design. In: M. Wooldridge, G. Weiss, and P. Ciancarini (eds.), Proc. of the Second International Workshop on Agent-Oriented Software Engineering, AOSE'01. Lecture Notes in CS, Springer Verlag. This volume.
8. Ferber, J. and Gutknecht, O. (1998). A meta-model for the analysis and design of organizations in multi-agent systems. In: *Proc. of the Third International Conference on Multi-Agent Systems (ICMAS '98) Proceedings.* IEEE Computer Society, 1998
9. Ferber, J. and Gutknecht, O. (1999). Operational Semantics of a role-based agent architecture. *Proceedings of the 6th Int. Workshop on Agent Theories, Architectures and Languages.* Lecture Notes in AI, Springer-Verlag.
10. Ferber, J., Gutknecht, O., Jonker, C.M., Mueller, J.P., and Treur, J., Organization Models and Behavioural Requirements Specification for Multi-Agent Systems (extended abstract). In: *Proc. of the Fourth International Conference on Multi-Agent Systems, ICMAS 2000.* IEEE Computer Society Press, 2000. Extended version in: *Proc. of the ECAI 2000 Workshop on Modelling Artificial Societies and Hybrid Organizations*, 2000.
11. Herlea, D.E., Jonker, C.M., Treur, J., and Wijngaards, N.J.E. (1999). Specification of Behavioural Requirements within Compositional Multi-Agent System Design. In: F.J. Garijo, M. Boman (eds.), *Multi-Agent System Engineering, Proc. of the 9th European Workshop on Modelling Autonomous Agents in a Multi-Agent World, MAAMAW'99.* Lecture Notes in AI, vol. 1647, Springer Verlag, 1999, pp. 8-27.
12. Jonker, C.M., and Treur, J., Compositional Verification of Multi-Agent Systems: a Formal Analysis of Pro-activeness and Reactiveness. In: W.P. de Roever, H. Langmaack, A. Pnueli (eds.), *Proceedings of the International Workshop on Compositionality, COMPOS'97.* Lecture Notes in Computer Science, vol. 1536, Springer Verlag, 1998, pp. 350-380
13. Kaminka, G.A., and M. Tambe. Robust agent teams via socially-atentive monitoring. In: *Journal of Artificial Intelligence Research*, 12:105--147, 2000.

14. Klein, M., and C. Dellarocas. Exception handling in agent systems. In O. Etzioni, J. Muller, and J. Bradshaw, editors, In: *Proceedings of the 3rd International Conference on Autonomous Agents (AA'99)*, pages 62--68, 1999.

15. Kontonya, G., and Sommerville, I. (1998). *Requirements Engineering: Processes and Techniques*. John Wiley and Sons, New York.

16. Malone, T. W., K. Crowston, J. Lee, B. Pentland, C. Dellarocas, G. Wyner, J. Quimby, C. S. Osborn, A. Bernstein, G. Herman, M. Klein, and E. O'Donnell. Tools for inventing organizations: Toward a handbook for organizatinal processes. In: *Management Science*, 45:425-443, 2000.

17. Minar, M., R. Burkhart, C. Langton, and M. Askenazy. *The Swarm simulation system: A toolkit for building multi-agent simulations*. Technical report, Santa Fe Institute, 1996. http://www.santafe.edu/projects/swarm/.

18. Parunak, H.V.D., and Odell, J., Representing Social Structures in UML. In: M. Wooldridge, G. Weiss, and P. Ciancarini (eds.), Proc. of the Second International Workshop on Agent-Oriented Software Engineering, AOSE'01. Lecture Notes in CS, Springer Verlag. This volume. In: M. Wooldridge, G. Weiss, and P. Ciancarini (eds.), Proc. of the Second International Workshop on Agent-Oriented Software Engineering, AOSE'01. Lecture Notes in CS, Springer Verlag. This volume.

19. Venkatraman, M., and M.P. Singh. Verifying compliance with commitments protocols: enabling open web-based multiagent systems. In: *Autonomous Agents and Multi-Agent Systems*, 2:217--236, 1999.

20. Zambonelli, F., N.R. Jennings, and M. Wooldridge. Organizational abstractions for the analysis and design of multi-agent systems. In: P. Ciancarini and M. Wooldridge, editors, *Agent-Oriented Software Engineering*, LNCS 1957. Springer-Verlag, 2001.

Agent Societies: Towards Frameworks-Based Design

Virginia Dignum[1], Hans Weigand[2], and Lai Xu[2]

[1] Achmea
C/O University Utrecht, Intelligent Systems Group, PO Box 80089,
3508 TB Utrecht, The Netherlands
virginia.dignum@achmea.nl
[2] Infolab, Tilburg University, PO Box 90153,
5000 LE Tilburg, The Netherlands
{weigand, l.xu}@kub.nl

Abstract. We present a framework and methodology for the design of agent societies that considers the influence of social organizational aspects on the functionality and objectives of the agent society and specifies the development steps for the design and development of an agent-based system for a particular domain. Our approach is to provide a generic frame that directly relates to the organizational perception of the problem. The methodology informs and supports the development of increasingly detailed models of the society and its components. For the implementation of each methodological step existing agent oriented software development methodologies can be used.

1 Introduction

The application of the agent paradigm to the development of different application calls for a development methodology that focuses not only on the internal organization of each of the intervening agents but also on the social aspects of the domain [26]. Generic SE methodologies are not tailored to deal with design aspects specific to agent systems, such as the capture of flexible and autonomous behavior of agents and the complexity of agent interactions and social organization of the system [35].

Currently, research on agent specific SE is a topic of great interest [34, 14]. A good overview and analysis of existing methodologies, applicable to Agent-Oriented Information Systems can be found in [1]. However, as yet, there is no well-established and all-encompassing agent-oriented methodology that covers the whole development process from early requirements acquisition to implementation. Most existing methodologies concentrate in just one part of the total picture or are too formal to be applicable in practice. Furthermore, most approaches start from the moment that the decision to use the agent paradigm has been made, and do not guide this choice. A methodology for designing multi-agent systems must be both specific enough to allow engineers to design the system and generic enough to allow the acceptance and implementation of multi-agent systems within an organization, allowing for the involvement of users, managers and project teams.

M.J. Wooldridge, G. Weiß, and P. Ciancarini (Eds.): AOSE 2001, LNCS 2222, pp. 33-49, 2002.

In order to make agent technology widely accepted and used in industry it is necessary to clearly specify the type of problems suitable for an agent approach and the benefits of agents above other technologies. An aspect that in our view will contribute to the acceptance and understanding of agents societies in organizations, is that the agent paradigm provides a natural way to view and characterize intelligent systems [32]. Intelligence and interaction are deeply and inevitably coupled, and multi-agent systems reflect this insight. Multi-agent systems can provide insights and understanding about poorly understood interactions between natural, intelligent beings as they organize themselves into groups, societies and economies in order to achieve improvement. Other important contributions to the success and acceptance of agent technology are the development of robust agent tools and of standard methodologies such as FIPA or the AUML effort [2].

Our aim is to develop a practical methodology that describes all the steps of development of a multi-agent system. The methodology takes the organizational perspective as starting point and specifies the development steps for the design and development of an agent-based system for a particular domain. Once these steps have been identified, existing, specific agent-based methodologies can be used for the development and modeling of each step. We believe that such a generic framework, based on the organizational view, will contribute to the acceptance of multi-agent technology by organizations. Furthermore the methodology proposed gives an answer to the development challenges posed by Sycara [29]:

1. How to engineer practical multi-agent systems.
2. How to decompose problems and allocate tasks to individual agents
3. How to coordinate agent control and communication
4. How to make multiple agents to act in a coherent manner
5. How to make each agent reason about the other agents and the state of coordination
6. How to reconcile conflicting goals between coordinating agents

Based on the organizational coordination model, we define a social framework for agent communities that 'implements' the generic interaction, cooperation and communication mechanisms (2 and 3) that occur in the problem domain. The proposed methodology (1) allows to tailor this generic coordination model to the specific application and to determine the specific agent roles and interactions (5). In the following steps the level of design detail will be successively increased to include the internal organization and reasoning capabilities of the agents (4). The reconciliation of conflicting goals (6) is one aspect of interaction. Depending on the organizational model, different reconciliation processes need to be specified.

Our work applies ideas from coordination theory research in organizational sciences to the design of agent societies. The resulting architecture of the agent society considers and reflects the implications of the coordination model of the real-life organization being modeled.

2   Coordination in Organizations

Organizational science and economics have since long researched coordination and organizational structures. Drawing on disciplines such as sociology and psychology, research in organization theory focuses on how people co-ordinate their activities in formal organizations.

An organization can be defined as a specific solution created by more or less autonomous actors to achieve common goals. In order to achieve their objectives, organizations depend on a facilitation layer, which provides the social organization of the environment, that is, the maintenance of the organization itself. Social interaction emerges from a set of negotiated social norms and is regulated by mechanisms of social control. The way that different societies organize and balance their objectives and their facilitation activities is dependent on their coordination model.

Software agents are 'advertised' as autonomous entities with reasoning and communicative capabilities, and therefore utmost suitable to implement, simulate or represent real-life entities presenting the same autonomy. Agent societies[1] represent the interactions between agents and are as such the virtual counterpart of real-life societies and organizations. Because of the proactive and autonomous behavior of agents it is natural to design agent societies mimicking the behavior and structure of human organizations [36]. Agents model specific roles in the system and interact with others as a means to accomplish their roles. This perspective makes the design of the system less complex since it reduces the conceptual distance between the system and the real-world application it has to model.

2.1 Models of Organizational Coordination

Relationships between and within organizations are developed for the exchange of goods, resources, information and so on. Williamson [33] argues that the transaction costs are determinant for the organizational model. Transaction costs will rise when the unpredictability and uncertainty of events increases, and/or when transactions require very specific investments, and/or when the risk of opportunistic behavior of partners is high. When transaction costs are high, societies tend to choose a hierarchical model in order to control the transaction process. If transaction costs are low, that is, are straightforward, non- repetitive and require no transaction-specific investments, then the market is the optimal choice. Powell [28] introduces networks as another possible coordination model. Networks stress the interdependence between different organizational actors and pay a lot of attention to the development and maintenance of (communicative) relationships, and the definition of rules and norms of conduct within the network. At the same time, actors are independent, have their own interests, and can be allied to different networks.

Coordination in markets is achieved mainly through a price mechanism in which independent actors are searching for the best bargain. Hierarchies are mainly coordinated by supervision, that is, actors that are involved in power-dependent relationships act according to routines. Networks achieve coordination by mutual interest and interdependency. The characteristics of the different forms of organization are captured in Table 1 (adapted from [22]).

---

[1] In order to stress the social aspects of agent interaction we use the term **agent society** instead of **multi-agent system**.

Table 1. Comparison of organizational forms

	Market	**Network**	**Hierarchy**
Coordination	Price mechanism	Collaboration	Supervision
Relation form	Competition	Mutual interest	Authority
Primary means of communication	Prices	Relationships	Routines
Tone or Climate	Precision/ suspicion	Open-ended/ mutual benefits	Formal/ bureaucratic
Conflict Resolution	Haggling (Resort to courts)	Reciprocity (Reputation)	Supervision

2.2   Agent Societies

Coordination is one of the cornerstones of agent societies and is considered an important problem inherent to the design and implementation of MAS [3]. However, the implications of the coordination model for the agent society architecture and design method have usually not been considered. So far, research about coordination in MAS has been mainly limited to the study of technical aspects of coordination, such as control and planning. Little attention has been paid to the organizational aspects of coordination in agent societies.

In multi-agent research, organizations are often viewed as a structural relationship between agents. Ferber and Gutknecht introduced AALAADIN in [11], a model for agent societies based on an organizational perspective that describes an organization based on the way that agents perform roles and are organized into groups to form a whole. This model is based on the basic notions of agent, role and group and has been used in requirements engineering [16] and to extend AUML [31]. In our view the concepts of agent, role and group model can be extended and refined to incorporate aspects of social coordination in organizations. Coordination structures define roles and interactions specific to that structure and that can be used to in the development of the agent society model. That is, the organization of a market will require different roles and interaction forms than a hierarchy. Our aim is to provide generic facilitation and interaction frameworks for agent societies that implement the functionality derived from the coordination model applicable to the problem domain. The type of coordination will determine the interaction patterns and functionality of the facilitation level of the agent society.

All societies are created and maintained to realize a certain objective, dependent on the domain goals and requirements. The fact that societies are designed to realise goals is a main difference between our notion of society and the concept of group in the AALAADIN model introduced in [11]. Groups in AALAADIN are defined as atomic sets of agents and do not incorporate the notion of goal. However, agent societies, like 'real' societies, are dependent on a layer of facilitation to organize and maintain the society itself. The type of social coordination determines the facilitation roles and interaction forms in the society. Therefore, it is our view that the design of agent societies should start with the identification of the overall type of coordination in the domain.

In agent societies coordination models describe the way interactions between agents are organized and the way the interface between the society and the 'outside world' is defined. That is, coordination models provide a framework to express interaction between agent activities and social behavior of the system [7].

The way organizational coordination models achieve coordination is determinant to the motivation of coordination in agent societies. Table 2 gives an overview of the characteristics of agent societies with different coordination models.

Table 2. Coordination in agent societies

	Market	**Network**	**Hierarchy**
Type of society	Open	Trust	Closed
Agent 'values'	Self interest	Mutual interest/ Collaboration	Dependency
Facilitation roles	Matchmaking Banking	Gatekeeping Registry Matchmaking	Interface Control

In **markets**, agents are self-interested (determine and follow their own goals) and value their freedom of association and own judgement above security and trust issues. Openness is thus per definition a feature of markets. Facilitation is, in the most extreme case, limited to identification and matchmaking activities. Interaction in markets occurs through communication and negotiation.

Network organizations are built around general patterns of interaction or contracts. Relationships are dependent on clear communication patterns and social norms. Agents in a network society are still self interested but are willing to trade some of their freedom to obtain secure relations and trust. Therefore, agents need to enter a social contract with the network society in which they commit themselves to act within and according to the norms and rules of the society. The society is responsible to make its rules and norms known to potential members. Coordination is achieved by mutual interest, possibly using trusted third parties, and according to well-defined rules and sanctions.

Finally, in a **hierarchy** interaction lines are well defined and the facilitation level assumes the function of global control of the society and coordination of interaction with the outside world. In a hierarchy, agents are cooperative, not motivated by self interest and all contribute to a common global goal. Coordination is achieved through command and control lines. Agents are cooperative and not motivated by self-interest. Such agents are said to be benevolent, that is, agents are assumed to always attempt to do what is request from them [21].

2.3   Coordination of Activities

In Computer Science coordination is defined as the art of managing interactions and dependencies among activities. Coordination languages are a class of programming notations that offer a solution to the problem of specifying and managing the interactions among computing agents. From this point of view coordination models are divided into two classes: control-driven and data-driven [27]. Control-driven models are systems made up of a well-defined number of entities and functions, in which the flow of control and the dependencies between entities need to be regulated. The data-driven model is more suited for open societies where the number of entities and functions is not known a priori and cooperation is an important issue.

The main difference between this classification and the classification introduced in section 2.1 is that the former takes an agent perspective and the later an organizational perspective. That, is where the classification of co-operation provided by organizational theory, as described in section 2.1 stems from social considerations and transaction costs, the data-driven, control-driven classification is concerned with the way interaction between agents happens. This classification can be seen as an extra dimension of interaction, and can be applied to all agent society models.

3   Agent Society Frameworks

In this section we will describe in more detail the social frameworks for agent societies that will implement these coordination models.

Different application contexts exhibit different needs with respect to coordination, and the choice of a coordination model will have great impact in the design of the agent society. Following this observation we argue that the first step in the development of an agent society is to identify its underlying coordination model.

So far, most agent-oriented design methodologies haven't considered the influence of the social organization model on the functionality and objectives of the agent society. In many cases the social organization is left implicit in the design of the agent society. However, the organization model determines important autonomous activities, which must be explicitly organized into autonomous entities in the conceptual model of the agent society.

Different coordination models result in different frameworks for agent societies. The overall goals of a society are domain dependent but all societies depend on a facilitation layer that provides the social backbone of the organization. Facilitation activities deal with the functioning of the society itself and are related to the underlying coordination model.

Once the social coordination model of a specific problem domain has been established, the corresponding agent society framework can be applied. In the next stage, this framework is extended with domain specific roles and interaction forms that characterize the problem. We can compare this process to the design a generic enterprise model including roles as accountants, secretaries and managers, as well as their job descriptions and relationships, and then extending it with a 'recipe' to build the functions necessary to achieve the objectives of the given enterprise. These are, for example, designers and carpenters if the firm is going to manufacture chairs, and programmers and system analysts if the enterprise is a software house. While the chosen coordination model determines the social part, domain roles are directly derived from the domain requirements.

3.1   Market Model

The market metaphor has been used to describe agent interaction, enhancing the adaptation, robustness, and flexibility of multi-agent systems. In a market model, agents representing (or providing) services and/or competencies compete to perform tasks leading to the satisfaction of their own individual objectives as well as to a possible overall system's goal [24].

The main goal of a market is to facilitate exchange between agents. In a market heterogeneous agents will strive to find partners or clients with whom to trade their services. Being open systems, market architectures assume the heterogeneity of its members, both in structure, goals and ways of acting. The degree of the organization of the facilitation aspects of the society will determine the level of freedom of agents in markets.

In a free market framework, social interaction is open and partners in a transaction are free to make their own agreements and contract rules. Markets are particularly suitable to situations in which resources are overlapping and agents need to compete for them. For example, the market architecture is a good selection to model product or service allocation problems. Being self-interested, agents will first try to solve their own local problem, and then agents can potentially negotiate with other agents to exchange services or goods in shortage or in excess.

The facilitation activities of such agent society are mainly limited to matchmaking, that is, help agents find suitable partners. **Matchmakers** keep track of agents in the system, their needs and possibilities and mediate in the matching of demand and supply of services. Market societies also provide **identification** and **reputation** facilities to build confidence for customers as well as offering guarantees to its members. Furthermore, it is necessary to define ways to value the goods to be exchanged and determine profit and fairness of exchanges. This is accomplished by some banking facilities and currency specification.

3.2   Networks

Networks are coalitions of self-interested agents that agree to collaborate to achieve a mutual goal. Agents in a network society are still self interested but are willing to trade some of their freedom to obtain secure relations and trust. Coordination is achieved by mutual interest, possibly using trusted third parties, and according to well-defined rules and sanctions. These coalitions have been studied in the area of game theory and Distributed Artificial Intelligence (DAI) [30].

Networks provide an explicit shared context, describing rules and social norms for interaction and collaboration. As in any market, the aim of agents when entering the society is to trade their knowledge, goods or services. An agent society based on the model must be able of describing its rules of interaction, regulations, facilities and legal guarantees to applying members.

Dellarocas introduces the concept of Contractual Agent Societies (CAS) as a model for developing agent societies [9]. CAS has been inspired by work in the areas of organizational theory, economy and interaction sociology, which model organizations and social systems after contracts. Social contracts govern the interaction of a member with the society. Furthermore, the society is responsible to enforce the contracts formed by its members and punish potential violators (for example, through loss of reputation or eventually banishment). New agents are admitted through a process or socialization during which the agent negotiates with the society the terms of its membership. As a result the terms of the social contracts of existing members may need to be renegotiated as well.

Facilitation level agents monitor and help form contracts, take care of introducing (teaching) new agents to the rules of the market, keep track of the reputation of agents. Furthermore, they keep and enforce the 'norms' of the agent community and ensure interaction. Besides matchmakers as in market frameworks, other types of facilitation level agents in networks are gatekeepers, notaries and monitoring agents. Gatekeepers are responsible for accepting and introducing new agents to the market. Agents entering the marketplace must be informed about the possibilities and capabilities of the market. **Gatekeepers** negotiate the terms of a social contract between the applicant and the members of the market. **Notaries** keep track of collaboration contracts between agents. **Monitoring agents** are trusted third parties. The marketplace must provide monitoring agents to interested parties. When a contract appoints a (set of) monitoring agents, this is the equivalent to the setting up of a (super) contract between the contracting agents and the environment (here personified by the monitoring agents). This super-contract (which can also be described using the contract language) specifies that the monitoring agents are allowed to check the contracting agents actions (ex. Look at agent states) and that the contracting agents must submit to the sanctions imposed.

3.3   Hierarchies

Hierarchies coordinate the flow of resources or information through adjacent steps by controlling and directing it at a higher level in the managerial hierarchy. Managerial decisions, and not negotiation and communication as in markets, determine interaction and design. Demand parties do not select a supplier from a group of potential suppliers: they simply work with a predetermined one. Vertical integration occurs where the hierarchy is a single firm. In other cases the hierarchy may span several separate firms in a close, perhaps electronically mediated relationship (vertical coordination). In vertical coordination hierarchies one can choose to integrate the hierarchies of each of the organizations involved or to model one organization as an agent participating in the hierarchy modeling the coordination.

In hierarchical systems, an agent reigns over an arbitrarily and usually statically defined sub-hierarchy, in many cases an administrative domain of some kind. For instance, a university could be managed as follows: an agent is in charge in each lab, whereas other agents each oversee a department and a single one rules the university. These domains do not reflect the easy routing parts of the network and do not evolve.

Environments such as automated manufacturing planning and control are also well suited to the hierarchical model. In such systems, reliable control of resources and information flow requires central entities that manage local resources and data but also need quick access to global ones. Hierarchical models of agents have been used for information agents [6] and for management of communication networks [12]. In a hierarchical model of information systems, each information agent is responsible for providing information about a specific domain. Information agents further down the hierarchy provide more specialized information about a domain. In response to a query, an information agent may cooperate with information agents in other domains or sub-domains, in order to generate a response. Communication network solutions are based on a hierarchy of autonomous intelligent agents, which have local decision making capabilities, but cooperate to resolve conflicts. Higher level agents arbitrate unresolvable disputes between peer agents.

In a hierarchic agent model agents at facilitation level are mainly dedicated to the overall control and optimization of the system activities. Some times, these facilitation activities are concentrated in one agent, typically the 'root' agent of the hierarchy.

Controllers will monitor and orient the overall performance of the system or of a part of the system. Autonomous agents have local perspective and their actions are determined by its local state. Therefore, in a hierarchical architecture, is necessary to have an agent which role is to control the overall performance of the system. **Interface agents** in a hierarchical model are responsible for the communication between the system and the 'outside world'. In this architecture communication lines between agents are predefined. Furthermore, agents are usually not free to enter or leave the system. Therefore communication with the outside must be regulated at the facilitation level.

4   Development Methodology

In this section we introduce a methodology for the development of agent societies based on the coordination frameworks described above. After accessing the applicability of the agent paradigm to the problem on hand, the methodology consists of the following levels, which provide a growing level of refinement of the resulting system into more structured and precise forms:

- **Coordination**: the structure of the domain is determined and a model is designed based on the collection of coordination models available in the library.
- **Environment**: based on the coordination model design in the previous step, this level describes the interaction between the society and its environment in terms of global requirements and domain ontology.
- **Behavior**: based on the models above, in this level the intended behavior of the society is described in terms of agent roles and interaction patterns. These process is supported by a library of roles and interaction patterns
- **Agent**: finally, the internal structure of agents is described in terms of requirements for communication, action, interface and reasoning behavior.

We intend to develop libraries of models, patterns, behaviors and components to inform this process. The methodological process is described in Figure 6 and will be described in more detail in the following sections.

These steps result in a complete model for the agent society. Furthermore, a verification process is needed to demonstrate that the designed system actually will show the required behavior. In the very least verification must demonstrate that system objectives and requirements are met by the design.

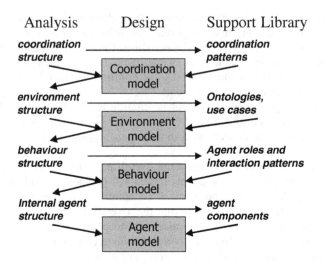

Fig. 1. Development methodology for agent societies

4.1   Determination of Agent Appropriateness

It is commonly accepted that the agent paradigm is appropriate for complex, distributed problems and reactive systems. Such systems maintain an ongoing interaction with some environment and are inherently quite difficult to design and correctly implement. Moreover, agents scan be seen as 'active objects', that is, objects with goals and communicative and deliberative capabilities. Therefore, agents are applicable in areas were the object paradigm has limitations, especially where communication is involved [13].

The aim of this pre-step to the methodology is to motivate the choice of an agent-based approach to the organization involved in the deployment of the system. It is clear that both empirical and methodological guidance is necessary for the identification of application areas for which agent-oriented approaches are the best. [25] indicates some empirical guidelines that have been identified by EURESCOM [19] to help a developer decide or not whether an agent-oriented approach is appropriate.

However, more research is needed in this area, in order to be able to define methods, libraries and heuristics supporting and informing the application of the agent paradigm to arbitrary problems. This need has been recognized both in the scientific as in the industrial communities and some work is already taking place. For instance, [25] describes a method to determine the best methodology for a particular problem, and compares both agent-oriented as object-oriented methodologies. In our opinion, this is a valid first step towards a methodological approach to the problem of evaluating the applicability of agent-oriented design approaches.

4.2   Coordination Level

In this stage a decision is achieved on which coordination model applies to the problem. Table 3 gives an overview of the specific characteristics of each coordination model, which can be used to determine the applicable model for the domain. The identification of the appropriate model will point out the type of social laws and norms of conduct and inform the organization on the interaction patterns and facilitation needs of the agent society, as described in section 3.

Table 3. Social characteristics of different frameworks

	Market	**Network**	**Hierarchy**
Society purpose	Exchange	Collaboration	Production
Goals	Individual goals (determined by the agent)	Both are possible	Determined by the global goals of the society
Relation forms	Negotiation (e.g. Contract Net Protocol)	Negotiable within society norms and rules	Fixed (e.g. Action/ Workflow loop)
Communication capabilities of agents	Interaction based on standards; communication concerns exchange only	Both the interaction procedures and exchange can be negotiated	Specified on design
Interface to outside world	Usually open for agents (after identification)	Admittance procedure for agents	Closed for agents; open for data (input and output)

So far, agent-based methodologies that consider both the social and the agent levels of analysis and design have been specified with a specific type of society in mind. For example, the Gaia methodology is intended to support the development of societies of agents, which constituents are known at design time and in which all agents are supposed to cooperate towards a common goal, and is thus not suitable to the development of market-like societies [34]. The Coordination Level of our methodology guides the choice of a coordination model and informs the further design process.

4.3   Environment Level

At the environment level we describe the external behavior of the society, that is, the interaction between society and its environment or external world. This includes the identification of the functionality of the society and the specification of the domain ontology.

Organizations and their environments are interdependent, and each can influence the other. The design of agent societies depends in many ways on the environment. In characterizing the environment, one has to decide what level of analysis is appropriate. The behavior of an agent society with respect to its environment can be defined in terms of the expected functionality of the society, that is, what is the society expected to do or produce. This can be expressed in terms of overall requirements or in terms of scenarios or use cases. Requirement Engineering is an important topic of research and several methods have been developed. However these methods are not always applicable to the specific needs of agent systems development. The Requirement Language described in [8, 15] has been developed specifically to specify behavioral requirements and scenarios for agent systems.

Another issue in this level is to identify the concepts and relationships relevant in the domain. Because each agent can have its own ontology, or "view of the world", a common ontology is used to bridge the different ontologies of agents. Depending on the domain and coordination model, the shared ontology can be the merge of the ontologies of each agent or it can concentrate on the concepts relevant for the interaction between agents. The merging approach is not scalable and is costly. Furthermore, the process must be repeated when new agents enter the society, and may not even be possible due to unresolvable inconsistencies between ontologies. In the distributed approach, only articulations between ontologies that serve specific application objectives need to be generated [20].

4.4   Behavior Level

The previous development steps have resulted in a coordination framework (Coordination Level) and the description of the intended behavior of the agent society in terms of requirements or use cases (Environment Level). The purpose of the Behavior Level is to populate the framework with the agent roles and interaction patterns needed to achieve the requirements.

At this level, whether or not an agent is intelligent, or how agents are internally structured is not important. We are concerned with only the high-level definition of the types of agents and their goals. The social rules and norms of conduct associated with each coordination framework will determine the interaction patterns between agents in the society. To support the identification and specification of agent roles, role catalogues have been developed (for instance at BT) [17]. These catalogues provide commonly occurring role models, which include many of the facilitation roles we have described in section 3. Interaction patterns can be modeled using for example Petri Nets or AUML interaction protocols [2].

A methodology that accounts for the analysis and design of social behavior of agent societies is SODA [26]. SODA views coordination as an interaction issue as described in section 2.3 and does not consider the organizational aspects of coordination. Our approach provides a structural way to specify the analysis and design of agent roles and interaction, specifying the coordination framework, and consequently the facilitation structure. This will direct the choice of a specific design methodology for the specification of the behavior of the agent system. In addition, we plan to develop a library of generic models for different agent roles and interaction patterns.

4.5   Internal Agent Level

At Agent Level the functionality of each agent role is specified in terms of specific requirements for interaction, communication, reasoning, goals behavior and interface. Depending on the application, agent societies can be open systems where foreign agents (which design cannot be determined a priori) can participate. Therefore, it is not possible to enforce a particular design for the internal structure of agents. However, agents living in a society must, besides the capability of performing its own task, be able to interact. This imposes some conditions to the internal model of the agent which are described in this level.

Furthermore, instead of designing each new agent from scratch a generic agent model can be used. This model can be adapted and filled up with components necessary to achieve the agent's functionality. GAM (Generic Agent Model) gives a formal design of a compositional agent model that can be reused as a template of pattern for a variety of agent types and application domains [5]. MaSE [10] and DESIRE [4] are other examples of methodologies for agent design.

5   Application Example

We are currently applying the methodology described in this paper to the development of K-Exchange, a knowledge exchange support system at Achmea. The objective of the system is to support intranet users to exchange knowledge with each other, in a way that preserves the knowledge, rewards the knowledge owner and reaches the knowledge seeker in a just-in-time, just-enough basis. Current users of the (pilot) intranet are project managers and developers of non-life insurance products. The contents of the intranet are (XML) documents representing knowledge about reports, people, applications, websites, projects, questions, etc.

The following meta-level requirements expressed by the project stakeholders are used to determine both the applicability of an agent-based solution and the desirable type of coordination:

−   The *organization* aims at supporting collaboration and extending synergy. Another aim of the organization is to preserve existing knowledge and make it available organization-wide.

−   *Knowledge owners* are willing to share their knowledge within a controllable, trusted group; however they wish to be able to decide on sharing decisions and conditions; added-value of the sharing effort and fair exchange is a must (that is, the feeling that one is rewarded for share)

−   *Knowledge seekers* are not aware of existing knowledge and knowledge owners; they also wish to be able to decide on acquisition conditions and partners, furthermore an accreditation and certification mechanism is desired, that enables checking the level of trust and knowledge of partners

These requirements identify a distributed system where different actors, acting autonomously on behalf of a user and each pursuing its own goals, need to interact in order to achieve their goals. Thus, communication and negotiation are paramount. Furthermore, the number and behavior of participants cannot be fixed a priori and the system can be expected to expand and change during operation. These characteristics indicate a situation for which the agent paradigm is well suited. Therefore, the methodology described in the previous sections can be followed in order to design the system. The choices and commitments taken at each methodological level can be very briefly described as follows:

Coordination level: The system needs to satisfy the global organizational requirement of supporting collaboration and synergy. Participants are aware of and collaborative with this requirement but also have their own objectives and constraints. Furthermore, the system implements a situation where collaboration and certification mechanisms are necessary. Participants wish to be free to determine their own exchange rules and to be assured that there is control over who are the other participants in the environment.

In this situation a market framework is not really suitable because negotiation in a market follows fixed rules (for example an auction model) and participants cannot negotiate their own exchange model with each other. Moreover, participation is often open to any agent, and restriction of role or access is not possible. Also the hierarchical model can be rejected because it imposes a fixed partnership relation that is not possible, since partners and sources are not a priori known.

On the other hand, the expressed requirements and wishes of the stakeholders point clearly to the **network** framework (see Table 3). The facilitation roles of gatekeeper, matchmaker and notary are deduced from the network framework and the characteristics of the application. The gatekeeper determines whether an agent can participate in the exchange or not and what kind of role can be fulfilled, the matchmaker matches supply and demand of knowledge between participants and the notary registers and oversees the exchange commitments decided upon between participants.

Environment level: The aim of this level is to identify the domain specific requirements. For the (brief) description of the knowledge exchange network above, the following requirements can be deduced (this list is only a very informal part of the complete requirement specification):

-      Knowledge owners provide knowledge sources
-      Knowledge seekers require knowledge sources (ask for answers)
-      Participants can negotiate exchange terms
-      Knowledge owners are rewarded for their input
-      The editorial board judges the validity and correctness of knowledge items
-      Experts are participants knowledgeable in a certain area
-      Experts (participants designed knowledgeable in a certain area) can be asked for answers and for opinion on knowledge sources

At this level, it is also necessary to specify the common ontology identifying and describing concepts that must be understood by participating agents, that is, the communication content. In K-Exchange three ontologies are needed:
-      *Exchange ontology* describing concepts related to exchange of knowledge such as knowledge owner, knowledge source and knowledge description.
-      *Non-life insurance ontology*, describing concepts related to the application domain, such as mobility, travel insurance, policy, etc.

- *Achmea ontology*, describing concepts related to the organization such as ABU (Achmea Business Unit), AKN (Achmea Knowledge Net, the intranet for knowledge workers) and knowledge center.

Behavior level: In this level the environment requirements described in the environment level need to be translated into domain roles and interaction rules of the system. Clearly the roles of knowledge seeker and knowledge owner are needed. Other roles, such as editor and expert relate to the desired functionality of the system. Editors are responsible to determine the validity and degree of expertise of knowledge items and knowledge owners, and experts can be consulted about a certain area and will be requested to answer questions of knowledge seekers. Furthermore, the role of visitor can be defined, referring to participants who are just browsing through the system, are able to consult the knowledge repository but cannot request most of the services.

Agent level: At this level, the internal components of each agent have to be described. However, at the moment we are still in the phase of defining the overall characteristics of the system and no work has been done yet on the internal characteristics of agents.

6   Conclusions

We have presented a global methodology for the design of agent societies. The methodology takes the organizational perspective as starting point and specifies the development steps for the design and development of an agent-based system for a particular domain. Although there are several agent-based software engineering methodologies (for example, [26, 35, 4, 10]) these are often either too specific or too formal and not easily used and accepted. Our approach is to provide a generic frame that directly relates to the organizational perception of a problem. If needed, existing methodologies can be used for the development, modeling and formalization of each step. We believe that this approach will contribute to the acceptance of multi-agent technology by organizations. One contribution of our research is that is describes the implications of the coordination model of the organization for the architecture and design method of the agent society being developed.

We are currently applying this methodology to the development of a Knowledge Management Environment. This will serve as well as a test case to the methodology. Our research will further continue in two directions. On one hand, we intend to further specify each step of the methodology and to develop libraries of conceptual interaction patterns, organizational and facilitation roles and agent components. These libraries will improve and facilitate the design agent societies. We also plan to look at the compatibility and integration of our ideas with current standardization efforts for agent development (for example the Agent UML effort [23]). On the other hand, we plan to develop tailored frameworks for specific applications domains such as Knowledge Management, Workflow Management and e-business.

References

1. Azary, O., Woo, C.: Analysis and design of Agent-Oriented Information Systems (AOIS). Working paper 99-MIS-004, Faculty of Commerce & Business Administration, Univ. of British Columbia, Vancouver, Canada (2000)
2. Bauer B., Mueller, J., Odell, J.: Agent UML: A Formalism for Specifying Multiagent Software Systems. In: Ciancarini, P., Wooldridge, M. (eds.): Agent-Oriented Software Engineering, LNCS 1957. Springer-Verlag (2001) 91-104
3. Bond, A., Gasser, L.: Readings in Distributed Artificial Intelligence. Morgan Kaufmann, (1988)
4. Brazier, F., Dunin-Keplicz, B., Jennings, N., Treur, J.: DESIRE: Modeling Multi-Agent Systems in a Compositional Formal Framework. In: Huhns, M., Singh M. (eds.): International Journal of Cooperative Information Systems, 6(1) (1997)
5. Brazier, F., Jonker, C., Treur, J.: Compositional Design and Reuse of a Generic Agent Model, Applied Artificial Intelligence Journal, vol. 14 (2000) 491-538
6. Castillo, A., Kawaguchi, M., Paciorek, N., Wong, D.: Concordia™ as Enabling Technology for Cooperative Information Gathering. In: Proceedings of Japanese Society for Artificial Intelligence Conference, Tokyo, Japan (1998)
7. Ciancarini, P., Omicini, A., Zambonelli, F.: Coordination Models for Multi-Agent Systems. In: AgentLink News, 3, July (1999)
8. Dastani, M., Jonker, C., Treur, J.: A Requirement Specification Language for Configuration Dynamics of Multi-Agent System. In this volume.
9. Dellarocas, C.: Contractual Agent Societies: Negotiated shared context and social control in open multi-agent systems. In: Proceedings of Workshop on Norms and Institutions in Multi-Agent Systems, Autonomous Agents-2000, Barcelona (2000)
10. DeLoach, S.: Multiagent Systems Engineering: A Methodology and Language for Designing Agent Systems. In: Proceedings of Workshop on Agent-Oriented Information Systems (AOIS'99) (1999)
11. Ferber, J., Gutknecht, O.: A meta-model for the analysis and design of organizations in multi-agent systems. In: Proceedings of the Third International Conference on Multi-Agent Systems (ICMAS'98), IEEE Computer Society, (1998)
12. Frei, C., Faltings, B.: A Dynamic Hierarchy of Intelligent Agents for Network Management. In: Proceedings of 2nd International Workshop on Intelligent Agents for Telecommunications Applications (IATA'98), Paris, France (1998) 1-16
13. Jennings, N., Wooldridge, M. (eds.): Agent Technology: Foundations, Applications and Markets. Springer-Verlag (1998)
14. Jennings, N.: On agent-based software engineering. Artificial Intelligence, 117 (2000) 277-296
15. Jonker, C., Klusch, M., Treur, J.: Design of Collaborative Information Agents, Cooperative Information Agents IV. In: Klusch M., Kerschberg, L. (eds.): Cooperative Information Agents IV. LNAI 1860, Springer-Verlag (2000) 262 – 283
16. Jonker, C., Letia, J., Treur, J.: Diagnosis of the Dynamics within an Organization by Trace Checking of Behavioral Requirements. In this volume.
17. Kendall, E.: Agent Software Engineering with Role Modeling, Agent-Oriented Software Engineering. In: Ciancarini P., Wooldridge, M. (eds.): Agent-Oriented Software Engineering, LNCS 1957, Springer-Verlag (2001) 163-170
18. Malone, T., Crowston, K.: The interdisciplinary study of coordination. ACM Computing Survey. 26(1), 1994 87-120
19. MESSAGE: Methodology for Engineering Systems of Software Agents – Initial Methodology. EURESCOM Project P907-GI, http://www.eurescom.de/~pub-deliverables/P900-series/P907/D1 (2000)
20. Mitra, P., Wiederhold, G., Jannink, J.: Semi-automatic Integration of Knowledge Sources. In: Proceedings of Fusion '99, Sunnyvale CA, July (1999)

21. Mohamed, A.M., Huhns, M.N.: Multi-agent Benevolence as a Societal Norm, Workshop on Norms and Institutions in Multi-agent Systems, at the 4th International Conference on Autonomous Agents (Agents 2000) Barcelona, Spain, (2000).
22. Nouwens, J., Bouwman H.: Living Apart Together in Electronic Commerce: The Use of Information and Communication Technology to Create Network Organizations. In: Steinfield, C. (ed.): Journal of Computer Mediated Communication, Special Issue in Electronic Commerce, Annenberg School for Communication, University of South California, http://www.ascusc.org/jcmc, 1(3) (1995)
23. Odell, J., Parunak, H., Bauer, B.: Extending UML for Agents. In: Proceedings of Workshop on Agent-Oriented Information Systems (AOIS'00) (2000)
24. Oliveira, E.: Applications of Agent-based Intelligent Systems. In: Proceedings of 4th SBAI-Brazilian Symposium of Intelligent Automation, S.Paulo, Brazil (1999)
25. O'Malley, S., DeLoach, S.: Determining When to Use an Agent-Oriented Software Engineering Paradigm. In this volume.
26. Omicini, A.: SODA: Societies and Infrastructures in the Analysis and Design of Agent-based Systems. In: Ciancarini P., Wooldridge, M. (eds.): Agent-Oriented Software Engineering, LNCS 1957, Springer-Verlag (2001)
27. Papadopoulos, G., Arbab, F.: Coordination Models and Languages. Advances in Computers, Academic Press (1998) 329-400
28. Powell, W.: Neither market nor hierarchy: Network forms of organisation. Research in Organizational Behavior, 12, (1990) 295-336
29. Sycara, K.: Multi-agent Systems. AI Magazine, 19(2) (1998) 79-92
30. Tsvetovat, M., Sycara, K., Chen, Y., Ying, J.: Customer Coalition in Electronic Markets. In: Dignum, F., Cortés, U. (Eds.): Agent-Mediated Electronic Commerce III, LNAI 2003 (2001) 121-138
31. E. Van Dike Parunak, H., Odell, J.: Representing Social Structures in UML. In this volume.
32. Weiss, G.: Multi-agent Systems: a Modern Approach to Distributed Artificial Intelligence. MIT Press (1999)
33. Williamson, O.: Markets and hierarchies: Analysis and antitrust implications. Free Press, New York, 1975
34. Wooldridge, M.: Agent-Based Software Engineering. IEEE Proc. Software Engineering, 144(1) (1997) 26-37
35. Wooldridge, M., Jennings, N., Kinny, D.: The Gaia Methodology for Agent-Orient Analysis and Design. Autonomous Agents and Multi-Agent Systems, 3(3) (2000) 285-312
36. Zambonelli, F., Jennings, N., Omicini, A., Wooldridge, M.: Agent-Oriented Software Engineering for Internet Applications. In: A. Omicini, Zambonelli, F., Klusch, M., Tolkdorf, R. (eds.): Coordination of Internet Agents: Models, Technologies, and Applications. Springer-Verlag (2001) 326 - 346

Bringing Coherence to Agent Conversations

Roberto A. Flores and Robert C. Kremer

University of Calgary, Computer Science Department,
2500 University Dr., NW, Calgary, Canada T2N 1N4
{robertof, kremer}@cpsc.ucalgary.ca

Abstract. In this paper, we present a social model for software agent conversations for action based on social commitments and their negotiation. We depart from the premises that conversations are cornerstone to support autonomous and heterogeneous agents, and that conversational coherence can be supported through public definitions of speech act and compositional semantics. We specify a unified social model for conversations in which speech act semantics is an emergent product of identity, conversational use, and potential consequences, and where conversational composition is guided by rules of conversational use and their application to the state of conversation instances. Lastly, we show the effectiveness of this novel approach by formally describing the evolution of a simple conversation for action.

1 Introduction

Internet software is evolving from being mere communication enablers to become active participants in automating the interactions of their users. More and more, these software programs (often called software agents) are being invested with the authority and intelligence to autonomously interact with other programs on behalf of their users.

In open environments such as the Internet these agents can be drawn from heterogeneous sources. The common denominator of these agents is not how they are built, but how they interact, and in the case of purely communicational agents, it is how they converse. Cornerstone to the notion of conversations is the issue of their coherence, i.e., the shared understanding of the meaning of messages (message semantics), and the connectedness between messages (compositional semantics) [8].

Agent communication languages (ACL) have customarily used speech acts and conversation protocols to support message meaning and their connectedness in conversations, respectively.

On the one hand, speech act semantics are mostly defined in terms of mental attitudes, such as beliefs, intentions and goals. This approach has been criticized as inadequate for open environments, since it cannot be verified whether the private beliefs of conversing agents comply with the definition of the speech acts being uttered without pre-established constrains on how agents are implemented.

On the other hand, conversation protocols are static structures that define the sequence of messages making a coherent conversation. Although very simple to imple-

M.J. Wooldridge, G. Weiß, and P. Ciancarini (Eds.): AOSE 2001, LNCS 2222, pp. 50–67, 2002.

ment, protocols are criticized for its lack of flexibility, i.e., the lack of compositional rules governing how they can be extended or merged.

An additional shortcoming is that current ACL define speech acts and protocols independently from each other; and although there have been attempts to combine these techniques into a comprehensive approach, these efforts have failed to recognize the dependencies between meaning and composition.

On the light of the above, our aim is to support coherency in conversations by integrating speech act semantics and connectedness of messages in a unified approach.

For that we propose a model for conversations where the meaning of speech acts is the emergent product of their identity, conversational use, and potential consequences; and where the connectedness of messages is guided by the rules of conversational use and their application to the state of conversation instances.

Central to this model is the notion of social commitments to action, i.e., engagements to a course of action taken by an agent relative to another agent on whose behalf these actions are done. We formally define a small set of fundamental rules to support the negotiation of shared commitments to action, which we see as instrumental for autonomous agents to negotiate and advance the state of their joint activities.

The structure of this paper is as follows: first, we give a brief account of current approaches to speech act semantics and conversations. This is followed by the description of our unifying social model for agent conversations, and a simple, formal example of its application.

2 Speech Act Semantics

Linguistic pragmatics is the area of linguistics that studies the use of language as action. One of the dominant theories in this area is that of speech act theory [1][17], which has been traditionally used in computer science to motivate speech act semantics in ACL.

Researchers have determined that ACL should yield definitions that are publicly accessible, such that any utterance of a speech act can be verified to comply with the state of the world [11][13][18][21].

Current ACL that define speech acts in terms of mental attitudes (e.g., Cohen & Levesque's Joint Intention Theory [3][4][5], KQML [10][15][16], and FIPA ACL [11]) have been criticized as inadequate to comply with this requirement. It is argued that, since mental attitudes are inherently private to agents, verifying the compliance of an utterance with its definition would require that agents be constructed in predefined ways to allow the inspection of their mental states [18]. We find this restriction unacceptable if a message semantics is to be applied to heterogeneous and autonomous agents.

As such, our first goal is:

To support the communication of autonomous and heterogeneous agents in open environments we require a public and verifiable speech act semantics.

To support this goal, we drew inspiration from existing social ACL (e.g., Singh's [19] and Colombetti's [6] models) and adopted social commitments as elements to support speech act meaning. Nevertheless, our model is built independently.

3   Compositional Semantics

There are two approaches to derive the sequencing of speech acts in conversations: the first one is to define conversation protocols, i.e., structures that specify which utterances can follow any given utterance independently of state; the second one is to define conversation policies, i.e., rules for deriving which utterances can follow any given utterance under specific states.

We favor the definition of policies over protocols since the former allows conversations to dynamically evolve according to their context of use, whether the latter only allows pre-specified patterns of interaction [12].

As such, our second goal is:

To support flexible conversations, we require a set of rules to specify conversational composition.

To support this goal, we define conversation policies to govern the sequencing of utterances according to the state of social commitments shared among conversing agents.

4   Integrating Speech Act and Compositional Semantics

Interestingly, in all the ACL we have studied (whether based on mental attitudes or social commitments) the sequencing of utterance in conversations is defined through protocols.[1] In fact, these ACL treat speech act semantics and protocols (as a palliative for conversation policies) as independent but pragmatically complementing definitions to support conversational coherence.

We do not share this view. Instead of dealing with speech act and compositional semantics as separate attributes for conversations, we aspire to integrate them under a unifying model.

As such, our third goal is:

To support a unifying model for speech acts and compositional semantics, we require a common set of principles from which these can be derived.

To support this goal, we define the meaning of speech acts as the emergent product of their identity, conversational use, and potential consequences; and where the connectedness of utterances is guided by rules of conversational use and their application to the state of conversation instances.

---

[1] In the case of Cohen and Levesque's JIT, Smith et al. [20] proposed an extension to accommodate for the sequencing of speech acts in the KAoS framework [2].

5 Modeling Conversations for Action

In this section, we specify a model for conversations based on social commitments to action, and introduce our definition of agents, speech acts, social commitments and various conversation policies for negotiating shared social commitments. We formalize these definitions using the Z formal notation [9].

5.1 Speech Acts

We use illocutionary points, i.e., the publicly intended perlocutionary effects, as the basic compositional elements of speech acts. This view allows us to describe the meaning of a speech act as the emergent property of its enclosed illocutionary points. Therefore, we define speech acts as structures composed of a set of illocutionary points.

```
__ SPEECH_ACT _____
  points: P ILLOCUTIONARY_POINT;
```

We also specify that a speech act is a kind of action (where other physical acts are also actions that could be included in this definition).

ACTION ::= SpeechAct 《SPEECH_ACT》

To complement this definition, we specify an utterance to be an event occurring at a certain moment in time involving a speech act between a speaker and an addressee.

```
__ EVENT _____
  time: TIME;
  action: ACTION
```

```
__ UTTERANCE _____
  EVENT;
  speaker, addressee: AGENT;
  speechAct: SPEECH_ACT
  _____
  action ∈ ran SpeechAct;
  speechAct = SpeechAct~ action
```

5.2 Social Commitments

We define a social commitment as a structure indicating a debtor committed to an action relative to a creditor on whose behalf the action is done. Interestingly, that speech acts have been declared as actions allows us to have social commitments entailing a speech act. We call this type of commitments conversational commitments.

```
┌─ SOCIAL_COMMITMENT ──────────────
│ debtor, creditor: AGENT;
│ action: ACTION;
│
└─────────────────────────────────
```

Based on the above definition, we specify that a shared social commitment is a structure with a commitment that is shared among agents.

```
┌─ SHARED_SOCIAL_COMMITMENT ───
│ SOCIAL_COMMITMENT;
│ among: P AGENT;
├─────────────────────────────
│ among ≠ ∅
│
└─────────────────────────────
```

Operations on Social Commitments. To denote that social commitments can be adopted or discharged we define the type OPERATION, which is defined in terms of a social commitment.

OPERATION ::= Add 《SOCIAL_COMMITMENT》 | Delete 《SOCIAL_COMMITMENT》

5.3 Agents

Succinctly, we conceptualize an agent in our model as an entity that maintains a set of shared social commitments and a history of the utterances it has witnessed.

```
┌─ AGENT ───────────────────────────────────
│ commitments: P SHARED_SOCIAL_COMMITMENT;
│ utterances: P UTTERANCE;
│
└───────────────────────────────────────────
```

Agents should be able to decide whether other agents can get them involved in a shared social commitment. This is, to support agent autonomy, social commitments should not be imposed on agents but rather should be negotiated by interacting agents. We support this process by implementing a negotiation protocol that we have called the Protocol for Proposals.

5.4 The Protocol for Proposals

We define a basic protocol for the negotiation of social commitments. This protocol, which we call the Protocol for Proposals (PFP), is informally described as follows:

The protocol starts with a proposal from a sender to a receiver to adopt or discharge a specified social commitment. Either the receiver replies with an acceptance, rejection, or counteroffer, or the sender issues a withdrawal or counteroffer.[2] All reply

---

[2] It is also possible that the addressee goes silent. In such cases, the elapsing of the expected reply time indicates to the speaker (or any observer) that the addressee either intentionally forfeited his obligation to reply or was unable to communicate as expected.

utterances except a counteroffer terminate that instance of the protocol. A counteroffer is deemed as a proposal, in the sense that it can be followed by the same speech acts that can reply to a proposal (but with speaker-addressee roles inverted if the previously proposed agent is the speaker of the counteroffer).[3] When an acceptance is issued both speaker and addressee simultaneously apply the proposed commitments to their record of shared social commitments.

Figure 1 shows the UML interaction diagram for the PFP. An example of how the PFP is applied to conversations is shown in a later section.

Requirements for the Protocol for Proposals. To support this protocol, we define the following requirements (and corresponding effects):

- *Requirement 1.* Agents shall be able to propose that other agents consider the shared uptake of social commitments.
  Effect a) A proposal commits proposed agents to reply.

- *Requirement 2.* Proposed agents shall be able to accept a proposal.
  Effect a) An acceptance releases proposed agents of the commitment to reply.
  Effect b) An acceptance (if uttered within the window of interaction[4] specified in the proposal) realizes the shared uptake of proposed social commitments.

- *Requirement 3.* Agents shall be able to reject a proposal.
  Effect a) A rejection releases proposed agents of the commitment to reply.

- *Requirement 4.* Agents shall be able to counteroffer a proposal.
  Effect a) A counteroffer releases proposed agents of the commitment to reply to the proposal.
  Effect b) A counteroffer commits counteroffered agents to reply within the window of interaction.

- *Requirement 5.* Counteroffered agents shall be able to accept a counteroffer.
  Effect a) An acceptance releases counteroffered agents of the commitment to reply.
  Effect b) An acceptance (if uttered within the window of interaction specified in the counteroffer) realizes the speaker and addressee shared uptake of counteroffered commitments.

- *Requirement 6.* Agents shall be able to reject a counteroffer.
  Effect a) A rejection releases counteroffered agents of the commitment to reply.

- *Requirement 7.* Agents shall be able to counteroffer a counteroffer.
  Effect a) A counteroffer releases previously counteroffered agents of the commitmento reply to that counteroffer within the window of interaction.
  Effect b) A counteroffer commits counteroffered agents to reply.

---

[3] In theory, a counteroffer can follow another counteroffer ad infinitum; in practice, however, the number of successive counteroffers might be limited by the reasoning, competence, or endurance of interacting agents.
[4] The window of interaction is a time interval in which a reply is expected

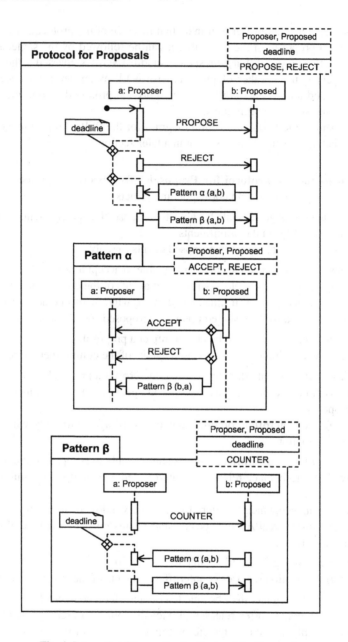

Fig. 1. Interaction Digram for the Protocol for Proposals

These requirements (and embedded effects) are supported by the definitions in the sections below.

Illocutionary Points. To model the PFP, we define four basic illocutionary points: PROPOSE, ACCEPT, REJECT, and COUNTER. We define them as illocutionary points as follows:

ILLOCUTIONARY_POINT   ::=   Propose 《PROPOSE》 | Accept 《ACCEPT》 |
                         Reject 《REJECT》 | Counter 《COUNTER》

Proposing. We define the illocutionary point PROPOSE to support requirement 1 (agents shall be able to propose to other agents that they consider the shared uptake of social commitments). These are supported by the specification of the variables proposing as the operation on a social commitment being proposed, and replyBy as the time indicating the window of interaction.

```
_ PROPOSE_____
proposing: OPERATION;
replyBy: TIME;
|_____
```

Accepting. We define the illocutionary point ACCEPT to support requirement 2 (proposed agents shall be able to accept a proposal) and requirement 5 (counteroffered agents shall be able to accept a counteroffer). These requirements are supported by the specification of accepting as the social commitment that is being agreed to uptake.

```
_ ACCEPT_____
accepting: OPERATION;
|_____
```

Rejecting. We define the illocutionary point REJECT to support requirement 3 (agents shall be able to reject a proposal) and requirement 6 (agents shall be able to reject a counteroffer). These requirements are supported by the specification of rejecting as the social commitment being rejected. Note that—from the standpoint of a speech act—there is no difference between rejecting and withdrawing, since both discard a previously made proposal. Rather, that one is rejecting or withdrawing is defined in the context of previously uttered speech acts. This point is addressed in a later section on conversational commitments.

```
_ REJECT_____
rejecting: OPERATION;
|_____
```

Counter-Offering. Lastly, we define the illocutionary point COUNTER to support requirement 4 (agents shall be able to counteroffer a proposal), requirement 7 (agents shall be able to counteroffer a counteroffer). These requirements are supported by the specification of COUNTER in terms of REJECT and PROPOSE, where the former indicates the commitment previously proposed and now being rejected, and the latter presents the new proposed commitment along with a time indicating the window of interaction.

```
 ┌─ COUNTER ─────────────────────
 │  REJECT;
 │  PROPOSE;
 │
 └──────────────────────────────
```

Conversational Commitments. We identify conversational commitments as those commitments that entail the utterance of a speech act. In this section, we present conversation policies for the adoption and discharge of commitments when uttering the illocutionary points for the PFP. These policies can be taken as norms of conversational behavior that agents are expected to follow in a society that mandates the use of the protocol.

Adopting Conversational Commitments. Policy 1A and Policy 1B support the expectation that agents being addressed by an utterance with a PROPOSE or a COUNTER illocutionary point (respectively) will commit to reply.

Policy 1A (Figure 2) supports effect 1a (a proposal commits the proposed agents to reply), and Policy 1B (not shown) supports effects 4b and 7b (a counteroffer commits addressees to reply).

This policy can be read as "for each PROPOSE illocutionary point in a just uttered speech act, agents add to their commitments database that speaker and addressee have

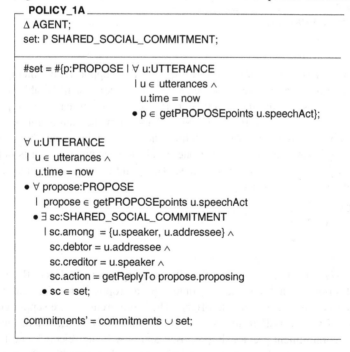

Fig. 2. A proposal commits addressee agents to reply.

as a shared social commitment that the addressee (debtor) will utter to the speaker (creditor) a reply speech act (action) with the same operation on commitment as the one found in the just uttered PROPOSE."

Policy 1B reads the same as this previous policy but with a COUNTER instead of the PROPOSE illocutionary point.

Discharging Conversational Commitments. Once that agents have adopted conversational commitments, they can expect their discharge when any of the following three conditions hold:

- *Condition 1.* A proposed (or counteroffered) agent utters a speech act containing an ACCEPT with the same operation on commitment as that of the previously uttered PROPOSE (or COUNTER). This condition is defined in Policy 2A (Figure 3), which supports effect 2a (an acceptance releases proposed agents of the commitment to reply) and effect 5a (an acceptance releases counteroffered agents of the commitment to reply).

- *Condition 2.* The proposing or the proposed agent utters a speech act containing a REJECT illocutionary point with the same operation on commitment as that of the previously uttered PROPOSE. This condition is defined in Policy 2B (not shown), which supports effect 3a (a rejection releases proposed agents of the commitment to reply) and effect 6a (a rejection releases counteroffered agents of the commitment to reply).

- *Condition 3.* The proposing or proposed (or counteroffering or counteroffered) agent utters a speech act containing a COUNTER illocutionary point rejecting the same operation on commitment as that of the previously uttered PROPOSE (or COUNTER). This condition is defined in Policy 2C (not shown), which supports effect 4a (a counteroffer releases proposed agents of the commitment to reply) and effect 7a (a counteroffer releases counteroffered agents of the commitment to reply).

Policy 2A can be read as "for each ACCEPT illocutionary point in a just uttered speech act that has an identical operation on commitment as that of a PROPOSE or a COUNTER previously uttered by the addressee to the speaker (and before the expiration time indicated in the PROPOSE or COUNTER has elapsed), agents delete from their commitments database that the speaker and addressee have as a shared social commitment that the speaker (debtor) will utter to the addressee (creditor) a reply speech act (action) with the same operation on commitment as the one found in the just uttered ACCEPT."

Conversational commitments, as defined in these policies, support the continuity of conversations. As a conversation evolves, conversational commitments are added and others are deleted. In this view, conversations end when there are no outstanding conversational commitments for that conversation instance.

POLICY_2A

Δ AGENT;
set: ℙ SHARED_SOCIAL_COMMITMENT;

#set = #{p:PROPOSE | ∀ u:UTTERANCE
     | u ∈ utterances ∧
     u.time = now
     • ∀ accept:ACCEPT
      | accept ∈ getACCEPTpoints u.speechAct
      • p = getaPROPOSEforthisACCEPT(utterances, u.speaker,
                 u.addressee, accept,
                 u.time)} +
   #{c:COUNTER | ∀ u:UTTERANCE
      | u ∈ utterances ∧
      u.time = now
      • ∀ accept:ACCEPT
      | accept ∈ getACCEPTpoints u.speechAct
      • c = getaCOUNTERforthisACCEPT(utterances, u.speaker,
                 u.addressee, accept,
                 u.time)};
∀ u:UTTERANCE
| u ∈ utterances ∧
u.time = now
• ∀ accept:ACCEPT
| accept ∈ getACCEPTpoints u.speechAct ∧
(existsaPROPOSEforthisACCEPT(utterances, u.speaker, u.addressee, accept, u.time) ∨
existsaCOUNTERforthisACCEPT(utterances, u.speaker, u.addressee, accept, u.time))
• ∃ sc:SHARED_SOCIAL_COMMITMENT
| sc.among = {u.speaker, u.addressee} ∧
sc.debtor = u.speaker ∧
sc.creditor = u.addressee ∧
sc.action = getReplyTo accept.accepting
• sc ∈ set;

commitments' = commitments \ set

Fig. 3. An acceptance releases proposed agents of the commitment to reply.

Agreeing to Uptake Social Commitments. Nevertheless, one thing is to uptake conversational commitments and another one to uptake proposed social commitments, i.e., the social commitments being negotiated. We consider that conversing agents are only justified to affect their set of shared commitments if there is the awareness that a speech act containing a PROPOSE or COUNTER illocutionary point is followed (within specified times) by a speech act containing an ACCEPT with the same operation on commitment as that of the PROPOSE or COUNTER previously uttered.

```
__ POLICY_3 _____
Δ AGENT;
setToAdd, setToDelete: ℙ SHARED_SOCIAL_COMMITMENT;
_____

#setToAdd +
#setToDelete = #{p:PROPOSE | ∀ u:UTTERANCE
                          | u ∈ utterances ∧
                          u.time = now
                        • ∀ accept:ACCEPT
                          | accept ∈ getACCEPTpoints u.speechAct
                            • p = getaPROPOSEforthisACCEPT( utterances, u.speaker,
                                                            u.addressee, accept,
                                                            u.time )} +

              #{c:COUNTER | ∀ u:UTTERANCE
                          | u ∈ utterances ∧
                          u.time = now
                        • ∀ accept:ACCEPT
                          | accept ∈ getACCEPTpoints u.speechAct
                            • c = getaCOUNTERforthisACCEPT( utterances,u.speaker,
                                                            u.addressee, accept,
                                                            u.time )};
∀ u:UTTERANCE
| u ∈ utterances ∧
u.time = now
• ∀ accept:ACCEPT
  | accept ∈ getACCEPTpoints u.speechAct ∧
  (existsaPROPOSEforthisACCEPT( utterances, u.speaker, u.addressee, accept, u.time ) ∨
  existsaCOUNTERforthisACCEPT( utterances, u.speaker, u.addressee, accept, u.time ))
  • ∃ c:SOCIAL_COMMITMENT
    | c = Add~ accept.accepting ∨
    c = Delete~ accept.accepting
  • ∃ sc:SHARED_SOCIAL_COMMITMENT
    | sc.among = {u.speaker, u.addressee} ∧
    sc.debtor = c.debtor ∧
    sc.creditor = c.creditor ∧
    sc.action = c.action
    • (accept.accepting ∈ ran Add   ∧ sc ∈ setToAdd) ∨
    (accept.accepting ∈ ran Delete ∧ sc ∈ setToDelete);

commitments' = (commitments ∪ setToAdd) \ setToDelete
```

Fig. 4. Accepting a proposal realizes the negotiated operation on commitment.

We define Policy 3 (Figure 4) to denote the uptake of social commitments upon the correct sequencing of a pair of utterances containing a PROPOSE or a COUNTER and an ACCEPT illocutionary points. These policies support effects 2b and 5b (an acceptance realizes the shared uptake of proposed/counteroffered commitments), respectively.

This policy can be read as "for each ACCEPT illocutionary point in a speech act uttered by a speaker to an addressee that has an identical operation on commitment as that of a PROPOSE or a COUNTER previously uttered by the addressee to the speaker (and before the expiration time indicated in the PROPOSE or COUNTER has elapsed), agents apply to their commitments database as a shared commitment between speaker and addressee the negotiated operation on commitment."

6   Example: Asking the Time

In the dynamics of our model, agents will join a society where the description of activities is specified in terms of roles, sequencing of communicational actions, and the description of actions and their results.

Currently our model only accounts for the expected sequencing of communicative actions in an activity. We acknowledge though the importance of action definitions, but such study will not be pursued here since they are not significant to define our rules of conversational composition.

In this section, we present a simple example of the application of our model to guide the evolution of conversations. This example is intended for agents that want to know about the time of the day. As such we specify an activity in terms of an action *getTime*, which we informally define as "to get the current local time," along with two policies to indicate the adoption and discharge of the commitment to communicate the obtained time.

The first policy, which we identify here as Policy 4 (Figure 5), indicates that the acceptance of a proposal for adopting the action *getTime* causes the automatic adoption of the shared commitment that the accepting agent will utter a speech act in which he proposes to discharge the commitment that he performs the action. This is, that an agent is accepting to do the action *getTime* causes the adoption as a shared commitment that he will propose its discharge. Although this commitment could have also being included in the proposing speech act, its definition as part of the activity description allows agents to know before hand how the interactions in the activity are expected to evolve.

Policy 5 (not shown) indicates that once the creditor agent has accepted the proposal to discharge the action *getTime*, there is the automatic shared commitment that the debtor has to propose discharging the action. That is, that the action has being discharged causes the release of the commitment that its discharge has to be proposed. At this point in a conversation, agents can expect that there will be no outstanding conversational commitments, and thus that the conversation is over.

Figure 6 shows one possible conversation for this activity. In this case, the conversation starts with the utterance of a speech act from agent A to agent B that contains a PROPOSE illocutionary point proposing the addition of a social commitment in which agent B is to perform the action *getTime* on behalf of agent A. As shown in the figure, this utterance triggers Policy 1A (uttering a proposal causes the shared conversational

```
_ POLICY_4 _____
Δ AGENT
set: ℙ SHARED_SOCIAL_COMMITMENT;
_____

#set = #{p:PROPOSE | ∀ u:UTTERANCE
                      | u ∈ utterances ∧
                      u.time = now
                      • ∀ accept:ACCEPT
                      | accept ∈ getACCEPTpoints u.speechAct ∧
                        isAcceptToGetTime( u.speaker, u.addressee, accept )
                      • p = getaPROPOSEforthisACCEPT( utterances, u.speaker,
                                                      u.addressee, accept,
                                                      u.time )};
∀ u:UTTERANCE
| u ∈ utterances ∧
u.time = now
• ∀ accept:ACCEPT
| accept ∈ getACCEPTpoints u.speechAct ∧
isAcceptToGetTime( u.speaker, u.addressee, accept ) ∧
existsaPROPOSEforthisACCEPT( utterances, u.speaker, u.addressee, accept, u.time )
• ∃ sc:SHARED_SOCIAL_COMMITMENT
| sc.among = {u.speaker, u.addressee} ∧
sc.debtor = u.speaker ∧
sc.creditor = u.addressee ∧
(∃ action:ACTION
| action ∈ ran SpeechAct ∧
(∃ s:SPEECH_ACT
| ∃ propose:PROPOSE
| propose ∈ getPROPOSEpoints s
• isDischargeOfGettingTime( u.speaker, u.addressee, propose )
• s = SpeechAct~ action)
• action = sc.action)
• sc ∈ set;

commitments' = commitments ∪ set
```

Fig. 5. The acceptance to commit to the action *getTime* causes the commitment to propose its discharge.

commitment that this proposal will be replied) which results in the addition of shared commitment number 1 to the state of shared commitments.

Next is an utterance from agent B to agent A in which the former accepts committing to do the action. This acceptance triggers the following policies: Policy 2A (the reply to a proposal discharges the commitment to reply), which deletes commitment number 1; Policy 3 (the acceptance of a proposal causes the shared uptake of the proposed commitment), which adds commitment number 2; and, Policy 4 (accepting to perform the action *getTime* causes the shared commitment that the agent doing the action will propose the discharge of the commitment to do the action—presumably

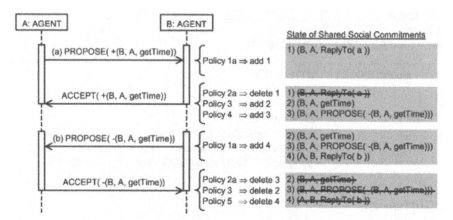

Fig. 6. Interaction diagram for a conversation asking the time

because he has done it, or because he is polite enough to communicate that he will not be able to do it), which causes the adoption of shared commitment number 3.

Next is an utterance from agent B to agent A in which he proposes to discharge that he is to do the action. This proposal triggers Policy 1A, which causes the addition of shared commitment number 4 (that this proposal for discharging will be replied).

As previously mentioned, that this proposal is accepted or not is for agent A to decide (e.g., the proposal may include the time obtained, or may provide a reason to forfeit performing the action). In this case, agent A graciously accepts the proposal, which triggers Policy 2A (which deletes commitment 3), Policy 3 (which deletes commitment 2), and Policy 5 (which deletes commitment 4).

At this point, all shared conversational commitments have been deleted, signaling the termination of the conversation.

7   Revisiting Goals

The major goals of our model (which were described in sections 2, 3, and 4) were:
1.   To support autonomous and heterogeneous agents in open environments we require publicly verifiable speech act semantics.
2.   To support flexible conversations, we require a set of rules to specify conversational composition.
3.   To integrate speech act meaning and conversational composition, we require a common set of principles from which these can be derived.

The remainder of this section elaborates on how these goals are achieved by our model.

7.1   Speech Act Semantics

In our model, speech act meaning is the emergent product of the following elements:

- *identity*: where a speech act is identified by their illocutionary points;
- *conversational use*: where the utterance of a speech act enables (and obligates) agents to utter other speech acts; and
- *consequences*: where a speech act specifies the actions it can bring about through negotiation. Agents can use speech acts in conjunction with the PFP to request the performance of actions.

To illustrate this point we describe the meaning of a proposing speech act; where its identity is that of a speech act containing the illocutionary point PROPOSE; its conversational use is that of a speech act that once uttered is expected to be replied (Policy 1A); and, its consequence is that of a speech act that (if replied within a specific time frame) can cause the mutual uptake in speaker and addressee of the proposed operation on a social commitment (Policy 3).

Furthermore, the definitions and policies specified in our model are defined in terms of the observable characteristics and effects of communications. As such we deemed these elements to be public and thus verifiable in open environments, thus fulfilling our first goal.

7.2 Composing Conversations

Flexible conversations require the specification of rules governing their sequencing. In our model, the PFP supports a simple yet powerful method to advance the state of conversations involving social commitments to action.

As we previously specified, the PFP starts with a proposal that can be accepted, rejected, or counteroffered by the addressee, or withdrawn or counteroffered by the speaker. An acceptance, rejection, or withdrawal terminates the interaction, while a counteroffer requires a reply in the form of a withdrawal, acceptance, rejection, or another counteroffer. In theory, a counteroffer can follow another counteroffer ad infinitum; in practice, the number of successive counteroffers might be limited by the reasoning, competence, or endurance of interacting agents. In any event, complex conversations for action can be dynamically composed to suite the context-dependent needs of agents, thus fulfilling our second goal.

7.3 Integrating Speech Acts and Composition

Our model implements a novel approach to speech act semantics in which conversational composition is an integral part of speech act meaning. As such we deem our model to support our last goal, i.e., to integrate message meaning and conversational composition under a common set of principles.

8 Conclusion

In this paper we set out to address the problem of the lack of conversational coherence supported by current ACL. Most ACL make use of conversation protocols, which are relatively inflexible, and message semantics based on mental attributes, which require unrealistic knowledge of the inner workings of other agents. Protocols and message semantics have also not been combined in a way that recognizes the dependencies between the two.

We have taken the approach of using only observable behavior and the concept of shared social commitments to drive the coherence of agent conversations for action. The choices an agent can make at any juncture in a conversation are guided by a small set of fundamental policies formally defined in our model. The atomic element of all conversations is a simple proposal followed by one of five responses (plus the possibility of no response at all): the receiver's acceptance, rejection, or counter-offer, and the sender's rejection or counteroffer. Acceptance messages imply the shared uptake of conversational and social commitments, which are the driving force behind larger conversation modules.

In this paper we presented a first step toward a unifying model of rational agent conversations. On the one hand, the basic conversation policies in our model can be applied for the off-line design of conversation protocols that simple agents (i.e., without complex rational mechanisms) could follow. These protocols would probably not be as rich and flexible as those of rational agents, but their interactions will nevertheless be consistent. Additionally, in the case of rational agents, we foresee that occurrences of communicative acts could be dynamically qualified (e.g., ascribed with mental attitudes) according to context, thus, helping agents to select engagements that do not lead to (potentially) conflicting goals, or undesirable communicational patterns (e.g. deadlocks, livelocks), for example.

We plan to further investigate these issues. Currently we are working on the formal specification of more complex interactions (such as the Contract Net protocol), and on the implementation of an experimental engine that agents can use to support our model in an environment where agents could be engaged in multiple simultaneous conversations.

Acknowledgments. Many thanks to Douglas Norrie. Michal Pechoucek, Martyn Fletcher, Frank Maurer, Jörg Denzinger, Brian Gaines, and the researchers at the Intelligent Systems Group at the University of Calgary for their thoughtful comments and suggestions to improve the material presented in this paper. We are also grateful to the anonymous reviewers for their suggestions to improve this paper. This work was supported by the Natural Sciences and Engineering Council of Canada (NSERC), Smart Technologies, Inc., the Alberta Software Engineering Research Consortium (ASERC), and the Alberta Informatics Circle of Research Excellence (iCORE).

References

1. Austin, J.L. How to Do Things with Words. Harvard University Press, 1962.
2. Bradshaw, J.M., Dutfield, S., Benoit, P. & Woolley, J.D. KAoS: Toward An Industrial-Strength Open Agent Architecture. Software Agents, J.M. Bradshaw (ed.), AAAI Press, 1997, pp. 375-418.

3. Cohen, P.R. & Levesque, H.J. Rational Interaction as the Basis for communication. Intentions in Communication, P.R. Cohen, J. Morgan & M.E. Pollack (eds.), MIT Press, 1990, pp. 221-255.

4. Cohen, P.R. & Levesque, H.J. Intention is Choice with Commitment. Artificial Intelligence, Number 42, Elsevier Science Pubblishers, 1990, pp. 213-261.

5. Cohen, P.R. & Levesque, H.J. Teamwork. Noûs, Special Issue on Cognitive Science and Artificial Intelligence, Volume 25, Number 4, 1991, pp. 487-512.

6. Colombetti, M. A Commitment-based Approach to Agent Speech Acts and Conversations. Fourth International Conference on Autonomous Agents, Workshop on Agent Languages and Conversation Policies, M. Greaves, F. Dignum, J. Bradshaw, and B. Chaib-draa (eds.), Barcelona, Spain, 2000, pp. 21-29.

7. Conte, R. & Castelfranchi, C. Cognitive and Social Action. University College London Press, 1995.

8. Craig, R.T. & Tracy K. (eds.) Conversational Coherence: Form, Structure, and Strategy, Sage Publications, 1983.

9. Diller, A. Z: An Introduction to Formal Methods. John Willey & Sons, 1990.

10. Finin, T., Labrou, Y. & Mayfield, J. KQML as an Agent Communication Language. Software Agents, J.M. Bradshaw (ed.), AAAI Press, 1997, pp. 291-316.

11. FIPA Agent Communication Language Specifications, Foundation for Intelligent Physical Agents, 1997 http://www.fipa.org/

12. Greaves, M., Holmback, H. & Bradshaw, J. What is a Conversation Policy? Third International Conference in Autonomous Agents, Workshop on Specifying and Implementing Conversation Policies, M. Greaves & J. Bradshaw (eds.), Seattle, WA, 1999, pp. 1-9.

13. Huhns, M.N. & Singh, M.P. Agents and Multiagent Systems: Themes, Approaches, and Challenges. Readings in Agents, M.N. Huhns & M.P. Singh (eds.), Morgan Kaufmann Publishers, 1999, pp. 1-23.

14. Karnow, C.E.A. Liability for distributed artificial intelligences. Berkeley Technology Law Journal, Volume 11, Number 1, 1996, pp.147–204.

15. Labrou, Y. Semantics for an Agent Communication Language. Ph.D. Thesis, Computer Science and Electrical Engineering Department, University of Maryland, 1997.

16. Labrou, Y. & Finin, T. Semantics and Conversations for an Agent Communication Language. Readings in Agents, M.N. Huhns & M.P. Singh (eds.), Morgan Kaufmann Publishers, 1999.

17. Searle, J. Speech Acts. Cambridge University Press, 1969.

18. Singh, M.P. Agent Communicational Languages: Rethinking the Principles. IEEE Computer, Volume 31, Number 12, 1998, pp. 40-47.

19. Singh, M.P. A Social Semantics for Agent Communication Languages. International Joint Conference in Artificial Intelligence, Workshop on Agent Communication Languages, F. Dignum, B. Chaib-draa & H. Weigand (eds.), Springer Verlag, Stockholm, Sweden, 1999.

20. Smith, I.A., Cohen, P.R., Bradshaw, J.M., Greaves, M. & Holmback, H. Designing conversation policies using joint intention theory. Third InternationalConference on Multi-Agent Systems, Paris, France, 1998, pp. 269-276.

21. Wooldridge, M. Verifiable Semantic for Agent Communication Languages. Third International Conference on Multi-Agent Systems, Y. Demazeau (ed.), IEEE Press, 1998.

Extended Modeling Languages for Interaction Protocol Design

Jean-Luc Koning[1], Marc-Philippe Huget[2], Jun Wei, and Xu Wang[3]

[1] Leibniz-Esisar
50, rue Laffemas - BP 54
26902 Valence, France
Jean-Luc.Koning@esisar.inpg.fr
[2] Magma-Leibniz
46, avenue Félix Viallet
38031 Grenoble, France
Marc-Philippe.Huget@imag.fr
[3] Institute of Software
Chinese Academy of Sciences
Beijing, China
wj@otcaix.iscas.ac.cn   xuwang@cs.ust.hk

Abstract. Successful development of agent interaction protocols requires modeling methods and tools that support a relatively complete development lifecycle. Agent-based systems are inherently complex but exhibit many similarities to object-oriented systems. For these reasons not only current modeling languages need to be extended, but also related tools should be provided for agent interaction protocol design to be supported. In this paper, we focus on the design stage of an agent interaction protocol development cycle. We start by giving general criteria for comparing agent modeling languages. The ones we take into consideration in this paper are extensions of Agent-UML and FIPA-UAML languages. We describe these languages and discuss some extensions on a simplified application of the Netbill electronic commerce protocol. We then briefly introduce a component-based formal specification language in order to support the protocol's design stage and present a tool built upon the FIPA norm (making use of the PDN or UAML notation) which supports the analysis and design of interaction protocols.

1   Introduction

The development cycle of agent interaction protocols (AIP) for multiagent systems does not account for as large a literature as the one dedicated to communication protocols in distributed systems. Let us quote El Fallah-Seghrouchni's work on interaction protocol engineering [16] where it comprises three main stages:

Design and validation. A dedicated way to tackle stage 1 is through the use of colored Petri nets since such a formalism supports concurrent processing. Besides a whole set of validation tools is available.

M.J. Wooldridge, G. Weiß, and P. Ciancarini (Eds.): AOSE 2001, LNCS 2222, pp. 68–83, 2002.

Observation of the protocols' execution. Stage 2 deals with a post-mortem analysis of the message scheduling.

Recognition and explanation of conversations. Stage 3 checks whether the interactions unfolded according to the protocol and that the overall behavior corresponds to what the designer expected. It also highlights the agents' behavior during those interactions and helps pinpoint possible causes of failure.

Because of the quite distinctive nature of the two sets of protocols found in distributed and multiagent systems, it is not possible to fully apply results from works in communication protocols to interaction protocols. Therefore, it is necessary to define a suited development cycle that, when possible, makes use of existing techniques from distributed systems, or otherwise derives new ones.

In this paper, we will focus on the design stage of an agent interaction protocol development cycle. Section 2 starts by giving general criteria for comparing agent modeling languages. The ones taken into consideration in this paper are extensions of Agent-UML and FIPA-UAML languages. We describe these languages and discuss some extensions on a simplified application of the Netbill electronic commerce protocol (section 3). Section 4 then briefly introduces a component-based formal specification language in order to support the protocol's design stage and presents a tool built upon the FIPA norm (making use of the PDN or UAML notation) which supports the analysis and design of interaction protocols. This tool also supports our extension of UAML.

2   Agent Modeling Languages

Essentially two families of agent modeling languages have been used for representing AIPs[1]: one is Agent-UML [12] and the other is FIPA-UAML [4]. In this section, we briefly compare these two families as well as their respective extension against a set of general criteria.

2.1   Unified Agent Modeling Language and UAMLe

UAML [4] is probably the first graphical language proposed (by FIPA) for representing AIPs. Most of the characteristics in UAML also appear in AUML: agents are denoted via their role, several types of message sendings along with possible added constraints are allowed (synchronous, asynchronous, broadcast, repeated sendings, temporal constraints, etc.). As shown in figure 1, concurrent messages are allowed. Sub-protocols are an interesting notion introduced in UAML that denotes a sequence of messages inside one protocol.

The letters attached to the edges represent a cardinal value, e.g., the first edge indicates that m copies of the message are to be sent and n (or o or p) answers ($n \leq m$) can be sent back and so on.

---

[1] Both of these forms were combined in 2000 and are now referred to simply as AUML.

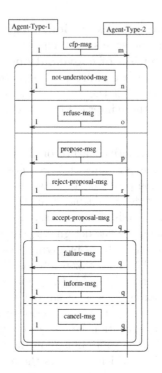

Fig. 1. Contract Net in UAML.

UAML represents alternatives in interaction states by means of boxes with separations between the possible cases. Each message is defined via a box containing a message (i.e., with an arrow). A sub-protocol (e.g., see the box starting with the message *not-understood-msg*) may contain other sub-protocols (as shown by two other nested boxes in figure 1). Possible choices are separated by lines and messages to be handled concurrently are separated by dotted lines (like between *inform-msg* and *cancel-msg*).

Compared with UAML, UAMLe essentially enables to synchronize one agent on several messages of different types and also introduces the notion of exception at the level of a single message as well as a set of messages. In the classical Contract Net protocol (with AUML [12] and with UAML [4]) the final message is a *cancel* message returned by the initiator after receiving the last inform message. Actually, it would be better to send a *cancel* message only if an exception arises. In UAMLe (figure 2) this exception handling is denoted by an *exception[cancel]... end exception* statement. Therefore the exception applies to the whole time interval that corresponds to the waiting for an answer by the agent in charge of the task. When the exception is caught the *cancel* message is sent to that agent.

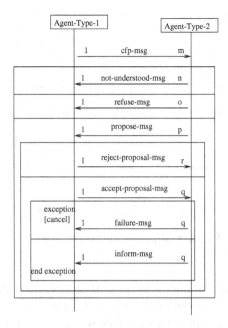

Fig. 2. Contract Net in UAMLe.

2.2 Agent-UML and EAUML

AUML [12] [13] is a proposal for the specification of agent-based systems. It has
been mainly applied to model protocols for multiagent interactions. AUML provides a set of extensions based on UML sequence diagrams, packages, templates:
protocol diagrams, agent roles, extended message semantics, multi-threaded lifelines, nested and interleaved protocols, and protocol templates. The core of these
extensions for AIPs is found in what could be called *protocol diagrams* that combine sequence diagrams with the notation of state diagrams for the specification
of AIPs.

In AUML messages are considered to be exchanged between agents that are
denoted by their role. Loops are taken care both at the level of single messages
and sets of messages. Conditional branching can be represented by means of standard *if-then-else* choice and also through some dedicated connectors representing
concurrent threads. Figure 3 respectively shows *and, xor* and *or* connectors.

On one hand the simplicity of UML sequence diagrams makes them suitable
for expressing requirement, but lack of semantics makes them sometimes ambiguous and therefore difficult to be interpreted. AUML's proposal has improved this
situation.

EAUML [19] is essentially based on AUML protocol diagrams. It brings forth
some simplifications and modifications in that it adopts a somewhat different
view from AUML as far as control threads for single agent and message char-

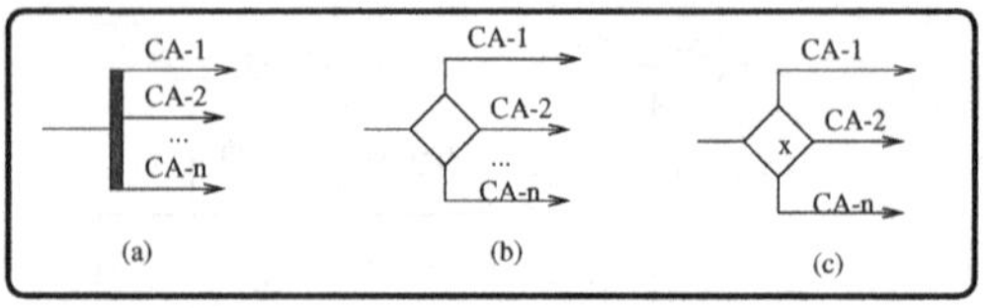

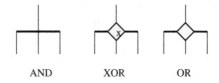

Fig. 3. Connectors for message sending in AUML.

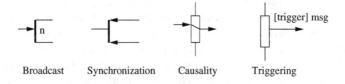

AND   XOR   OR

Fig. 4. Connectors for lifeline in AUML.

acterization. EAUML should not be seen as a competing alternative to AUML but rather as a way of viewing AIP visual modeling from another angle.

The extended notations for agent lifelines (see figure 4) and message sending (see figure 3) in AUML are kept but with a different semantics as far as the inclusive-or lifeline. Also only an asynchronous semantics is kept for messages. Besides, these messages are abstract symbolic messages rather than mere speech act messages.

Broadcast   Synchronization   Causality   Triggering

Fig. 5. Connectors in EAUML.

The extensions EAUML provides essentially deal with message passing within sequence diagrams. Figure 5 shows four new connectors. *Message broadcast* corresponds to sending a message n times. *Message triggering* corresponds to the guarded messaging in UML and AUML but in EAUML this also implies some internal events trigger the message sending. *Message synchronization* and the keyword "*silent*" have no direct counterpart in AUML. The former means an agent has to wait for several messages to arrive. The latter is a constraint that can be placed on messages to denote that the sending or receiving of a message has no effect on the current state. *Message causality* is introduced to indicate a causal relationship between two messages. The purpose of this construct is to simplify the dynamic model.

Figure 6 depicts the contract net protocol expressed as a EAUML sequence diagram. This example very much looks like the one given by Odell et al. [12]. The major difference with the AUML sequence diagram deals with the handling of message *Cancel*. This is not a regular message since it appears only in case of trouble we can make use of the fourth connector of figure 5.

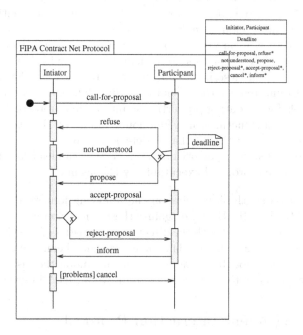

Fig. 6. Contract Net in EAUML.

Regarding organizational structures, some further extensions to AUML have recently been addressed [14]. Among other things they refine the concept of role agents may endow from a behavioristic perspective.

2.3   Some General Criteria on Agent Modeling Languages

In order to compare agent modeling languages, let us list a series of nine general criteria one may want to see supported by AIPs one way or another.

Roles: Agents are not represented by their name but according to their role within the interaction protocol. Such an approach enables to easily take into account a variable number of agents. Once those roles are identified there is no need to modify the design of the interaction protocol when a new agent is brought into place.

Synchronous/asynchronous communication: When agents send messages to one another they wait (resp. do not wait) till those messages are read prior to keep on running.

Concurrency: A number of messages can be sent or received at the same time.

Loop: A set of messages is sent a number of times. Either this number is explicitly known or the loop is based on a condition that must be true for the loop to keep on being activated.

Temporal constraints: An agent specifies a deadline that corresponds to a point in time before which some messages are expected.

Exception: A way to handle unexpected events that could either stop the course of an interaction or lead to a failure.

Design: Connected to the visual modeling langage a set of algorithms and/or tools to go to a formal corresponding definition is provided. This may involve a translation of the description into finite state machines (FSM).

Validation: Connected to the visual modeling langage a set of algorithms and/or tools for validating properties on interaction protocols is provided. It may either be a structural or a functional validation. For this purpose one may rely on the SPIN/PROMELA model-checker [6].

Protocol synthesis: Some algorithms and/or tools can lead to some code generation to make a protocol executable by the agents.

Table 1 gives a synthesized view on the following four graphical languages AUML, EAUML, UAML, UAMLe against these nine criteria.

The first six criteria deal with the direct characteristics of the visual language, and as a matter of fact, all four languages provide them. Sharper differences between these agent modeling languages appear among the last three criteria, i.e., when one considers them as a stage of an overall AIP life-cycle.

3   Designing Agent Interaction Protocol

3.1   Designing the Netbill Protocol Using EAUML

In order to clarify the extension in EAUML sequence diagrams, let us look at the agent-based Netbill [3] purchase protocol. Although we give here a simplified version of the Netbill protocol (see figure 7) it embodies the primary characteristics of agent interaction protocols in electronic commerce, including asynchronous messaging, distributed processing, concurrency, communication uncertainties, etc. The agent-based modeling of this protocol can be abstracted to involve only three agents, one consumer, one merchant and a commonly trusted bank. Consumers buy e-goods through a web-browser from the merchant. Payment between them is settled by the bank.

Figure 7 illustrates the interaction pattern among the three parties. Message passing is asynchronous. Causal messaging relates in/out messaging into one action such as on the Merchant lifeline where in-message "endorsed electronic payment order" (EEPO) and "electronic payment order" (EPO) are causally related. The triggered messaging implies that some internal event happened so that one message sending is triggered. The triggered messaging on the lifeline of Consumer expresses that the timeout event occurred and then caused message "transaction enquiry" (TE) to be sent out. XOR and OR message sendings are

Table 1. Some criteria for comparing agent modeling languages.

	AUML	EAUML	UAML	UAMLe
Roles	✓			
Sync./ Async.	Both	Asynchronous	Both	
Concurrency	Specific connector		Separation of the various messages using boxes	
Loop	At the level of a message or a group of message			
Time	Through deadlines			
Exception		By means of a special connector for triggering actions	Not directly	Upon a set of messages
Design	Possible augmented UML tools	Algorithms for translation into FSM	No graphical tools	Graphical tool DIP
Validation	No direct bridge to validators	Algorithms for translation into PROMELA for use with SPIN	No direct bridge to validators	Translation to FSM for reachability analysis and translation to PROMELA for model-checking
Protocol synthesis	No known algorithm for protocol synthesis	Code generation	No known algorithm for protocol synthesis	Code generation

selected depending on some state condition. The XOR message sending between "payment slip" (PS) and "no payment" (NP) on the bank lifeline is chosen based on a state condition about payment transaction status. The *silent* message "no record" (NR) does not affect the state of the recipient (Consumer) nor the sender (Bank). GR refers to "Good Request" and EG to "Electronic Good".

3.2   Designing the Netbill Protocol Using UAMLe

The Netbill protocol is represented with UAMLe in figure 8.

In conjunction with the UAMLe modeling language a formal description is provided. We give such a detailed description of the Netbill protocol in section 4.2.

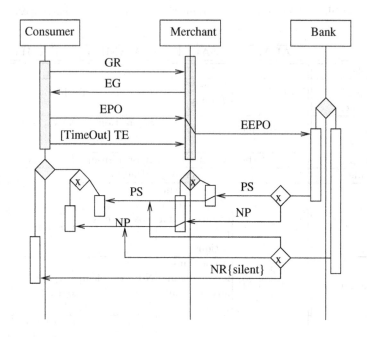

Fig. 7. Transaction Protocol of NetBill in EAUML.

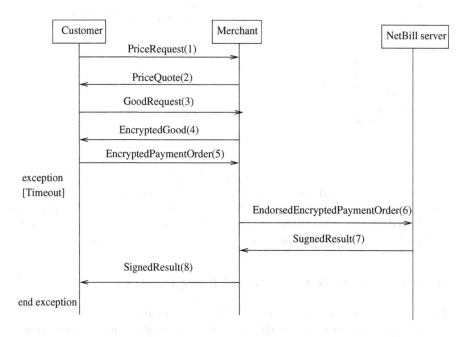

Fig. 8. Complete Transaction Protocol of NetBill in UAMLe.

4   Towards a Component-Based Specification

4.1   Protocols and Micro-Protocols

It is important for an interaction protocol to be reusable, i.e., a piece of a protocol could be replaced by another without having to start a whole new development cycle and to globally think out the protocol but to be able to reuse parts of a protocol. This idea has been introduced by Singh [17] and Burmeister et al. [2].

One could define interaction protocols as sets of components, called micro-protocols (i.e., they represent interaction units that themselves contain a set of performatives[2] and whose contents is the piece of information to be passed on), that can be assembled in a protocol via a dedicated composition language called CPDL. See [9] for an extended article on issues related to the modeling of component-based interaction protocols.

Like components in software engineering, a micro-protocol is defined by an *executable* part which is a set of performatives and an *interface* part for connecting micro-protocols together. Such a micro-protocol is composed of four attributes:

- Its *name* identifies a unique micro-protocol.
- Its *semantics* is used to help designers know its meaning without having to analyze its definition. These two fields make up the micro-protocol's signature. The other two attributes refer to its implementation.
- Its *parameters' semantics*. When making use of a micro-protocol it is necessary to know all the parameters' semantics since they are used for building messages.
- Its *definition* corresponds to the ordered set of performatives constituting the micro-protocol. Each performative is described along with its parameters like the sender, the receiver and the message's content.

Combining micro-protocols into a general interaction protocol can be done with some logic-based formulae encompassing a sequence of micro-protocols. The relation between the micro-protocols' parameters should also be specified by telling which are the ones matching. Suppose two parameters u and v are used in a same protocol, if they handle an identical parameter, this parameter should have a unique name. This facilitates the agents' work in allowing them to reuse preceding values instead of having to look for their real meaning. This approach is very much oriented towards data reuse.

CPDL is a description language for interaction protocols based on a finite state automaton paradigm which we have endowed with a set of features coming from other formalisms such as:

- *tokens* in order to synchronize several processes as this can be done with high-level Petri nets.
- *timeouts* for the handling of time in the other agents' answers. This notion stems from, for example, temporal Petri nets.

---

[2] A performative is related to speech act [15] and is a verb plus a content.

– *beliefs* that must be taken into account prior to firing a transition. This notion is present in predicate/transition Petri nets as well as in temporal logic. Beliefs within the protocol's components as it is the case in AgenTalk [11].

Compared with a finite state automaton a CPDL formula includes the following extra characteristics:

1. a conjunction of predicates in first order logic that sets the conditions for the formula to be executed.
2. the management of loops that enable a logic formula to stay true as long as the premise is true, with a **loop** predicate.

These following characteristics are included in micro-protocols:

1. the synchronization of processes through the handling of tokens. Such behavior is given through the **token** predicate.
2. the management of time and time stamps in the reception of messages with the **time** predicate. A CPDL well-formed formula looks like:

$$\alpha, \{b \in \mathcal{B}\}^\star, loop(\bigwedge p_i) \mapsto \text{micro-protocol}^\star, \beta$$

A CPDL formula corresponds to an edge going from an initial vertex to a final one in a state transition graph. Such an arc is labeled with the micro-protocols, the beliefs and the loop conditions. α denotes the state the agent is in prior to firing the formula and β denotes the state it will arrive in once the formula has been fired. The star on the micro-protocols denotes that one can have zero micro-protocol in this formula.

$\{b \in \mathcal{B}\}^\star$ represents the guard of a formula. Such a guard is a conjunction of first-order predicates that needs to be evaluated to true in order for the formula to be used. $\mathcal{B}$ is the set of the agent's beliefs. This guard is useful when the set of formulae contains more than one formula with a same initial state. Only one formula can have a guard evaluated to true, and therefore it is fired. This requires that no formula be nondeterministic and that two formulae cannot be fired at the same time. In the current version of CPDL, predicates used for beliefs are defined within the language, and agents have to follow them.

As indicated earlier the **loop** predicate aims at handling loops within a formula. Its argument is a conjunction of predicates. It loops on the set of micro-protocols involved in the formula while it evaluates to true.

4.2   Description of Netbill in CPDL

Given that there are three different roles in the Netbill protocol (see figure 8) it is divided into three interaction parts: *PriceRequest* where one consumer asks to the merchant how much is one particular electronic good, *GoodsDelivery* where the merchant sends encrypted electronic goods to the consumer and *Payment* involving the three roles where the consumer purchases the goods to the merchant via the bank represented by a Netbill server. The consumer receives a key in order to decrypt the good.

The CPDL expression of the latter protocol is given as

> init $\mapsto$ PriceRequest(C,M,G), A1
> A1, exception{timeout = exit} $\mapsto$ GoodsDelivery(C,M,G), A2
> A2 $\mapsto$ Payment(C,M,G), end

Variables C, M and N correspond to the consumer, the merchant and the bank. The definition of micro-protocol *PriceRequest* is:

> request-price(C,M,G).inform(M,C,P)

The one for *GoodsDelivery* is:

> request(C,M,G).send(M,C,G)

Micro-protocol *Payment* is defined as:

> pay(C,M,EPO).pay(M,N,EEPO).inform(N,M,R).inform(M,C,R)

Variable G corresponds to the requested good and P stands for its price. *request-price* is a performative. Performatives *inform* and *request* have the same semantics as the one in FIPA-ACL [4]. Performative *send* corresponds to the sending of good G.

Variable EPO corresponds to the Electronic Payment Order sent by the consumer. When it is passed from the merchant agent to the bank agent, the former agent is adding a key that is necessary for deciphering the good G, thus leading to the variable $EEPO$ (Endorsed EPO). Variable R is the result of the financial transaction as well as the key need for deciphering. The semantics of performative *pay* is the payment of good G.

The exception inside the second formula corresponds to the case where the consumer agent is refusing the price given by the merchant agent. In Netbill, nothing is said concerning whether the consumer agent has to let know the merchant agent that the interaction is over. Therefore an exception allows to take into consideration the fact that a client agent presumably closed the interaction whenever the duration between the price offer and the request for the good is too long.

4.3   A Tool for Supporting AIP Design

We have developed a platform with a tool dedicated to helping design interaction protocols (DIP). This platform also contains a tool for validation (TAP) and a tool for conformance testing (CTP). DIP follows the component-based approach presented here above. As shown on figure 9, such a tool enables to design and bring into play a protocol in a graphical manner by relying on micro-protocols and on the compositional language CPDL.

Our platform is endowed with a true graphic editor that enables to define interaction protocols in the graphic language UAMLe (cf. figure 9). Such a tool allows to (1) build and (2) modify protocols. For this, DIP maintains some information about a protocol: its name, its set of micro-protocols, its semantics and its set of CPDL formulas

Another feature is (3) the automatic translation into CPDL of a protocol represented by a high-level Petri net. (4) DIP allows to display a protocol in the alternate FIPA's notation called the *Protocol Description Notation* (PDN). Unlike UAML (and UAMLe), PDN is a tree-like description of a protocol where each node represents a protocol state and the transitions going out of a node correspond to the various types of message that can be received or sent at the time the interaction takes place. Since DIP is also used in analysis and protocol synthesis phases, it is possible to store a description of the protocol in natural language and the designer can generate a skeleton of the protocol in a programming language.

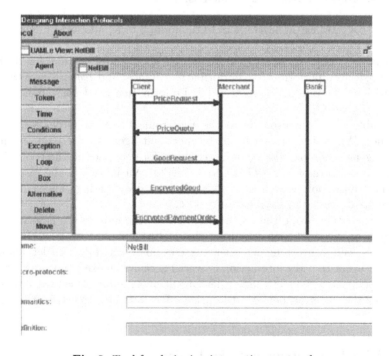

Fig. 9. Tool for designing interaction protocols.

5   Discussion

In the field of multiagent systems, there are very few tools supporting the design of interaction protocols to date. Let us mention AgentBuilder [18] and AgentTool [1].

As opposed to the approach advocated in this paper, AgentBuilder does not allow for an easy reuse of existing protocols in order to build new ones as with DIP. Protocols in AgentBuilder are defined by means of finite state automata which unfortunately do not efficiently handle synchronization among agents. Furthermore, AgentBuilder leans on a proprietary protocol's structure which makes it very difficult to utilize any external tool to perform validation tests.

It is also impossible to import protocols expressed in some other formalism which limits reusing. In the approach we have presented, interaction protocols are given in an open formalism which makes it possible to import foreign protocols expressed by means of Petri nets for instance.

In the domain of distributed systems protocol engineering has been tackled for a long time. This has led to numerous effective tools. Let us mention Design/CPN [7] which allows to manage protocols by means of colored Petri nets.

Design/CPN enables to graphically design and test Petri nets. Such a software tool is capable of simulating the execution of a protocol but is not open to other tools. Its proprietary formalism for representing protocols forces designers to address the protocol implementation issue with still another formalism which is not adequate as far as validation is concerned. On the other hand DIP aims at keeping a same formalism up to the point of validation [9].

Our work on graphically designing interaction protocols and on CPDL is included in a whole interaction protocol engineering [10]. This engineering is decomposed in five phases coming from analysis to conformance testing. In a very first time, the designer specifies the document of protocol's requirements, then formally describes it (with CPDL and UAMLe). The next step is to check if the protocol fulfills the properties defined in the document written before. The last two steps of our proposal of interaction protocol engineering tackle on an executable version of the protocol. First, one generates a program corresponding to the protocol and finally, one checks if the protocol always fulfills properties defined before. This proposal of interaction protocole engineering makes benefit of work in distributed systems where one can find one communication protocol engineering [5].

Acknowledgments. This work was partially supported by the Sino-French Advanced Research Program (PRA SI 00-06). CIPE project: *Component-based Interaction Protocol Engineering*. J.-L. KONING & WEI Jun).

References

1. Agenttool information page. http://en.afit.af.mil/ai/agentool.htm, 2000.
2. B. Burmeister, A. Haddadi, and K. Sundermeyer. Generic, configurable, cooperation protocols for multi-agent systems. In C. Castelfranchi and J.-P. Muller, editors, *From Reaction to Cognition*, volume 957 of *Lecture notes in AI*, pages 157–171, Berlin, Germany, 1995. Springer Verlag. Appeared also in MAAMAW-93, Neuchatel.
3. B. Cox, J. Tygar, and M. Sirbu. Netbill security and transaction protocol. In *Proceedings of the First USENIX Workshop in Electronic Commerce*, july 1995.
4. FIPA. *Specification: Agent Communication Language*. Foundation for Intelligent Physical Agents, http://www.fipa.org/spec/fipa99spec.htm, September 1999. Draft-2.
5. G. J. Holzmann. *Design and Validation of Computer Protocols*. Prentice-Hall, 1991.
6. G. J. Holzmann. The model checker spin. *IEEE Transactions on Software Engineering*, 23(5), May 1997.
7. K. Jensen. *Coloured Petri Nets. Basic Concepts, Analysis Methods and Practical Use*, volume 1, Basic Concepts of *Monographs in Theoretical Computer Science*, chapter 6, Overview of Design/CPN. Springer-Verlag, 1992. ISBN: 3-540-60943-1.
8. J.-L. Koning and M.-P. Huget. A component-based approach for modeling interaction protocols. In *10th European-Japanese Conference on Information Modelling and Knowledge Bases*, Finland, May 2000.
9. J.-L. Koning and M.-P. Huget. A semi-formal specification language dedicated to interaction protocols. In H. Kangassalo, H. Jaakkola, and E. Kawaguchi, editors, *Information Modelling and Knowledge Bases XII*, Frontiers in Artificial Intelligence and Applications. IOS Press, Amsterdam, 2001.
10. J.-L. Koning, M.-P. Huget, J. Wei, and X. Wang. Engineering electronic commerce interaction protocols. In *Proceedings of Intelligent Agents, Web Technologies and Internet Commerce (IAWTIC 01)*, Las Vegas, NV, USA, July 2001.
11. K. Kuwabara, T. Ishida, and N. Osato. AgenTalk: Describing multiagent coordination protocols with inheritance. In *Seventh IEEE International Conference on Tools with Artificial Intelligence*, pages 460–465, Herndon, Virginia, November 1995.
12. J. Odell, H. V. D. Parunak, and B. Bauer. Extending uml for agents. In G. Wagner, Y. Lesperance, and E. Yu, editors, *Proceedings of the Agent-Oriented Information Systems Workshop at the 17th National conference on Artificial Intelligence*, Austin, Texas, july, 30 2000. ICue Publishing.
13. J. Odell, H. V. D. Parunak, and B. Bauer. Representing agent interaction protocols in uml. In P. Ciancarini and M. Wooldridge, editors, *Proceedings of First International Workshop on Agent-Oriented Software Engineering*, Limerick, Ireland, june, 10 2000. Springer-Verlag.
14. H. V. D. Parunak and J. Odell. Representing social structures in uml. In M. Wooldridge, G. Weiss, and P. Ciancarini, editors, *Second International Workshop on Agent-Oriented Software Engineering (AOSE-2001)*, LNCS, Montreal, Canada, May 2001. Springer-Verlag.
15. J. Searle. *Speech Acts: An Essay in the Philosophy of Language*. Cambridge University Press, Cambridge, 1969.
16. A. E.-F. Seghrouchni, S. Haddad, and H. Mazouzi. A formal study of interaction in multi-agent systems. In *Modelling Autonomous Agents in Multi-Agent Worlds (MAAMAW)*, 1999.

17. M. P. Singh. Toward interaction oriented programming. Technical Report TR-96-15, North Carolina State University, May 1996.
18. R. Systems. Agentbuilder, an integrated toolkit for constructing intelligent software agents. Technical report, Reticular Systems, 1999.
19. J. Wei, S.-C. Cheung, and X. Wang. Towards a methodology for formal design and analysis of agent interaction protocols : An investigation in electronic commerce. In *International Software Engineering Symposium*, Wuhan, Hubei, China., March 2001.

A Policy Language for the Management of Distributed Agents

Naranker Dulay, Nicodemos Damianou, Emil Lupu, and Morris Sloman

Department of Computing, Imperial College,
180 Queensgate, London SW7 2BZ, United Kingdom
{nd, ncd, e.c.lupu, mss}@doc.ic.ac.uk

Abstract. A key issue in managing distributed agents is the provision of effective policy-based frameworks. To help realise such frameworks we have developed a new policy language that features dynamic fine-grained access controls and event-triggered condition-action rules, with abstractions for grouping objects/agents (domains), and grouping policies (roles, relationships and management structures). In our language policies apply to domains of objects. By changing a policy we change the behaviour of a system. By adding an object or agent to a domain we cause the domain's policies to be applied to the newly added object. The language is declarative, strongly typed and object-oriented, which makes the language flexible, extensible and adaptable to a wide range of management requirements

1 Introduction

The growth of computer networks and the ever-growing integration of diverse applications and technologies make the task of managing complex distributed agent systems ever more challenging. Distributed systems are increasingly dependent on interaction with other distributed systems, as well as with users and services on the Internet. At the same time distributed agent systems are often required to continue to support legacy applications built with dated tools and technologies.

A promising approach is the use of policy-based frameworks to provide effective management support and for specifying security. Policies are rules that define a choice in the behaviour of a system. Separating policies from the implementation of a system permits policies to be modified in order to dynamically change the strategy for managing the system – and hence modify the behaviour of a system without changing its underlying implementation.

Policy models and implementations are emerging in the research community, what is lacking is a unified approach to expressing policy. There is a need to express and enforce both management and security policies for heterogeneous distributed systems in a single language and to be able to communicate policies between systems administrators and across administrative boundaries. This paper describes PONDER, a declarative language that provides a uniform means for specifying policies that map onto various access control implementation mechanisms such as firewalls, operating systems, databases and Java. Equally importantly, PONDER provides a uniform means for dealing with events that occur in a distributed system such as those related to

M.J. Wooldridge, G. Weiß, and P. Ciancarini (Eds.): AOSE 2001, LNCS 2222, pp. 84-100, 2002.
© Springer-Verlag Berlin Heidelberg 2002

faults, auditing, backups, security violations, resource consumption, performance degradation, QoS. PONDER aims to be easy to use and to facilitate improved management interfaces and tools.

The next section outlines our requirements for a distributed systems policy language. Section 3 presents the PONDER language and shows how it can be used to specify policies for distributed systems. Section 4 presents a small example, while section 5 covers related work on policy languages. Section 6 presents our conclusions.

2   Requirements

Many requirements need to be satisfied in order to manage complex distributed systems. This paper does not address all such requirements, but focuses on the requirement of developing a policy-driven language for distributed systems. We take the view that building a framework that supports policy specification and enforcement can significantly enhance the management of any distributed system, but particularly large heterogeneous systems.

We identify the following requirements for policy-driven distributed systems:

- the ability to specify and enforce the policies for a distributed system separately from the implementation of the objects within the system (*separation of concerns*);

- the ability to change policies and hence change the behaviour of a running system without having to re-implement the objects within the system (*evolvability*);

- the ability to apply policies to distributed, hierarchical and heterogeneous groups of objects (*domains*)

- the ability to group policies relating to a single entity (*roles*);

- the ability to define and group policies between roles (*relationships*);

- the ability to group roles and relationships (*management structures*);

- the ability to define what actions an object is permitted or forbidden to perform on available resources, or on other objects (*authorisation policies*);

- the ability to define the management actions that need to be performed periodically, when triggered by events or simply need to be performed depending on dynamic factors such as the current state of an application (*obligation policies*);

- the ability to define constraints on a set of policies (*meta policies*);

- the ability to handle policy conflicts (*conflict prevention, detection, resolution*);

- the ability to treat policies and domains as objects and subject them to policy control (*self management*).

The following section gives an overview of the PONDER policy specification language that we have designed to address the policy requirements outlined above. PONDER is declarative, strongly typed and object-oriented (see [5][6] for details on the type system), which makes the language flexible, extensible and adaptable for management of agent communities. PONDER offers a high degree of customisation by supporting parameterisation of any parts of a specification. The language assumes a class-based object-oriented view of the underlying distributed system where interaction occurs through remote object invocations and asynchronous event notifications. PONDER's types and instances are implemented as objects in the system and therefore policies may also apply to these objects.

3   PONDER Language

PONDER is a language for specifying enforceable policies for management and security of distributed systems [5][6]. Policies are rules that are used to control access to resources as well as to define the actions automated agents must perform when specific events occur. The abstractions supported by PONDER are summarised in Fig. 1.

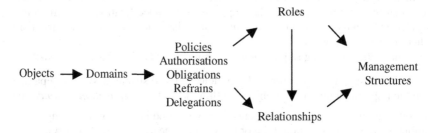

Fig. 1. Summary of Abstractions in PONDER

In our prototype implementation policies are compiled into enforcement objects that either directly carry out the enforcement, or into enforcement objects that interact with underlying mechanisms to perform the enforcement. In a distributed environment a single policy will normally generate an enforcement object for each agent or object to which the policy applies. This implies, where possible, that policies are enforced locally where objects execute. This helps in producing scalable implementations but also allows policies to be written that apply to heterogeneous environments where a single policy will produce different enforcement code for different platforms.

3.1   Objects and Domains

The basic unit of management in PONDER is an object which could be an intelligent agent, a resource or represent a person. In our framework a distributed system is considered to be a large collection of managed objects. Objects that provide no means of being managed lie outside the scope of PONDER. At the simplest level, a policy-based management system needs to be able to create, reference, and destroy objects via a management interface. Typically objects will also provide methods that can be invoked by other objects to perform various actions. In our framework these actions are invocable by the policy management system in order to effect high-level policies. Furthermore, given a suitable underlying access-control mechanism, access to object methods can be restricted by policies that configure the access-control mechanism.

The unit of object grouping in PONDER is the domain. Domains are a unit of management akin to file directories in operating systems. Domains provide hierarchical structuring of objects like directories, but also support policy-based management by allowing policies to be applied to them. Thus, each domain holds references both to the objects within the domain and to the policies that currently apply to the domain. Domains are objects themselves, and so can be included in other domains and have policies applied to them. This allows hierarchical structuring and self-management policies that apply to domains themselves. In order to increase flexibility further, objects and domains can be members of more than one domain, which supports scenarios where objects/agents are members of different groups.

Domain membership is dynamic. Objects can be added to, or removed from, a domain as needed. If an object is added to a domain, the policies that currently apply to that domain will subsequently apply to the newly added object. Conversely, if an object is removed from a domain, the policies for the domain will no longer be applied to the object. Objects can thus be managed either by (i) modifying the policies applying to the domains of which the objects are members or (ii) adding or removing the objects from domains to which specific policies apply.

An enterprise domain defines the boundary for policy management. In situations where objects interact across or move between different enterprise domains, policy-driven management requires a trust infrastructure between them and support for exchanging policies. Where agents external to the enterprise domain (e.g. agents on the Internet) wish to interact with objects within the enterprise domain, admission control policies are needed that identify the external agents and add them to domains with appropriate policies.

3.2   Policies

The four basic types of policy are summarised in table 1. Authorisations, refrains and delegation policies provide access control, while obligation policies are event-triggered scripts that carry out management actions. An additional policy type, is available, the meta-policy type, which allows constraints to be written about policies.

Authorisation policies are designed to protect *target* objects and are conceptually propagated to and enforced by each target object. In practice, the target objects of authorisation policies are off-the-shelf components and are unable to directly enforce policies themselves. Instead, authorisation policy enforcement is performed by PONDER generated enforcement objects, that either directly perform the enforcement (e.g. special PONDER permission classes for Java), or more typically configure an underlying access control mechanism (e.g. firewalls, database access systems, operating systems). While the subjects of an authorisation policy can be any objects that initiate actions on targets, the subjects of refrain and obligation policies are instances of special enforcement objects called *obligation agents* that implement a virtual machine for the execution of any obligation or refrain policy.

The four basic policy types have some features in common. Each assumes that the objects managed by the policy are drawn from the domain structure of the distributed system. The S, T, G and H (subjects, targets, grantors, grantees respectively) in the table are all domains, and a policy normally applies between all objects in the subject domain and the target domain. Each policy type can also be qualified by a run-time constraint to limit the applicability of the policy.

Table 1. Basic Policy Types in PONDER

Policy Type	Abstract Form	Enforced by	Meaning
Authorisation +	S → T.A ? C	Target	S is authorised to invoke action T.A if C
Authorisation −	S →│ T.A ? C	Target	S is not authorised to invoke action T.A if C
Refrain	S ↦ T.A ? C	Subject	S must refrain from invoking action T.A if C
Delegation +	G [S→T.A] → H ? C	Policy System	G ⊆ S is authorised to create a policy H→T.A if C
Delegation −	G [S→T.A] →│ H ? C		G ⊆ S is not authorised to create a policy H→T.A if C
Obligation	E, S → M ? C	Subject	On event E, S is obliged to execute method M if C
S – subjects, T – targets, G – grantors, H – grantees, C – constraint, E – event, A – action implemented by each target object,			

3.3   Positive Authorisation Policies

The *positive authorisation policy*: S → T.A ? C, states that all objects of the subject domain S are authorised to invoke an action A on any object of the target domain T if constraint C is satisfied. The policy can also be read from the point of view of the target object i.e., that all members of the target domain T are authorised to accept action A from any object of the subject domain S if constraint C is satisfied. Although not shown in the table, it is also possible to write authorisation policies that process the parameters of an action (filtering policies).

Example: The following policy states that laptop applications of trusted visitors are authorised to print to a colour printer provided the document to be printed is no more than 10 pages long.

```
inst auth+ P1 {
        subject /visitor/trusted/laptop_app/
        target  /printer/colour/
        action  print (doc)
        when    doc.pages <= 10
}
```

By default, policies apply to all objects in nested sub-domains, so we can hierarchically structure both subject and target domains as shown in Fig. 2.

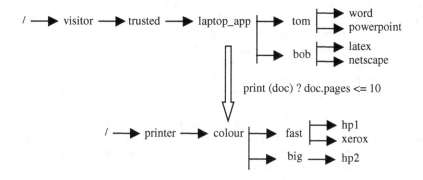

Fig. 2. Subject and Target Domain Structures

Conceptually each printer object in the colour printer domain enforces the policy. When a colour printer object receives a print action, it checks that the object invoking the action is in the laptop applications domain and that the constraint is satisfied before processing the action.

3.4 Negative Authorisation Policies and Refrain Policies

The *negative authorisation policy*: S →| T.A ? C states that no object of the subject domain S is authorised to invoke an action A on any object of the target domain when constraint C is satisfied. Negative authorisations are required in situations where any action that is not explicitly denied is authorised by default or for revocation of authorisation. In those systems where actions are denied by default, negative authorisations are still useful as they permit the explicit definition of an action that must be denied and this can give rise to a helpful alert when an attempt is made to apply a conflicting positive authorisation policy.

Example: The following policy states that Bob's laptop applications are not authorised to print to big colour printers.

```
inst auth- P2 {
        subject /visitor/trusted/laptop_app/bob/
        target  /printer/colour/big/
        action  print
}
```

Example: The following policy states that by default, no action is permitted from any object in the system on any object.

```
inst auth- default {
        subject /
        target  /
        action  *
}
```

In a system with conflicting policies, e.g. policies P1 and P2, rules are necessary to decide which policy takes precedence. Many approaches are possible, for example, we can give precedence to negative authorisations over positive authorisations, or we can have explicitly defined precedence rules, for example, a policy for a sub-domain takes precedence over a policy for a parent domain, or a policy defined textually before another takes precedence. For details of our approach see [15]. PONDER meta policies (see section 3.8) can also be used to specify application specific precedence between conflicting policies.

Refrain policies are similar to negative authorisations but are enforced by the subjects of the policy and define what actions subjects must not invoke. Refrains are useful in situations where subjects can assist the enforcement process by carrying out the enforcement process at the source or where targets do not want to be protected e.g to prevent access to untrusted resources. If subjects are unable or unwilling to carry out a refrain policy, then an equivalent negative authorisation policy is needed to protect targets from rogue subjects. In our implementation, refrains are enforced by policy management agents that correctly enforce obligation and refrain policies.

Example: The following policy states that Tom's laptop applications must refrain from printing documents greater than 10 pages to big colour printers.

```
inst refrain P3 {
        subject  /visitor/trusted/laptop_app/tom/
        target   /printer/colour/big/
        action   print (doc)
        when     doc.pages > 10
}
```

3.5   Delegation Policies

The positive delegation policy: G [S→T.A] → H ? C, takes an existing authorisation policy S → T.A and defines a policy that states that any object of G (where G is a subset of the objects of S) is authorised to create a new authorisation policy H → T.A if C is satisfied. We call G the *grantors*, and H the *grantees*. When a grantor performs a positive delegation action (on the policy system), a new authorisation policy H → T.A is created. Since H → T.A is identical to S → T.A except for a new subject domain, the implementation and enforcement of delegated policies is the same as that for authorisation policies.

Example: The following delegation policy states that Tom's Word application is authorised to create a new authorisation policy that would allow Jim's Word application to print to a colour printer provided the document to be printed is no more than 10 pages long (see policy P1 earlier)

```
inst deleg+ P4 (P1) {
        grantor  /visitor/trusted/laptop_app/tom/word
        grantee  /visitor/untrusted/jim/word
}
```

Delegation in PONDER does not transfer access rights from grantors to grantees; grantors continue to retain their access rights after a delegation is performed. Delegation policies that delegate over other delegation policies are also supported (cascaded delegation policies), as are negative delegation policies.

3.6 Obligation Policies

Authorisations and refrains are access control policies; in contrast, obligations are management tasks that subjects must perform. The obligation policy: E, S → M ? C states that all objects of the subject domain S execute method M each time event E occurs provided constraint C is satisfied. Obligation methods are defined as sequences of sequential or parallel actions on the targets and/or the subjects of the policy. Events can either be simple named events or composite events such as E1 -> E2 ! E3 for event E1 followed by event E2 with no interleaving event E3 occurring in between. Events can also be parameterised and the parameters used in invoked actions or in constraints to limit the policy.

Example: The following policy specifies that if a print job fails that the printing agent will email the user and retry printing the job after 10 mins. Only one attempt will be made.

```
inst oblig P5 {
        on        printing_failure (job)
        subject s = /agent/printing
        target  t = /agent/mailing
        do        t.email(job.user, "print job failed")
                  s.printwithdelay(job, 10)
        when      job.attempts == 0
}
```

Example: The following policy specifies that the domain system agent will add trusted new visitors to the trusted user domain and their apps to the trusted laptop domain. Note: The inclusion of objects in a domain implies that they acquire the current policies for that domain.

```
inst oblig P6 {
        on        new_visitor (v)
        subject s = /agent/domainsystem
        do        s.add (v, "/visitor/trusted/user/")
                  s.add (v.apps,"/visitor/trusted/laptop_app/")
        when      trusted_user (v)
}
```

3.7 Roles, Relationships, and Management Structures

In order to support *policy-specification-in-the-large* and to model the people, agents and structures of an organisation, PONDER provides 3 distinct abstractions for policy groupings: roles, relationships and management structures.

Roles provide the means of grouping policies related to a position in an organisation such as a staff member, customer support manager or Chief Executive Officer (CEO). A role can also group policies relating to a specific agent such as one that registers new users or adaptively manages Quality of Service in a network. Roles allow us to write the basic policies for a subject in a single specification. A role thus conveniently groups the authorisations (+ and −), obligations and refrains for an agent or position. A person or an agent can then be assigned to (or removed from) a role and so acquires all the policies applying to the role Since the subject domain of a role is common for all policies in the role, it is omitted from the policies within a role for clarity.

Relationships between roles are used to define additional policies which are not part of the individual roles but specify how the roles interact e.g. that a manager agent is permitted to perform specific actions on a worker agent and the worker needs to periodically report ist status to the manager agent. Roles and relationships can be further composed into management structures, and these can be grouped within other management structures, allowing a policy hierarchy to be formed that reflects the organisational roles and structures of an enterprise. Fig. 3 shows an example of a management structure with three roles, and one relationship with two policies between the subjects of the roles.

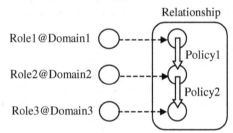

Fig. 3. Management Structure of Roles and Relationships

3.8 Meta Policies

Meta policies are constraints over a set of policies, either policies within a policy grouping, or policies within a domain. Meta policies are written as a sequence of Object Constraint Language (OCL) expressions. If the last OCL expression of a meta policy evaluates to true a conflict exception is raised. Meta policies are used to check for dynamic semantic conflicts such are separation of duties and self-management.

Example: The following policy prevents a conflict of duty in which the same agent both approves and submits a budget. It checks for polices with the same subject and target budget that have actions submit and approve.

```
Inst meta P7 raises separationOfDutyConflict {
        [z] = self.policies -> select (pa, pb |
              pa.subject->intersection (pb.subject)
                  -> notEmpty and
              pa.exists (act | act.name = "submit") and
              pa.exists (act | act.name = "approve") and
              pb.target->intersection (pa.target)
```

```
                    -> oclIsKindOf(budget));
        z -> notEmpty
}
```

Example: The following policy checks that there is no policy authorising a management object to retract policies for which it is the subject. This can happen, for example, within a single authorisation policy with overlapping subjects and targets.

```
Inst meta P8 raises selfManagementConflict (pol) {
        [pol] = this.authorisations -> select (p |
            p.action->exists ( a |
                a.name = "retract" and a.parameter ->
                    exists (p1 |
                        p1.oclType.name = "policy" and
                            p1.subject = p.subject)));
        pol -> notEmpty ;
}
```

4   Example Scenario

Lets consider a scenario of a small company with a network of computers (servers, desktops). We'll assume that the systems manager has already configured the hardware, set-up firewall and network controls, created users and user groups, configured mail and web servers, installed a database for the database administrator, set-up software to monitor the distributed system for problems (e.g. resource consumption, intrusion), automated repetitive task (e.g. backups) and so on. The company then hires a new customer support person (Alice), who'll need access to customer records, printing and email services. The systems manager will need to acquire a new computer, install the OS and applications on it, create new user and database accounts, update email, web and other servers, update firewall rules, and so on. Typically this involves editing configuration information or running commands, often with different conventions and in different places. With PONDER we can simplify this process by defining policies for access control and automating tasks such as account creation and using a policy management system to enforce the policies.

4.1 Domain Structure

Fig. 4 gives a partial view of the top-level domain structure for the company. The users are grouped together under the `staff` domain, the system services under the `sys` domain, while the automated policy management agents are grouped under the `agent` domain. The default access control policy for all objects is:

```
inst auth- default {subject /; target /; action *}
```

which forbids all actions. In practice this policy is too limiting and needs to be specified lower down the domain hierarchy.

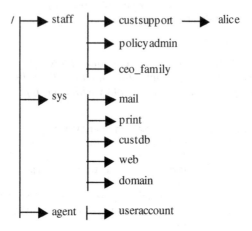

Fig. 4. Company Domain Structure

4.2 Staff Roles

The policies for staff are defined by a general role (R1) for the staff domain and specific roles for ist sub-domains. The general role is:

```
inst role R1 {
        auth+ P0 {target /sys/mail;    action send}
        auth+ P1 {target /sys/mail;    action receive}
        auth+ P2 {target /sys/print;   action print}
} @ /staff/
```

The role allows all staff to send and receive email (P0, P1), as well as send documents to the print server (P2). Customer support staff (role R2) can in addition read customer database records (P3) and browse the Web after hours (P4):

```
inst role R2 {
        auth+ P3 {target /sys/custdb;  action read}
        auth+ P4 {target /sys/web;     action browse;
                   when time.between (1800, 2100) }
} @ /staff/custsupport/
```

In order to create the policies for a new employee Alice, all we need to do is create a domain for her, and add the domain as a sub-domain under the custsupport domain:

```
mkdomain /staff/custsupport/alice/
```

We also need to add references to suitable client applications to her domain. This can either be done manually or with an obligation policy (see role useraccount later). If we wished to deny Alice access to the Web we could define a specific Alice role (R3) with a policy that overrides the customer support web policy (P5):

```
inst role R3 {
        auth- P5 {target /sys/web;     action browse}
} @ /staff/custsupport/alice
```

The following role policy administration role uses policies to restrict the instantiation of policies to domains (P6), and the creation of domains (P7), to policy administrators:

```
inst role R4 {
        auth+ P6 {target /sys/domain; action instpolicy}
        auth+ P7 {target /sys/domain; action mkdomain}
} @ /staff/policyadmin
```

As a final example, lets consider allowing members of the Chief Executive Officer's (CEO) family to have access to the web at all times (P8), but no access to any other services. Unfortunately the ceo_family domain is grouped under the staff domain. This means that the policies for staff (P0, P1, P2) will also apply to CEO family members. One solution would be to move the ceo_family domain out of the staff domain while another solution is to override and disable staff policies (P9) within the CEO family's role:

```
inst role R5 {
        // policy P8 has precedence over policy P9
        auth+ P8 {target /sys/web;     action browse }
        auth- P9 {target /sys;         action *}
} @ /staff/ceo_family/
```

4.3 User Account Agent

The useraccount role illustrates the use of obligation policies. Whenever a new member of staff is added under the staff domain, the user account agent creates an operating system account (policy P10). Additionally, when a new customer support staff member is added, the agent creates a database account (P11) and populates the new member of staff's individual sub-domain with 3 client applications (P12).

The role assumes that domain membership operations generate events, in this case, a newDomainMemberEvent with 2 parameters: (i) a reference to the domain added to, and (ii) a reference to the object or domain that is added.

```
Inst role useraccount {
        oblig p10 {
            target k=/sys/kerberos;
            on    newDomainMemberEvent (d, m)
            do    k.createaccount (m)
            when  startswith (d.path, "/staff/")
        }
        oblig p11 {
            target db=/sys/custdb;
            on    newDomainMemberEvent (d, m)
            do    db.createaccount (m)
            when  startswith (d.path, "/staff/custsupport")
        }
```

```
oblig p12 {
    target dm=/sys/domain;
    on      newDomainMemberEvent (d, m)
    do      dm.add (d, emailClient)
            dm.add (d, dbClient)
            dm.add (d, webClient)
    when    startswith (d.path, "/staff/custsupport")
}
} @ /agent/useraccount
```

5   Related Work

Most other work on policy specification relates to security policies and conflict resolution. None include the range of policies available in PONDER and most lack abstractions to support policy-specification-in-the-large.

PDL [14][21] is an event-based policy language which is used to define policies of the form *event causes action if condition*. Events can be compound event expressions and the actions can be local or remote method calls, complex workflows or actions that trigger other events to form a hierarchical policy chain. PDL has been used to program the SARAS softswitch and other aspects of network operations and management. PDL lacks support for policy grouping and does not support access control policies. SPL [19] is also an event-based policy language but supports access-control, history-based and obligation-based policies. SPL is implemented by an event monitor that for each event decides whether to allow, disallow or ignore the event. Conflicts between positive and negative authorisation policies are avoided by using a tri-value algebra that prioritises policies when they are grouped together.

LGI [16] is an approach for specifying laws on the interactions of a distributed group of agents. Laws are specified in Prolog and regulate the exchange of messages between agents. Laws are implemented by special controller agents (typically one per agent) that intercept each outgoing and incoming message and enforce the laws of the system. The use of Prolog allows arbitrarily complex policies to be expressed, but can also be costly since each communication has an additional overhead to check the laws and this cost will increase as group size increases and agents become members of several groups.

LaSCO [11] is a graphical approach for specifying security constraints on objects, in which a policy consists of two parts: the domain (assumptions about the system) and the requirement (what is allowed assuming the domain is satisfied). Policies defined in LaSCO have the appearance of conditional access control statements. The scope of this approach is restricted to satisfy the requirements of security management.

The IETF Policy Group are defining a policy framework that can be used for classifying packet flows as well as specifying authorisations for network resources and services [17]. IETF policies are of the form *if (a set of conditions) then do (a set of actions)*. They do not have the concepts of subject and target that can be used to determine to which objects a policy applies, so the mapping of policies to objects has to be done by some other means. Directories are used for storing policies but not for grouping objects.

Trust management frameworks combine authentication with authorisation. In [2][8], signed queries of the form *"does request r, supported by credential set C, comply with policy P?"* are used for applications such as web based labelling, signed email and active networks. The credentials can be public key certificates with anonymous identity. Both policies and credentials are predicates specified as simple C-like expression and regular expressions. Similar functionality aimed at e-commerce applications is proposed in [9]. Here XML is used for specifying trust policies and permit negative authorization as well as positive. The credentials result in a client being assigned to a role which specifies what the client is permitted to do.

Role based access control (RBAC) structures using a direct inheritance of permissions between role instances are defined in [20]. These permit reuse of permissions and follows an organisational structure in that more senior roles inherit the access rights of junior roles. However, this instance based inheritance model violates organisational control principles and introduces the need to cater for a substantial number of exceptions as often some access rights should not be inherited by senior roles from junior roles. Tower, a recent role-based access language is proposed in [10]. It includes the classical concepts of RBAC such as role, users, and permissions and applies them to object-oriented systems. Tower uses meta-variables and role-constraints to define dynamic policies such dynamic separation of duty, Chinese wall policies, and joint action based policies.

Formal logic-based approaches to policy specification and conflict resolution are generally not intuitive and do not easily map onto implementation mechanisms. They assume a strong mathematical background, which can make them difficult to use and understand. ASL [12] is a formal logic language for specifying access control policies. The language includes a form of meta-policies called integrity rules to specify application-dependent rules that limit the range of acceptable access control policies. Although ASL provides support for role-based access control, the language does not scale well to large systems because there is no way of grouping rules into structures for reusability. A separate rule must be specified for each action. There is no explicit specification of delegation and no way of specifying authorisation rules for groups of objects that are not related by type. In [18] a modal logic based on deontic logic is used to express security policies in information systems based on the logic of permissions and obligations. Standard deontic logic centres on impersonal statements instead of personal; we see the specification of policies as a relationship between explicitly stated subjects and targets instead. In his approach he accepts the axiom $Pp = Op$ ("permitted p is equivalent to not p being not obliged") as a suitable definition of permission. This axiom is not suitable for the modelling of obligation and authorisation policies; the two need to be separated. Deontic logic is also used to express obligation policies for security in [4]. Other approaches to conflict resolution can found in [1] and [13] which prioritise rules using concepts such as rule authorship, specificity and recency.

6   Conclusions

In large scale distributed computing systems, the ability to flexibly manage the resources and users of the system is highly desired. We believe that the use of a common policy specification language is an important technique for simplifying the management of complex distributed systems. By keeping the language simple and by focussing on implementable policies, we believe that the language can be integrated and effectively used in management frameworks that govern the behaviour of large-scale distributed systems.

With PONDER all the managed objects in a distributed system are organised into hierarchical domains. Policies are then written in terms of domains, and domain membership is evaluated whenever policy enforcement is performed. This means that there is normally no need to write policies specific to an object. Instead, whenever an object is added to a domain, the policies that apply to that domain will automatically be applied to the object, until either the object is removed from the domain or the policy disabled. The use of domains supports the management of systems with large numbers of objects.

PONDER policies can be divided into three broad categories: access control, automated management and meta-level. Each plays an important role. Access control policies allow us to capture the wide range of access control rules that a typical distributed system will implement, from rules for firewalls, to access controls for the users of services (databases, web), to standard operating system controls. The advantage of our approach is that a single language is used to specify all these policies and the policy writer can use an abstract model for specification, leaving the translation of PONDER policies to underlying mechanisms, to software tools. The ability to automatically take appropriate actions when particular events occur in a distributed system is addressed by PONDER's obligation policies, which allow us to define the management actions that need to be taken when specific events occur. The use of a unified model for access control and automated management allows us to easily group different types of policies into roles, and to group roles into management structures. Policy grouping is an important and powerful technique for policy-specification-in-the-large and often lacking in the other languages. Meta-level policies are the third category of policy in PONDER. They allow the global constraints of a system to be preserved by restricting the applicability of policies. In particular, meta policies can be used to check for dynamic semantic conflicts such are separation of duties and self-management. At a formal level, an operational semantics is being developed to precisely define the language and extensions to the language that incorporate the specification of policies for interaction protocols between objects are under consideration.

A Java-based toolkit for PONDER is under development. It comprises a PONDER compiler written using SableCC, with experimental backends for Windows NT/2000 access control; Linux ipchains, PAM modules, DNS and Samba. Work is in progress in producing a backend for DiffServ quality of service management as well as a backend that compiles parts of PONDER to field programmable gate arrays (FPGAs). Details of the PONDER deployment and enforcement model can be found in [7]. A different implementation that maps PONDER into an agent-based system is being developed at the University of Bologna [3]. Other tools in the toolkit include a domain and policy browser that uses hyperbolic tree navigation and a graphical policy editor. The current implementation needs further work in several areas, in particular, policy groups and meta-policies are not fully supported by backends, the implementation is centralised, and change management is non-transactional. Tools for policy analysis and reasoning also need to be developed.

Acknowledgements. We gratefully acknowledge the support of the EPSRC for research grants GR/L96103 (SecPol) and GR/M 86019 (Ponds) as well as BT for support on the Alpine project.

References

1. Bertino, E., Buccafurri, F., Ferrari, E., and Rullo, P.: A Logical Framework for Reasoning on Data Access Control Policies, In Proceeding of the 12th IEEE Computer Security Workshop, IEEE Computer Society Press, 1999.
2. Blaze, M., Ioannidis, J., Keromytis, A.D.: Trust Management and Network Layer Security Protocols, In Cambridge Protocols Workshop. Cambridge. Available from http://www.crypto.com/papers/ networksec.pdf, 1999.
3. Corradi, A., Dulay, N., Montanari, R., Stefanelli C.: Policy-Driven Management of Agent Systems, In: Sloman, M., Lobo, J., Lupu, E.C. (eds): Policies for Distributed Systems and Networks. Lecture Notes in Computer Science, Vol. 1995. Springer-Verlag, Berlin Heidelberg New York (2001) 214–229.
4. Cuppens, F., Saurel, C.: Specifying a security policy: A Case Study. In IEEE Computer Society Computer Security Foundations Workshop (CSFW9), 1996, 123–135.
5. Damianou, N., Dulay, N., Lupu, E., Sloman, M.: The Ponder Policy Specification Language, In: Sloman, M., Lobo, J., Lupu, E.C. (eds): Policies for Distributed Systems and Networks. Lecture Notes in Computer Science, Vol. 1995. Springer-Verlag, Berlin Heidelberg New York (2001) 18–38.
6. Damianou, N., Dulay, N., Lupu, E., Sloman, M.: Ponder: A Language for Specifying Security and Management Policies for Distributed Systems, Language Specification 2.3, Imperial College Research Report DoC 2000-1, October 2000. Available from http://www-dse.doc.ic.ac.uk/policies.
7. Dulay, N., Lupu, E., Sloman, M., Damianou, N.: A Policy Deployment Model for the Ponder Language, In: Pavlou, G., Anerousis, N., Liotta, A. (eds): Integrated Network Management VII, IEEE (2001) 529–543.
8. Feigenbaum, J.: Overview of the AT&T Labs Trust Management Project: Position Paper in Proceedings of the 1998 Cambridge University Workshop on Trust and Delegation, Lecture Notes in Computer Science. Springer Verlag, 1998
9. Herzberg, A., Mass, Y., Michaeli, J., Naor, D., Ravid, Y.: Access Control Meets Public Key Infrastructure, or: Assigning Roles to Strangers, In Proceedings of the 2000 IEEE Symposium on Security and Privacy.
10. Hitchens, M., Varadharajan, V.: Tower: A Language for Role Based Access Control, In: Sloman, M., Lobo, J., Lupu, E.C. (eds): Policies for Distributed Systems and Networks. Lecture Notes in Computer Science, Vol. 1995. Springer-Verlag, Berlin Heidelberg New York (2001) 88–106.
11. Hoagland, J.A., Pandey, R., Levitt, K. N.: Security Policy Specification Using a Graphical Approach. Technical report CSE-98-3, UC Davis Computer Science Department, 1998.
12. Jajodia, S., Samarati, P., Subrahmanian, V. S.: A Logical Language for Expressing Authorizations, In IEEE Symposium on Security and Privacy, Research in Security and Privacy, Oakland, CA, 1997. IEEE Computer Society Press 31-34.
13. Li, N., Feigenbaum, J., Grosof, B. N.: A Logic-Based Knowledge Representation for Authorization with Delegation, In Proceeding of the 12th IEEE Computer Security Workshop. IEEE Computer Society Press, 1999.
14. Lobo, J., Bhatia, R., Naqvi, S.: A Policy Description Language. In Proceedings of the AAAI, Orlando, Florida, USA, July 1999.
15. Lupu, E.C., Sloman, M.: Conflicts in Policy-Based Distributed Systems Management. In IEEE Transactions on Software Engineering, Vol 25(6): 852-869, Nov.1999.

16. Minsky, N.H., and V. Ungureanu, V.: Unified Support for Heterogeneous Security Policies in Distributed Systems, In Proceedings of the 7th USENIX Security Symposium (SECURITY-98), Berkeley, Usenix Association, 1998, 131–142.
17. Moore, B. Strassner J. Elleson, E.,: Policy Core Information Model V1, Available from http://www.ietf.org/draft-ietf-policy-core-info-model-05.txt, March 2000
18. Ortalo, R.: A Flexible Method for Information System Security Policy Specification. In Proceedings of the 5th European Symposium on Research in Computer Security (ESORICS 98). Louvain-la-Neuve, Belgium, Springer-Verlag. 1998.
19. Ribeiro, C., Zuquete, A., Ferreira, P., Guedes, P.: SPL: An Access Control Language for Security Policies with Complex Constraints, In: Network and Distributed System Security Symposium (NDSS 01), San Diego, Internet Society, Feb 2001.
20. Sandhu, R., Coyne, E., Feinstein, H., Youman, C.: Role-Based Access Control Models, IEEE Computer, 29(2):38–47, 1996.
21. Virmani, A., Lobo, J., Kohli, M.: Netmon: Network Management for the SARAS Softswitch, In: Hong, J., Weihmayer, R. (eds): IEEE/IFIP Network Operations and Management Symposium, (NOMS2000), Hawaii, May 2000, 803-816.

UML Class Diagrams Revisited in the Context of Agent-Based Systems

Bernhard Bauer

Siemens AG, Corporate Technology, Information and Communications
Otto-Hahn-Ring 6
81739 Munich, Germany
bernhard.bauer@mchp.siemens.de

Abstract. Gaining wide acceptance for the use of agents in industry requires both relating it to the nearest antecedent technology (object-oriented software development) and using artifacts to support the development environment throughout the full system lifecycle. We address both of these requirements using AUML, the Agent UML (Unified Modeling Language) — a set of UML idioms and extensions. This paper illustrates the next steps of our approach by presenting notions for the internal behavior of an agent and its relation to the external behavior of an agent using and extending UML class diagrams.

1 Introduction

Agent technology enables the specification, design and implementation of future software systems characterized by situation awareness and intelligent behavior, distributedness, complexity as well as mobility support. Agent technology has the potential to play a key role in reaching goals of future applications and services like automating daily processes, supporting the (nomadic) user with pro-active and intelligent assistance providing adaptive and self-organizing system functionality, opening the way to new application domains while supporting the integration of existing and new software, and make the development process for such applications easier and more flexible. However successful industrial deployment of agent technology requires to present the new technology as an incremental extension of known and trusted methods, and to provide explicit engineering tools that support industry-accepted methods of technology deployment.

Accepted methods of industrial software development depend on standard representations for artifacts to support the analysis, specification, and design of agent software. Three characteristics of industrial software development require the disciplined development of artifacts throughout the software lifecycle:

- The scope of industrial software projects is much larger than typical academic research efforts, involving many more people across a longer period of time, and artifacts facilitate communication.
- The success criteria for industrial projects require traceability between initial requirements and the final deliverable — a task that artifacts directly support.

M.J. Wooldridge, G. Weiß, and P. Ciancarini (Eds.): AOSE 2001, LNCS 2222, pp. 101-118, 2002.
© Springer-Verlag Berlin Heidelberg 2002

- The skills of developers are focused more on development methodology than on tracking the latest agent techniques, and artifacts can help codify best practice.

Agent technology is based on existing basic technologies like software technology, e.g. object-orientation, components, or plug-and-play technologies. The content is described using standards like XML (eXtensible Markup Language); existing communication mechanisms are applied within agent technology. But agent technology provides additional features to these technologies. On the one hand additional functionality is added, like matchmaking, agent mobility, cooperation and coordination facilities or adaptive preferences model. On the other hand the supported agent infrastructure consists of application frameworks that can be instantiated for special purposes. Moreover agent platforms allow an easy implementation of agent based applications and services. These pillars of agent technology result in personalized added value services, supporting the (nomadic) user with intelligent assistance, based on search, integration and presentation of distributed information and knowledge management, advanced process control support, and mobile & electronic commerce and enterprise applications.

Unfortunately the potential of agent technology from a software engineering point of view is not studied sufficiently to derive exact numbers about cost saving doing an agent oriented software development process. But having a look at the already performed projects we assume the usage of agent-oriented patterns, like communication protocols or agent architectures, can reduce the development and the risks inherent in any new technology.

At the moment no sufficient software processes and tools are available being well suited for industrial projects. The Unified Modeling Language (UML) is gaining wide acceptance for the representation of engineering artifacts in object-oriented software. Our view of agents as the next step beyond objects leads us to explore extensions to UML and idioms within UML to accommodate the distinctive requirements of agents. The result is Agent UML (AUML) (see e.g. [1, 2] and the paper on MESSAGE and of Odell et al. in this volume). This paper reports UML class diagrams revisited in the context of agent-based systems, namely the representation of the agent's internal behavior and relating it to the external behavior of an agent. In contrast to MESSAGE (see the paper on MESSAGE in this volume) with a focus on the analysis phase, our extensions support the design phase.

The rest of this paper is organized as follows. In section 2 the background on Agent UML is given. Afterwards UML class diagrams are revisited and extended in the framework of agents, having also a look at inheritance. The paper finishes with some evaluation and conclusions.

2 Background

Agent UML (AUML) synthesizes a growing concern for agent-based software methodologies with the increasing acceptance of UML for object-oriented software development.

In [2] we have shown how Agent UML differs from the other existing agent software methodologies, as presented in [4, 5, 6, 8, 9, 10, 11, 12, 13, 14, 15, 16, 18, 19, 20, 21, 22, 23, 24, 26, 27].

This wide-ranging activity is a healthy sign that agent-based systems are having an increasing impact, since the demand for methodologies and artifacts reflects the growing commercial importance of our technology. Our objective is not to compete with any of these efforts, but rather to extend and apply a widely accepted modeling and representational formalism (UML) — one that harnesses insights and makes them useful for communicating across a wide range of research groups and development methodologies.

To make sense of and unify various approaches on object oriented analysis and design, an Analysis and Design Task Force was established within the OMG. By November 1997, a de jure standard was adopted by the OMG members called the Unified Modeling Language (UML) [3, 17, 21]. UML unifies and formalizes the methods of many approaches to the object-oriented software lifecycle, including Booch, Rumbaugh, Jacobson, and Odell.

In a previous paper, we have argued that UML provides an insufficient basis for modeling agents and agent-based systems [1, 2]. Basically, this is due to two reasons: *Firstly*, compared to objects, agents are active because they can take the initiative and have control over whether and how they process external requests. *Secondly*, agents do not only act in isolation but in cooperation or coordination with other agents. Multi-agent systems are social communities of interdependent members that act individually.

To employ agent-based programming, a specification technique must support the whole software engineering process — from planning, through analysis and design, and finally to system construction, transition, and maintenance.

A proposal for a full life-cycle specification of agent-based system development is beyond the scope of this paper. Therefore we will focus on a new subset of an agent-based UML extension for the specification of the agent's internal behavior and relating it to the external behavior of an agent using and extending UML class diagrams. This extension and considerations extends our effort on AUML for the software engineering process, because this topic closes the gap between the agent interaction protocol definition as shown e.g. in [2] and the internal behavior of an agent and its relation to the agent interaction protocols.

The definition of the internal behavior is part of the specification of the dynamical model of an agent system, as well as the static model of an agent.

3 UML Class Diagrams – Revisited

First of all let us have a closer look at the concepts of object oriented programming languages, namely the notions of object and class and adapt it afterwards to agent-based systems.

3.1 Basics

In object oriented programming languages an object consists of a set of instance variables, also called attributes or fields, and its methods. Creating an object its object identity is determined. Instance variables are identifiers holding special values, depending on the programming languages these fields can be typed. Methods are operations, functions or procedures, which can act on the instance variables and other objects. The values of the fields can be either pre-defined basic data types or references to other objects.

A class describes a set of concrete objects, namely the instances of this class, with the same structure, i.e. same instance variables, and same behavior, i.e. same methods. Usually a standard method 'new' exists, to create new instances of a class. A class definition consists of the declaration of the fields and the method implementations, moreover of a specification or an interface part as well as of an implementation part.

The *specification part* describes the methods and their functionality supported by the class, but nothing is stated about the realization of the operation.

The *implementation part* defines the implementation / realization of the methods and is usually not visible to the user of the method.

The access rights define visibility of methods for specific users. In most programming languages classes define types, i.e. each class definition defines a type of the same name.

Some programming languages allow class variables within the definition of a class shared by all classes, in contrast to instance variables belonging to a single object. I.e. each instance of a class has its own storage for its instance variables, in contrast to class variables sharing the same storage. Beyond class variables, class methods can be called independently of a created object. Both class variables and class methods can be used as global variables and global procedures, respectively.

3.2 Relating Objects with Agents

In contrast to an object that invokes its methods (see figure 1), an agent is able to evaluate incoming messages (communicative acts, CA for short) with respect to its goals, plans, tasks, preferences, and to the internal world model.

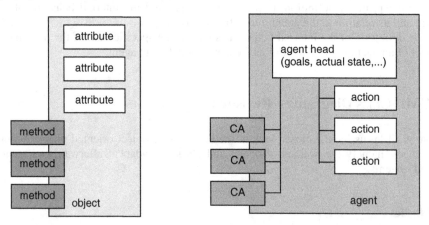

Fig. 1. Comparison object and agent

In contrast to distributed objects an agent is characterized by

- non-procedural behavior,
- balance between reactivity and pro-activity,
- high-level typed messages, like FIPA-ACL or KQML, and
- patterns and interaction protocols, not just client-server architecture.

In particular an agent is characterized by

- autonomy, i.e. deciding whether an action or behavior should be performed, not only method calls and returning results to other objects, especially not reacting based on hard-coded behavior
- pro- and re-activity, i.e. acting on events and messages as well as on self-triggered actions by the agents, in contrast to pure method invocation or events in the object oriented world
- the communication is based on speech act theory (communicative acts, CA for short), in contrast to method invocation with a fixed pre-defined functionality and behavior,
- the internal state is more than only fields with imperative data types, but include believes, goals and plans.

Among others these concepts have to be supported by a class diagram for agents.

3.3 Agent Class Diagrams

We start with some motivation and basics on agents, discuss afterwards the technical details, followed by agent head automaton and a look on generalization and inheritance for agents.

3.3.1 Motivation and Basics

An agent can be divided into

- the communicator - doing the physical communication,
- the head - dealing with goals, states, etc. of an agent and
- the body - doing the pure actions of an agent.

The communicator is responsible for the transparent dispatching of messages usually supported by agent platforms. For the internal view of an agent we have to specify the agent's head and body. The aim of the specification of an agent's internal behavior is to provide possibilities do define e.g. BDI, reactive, layered as well as interacting agent architectures and pure object oriented agents.

In particular the semantics of the communicative acts and the reaction of an agent to incoming messages have to be considered, established either by the designer of the multi-agent system or left open in the design phase and derived during run-time by the agent with reasoning functionality. The definition of a procedural as well as a declarative process description is supported using e.g. activity diagrams or the UML process specification language.

Not only methods can be defined for an agent which are only visible to the agent itself, but actions which can be accessed by other agents. But in contrast to object orientation the agent decides itself whether some action is executed.

Abstract actions are characterized with pre-conditions, effects and invariants. Moreover the usual object oriented techniques have to be applied to agent technology, supporting efficient and structured program development, like inheritance, abstract agent types and agent interfaces, and generic agent types.

Single, multi, and dynamic inheritance can be applied for states, actions, methods, and message handling.

Associations are usable to describe e.g. agent A uses the services of agent B to perform a task (e.g. client, server), with some cardinality and roles. Aggregation and composition show e.g. car park service and car park monitoring can be part of a car park agent.

The components can either be agent classes or usual object oriented classes. Several times we have argued that agent and objects are different things. Therefore we have to distinguish in our specifications between agents and objects. Especially an agent can be build using some object as part of its internal state (see fig 2). Therefore different notations between agents and objects have to be used either directly or using stereotypes.

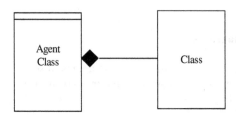

Fig. 2. Object part of an agent

3.3.2 Technical Details

In the agent oriented paradigm we have to distinguish between an *agent class*, defining a blue print for and the type of an individual agent, and *individual agents* being an instance of an agent class.

UML distinguishes different specification levels, namely the *conceptual*, the *specification* and the *implementation level*.

For the agent-oriented point of view in the *conceptual level* an agent class corresponds to an agent role (for a detailed description see Odell et al. in this volume) or agent classification, e.g. monitoring and route planning can be defined in different agent classes. E.g. we can have an individual traffic (IT) route planning (RP) agent and an IT Monitoring agent.

Fig. 3. Conceptual level

On the *specification level* or *interface level* an agent class is a blueprint for instances of agents, e.g. the monitoring and route planner are part of one agent class. But only the interfaces are described and not their implementation, i.e. the behavior of the agent to e.g. incoming messages is missing. Only the internal states and the interface, i.e. the communicative acts supported by the agent, are defined.

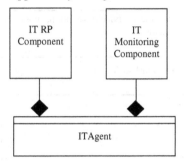

Fig. 4. Specification level

The *implementation level* or *code level* is the most detailed description of a system, showing how instances of agents are working together and how the implementation looks like. On this level the agent head automaton (see below) has to be defined, too.

In the following we show how usual UML class diagrams can be used and extended in the framework of agent oriented programming development. We will use the following notation to distinguish between different kinds of agent classes and instances.

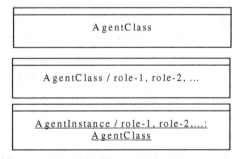

Fig. 5. Different kinds of agent classes

The first one denotes an agent class; the second an agent class satisfying distinguished roles and the last one defines an agent instance satisfying distinguished roles. The roles can be neglected for agent instances. According to the above descriptions the agent class diagram shown in figure 6 specifies agent classes.

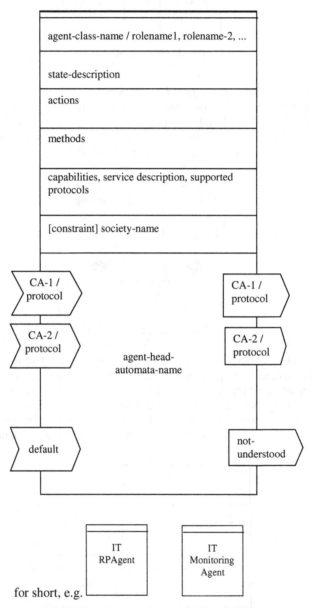

Fig. 6. Agent class diagram and its abbreviations

The usual UML notation can be used to define such an agent class, but for more readable reasons we have introduced the above notation. Using stereotypes an agent class written as a class diagram is shown in fig. 7.

Agent Class Descriptions and Roles

In UML, *role* is an instance-focused term. In the framework of agent oriented programming by *agent-role* a set of agents satisfying distinguished properties, interfaces, service descriptions or having a distinguished behavior is characterized. UML distinguishes between multiple classification (e.g., a retailer agent acts as a buyer and a seller agent at the same time), and dynamic classification, where an agent can change its classification during its existence. Agents can perform various roles within e.g. one interaction protocol. In an auction between an airline and potential ticket buyers, the airline has the role of a seller and the participants have the role of buyers. But at the same time, a buyer in this auction can act as a seller in another auction. I.e., agents satisfying a distinguished role can support multiple classification and dynamic classification. Therefore, the implementation of an agent can satisfy different roles. An agent role describes two variations, which can apply within a multi agent system. It can be defined at the level of concrete agent instances or for a set of agents satisfying a distinguished role and/or class. An agent satisfying a distinguished agent role and class is called agent of a given agent role and class, respectively. The general form of describing agent roles in agent UML (as we have shown in [2], for a detailed discussion on roles and agents see Odell et al. in this volume) is

instance-1 ... instance-n / role-1 ... role-m : class

denoting a distinguished set of agent instances instance-1,..., instance-n satisfying the agent roles role-1,..., role-m with n, m $\geq$ 0 and class it belongs to. Instances, roles or class can be omitted, for classes the role description is not underlined.

State Description

A *state description* is similar to a field description in class diagrams with the difference that a distinguished class *wff* for *well-formed formula* for all kinds of logical descriptions of the state is introduced, independent of the underlying logic. This extension allows the definition of e.g. BDI agents. Beyond the extension of the type for the fields, visibility and a persistency attributes can be added. E.g. in our personal travel assistance scenario the user agent has an instance variable storing the planned and booked travels. This field is persistent (denoted by the stereotype <<persistent>>) to allow the user agent to be stopped and re-started later in a new session. Optionally the fields can be initialized with some values.

In the case of BDI semantics three instance variables can be defined, named *beliefs*, *desires*, and *intentions* of type *wff*. Describing the beliefs, desires, and intentions of a BDI agent. These fields can be initialized with the initial state of a BDI agent. The semantics state that the *wff* holds for the beliefs, desires, and intentions of the agent.

In a pure goal-oriented semantics two instance variables of type *wff* can be defined, named *permanent-goals* and *actual-goals*, holding the formula for the permanent and actual goals.

Usual UML fields can be defined for the specification of a plain object oriented agent, i.e. an agent implemented on top of e.g. a Java-based agent platform.

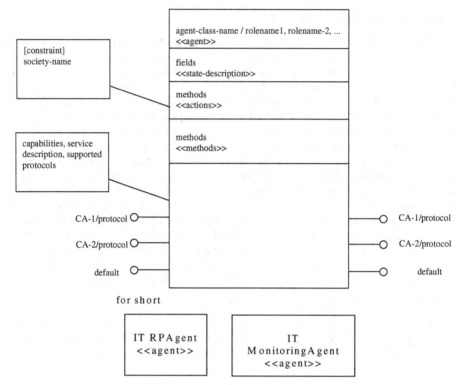

Fig. 7. Using UML class diagrams to specify agent behavior and its abbreviations

However in different design stages different kinds of agents can be appropriate, on the conceptual level BDI agents can be specified implemented by a Java-based agent platform, i.e. refinement steps from BDI agents to Java agents are performed during the agent development.

Actions

Pro-active behavior is defined in two ways, using pro-active actions and pro-active agent head automaton. The latter one will be considered later. Thus two kinds of actions can be specified for an agent:

- pro-active actions (denoted by the stereotype <<pro-active>>) are triggered by the agent itself, if the pre-condition of the action evaluates to true.
- re-active actions (denoted by the stereotype <<re-active>>) are triggered by another agent, i.e. receiving a message from another agent.

The description of an agent's actions consists of the action signature with visibility attribute, action-name and a list of parameters with associated types. Pre-conditions, post-conditions, effects, and invariants as in UML define the semantics of an action.

Methods

Methods are defined as in UML, eventually with pre-conditions, post-conditions, effects and invariants.

Capabilities

The capabilities of an agent can be defined either in an informal way or using class diagrams e.g. defining FIPA-service descriptions.

Sending and Receiving of Communicative Acts

Sending and receiving communicative acts characterize the main interface of an agent to its environment. By communicative act (CA) the type of the message as well as the other information, like sender, receiver or content in FIPA-ACL messages, is covered in this paper. We assume that classes and objects represent the information about communicative acts. How ontologies and classes / objects are playing together is beyond this paper and are reason for future work.

The incoming messages are drawn as and the outgoing messages are drawn as . The received or sent communicative act can either be a class or a concrete instance.

The notation *CA-1 / protocol* is used if the communicative act of class *CA-1* is received in the context of an interaction protocol *protocol*. In the case of an instance of a communicative act the notation *CA-1 / protocol* is applied. As alternative notation we write *protocol[CA-1]* and *protocol[CA-1]*. The context / *protocol* can be omitted if the communicative act is interpreted independent of some protocol. In order to re-act to all kinds of received communicative acts, we use a distinguished communicative act *default* matching any incoming communicative act. The *not-understood* CA is sent if an incoming CA cannot be interpreted.

Between instances and classes is distinguished, because an instance describes a concrete communicative act with a fixed content or other fixed values. Thus having a concrete request, say "start auction for a special good", an instance of a communicative act would be appropriate. To allow a more flexible or generic description, as "start auction for any kind of good", agent classes are used.

Matching of Communicative Acts

A received communicative act has to be matched against the incoming communicative acts of an agent to trigger the corresponding behavior of the agent. The matching of the communicative acts depends on the ordering of them, namely the ordering from top to bottom, to deal with the case that more than one communicative act of the agent matches an incoming message.

The simplest case is the default case, *default* matches everything and *not-understood* is the answer to messages not understood by an agent. Since instances of communicative acts are matched, as well as classes of communicative acts, free variables can occur within an instantiated communicative act, shown in figure 8 (class diagram for communicative acts where the instance variables have the type *undef*). Note, that classes without methods define communicative acts.

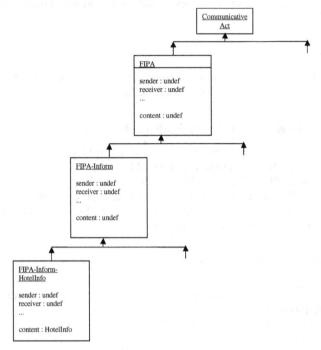

Fig. 8. Instance hierarchy on communicative acts, being an instance of the corresponding class hierarchy.

An input communicative act CA *matches* an incoming message CA', iff
- CA is a class, then
  - CA' must be an instance of class CA or
  - CA' must be a subclass of class CA or a subclass of it.
- CA is instance of a class, then
  - CA' is instance of the same class as CA and
  - CA.field matches CA'.field for all fields *field* of the class CA, defined as
    - CA.field matches CA'.field, if CA.field has the value *undef*.
    - CA.field matches CA'.field, if CA.field is equal to CA'.field with CA.field not equal to *undef* and the type of *field* is a basic type.
    - CA.field matches CA'.field, if CA.field is unequal to *undef* and the type of field is not a basic data type and CA.field are instance of the same class C and CA.field.cfield matches CA'.field.cfield for all fields *cfield* of class C.

In the case of a communicative act in the context of a protocol, *protocol[CA]* matches *protocol'[CA']*, if CA matches CA' and *protocol'* is equal to *protocol*.

The analogous holds for outgoing messages, the communicative act has to match the result communicative acts of the agent head automaton.

3.4 Agent-Head-Automaton

The agent head automaton defines the behavior of an agent's head. We had defined an agent consisting of an agent's communicator, head and body.

The main functionality of the agent is implemented in the agent body, like existing legacy software coupled with the MAS using wrapper mechanisms.

The agent's head is the "switch-gear" of the agent. Its behavior is specified with the agent head automaton. In particular incoming messages are related to the internal state, actions and methods and the outgoing messages, called the *re-active behavior* of the agent. Moreover *pro-active behavior* of an agent, i.e. automatically triggering different actions, methods and state-changes depending on the internal state of the agent is specified. An example of a pro-active behavior is to do an action at a specific time point, e.g. an agent migrates at pre-defined times from one machine to another one, or it is the result of a request-when communicative act.

UML supports four kinds of diagrams for the definition of dynamic behavior: sequence diagrams, collaboration diagrams on the object level, state and activity diagrams for other purposes. Sequence diagrams and collaboration diagrams are suitable for the definition of an agent's head behavior, since it is an instance-focused diagram. Thus the concrete behavior, based on actions, methods and state changes, can be easily defined. It is up to the preferences of the designer to apply one of these two diagrams. The state and activity diagram are more suitable for an abstract specification of an agent's behavior. Again it is up to the designer to select one of these two diagrams.

For the re-active behavior we specify how the agent reacts to incoming messages using an extended state automaton (see fig. 9). In contrast to standard state automaton the CA-notation of the class diagram is used to trigger an automaton (initial states) and the final states match with the outgoing communicative acts.

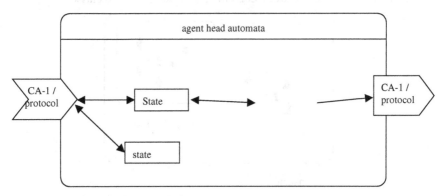

Fig. 9. Extended state automaton

Pro-active behavior is not triggered by incoming messages, but depends on the validity of constraints or conditions where the initial state(s) are marked with them.

3.5 Inheritance / Generalization on Class Diagrams

One main characteristic and THE modularization and structuring mechanism of object oriented programming languages is inheritance. This feature is applicable as well to agent-based systems.

Usually the following kinds of inheritance can be found in the literature:

- single inheritance,
- multiple inheritance and
- dynamic inheritance.

Reasons for introducing and using inheritance are

- the class hierarchy defines a type hierarchy
- inheritance supports re-usability and changeability
- inheritance supports to share common behavior.

Usually an object belongs either to a class A or to a class B, but it is impossible that an object of class A as well as to class B, see e.g. [28].

instances of class A   instances of class B

But sometimes it is better to have a class to be an instance of two classes:

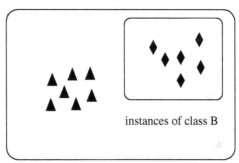

instances of class B

instances of class A

I.e. the instances of class B are also instances of class A. In agent's words, e.g. we have a buyer agent being in addition a seller agent. This inclusion property can be expressed using simple inheritance. Simple inheritance defines some type hierarchy, namely class B is some subtype of class A and the instances of class B are a subset of the instances of class A. If class B inherits from class A then B is subclass of A and A is super class of B.

Using single inheritance allows expressing, that an instance of class A and instances of class B can also be instances of class C.

For the implementation of the inheritance relation two views are well known:

- copy-view: inherits a class B from a class A, class B posses all components of class A, i.e. the instance variables and methods of class A. This is e.g. realized in the function tables of C++.
- search-view: An alternative view is obtained, if the access to instance variables and methods is done in the actual class. If the component is not present in this class, the super classes are searched for it. This technique is e.g. used in Smalltalk-80 and Java.

On the one side the concept of inheritance simplifies the implementation and on the other side makes the implementation more secure.

The implementation is simplified, since the code can be re-used, modified or extended using inheritance without re-writing all code. Methods can be re-defined, to specialize them for specific cases as well as define new methods to extend the functionality of a given class. Therefore the implementation is more secure, since tested code can be applied.

Thus inheritance supports top-down as well as bottom-up software development. Fixing the data type and their interfaces software systems can be developed top-down. Using class libraries and combining these classes with other classes results in a bottom-up software approach.

Generalization and specialization of class can be expressed as well using inheritance, since inheritance defines a type hierarchy, allowing an object to belong to more than one class. A generalization of classes is obtained, extracting common components of a class (instance variables and methods), which are used in different classes and defining them in an own class. This new class is a super class of the modified original class.

A specialization is realized, defining a new class B, which inherits from class A. Afterwards new components can be added in class B not included in class A.

A first draft characterization of simple inheritance for agents can look like

- subclass inherits all roles of the super class.
- state description:
  - additional fields can be defined, with new name and type
  - fields defined in a super class can be initialized
  - initialization can be re-defined, i.e. same type and field-name
- actions
  - are inherited from the super class
  - re-definition: same functionality, i.e. same argument types and result type as the super class; another new action is defined with different functionality, distinction between result types not possible.
- methods, like for actions but with possible result type and are not visible to other agents.
- capabilities are inherited , "everything" the super class can do, the actual class can do, too.
- societies
  - [constraint-1] society-name in super class and [constraint-2] society-name in subclass assumes that constraint-1 is stronger or weaker than constraint-2. Both cases are possible.
  - new societies can be added in the subclass

- old ones are inherited and can be restricted or extended, see above.
- CAs
  - the search is performed like for method-calls in object-oriented programming languages, i.e. try to match the incoming CA with one of the input CAs starting with the first one from top to bottom. If no input CA matches the incoming CA than try to find a matching CA in the super class(es). If no CA matches with the exception of the "default" input CA, then the default input CA of the actual class is used, if defined otherwise the "default" input CA is recursive searched in the super class(es)
  - the output CAs are determined by the agent head automaton. Here the same holds, that all output CAs have to be defined in the class hierarchy.
- agent head automaton
  - are inherited from the super class
  - can be redefined with the same name
  - additional behavior to the agent can be added

This is a first draft characterization, but show that inheritance is also a very interesting aspect in the design of multi-agent systems, but a topic for future research.

4 Evaluation and Conclusion

The artifacts for agent-oriented analysis and design were developed and evaluated in the German research project MOTIV-PTA (Personal Travel Assistant), aiming at providing an agent-based infrastructure for travel assistance in Germany (see www.motiv.de). MOTIV-PTA run from 1996 to 2000. It was a large-scale project involving approximately 10 industrial partners, including Siemens, BMW, IBM, DaimlerChrysler, debis, Opel, Bosch, and VW. The core of MOTIV-PTA is a multiagent system to wrap a variety of information services, ranging from multimodal route planning, traffic control information, parking space allocation, hotel reservation, ticket booking and purchasing, meeting scheduling, and entertainment.

From the end user's perspective, the goal is to provide a personal travel assistant, i.e., a software agent that uses information about the users' schedule and preferences in order to assist them in travel, including preparation as well as on-trip support. This requires providing ubiquitous access to assistant functions for the user, in the office, at home, and while on the trip, using PCs, notebooks, information terminals, PDAs, and mobile phones.

From developing PTA (and other projects with corporate partners within Siemens) the requirements for artifacts to support the analysis and design became clear, and the material described in this paper has been developed incrementally, driven by these requirements. So far no empirical tests have been carried out to evaluate the benefits of the Agent UML framework. However, from our project experience so far, we see two concrete advantages of these extensions: Firstly, they make it easier for users who are familiar with object-oriented software development but new to developing agent systems to understand what multi agent systems are about, and to understand the principles of looking at a system as a society of agents rather than a distributed collection of objects. Secondly, our estimate is that the time spent for design can be reduced by a minor amount, which grows with the number of agent-based projects. However, we expect that as soon as components are provided to support the implementation based on Agent UML specifications, this will widely enhance the benefit.

Areas of future research include aspects such as

- description of mobility, planning, learning, scenarios, agent societies, ontologies and knowledge
- development of patterns and frameworks
- support for different agent communication languages and content languages
- development of plug-ins for existing CASE-tools

At the moment we plan to extend the presented framework and take inheritance and the benefits and problems of inheritance into consideration.

References

1. AUML: http://www.auml.org
2. Bauer, B.; Müller, J. P.; Odell, J.: An Extension of UML by Protocols for Multiagent Interaction, Proceeding, Fourth International Conference on Multi Agent Systems, ICMAS 2000, Boston, IEEE Computer Society, 2000.
3. Booch, G., Rumbaugh, J., Jacobson, I., *The Unified Language User Guide*, Addison-Wesley, Reading, MA, 1999.
4. Brazier, F.M.T., Jonkers, C.M., Treur J., ed., *Principles of Compositional Multi-Agent System Development* Chapman and Hall, 1998.
5. Bryson, J., McGonigle, B. "Agent Architecture as Object Oriented Design," in: *Intelligent Agents IV: Agent Theories, Architectures, and Languages.* 1998.
6. Burmeister, B., ed., *Models and Methodology for Agent-Oriented Analysis and Design* 1996.
7. Burmeister, B., Haddadi A., Sundermeyer K., Generic, Configurable, Cooperation Protocols for Multi-Agent Systems, Lecture Notes in Computer Science, Vol. 957, 1995.
8. Garijo, F. J., Bomaned J., ed., *Multi-Agent System Engineering: Proceedings of MAAMAW'99,* 1999.
9. Gustavsson, R. E., "Multi Agent Systems as Open Societies," in: *Intelligent Agents IV: Agent Theories, Architectures, and Languages,* 1998.
10. Herlea, D. E., Jonker C. M., Treur J., and Wijngaards N.J.E., in: *Specification of Behavioural Requirements within Compositional Multi-Agent System Design,* 1999.
11. Iglesias, C. A., Garijo, M., González J.E., *A Survey of Agent-Oriented Methodologies,* in: *Intelligent Agents V: Agent Theories, Architectures and Languages* (ATAL-98), 1998.
12. Iglesias, C. A., Garijo, M., González, J. C., Velasco, J. R. "Analysis and Design of Multiagent Systems using MAS-CommonKADS," in: *Intelligent Agents IV: Agent Theories, Architectures, and Languages,* 1998.
13. Jonker, C. M., Treur, J., in: *Compositional Verification of Multi-Agent Systems: a Formal Analysis of Pro-activeness and Reactiveness,* 1997.
14. Kinny, D., Georgeff, M., "Modelling and Design of Multi-Agent Systems," in: Proceedings ATAL'96, 1996.
15. Kinny, D., Georgeff, M., Rao, A., "A Methodology and Modelling Technique for Systems of BDI Agents," in: *MAAMAW'96,* 1996.
16. Lee, J., Durfee, E. H., "On Explicit Plan Languages for Coordinating Multiagent Plan Execution," in: *ATAL 98,* 1998.

17. Martin, J., Odell, J., *Object-Oriented Methods: A Foundation*, (UML edition), Prentice Hall, 1998.

18. Nodine, M. H., Unruh, A., "Facilitating Open Communication in Agent Systems: the InfoSleuth Infrastructure," *ATAL 98,* 1998.

19. Parunak, H. Van D., *Visualizing Agent Conversations: Using Enhanced Dooley Graphs for Agent Design and Analysis,* in: *Proceedings of the First International Conference on Multi--Agent Systems,* MIT Press, 1995.

20. Parunak, H. Van D., Odell J., *Engineering Artifacts for Multi-Agent Systems*, ERIM CEC, 1999.

21. Parunak, H. Van D., Sauter, J., Clark, S. J., *Toward the Specification and Design of Industrial Synthetic Ecosystems*, in: *ATAL 98,*1998.

22. Rumbaugh, J., Jacobson, I., Booch G., *The Unified Modeling Language Reference Manual*, Addison-Wesley, 1999.

23. Schoppers, M., Shapiro, D., *Designing Embedded Agents to Optimize End-User Objectives*, in: ATAL 98, 1998.

24. Singh, M. P., *A Customizable Coordination Service for Autonomous Agents*, in: ATAL 98, 1998.

25. Singh, M. P., *Towards a Formal Theory of Communication for Multi-agent Systems,* Proceedings of the 12th International Joint Conference on Artificial Intelligence, pp. 69-74, Morgan Kaufmann, August 1991.

26. Wooldridge, M., Jennings, N. R., Kinny, D., "The Gaia Methodology for Agent-Oriented Analysis and Design," International Journal of Autonomous Agents and Multi-Agent Systems, 3, 2000.

27. Ciancarini, P., Wooldridge, M. J., eds, Agent-Oriented Software Engineering, First International Workshop, AOSE 2000, Limerick, Irland, June 2000, 2001.

28. A. Goldberg, D. Robson: Smalltalk-80: The Language and its Implementation. Addison-Wesley, Reading, MA, 1983

Agent Oriented Analysis Using Message/UML

Giovanni Caire[1], Wim Coulier[2], Francisco Garijo[3], Jorge Gomez[3], Juan Pavon[3],
Francisco Leal[4], Paulo Chainho[4], Paul Kearney[5], Jamie Stark[5], Richard Evans[6], and
Philippe Massonet[7]

[1]Telecom Italia LAB, Via Reiss Romoli 274, 10148 Turin – Italy
giovanni.caire@tilab.com
[2]Belgacom, E. Jacqmainlaan 177, 1210 Brussels, Belgim
wim.coulier@belgacom.be
[3]Telefónica I+D, Emilio Vargas, 28043 Madrid, Spain
fgarijo@tid.es
[4]PT Inovação, Largo de Mompilher, 22 – 3º, 4050-392 Porto, Portugal
fleal@ptinovacao.pt
[5]BtexaCT, Adastral Park, Martlesham Heath, Ipswich IP53RE, UK
paul.3.kearney@bt.com
[6]Broadcom Eireann Research Ltd, Kestrel House, Clanwilliam Place, Dublin 2, Ireland
re@broadcom.ie
[7]CEDITI, Av. Georges Lemaître,21, 6041 Charleroi, Belgium
phm@info.ucl.ac.be

Abstract. This paper presents the MESSAGE/UML agent oriented software engineering methodology and illustrates it on an analysis case study. The methodology covers MAS analysis and design and is intended for use in mainstream software engineering departments. MESSAGE integrates into a coherent AOSE methodology some basic agent related concepts such as Organization, role, goal and task, that have so far been studied in isolation. The MESSAGE notation extends the UML with agent knowledge level concepts, and diagrams with notations for viewing them. The proposed diagrams extend UML class and activity diagrams.

1. Introduction

1.1 Agent Oriented Software Engineering

The agent-oriented (AO) approach promises the ability to construct flexible systems with complex and sophisticated behaviour by combining highly modular components. The intelligence of these components – the agents – and their capacity for social interaction results in a multi-agent system (MAS) with capabilities beyond those of a simple 'sum' of the agents. The availability of agent-oriented development toolkits has allowed the technology to be assessed for industrial use. Many case studies have been carried out, yielding promising results that have aroused industrial interest in the technology.

M.J. Wooldridge, G. Weiß, and P. Ciancarini (Eds.): AOSE 2001, LNCS 2222, pp. 119-135, 2002.
© Springer-Verlag Berlin Heidelberg 2002

Most recent software engineering methodologies are designed for an object-oriented approach. Engineering of commercial MAS requires the availability of agent oriented software engineering (AOSE) methodologies. Most MAS systems will be implemented with object and component based technology in the near future unless a widely accepted agent programming language emerges. In this case, viewed at a detailed level, an agent is a relatively complex object or component. However, this is like considering that a house is a pile of bricks, but it is more convenient to view a house in terms of higher level concepts such as living room, kitchen and bedroom. When an agent is viewed at a more abstract level, structures come into focus that are not found in conventional objects or components. Agent-orientation is thus a paradigm for analysis, design and system Organization. An agent-oriented modelling language must provide primitives for describing these higher-level structures, the inspiration for which derives from cognitive psychology and social modelling via artificial intelligence.

MESSAGE[1] [5] (Methodology for Engineering Systems of Software Agents) is an AOSE methodology which builds upon current software engineering best practices covering analysis and design of MAS which is appropriate for use in mainstream software engineering departments. It has well defined concepts and a notation that is based on UML whenever appropriate.

1.2 Comparison to Other Approaches

Work toward an AOSE methodology can be divided into two broad categories. The first category aims to apply existing software engineering methodologies to AOSE. AgentUML (AUML) [9] for example defines extensions to UML with notations suited for agent concepts. AUML has extended UML's interaction diagrams to handle agent interaction protocols. Although this notation is useful and has been adopted within MESSAGE, it does not have the concept of agent at its centre, i.e. specifying an object's behaviour in terms of interaction protocols does not make it an agent.

The second category of work aims at developing a methodology from agent theory, mainly covering analysis and design. Typically these methodologies define a number of models for both analysis and design [8] such as Gaia [6] and MAS-CommonKads [7]. The Gaia methodology has two analysis models and three design models. While the analysis models are based on well-defined concepts, these only represent a subset of the concepts required for agent oriented analysis. The design models are not clearly explained and the authors envisage OO methods being used for detailed design. Mas-Common-Kads has six models for analysis, and three for design. While these models are comprehensive, the method lacks a unifying semantic framework and notation. In addition to this work, goal analysis techniques have been shown to be very useful [4, 10]. The techniques range from informal to formal analysis and cover functional and non-functional goal analysis. MESSAGE combines the best features of the above approaches.

---

[1] MESSAGE was a two year collaborative project funded by EURESCOM. EURESCOM is a research organization owned by European telecommunications companies, http://www.eurescom.de/.

1.3 Outline and Contributions

The MESSAGE/UML methodology covers MAS analysis and design and is designed for use in mainstream software engineering departments.

This article focuses on analysis of MAS using MESSAGE/UML. Section 2 describes the principal "knowledge level" agent-oriented MESSAGE concepts and describes different views on the analysis model. Section 3 describes the MESSAGE analysis process. Section 4 describes an analysis case study using the MESSAGE/UML notation. The following diagram types are introduced: Organization, goal, task, delegation, workflow, interaction and domain. All are extensions of UML class diagrams, except for the task diagram, which extends the UML activity diagram. The use of schemas to textually describe the concepts is also illustrated.

The contributions of MESSAGE are the agent knowledge level concepts, and the diagrams for viewing these concepts in the analysis model that have been added to UML. MESSAGE integrates into a coherent AOSE methodology that can be used by mainstream software engineering departments some basic agent related concepts such as Organization [11, 15], role [12], goal [4] and task [13], that have so far been studied in isolation. The case-study focuses on illustrating these new agent related concepts and the new diagrams to visualise them. A complete case study can use existing UML notation in addition to the new notation.

2. Message Description

2.1 Extending UML for Agent Modelling

UML is a convenient starting point for an agent-oriented modelling language for the following reasons:

- UML is widely accepted as a *de facto* standard for object-oriented modelling, many software engineers are trained in its use, and commercial software tools are available to support it (some of which are extendable).

- The object- and agent-oriented paradigms are highly compatible. Agent-oriented concepts can readily be defined in terms of object-oriented ones.

- UML is based on a meta-model (UML uses the MOF meta-modelling language [3]), which makes it extendable[1].

The MESSAGE modelling language is related to UML as follows:

1. It shares a common metamodelling language (meta-metamodel) with UML and MOF

2. It extends the UML metamodel with 'knowledge level' agent-oriented concepts.

A more complete description of the relationship between the MESSAGE metamodel and the UML metamodel is given in [5].

2.2 Main MESSAGE Concepts

2.2.1 Foundations

MESSAGE takes UML as a starting point and adds entity and relationship concepts required for agent-oriented modelling. Agent-oriented modelling borrows from the study of human Organizations and societies in describing the way in which agents in a Multi-Agent System work together to achieve a collective purpose, and from artificial intelligence (AI) and cognitive psychology to describe the agents themselves. These additional concepts can be defined in terms of object-oriented ones, but deal with ideas and structures at a higher conceptual level. In AI this higher level is often referred to as "the knowledge level", contrasting knowledge with data. Essentially, MESSAGE uses standard UML as its "data level" modelling language, but provides additional "knowledge level" concepts. These additional concepts are defined in the MESSAGE metamodel [5]. The metamodel also gives a declarative interpretation to some UML concepts used to describe behaviour. The most significant of these is "State" which is described hereafter.

The MESSAGE interpretation of State can be described as follows. A UML model is a collection of objects. A full description of this model at a point in time consists of a description of the value of every attribute of every object. Let us call such description a micro-state. It is rarely practical or useful to work directly with micro-states, however. A State is characterised by a partial description of the model, i.e. a constraint restricting the micro-state of model to being one of a set of possible micro-states. The simplest form of constraint would be to give the value of one attribute of one object in the model. Because States are sets (of micro-states), the language of Boolean algebra can be used to describe their relationships (set union, intersection and containment are equivalent to logical or, and implication).

Note that this is entirely consistent with the UML State concept. From the UML 1.3 specification [1]:

A state is an abstract metaclass that models a situation during which some (usually implicit) invariant condition holds. The invariant may represent a static situation such as an object waiting for some external event to occur. However, it can also model dynamic conditions such as the process of performing some activity (i.e., the model element under consideration enters the state when the activity commences and leaves it as soon as the activity is completed).

The rest of this section describes the knowledge level concepts that feature most prominently in the MESSAGE methodology as it stands at the moment, particularly those that appear explicitly in diagrams.

2.2.2 Knowledge-Level Concepts

Most of the MESSAGE knowledge level entity concepts fall into the main categories: *ConcreteEntity*, *Activity*, and *MentalStateEntity*. The main types of ConcreteEntity are:

Agent: An Agent is an atomic autonomous entity that is capable of performing some (potentially) useful function. The functional capability is captured as the agent's *services*. A *service* is the knowledge level analogue of an object's *operation*. The quality of autonomy means that an agent's actions are not solely dictated by external events or interactions, but also by its own motivation. We capture this motivation in an attribute named *purpose*. The purpose will, for example, influence whether an agent agrees to a request to perform a service and also the way it provides the service. SoftwareAgent and HumanAgent are specialisations of Agent.

Organization: An Organization is a group of Agents working together to a common purpose. It is a virtual entity in the sense that the system has no individual computational entity corresponding to an Organization; its services are provided and purpose achieved collectively by its constituent agents. It has structure expressed through *power relationships* (e.g. superior-subordinate relationships) between constituents, and behaviour/co-ordination mechanisms expressed through Interactions between constituents.

Role: The distinction between Role and Agent is analogous to that between Interface and (object) Class: a Role describes the external characteristics of an Agent in a particular context. An Agent may be capable of playing several roles, and multiple Agents may be able to play the same Role. Roles can also be used as indirect references to Agents. This is useful in defining re-usable patterns.

Resource: Resource is used to represent non-autonomous entities such as databases or external programs used by Agents. Standard object-oriented concepts are adequate for modelling Resources.

The main types of Activity are:

Task: A Task is a knowledge-level unit of activity with a single prime performer. A task has a set of pairs of Situations describing pre- and post-conditions. If the Task is performed when a pre-condition is valid, then one can expect the associated post-condition to hold when the Task is completed. Composite Tasks can be expressed in terms of causally linked sub-tasks (which may have different performers from the parent Task). Tasks are StateMachines, so that e.g. UML activity diagrams can be used to show temporal dependencies of sub-tasks.

Interaction and **InteractionProtocol**: The MESSAGE concept of Interaction borrows heavily from the Gaia methodology [6]. An Interaction by definition has more than one participant, and a purpose which the participants collectively must aim to achieve. The purpose typically is to reach a consistent view of some aspect of the problem domain, to agree terms of a service or to exchange to results of one or more services. An InteractionProtocol defines a pattern of Message exchange associated with an Interaction.

The internal architecture of an agent typically is based on one of several models derived from cognitive psychology. MESSAGE is intended to be applicable to a variety of agent cognitive architectures. However, without some basic abstract reference model it is difficult to say anything meaningful. We suppose that the architecture separates an inference mechanism from a knowledge base and a working memory. The knowledge base contains fixed or slowly changing domain or problem-solving knowledge in a declarative form. The working memory contains more transient sensed or derived information. We view this working memory as an abstract database holding instances of MentalStateEntities, and its contents define the Agent's mental state. For present purposes we focus on one type of MentalStateEntity: Goal.

Goal: A Goal associates an Agent with a Situation. If a Goal instance is present in the Agent's working memory, then the Agent intends to bring about the Situation referenced by the Goal. Some Goals are intrinsic to the agent's identity, and are derived from its purpose. These persist throughout the life of the Agent. Others are transient tactical Goals. It is often useful to express the purpose in terms of a utility function that associates 'goodness values' with Situations. The target situation of the Goal is then the one that is estimated to maximise utility (determined dynamically). Note that the agent's knowledge base needs to include 'rules' governing assertion and deletion of (tactical) Goals. One fairly standard rule would be to assert a Goal to provide a given service whenever the Agent agrees with another Agent to do so.

Two other simple but important concepts used in MESSAGE are: **InformationEntity** (an object encapsulating a chunk of information) and **Message**. The agent-oriented concept of Message differs from the object-orient one in a number of respects. In UML, a Message is a causal link in a chain of behaviour, indicating that an Action performed by one object triggers an Action by another object. In MESSAGE, a Message is an object communicated between Agents. Transmission of a Message takes finite time and requires an Action to be performed by the Sender and also the receiver. The attributes of a Message specify the sender, receiver, a speech act (categorising the Message in terms of the intent of the sender) and the content (an InformationEntity).

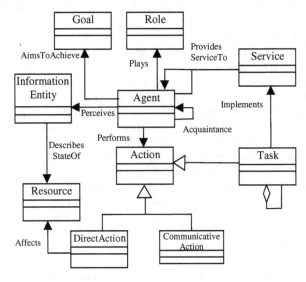

Fig. 1. Agent centric MESSAGE concepts

Figure 1 gives an informal agent-centric overview of how these concepts are inter-related, showing their relationship to the agent concept. A complete description of the MESSAGE metamodel can be found in [5].

2.3 Analysis Model Views

An analysis model is a complex network of inter-related classes and instances derived from concepts defined in the MESSAGE/UML metamodel. MESSAGE defines a number of views that focus on overlapping sub-sets of entity and relationship concepts.

Organization view (OV) – This shows ConcreteEntities (Agents, Organizations, Roles, Resources) in the system and its environment and coarse-grained relationships between them (aggregation, power, and acquaintance relationships). An acquaintance relationship indicates the existence of at least one Interaction involving the entities concerned.

Goal/Task view (GTV) – This shows Goals, Tasks, Situations and the dependencies among them. Goals and Tasks both have attributes of type Situation, so that they can be linked by logical dependencies to form graphs that show e.g. decomposition of high-level Goals into sub-goals, and how Tasks can be performed to achieve Goals. Graphs showing temporal dependencies can also be drawn, and we have found UML Activity Diagram notation useful here.

Agent/Role view (AV) – This focuses on the individual Agents and Roles. For each agent/role it uses schemata supported by diagrams to its characteristics such as what Goals it is responsible for, what events it needs to sense, what resources it controls, what Tasks it knows how to perform, 'behaviour rules', etc.

Interaction view (IV) – For each interaction among agents/roles, shows the initiator, the collaborators, the motivator (generally a goal the initiator is responsible for), the relevant information supplied/achieved by each participant, the events that trigger the interaction, other relevant effects of the interaction (e.g. an agent becomes responsible for a new goal). Larger chains of interaction across the system (e.g. corresponding to uses cases) can also be considered.

Domain view (DV) – Shows the domain specific concepts and relations that are relevant for the system under development (e.g. for a system dealing with making travel arrangements, this view will show concepts like trip, flight, ticket, hotel....).

Provisional ideas on notation, diagrams and schemas to visualize the views are illustrated in the case study section below.

3. Analysis Process

The purpose of Analysis is to produce a model (or collection of models) of the system to be developed and its environment, that is agreed between the analyst and the customer (and other stakeholders). It aids communication between the development team and the customer, and provides a basis from which design can proceed with confidence. The analysis models are produced by stepwise refinement.

Refinement Approach: The top level of decomposition is referred to as level 0. This initial level is concerned with defining the system to be developed with respect to its stakeholders and environment. The system is viewed as a set of Organizations that interact with resources, actors, or other Organizations. Actors may be human users or other existing agents. Subsequent stages of refinement result in the creation of models at level 1, level 2 and so on.

At level 0 the modelling process starts building the Organization and the Goal/Task views. These views then act as inputs to creating the Agent/Role and the Domain Views. Finally the Interaction view is built using input from the other models. The level 0 model gives an overall view of the system, its environment, and its global functionality. The granularity of level 0 focuses on the identification of entities, and their relationships according to the metamodel. More details about the internal structure and the behaviour of these entities are progressively added in the next levels.

In level 1 the structure and the behaviour of entities such as Organization, agents, tasks, goals domain entities are defined Additional levels might be defined for analysing specific aspects of the system dealing with functional requirements and non functional requirements such as performance, distribution, fault tolerance, security. There must be consistency between subsequent levels. In the MESSAGE project only level 0 and level 1 have been considered.

Analysis Refinement strategies: Several strategies are possible for refining level 0 models. Organization-centered approaches focus on analysing overall properties such as system structure, the services offered, global tasks and goals, main roles, resources. The agents needed for achieving the goals appear naturally during the refinement process. Then co-operation, possible conflicts and conflict resolution may be analysed.

Agent centred approaches focus on the identification of agents needed for providing the system functionality. The most suitable Organization is identified according to system requirements. Interaction oriented approaches suggest progressive refinement of interaction scenarios which characterise the internal and external behaviour of the Organization and agents. These scenarios are the source for characterising task, goal, messages, protocols and domain entities.

Goal/task decomposition approaches are based on functional decomposition. System roles, goals and tasks are systematically analyzed in order to determine the resolution conditions, problem-solving methods, decomposition and failure treatment. Task preconditions, task structures, task output and task post-condition may determine what Domain Entities are needed. Goals and tasks must be performed by agents playing certain roles. Consequently looking at the overall structure of goal and tasks in the Goal/task view decisions can be made on the most appropriate agents and Organization structure for achieving those goals/tasks.

The experience in MESSAGE shows that the different views of the system leave the analyst free to choose the most appropriate strategy. In practice a combination of refinement strategies with frequent loop-backs among them are used. The analysis process might start with the OV, then switch to the AV and continue with the IV. The results of the analysis of specific interaction scenarios may lead to reconsider part of OV, and starting again refining and adapting OV constituents.

4. Message/UML Case Study

This section illustrates the MESSAGE/UML concepts and views on a case study. MESSAGE diagrams are introduced with proposed notations. The analysis process is illustrated by describing level 0 and then refining it into level 1.

4.1 Case Study Description

The system under development is a knowledge management system to be used by a team of engineers of a telecom operator company (TOC) that perform equipment installation and maintenance operations on a given territory.

Context: Each engineer in the team gets the list of jobs assigned to him from a co-ordination centre and performs them sequentially moving on the territory in his van. At the end of each job he fills in a proper paper form where he reports the type of problem, if and how the problem was solved. These forms are then sent back to the co-ordination centre where the relevant information is stored in a database. Moreover the TOC owns a database storing all the technical documentation about the equipment deployed in the fields.

Requirements: The TOC wants now to improve the efficiency of the whole process by giving each engineer a proper wireless terminal and developing a system (distributed both on these terminals and on the terrestrial network) that

- Automatically notifies engineers about the jobs they are assigned,

- Automatically and/or on request retrieves the relevant documentation for the job to be carried out,

- Automatically and/or on request identifies other engineers in the team who can provide help in the job to be performed (e.g. because they have proper skills or because they recently solved similar problems) so that it is possible for an engineer to directly receive assistance from another qualified engineer,

- Allows engineers to report about performed jobs filling an electronic form so that the relevant information are directly inserted into the report database.

Appropriateness of an Agent Approach to the case-study: Since the documentation relevant to a job must be proactively provided to the engineer who is going to perform that job, the system to be developed requires its components to show a high degree of autonomy. Moreover it is almost impossible to exactly foresee all possible faults that can happen in the equipment to be maintained and therefore goal oriented behaviour will be needed. Finally finding an engineer with proper skills to provide assistance in a certain job may require some form of negotiation and distributed co-ordination.

4.2 Level 0 Analysis

4.2.1 Organization View
The analysis starts at level 0 viewing the system to be developed as a black box and focusing on its relationships to the entities in its environment (users, stakeholders, resources, ...).

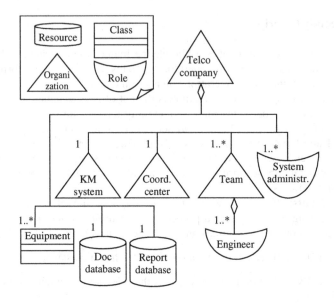

Fig. 2. Level 0 Organization Diagram (Structural relationships)

Two diagrams from the level 0 Organization view are reported as examples showing the main (from the system point of view) structural and acquaintance relationship in the TOC.

Figure 2 describes structural relationships in a level 0 Organization diagram. The diagram shows that the Knowledge Management (KM) system is owned by the TOC. An Engineer is part of a team and there are several teams in the TOC. It should be noticed that this Organization diagram is a UML class diagram where proper icons have been associated to different stereotypes. At level 0 the system under development, i.e. the KM system, is seen itself as an Organization that will be analysed at level 1.

Figure 3 shows the acquaintance relationships in the level 0 Organization diagram. The KM system interacts with two roles, the System Administrator and the Engineer and with two external systems (resources), the Technical Documentation DB to retrieve documentation and the Report DB to insert the job reports filled by the engineers. Moreover it interacts with the Coordination centre to get the list of jobs to perform. An Engineer also interacts with other Engineers to get direct help. It has to be noticed that an engineer does not interact directly with the Documentation DB and the Report DB. All these interactions are carried out through the KM system.

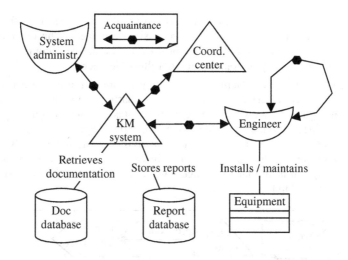

Fig. 3. Level 0 Organization Diagram (Acquaintance relationships)

4.2.2 Goal/Task View

As for the Goal view the main goal of the system (i.e. providing assistance to the engineers) is and/or decomposed according to the Goal/Task implication diagram in Figure 4.

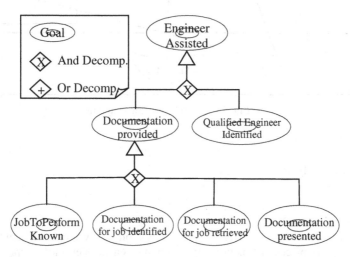

Fig. 4. Level 0 Goal/Task Implication Diagram

The diagram in figure 4 shows that the main goal of the system (EngineerAssisted) is satisfied when the relevant documentation for the current job is provided and the name of a qualified engineer to possibly request direct help to is identified. The DocumentationProvided goal on its turn is satisfied when the job to be performed is known, the documentation required to perform the job has been identified/retrieved, and that documentation is presented to the assisted engineer. The decomposition of the QualifiedEngineerIdentified goal is not shown. Alternative decompositions can be modelled with or-decomposition notation not illustrated here.

Alternatively, or in conjunction with goal/task implication diagram it is useful to analyse how a given service is realised by a partially ordered set of tasks. The example in figure 5 shows the workflow of tasks implementing the Identify-Qualified-Engineer service by means of a workflow diagram (i.e. a UML Activity Diagram where tasks are shown instead of activities). The diagram also shows the classes that are input/output of tasks using object flows and the roles that perform the tasks. This diagram is similar to the agent head automata, which is an extended state automata, proposed in [14].

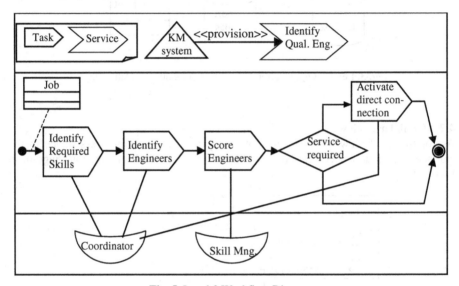

Fig. 5. Level 0 Workflow Diagram

4.3 Level 1 Analysis

4.3.1 Organization View
Moving from level 0 to level 1, analysis focuses on the system itself identifying at a glance the main pieces of functionality required (seen as roles and/or types of agents). The approach followed in this simple case study is to consider only roles initially and to define what agents will populate the system and what roles each agent will play at the beginning of the design process. However the developer is free to start identifying agents during analysis.

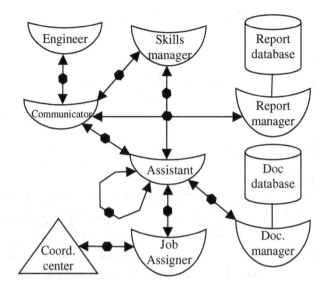

Fig. 6. Level 1 Organization Diagram (Acquaintance relationships)

Figure 6 shows the level 1 acquaintance relationships in an Organization diagram. The skills manager maintains knowledge of engineer's skills on the basis of the jobs he carries out. The interaction between Assistants requires a contract-net to identify another engineer who has the right skills to provide assistance for a given job.

4.3.2 Agent/Role View
Delegation, Workflow structure diagrams, and textual Agent/Role schemas are useful to describe the view.

A delegation structure diagram shows how the sub-goals obtained decomposing a goal of an Organization are assigned to the agents/roles included in the Organization. Clearly this diagram is strictly related to (and must be consistent with) both the goal decomposition diagram showing the decomposition of the Organization goal and the Organization diagram showing the agents/roles inside the Organization.

Figure 7 shows a Delegation structure diagram. Only the root and the leaves of the decomposition of the parent Organization goal are shown.

Similarly a workflow structure diagram shows the roles in an Organization that must perform the tasks necessary to implement a given service provided by the Organization.

For each agent/role there is one Agent/Role schema that describes its characteristics. At the analysis level this information is typically quite informal and therefore free text is preferred to a graphical notation. The schema below describes the Assistant role.

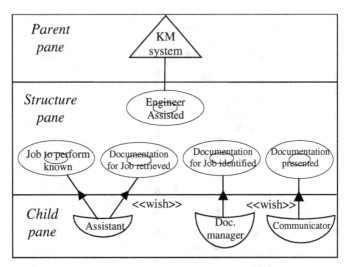

Fig. 7. Level 1 Delegation Structure Diagram

Table 1. Role schema

Role Schema	Assistant
Goals	JobToPerformKnown, DocumentationForJobRetrieved
Capability	Some learning capability is required to keep the profile of the engineer updated on the basis of the completed job.
Knowledge, Beliefs	A profile of the skills of the engineer to be used to evaluate if and how the engineer can provide help to a colleague requesting assistance A profile
Agent requirements	This role will be played by the agent that actually assists the Engineer.

4.3.3 Interaction View

This view highlights which, why and when agents/roles need to communicate leaving all the details about how the communication takes place to the design process.

The interaction view is typically refined through several iterations as long as new interactions are discovered. It can be conveniently expressed by means of a number of interaction diagrams. These diagrams are interaction centric (i.e. there is one of such diagram for each interaction) and show the initiator, the responders, the motivator (often a goal of the initiator) of an interaction plus other optional information such as the trigger condition and the information achieved and supplied by each participant.

The following picture shows as an example the interaction diagram describing the Documentation Request interaction between the Assistant and the Documentation Manager roles. Figure 8 shows an Interaction diagram.

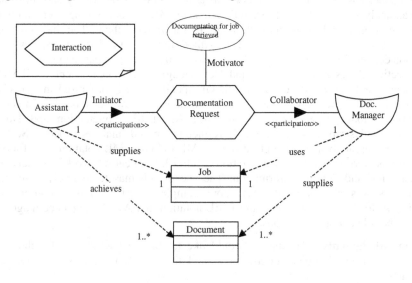

Fig. 8. Level 1 Interaction Diagram

The details of the interaction protocol and the messages that are exchanged between roles can be represented using AUML sequence diagram [2].

4.3.4 Domain View

The domain view can be conveniently represented by means of typical UML class diagrams where classes represent domain specific concepts and named association represent domain specific relations. It is typically built in parallel to the other views by adding new concepts and relations as long as they are needed in the other views. Figure 9 shows a provides a very simplified example related to the considered case study.

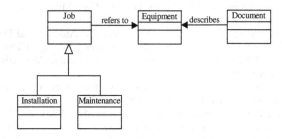

Fig. 9. Domain Information Diagram

5. Conclusions

This paper has presented the MESSAGE/UML AOSE methodology and illustrated it on an analysis case study. MESSAGE extends UML by contributing agent knowledge level concepts, and diagrams with notations for viewing them. The diagrams extend UML class and activity diagrams. The methodology covers MAS analysis and design and is designed for use in mainstream software engineering departments.

Section 2 described the principal "knowledge level" agent-oriented MESSAGE concepts and described how a MESSAGE specification is organised in terms of an analysis model and views. The following overlapping views have been defined on the analysis model: Organization, Goal/Task, Agent/Role, Interaction and Domain. Section 3 described the MESSAGE refinement based analysis process. Section 4 described an analysis case study using the MESSAGE/UML notation. The following diagrams were illustrated: Organization, goal/task implication, workflow, delegation, interaction and domain information. The use of schemas to textually describe the concepts was also illustrated. A more complete analysis model completes the MESSAGE diagrams with existing UML notation and AUML sequence diagrams to describe role/agent interactions.

Acknowledgments. The authors would like to thank EURESCOM for the project support, all P907 project contributors, and the AOSE reviewers for their useful comments.

References

1. OMG Unified Modeling Language Specification Version 1.3. Object Management Group, Inc., http://www.rational.com/uml/resources/documentation/index.jtmpl, June 1999.
2. Bauer, B. et al. Response to the OMG Analysis and Design Task Force UML 2.0 Request for Information: Extending UML for the specification of Agent Interaction Protocols. ftp://ftp.omg.org/pub/docs/ad/99-12-03.pdf .OMG, December 1999.
3. OMG Meta Object Facility (MOF) Specification. ftp://ftp.omg.org/pub/docs/ad/99-09-04.pdf., September 1999.
4. Dardenne, A., van Lamsweerde, A. and Fickas, S. Goal-Directed Requirements Acquisition. Science of Computer Programming Vol. 20, North Holland, 1993, 3-50.
5. MESSAGE website, http://www.eurescom.de/Public/Projects/p900-series/P907/P907.htm
6. Wooldridge, M., Jennings, N.R., Kinny D. "The Gaia Methodology for Agent-Oriented Analysis and Design". Kluwer Academic Press, 2000.
7. Iglesias, C., Garijo M., Gonzalez, J. and Velasco, J.R. Analysis and Design of multiagent systems using MAS-CommonKADS. Intelligent Agents IV: Agent Theories, Architectures and Languages, 1997, Singh, M. P., Rao, A. and Wooldridge, M.J., eds., Lecture Notes in Computer Science 1365.
8. Iglesias, C., Garrijo, M., Gonzalez, J. A survey of agent-oriented methodologies. Agent Theories, Architectures and Languages, 1998.
9. Odell, J., Van Dyke Parunak, H., Bauer, B. Extending UML for Agents. Proc. Of the Agent-Oriented Information Systems Workshop at the 17 th National Conference on Artificial Intelligence, Wagner, G., Lesperance, Y., and Yu, E. eds. 2000.
10. Mylopoulos, J., Chung, L., Liao, S., Huaiqing Wang, Yu, E. Exploring alternatives during requirements analysis. IEEE Software, Vol. 18, N. 1, 2001, 92 –96.

11. Zambonelli, F., Jennings, N.R., Wooldridge M. Organizational Abstractions for the Analysis and Design of Multi-agent Systems. In P. Ciancarini, M.J. Wooldridge, Agent-Oriented Software Engineering, vol. 1957 LNCS, 235-251. Springer-Verlag: Berlin, Germany 2001.

12. Kendall, E.A. Agent Software Engineering with Role Modelling. In P. Ciancarini, M.J. Wooldridge, Agent-Oriented Software Engineering, vol. 1957 LNCS, 163-169. Springer-Verlag: Berlin, Germany 2000.

13. Omicini, A. SODA: Societies and Infrastructures in the Analysis and Design of Agent-Based Systems. In P. Ciancarini, M.J. Wooldridge, Agent-Oriented Software Engineering, vol. 1957 LNCS, 185-193. Springer-Verlag: Berlin, Germany 2000.

14. Bauer, B. UML Class diagrams Revisited in the Context of Agent-Based Systems. In this volume.

15. Van Dyke Parunak, H., Odell, J. Representing Social Structures in UML. In this volume.

Specifying Agent Interaction Protocols with Standard UML

Jürgen Lind

iteratec GmbH
Inselkammerstr. 4
D-82008 Unterhaching, Germany
jli@agentlab.de

Abstract. In this paper, I will demonstrate how the Unified Modeling Language (UML) can be used to describe agent interaction protocols. The approach that is presented in this paper does not propose enhancements or completely new diagrams but instead relies on existing UML elements and the UML extension mechanism that is part of the standard. This conformity with the base UML is a major advantage of the idea as it prevents a diversification of the UML into different potentially incompatible dialects. The practical use of the method is demonstrated with an example on how to specify a realistic agent interaction protocol.

1 Introduction

One of the currently most popular graphical design languages is the Unified Modeling Language (UML) [3], [17] that aims at a global standard for the description of software systems. Such standardized blueprint languages already exist for electrical, mechanical or civil engineering for several years. The advantage of a blueprint language for software systems is that it provides a set of symbols and mechanisms together with well defined semantics that enables software designers from all over the world to express, exchange and work on their ideas without complicated and error-prone translation processes. Furthermore, a unified language increases the inter-operability among software design tools and allows software developers to become more independent of particular development environments and to assemble customized environments out of different tool suites. The UML combines original ideas with established features of other graphical design languages into a coherent framework that allows for the specification of a broad range of design aspects of a software system.

Due to the strong focus on object-oriented software design, however, the UML is not right away suitable for agent-based systems. In order to make it fit some special requirement of agent-oriented software, there are two possible ways to be taken. One way is to extend the UML by providing new structural elements and diagrams that enhance the expressive power of the base language. This way is favored by the developers of AUML [2], [1], [14] which proposes an extension of the UML with respect to agent-oriented concepts. This approach, however, has the major drawback that it violates the idea of the UML as a general design language. To quote from [17], p. 103: "Many modelers wish to tailor a modeling language for a particular application domain. This

M.J. Wooldridge, G. Weiß, and P. Ciancarini (Eds.): AOSE 2001, LNCS 2222, pp. 136–147, 2002.

carries some risk, because the tailored language will not be universally understandable, but people nevertheless attempt to do it." Thus, if each group within the computer science community added their own UML extension according to their particular needs, the base language is likely to be split up in several increasingly unrelated dialects. The result, as it can be observed with programming languages such as Basic, is a collection of inconsistent language fragments. Besides this not being the idea of a standard language, it introduces the additional difficulty of having to learn a new dialect when switching between two specialized application fields. Furthermore, tool support is usually not available for special purpose diagrams.

As a consequence from the above considerations, I suggest to take another approach to the use of the UML for describing agent-specific aspects of a software system. A major goal is to remain within the boundaries of the original language and to use only those extension mechanisms that were explicitly admitted by the language designers [3]. Thus, I will not introduce completely new diagram types or the like but instead rely on the provided structural elements and use them to model the system of agent-based applications.

In this paper, I will demonstrate how the UML can be used to capture one of the core concepts of multiagent systems – *interaction*. Interaction is the foundation for cooperative or competitive behavior among several autonomous agents and thus encapsulates the most fundamental design decisions within the development of multiagent systems. Before interaction can take place, however, some technical and conceptual difficulties must be solved. First of all, the agents must be able to understand each other. Mutual understanding is achieved by relying of accepted formal or informal standards where the de-facto standard of todays agent applications seems to be KQML [7], others can be found in [5] or [8]. Although agent communication languages are an important aspect of multiagent systems design, these aspects are not covered by this investigation of the UML as interaction description language. Instead, this paper will focus on the second important aspect of agent interaction which is that the agents must know which messages they can expect in a particular situation and what the are supposed to do (e.g. sending a reply message) when a certain message arrives (or does not arrive for a given period of time). This part of the interaction process is controlled by *interaction protocols* (or simply protocols).

For an example of an interaction protocol, consider an English auction. There, an auctioneer offers a product at a particular price to a group of bidders. Each of the bidders individually decides to accept that price or to decline the offer. If one of the bidders accepts the current price, the auctioneer raises the price by a fixed rate and asks the group of bidders again if any of them accepts the new price. If this is the case, the price is raised again and the cycle repeats until none of the bidders is willing to pay the current price. Then, the last bidder who accepted the price is given the product.

In this example, we can identify the major elements of interaction protocols. First, we can separate the participating agents into different groups. In this case, we have two groups: the auctioneer and the bidders. Each group has a set of associated incoming and outgoing messages an internal functions that decide about their next action. I will refer to the set of messages and behaviors that are associated with a group of agents as a *role* that can be played by an agent. Please note that agents are not limited to a single role, e.g. the auctioneer in the previous example can be a bidder in another auction at the same time. The second important aspect of an interaction protocol besides the participating roles is the temporal ordering of function evaluation and the messages that are exchanged. For example, it would not make sense or would be impossible for the bidder to decide on an offer and to decline it before it has even received the offer. Therefore, the interaction protocol determines the flow of control within each role as well as between different roles.

It is precisely the dualism mentioned in the previous paragraph that makes protocol design a difficult task. There are not only intra-role aspects to consider during the design process, but also inter-role dependencies induced by the other roles. Even worse, there is currently only little software engineering support for the design of interaction protocols. A number of protocol specification languages have been proposed ranging from specification languages for low level communication protocols [18], [9] up to high level specification languages for multiagent applications [4], [10]. Up to now, however, none – perhaps except for Estelle – of these languages has gained wide-spread acceptance. Estelle [18], is a specification language for service description and system behavior in telecommunications that uses extended finite automata to describe the intended behavior. Extended finite state machines are normal finite state machines plus (typed) variables. The state in the finite state machine has a set of associated variables that can be queried and/or manipulated in the transition specifications. In Estelle, a protocol is a collection of several distinct automata where each automaton can have an arbitrary number of inter-action points with other automata. These interaction points are called *channels* and they control the message exchange between different automata. Estelle is a very powerful language that was mainly developed for the specification of low level protocols. It is therefore not directly suitable for the use in multiagent applications.

One reason for the lack of acceptance mentioned above is probably the fact that protocol description languages usually provide only a text-based representations for the interaction protocols. This makes it hard, especially for complex protocols, to understand the flow of control within the protocol. An alternative for these text-based languages are therefore graphical languages that make the described protocols more accessible for the reader. As mentioned above, I argue that the UML allows the software engineer to specify the interaction schemes that can be found within a multiagent system. In an earlier approach described in [12], I have proposed a method to describe interaction diagrams using a standard diagram type provided by the UML with minor modifications of the proposed standard elements. The modification that I found necessary in my earlier work, however, have shown to be unnecessary now that I have gained greater knowledge of the UML meta-model that allows for defining new UML elements within well-defined bounds. Basically, this paper is a revised version of the Section in [12] that corrects the errors that have been made there.

2   Related Work

In the previous section, I have already mentioned some protocol specification languages that have been proposed to describe interaction protocols within agent-based systems.

One of the most recent approaches for modeling agent-specific aspects of a software system is the AUML approach mentioned above. As part of AUML, the authors suggest an extension of the UML by introducing a completely new diagram type called *protocol diagrams*. These diagrams combine elements of UML interaction diagrams and state diagrams to model the roles that can be played by an agent in the course of interacting with other agents. The new diagram type allows for the specification of multiple threads within an interaction protocol and supports protocol nesting and protocol templates based on generic protocol descriptions. In [19], an extension of this UML extension is proposed; a comparison of the two approaches can be found in [11]. As I have argued earlier, however, I see a major problem in this approach as it supports a diversification within the UML community that may not be in the sense of the original inventors.

The Protoz [15] protocol specification environment features a specification language that is related to Estelle [18] and that is based on a similar computational concept. However, due to the focus on multiagent specific aspects, Protoz provides a more accessible interface to protocol design. The main tool of the protocol environment is a compiler that generates Oz code [16] from a given protocol specification, a graphical notation is currently not available. In the Protoz environment, a protocol is defined by a collection of roles where each of these roles is specified as an extended finite state machine. The state machine transitions fire upon incoming messages; messages can stem from other agents or from internal procedures. These internal procedures implement the connection to the application and allow for a uniform modeling of internal and external communication.

The ZEUS development environment [13] from BT is a a design method and tool collection for the engineering of distributed multiagent applications. The ZEUS tools all encompass the direct-manipulation metaphor and allow the designer to use drag-and-drop technology to assemble the application from pre-defined components. The tool-kit allows the designer to specify models for different types of agents, for the organizational structure of agent societies and for negotiation models. The negotiation models are either pre-defined or the can be build by the designer if no appropriate pre-defined model is available for a particular task. In [6] a notation for role models is presented that originates from UML class diagram notation and that contains also elements from UML interaction diagrams (e.g. message sequencing). The ZEUS role models capture structural (static) relationships between roles as well as communicative acts that describe the dynamic aspects of inter-agent communication. The pre-defined role models that are provided by the ZEUS environment include various protocols from the trading domain as well as business processes such as supply chain management.

3   UML Activity Diagrams

Activity diagrams in UML models provide a number of structural elements as shown in in Figure 1 to describe algorithms in a flowchart like manner. To this end, each computation is expressed in terms of *states* and the progression through these states. In order to allow for a hierarchical modeling, the UML distinguishes between two classes of states. *Action states* are atomic entities that cannot be decomposed and that relate to atomic statements in a programming language, eg. variable assignment. *Activity states*, on the other hand, represent a collection of atomic states and can thus be decomposed into these atomic

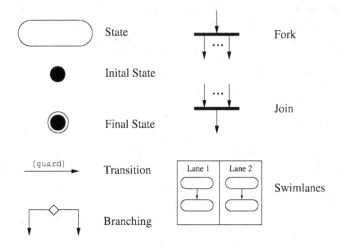

Fig. 1. Structural Elements of UML Activity Diagrams

states. Furthermore, the execution of an activity can be interrupted between any two subsequent states. In terms of programming languages, actions relate to statements and activities relate to subroutines.

The states of an activity diagram are linked with each other through *transitions* that indicate the control flow within the activity diagram. Each transition can have a *guard* condition that controls the flow of control in that it only allows a transition to fire if the guard condition is true. Because of the basic requirement that each transition must have at least one start and one end point, special states are introduced that represent the beginning and the end of an activity diagram, respectively.

The control flow within an activity diagram is not necessarily linear, otherwise it would be impossible to express anything other then trivial algorithms. Therefore, *branching* elements that represent the decision points within a diagram are provided. Each branching points stands for a boolean decision, i.e. the flow of control can proceed along two different paths.

Many modern programming languages provide some notion for pseudo-parallel program execution within a single operating system process. These light-weight processes – usually referred to as "threads" – can be modeled in UML activity diagrams by using two structural elements. A *fork* operation splits a single thread of execution into two or more threads that are subsequently executed in parallel. Thus, a fork bar has one incoming transition and several outgoing transitions. In order to merge several of these parallel threads into a single thread again, UML activity diagrams provide the *join* element. Thus, a join barrier has several incoming transitions and only a single outgoing transition, it can therefore be used to synchronize several parallel threads of execution. Note that a join barrier waits until *all* incoming threads have arrived at the barrier before proceeding with the single master thread.

Because of the fact that activity diagrams tend to become somewhat confusion with growing in size, UML activity diagrams can contain so-called *swimlanes* that are used to partition an activity diagram into several conceptually related parts. Within an activity diagram, each swimlane must have a unique name and each activity must belong to exactly one swimlane.

4   Tailoring UML

The UML has built-in extension mechanisms based on *constraints, tagged values*, and *stereotypes* that makes it possible to create UML profiles for particular application domains. A UML profile is a collection of modeling elements together with well defined semantics of these elements and the possible relations between them. For the purpose of this paper, stereotypes are sufficient; for a general UML profile for agent-based applications, all three extension mechanisms are likely to be necessary.

Stereotypes are new model elements that are declared within the model itself, i.e. stereotypes extend the modeling capabilities by introducing new classifiers that may extend the semantics but not the structure of existing meta-model classes. As an example for a stereotype, consider a business application where we want to deal with business processes explicitly. We can then introduce the business process stereotype as a means to describe a special kind of classes with attributes and methods but with additional constraints on usage and allowed structural relationships within the design model. Each stereotype must be based on an existing modeling element, this enables tools to deal with arbitrary stereotypes in the same way as with the respective base elements. To visually distinguish stereotypes and standard UML modeling elements, each stereotype can have its own icon. Furthermore, it is possible to define hierarchies of stereotypes with inheritance between them and using meta-model class diagrams to visualize the relationships between stereotypes. To store additional information about an instance of a stereotype, the creator of a stereotype can define a list of required tags that must be set whenever a stereotype instance is created. The information kept in the tagged values can, for example, be used by automatic code generators.

In the following section, I will define a couple of stereotypes that are necessary to model agent interaction protocols. For other aspects of agent-based systems, additional stereotypes will be needed.

5   Protocol Specification with Activity Diagrams

In this paper, I propose a notation for interaction protocols that is based on the basic elements of UML activity diagrams. In order to make them more usable to describe agent interaction protocols, I will introduce several stereotypes that relate the basic elements to the specific application area. First of all, I will extend the idea of swimlanes as a means to describe the *roles* (stereotype <<role>>) that occur within the application. In my view, these swimlanes are interpreted as physically – as opposed to conceptually – separated flows of control. I will sometimes refer to these independent flows of control as *control flow spaces* in the rest of this paper. The roles within the diagrams are linked with each other via explicit communication *channels* (<<channel>>) that manage the message

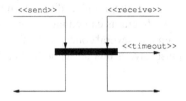

Fig. 2. Synchronization Point

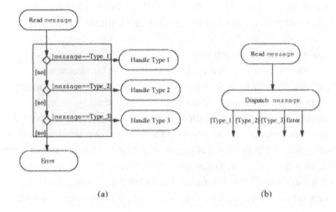

(a)   (b)

Fig. 3. Defining Macros

exchange between two roles. The message exchange itself is modeled in *synchronization points* (<<synchronization point>>) that denote the sending and the reception of messages, respectively. The graphical representation of a synchronization point is shown in Figure 2 where the arrows on either side denote the the control flow of the sender and the control flow of the receiver, respectively.

Each synchronization point has several incoming transitions out of which exactly one must be a <<send>> operation. The other transitions are the receivers of the respective message. Whenever the control flow of a receiver enters a synchronization point, the receiver suspends until a message has been delivered. This happens whenever the control flow of the sender reaches the synchronization point. After the massage has been delivered, the control flow of the sender and the control flow of the receivers resumes after the synchronization point. In order to prevent the receivers from infinite blocking while waiting for a message that never arrives, an additional <<timeout>> transition for each receiver can be attached to the synchronization. Whenever the timeout is reached and no message has been delivered, the control flow of the respective receiver resumes at the state pointed to by the timeout transition.

Note that the <<synchronization point>> stereotype includes a *semantic* extension of the UML because no such thing as a "timeout" is defined for join elements of standard activity diagrams. As explained in the previous paragraph, however, this

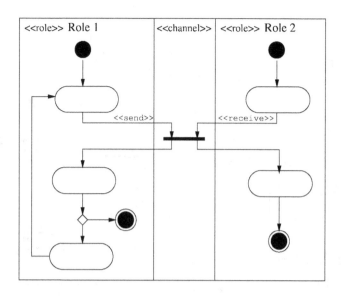

Fig. 4. Augmented Activity Diagram

semantic extension (which is still covered by the bounds of the extension mechanisms described above) is necessary to prevent either sender or receiver from infinite blocking. Note also, that it is not possible to express *asynchronous* message exchange with the protocol description mechanisms presented in this paper. For such diagrams, another modeling element would have to be defined either as stereotype or as new UML elements. Thus, here we might have the case that the UML is not sufficient and would need some extension. I will return to this later in the conclusion.

A very important feature of UML diagrams is that they provide a powerful structuring mechanism that can be used to make protocol mode readable. Since activity states can represent complete automata, it is straightforward to use them for macro definitions that can be used in interaction protocols. Figure 3 illustrates the idea. Figure 3 (a) shows an activity diagram for dispatching an incoming message according to the message type. Using the UML rule that a state can have several outgoing transitions that are labeled with conditional statements, we can rewrite the shaded part of the original automaton that contains three branching points into a single state as shown in 3 (b)[1]. Collapsing several states into a single macro state has not only the advantage to make a diagram more readable, it is also important that the macro state can be given a speaking name that highlight its purpose. Although the overall gain seems to be pretty small in the above example, the gain soon becomes apparent in more complex protocols where each decision point or loop construction that is hidden improves the readability of the protocol. Furthermore, this mechanism can be used to embed protocols into others, allowing for a hierarchical structuring, flexible combination and re-use of protocols.

---

[1] Note that conditions on the outgoing transitions are abbreviated in the example.

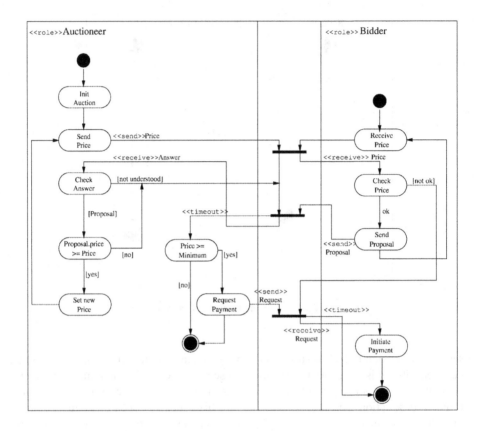

Fig. 5. English Auction

The use of the various modeling elements for specifying agent interaction protocols is shown in Figure 4. The swimlanes indicate the control flow spaces that are associated with each role within the agent interaction protocol. The control flow of each of these roles is modeled using the structural elements that are provided by standard UML activity diagrams. The self-contained control flow spaces are linked via a communication channel that holds one synchronization point that links the activity diagrams of the interacting roles. In the following section, we will see, how the modeling elements and the new stereotypes can be used to specify real agent interaction protocols.

6   Example

In order to illustrate the use of UML activity diagrams for interaction protocol specification on a realistic example, recall the English Auction that was mentioned in the introductory section. In Figure 5, I have depicted an interaction protocol that describes the course of actions and message exchanges within the auction more formally.

The first step in the interaction design process is to identify the roles that interact with each other. In the example, we have already identified the *auctioneer* and the *bidder* as the participating roles. Now, we create a control flow space that will later hold the finite automaton that describes the behavior of the agent playing a particular role. It is usually a good idea to develop an initial version of each automaton without considering the other automata, i.e. without switching back and forth between different automata. Thus, for the auctioneer, the auction starts with an initialization of its internal data, e.g. with determining the initial price of the product. Then, the auctioneer sends out a proposal to the bidders and waits for the incoming replies. In order to make the example more realistic, we shall assume that a bidder can indicate that the proposal was not understood, e.g. because the bidder is not familiar with the ontology used. In that case, the auctioneer simply ignores the message and continuous to wait for further messages. If, on the other hand, the price is accepted by the bidder, the auctioneer raises the price according to a fixed rate and the cycle starts from the beginning. In the offer is not accepted by the bidder, the auctioneer continuous to wait for incoming replies until a fixed timeout. When the timeout has expired and no bidder has accepted the offer, the product is given to the last bidder that has accepted the price (if that price exceeds a previously defined minimal acceptable price). Please note, that the *CheckAnswer* state uses the macro mechanism explained earlier to dispatch the incoming messages.

Now that the behavior of the auctioneer has been fully specified, we can turn to the bidder role. In the example, the bidder goes into a waiting loop as soon as the protocol execution is started. It leaves this loop when it receives an offer proposed by the auctioneer and checks whether to offered price is acceptable according to its individual goals. If this is the case, the bidder sends out a positive reply and re-iterates the waiting process. If the actual price is not acceptable, the bidder waits for a message from the auctioneer that indicates if the bidder is given the product or nor. Obviously, this can only happen when the bidder has issued a positive reply during the auction. To avoid an infinite blocking of the bidder, a timeout is applied to terminate the waiting process after a finite time. The bidder that receives the positive acknowledgment from the auctioneer will immediately initiate the payment process to finally receive the product.

This small example should be sufficient to provide the reader with an impression on how to apply the suggested method to arbitrary agent interaction protocols. The best way to see how the method works in practice is to pick an (preferably easy) protocol from the application domain of interest and then to simply start right away with an iterative modeling process. The value of the diagrams will then quickly become apparent.

7 Conclusion

In this paper, I have demonstrated how UML activity diagrams can be used for the specification of agent interaction protocols. The suggested method uses existing UML concepts and requires no additional elements, therewith making it easy for UML users to understand the interaction protocols without having to learn a completely new type of diagram. The method that was explained in this paper has been used in practical situations and has shown to be a valuable tool for modeling, understanding and communicating agent interaction protocols.

At the beginning of the paper, I have argued that, in my view, a special UML version only for agent-based systems is not desirable because of the potential emergence of mutually incompatible UML dialects. This does not mean, however, that the UML in its current version is perfect. Certainly there are aspects that need further elaboration and improvements and the requirements in the design of agent-based applications that provide input on which features should be added or improved are absolutely necessary. Approaches such as AUML can help to identify the potentially problematic or insufficient parts of the UML. The resulting extensions and improvements of the UML, however, should be chosen such that they are useful not only for agent-based systems, and they should be part of the general standard and not just a dialect thereof. In this sense, we shall continue to identify agent-specific requirements for the UML, try to solve the upcoming problems within the standard and suggest extensions only in those cases where solutions within the standard are not possible.

Acknowledgments. I would specifically like to thank Jeremy Pitt for the discussion on the weak points of an earlier version of this paper. His comments caused me to investigate the UML extension mechanism in greater depth in order to get the problems fixed.

References

1. Bernhard Bauer. UML Class Diagrams Revisited in the Context of Agent-Based Systems. In *Proceeedings of the Second International Workshop on Agent-Oriented Software Engineering (AOSE-2001)*, Montreal, Canada, 2001.
2. Bernhard Bauer, Jörg P. Müller, and James Odell. Agent UML: A Formalism for Specifying Multiagent Software Systems. In *Proceeedings of the First International Workshop on Agent-Oriented Software Engineering (AOSE-2000) held at the 22nd International Conference on Software Engineering*, Limerick, Ireland, 2001. Springer Verlag.
3. G. Booch, J. Rumbaugh, and I. Jacobson. *The Unified Modeling Language User Guide*. Addison Wesley, 1999.
4. B. Burmeister, A. Haddadi, and K. Sundermeyer. Generic configurable cooperation protocols for multi-agent systems. In C. Castelfranchi and J.-P. Müller, editors, *From Reaction to Cognition — 5th European Workshop on Modelling Autonomous Agents in a Multi-Agent World (MAAMAW'93)*, volume 957 of *LNAI*, pages 157–171. Springer-Verlag, 1995.
5. S. Bussmann and H. J. Müller. A Communication Structure for Cooperating Agents. *Computers and AI*, I, 1993.
6. J. Collins and D. Ndumu. The ZEUS Role Modelling Guide. Technical report, BT, Adastral Park, Martlesham Heath, 1998.
7. T. Finin and R. Fritzson. KQML — a language and protocol for knowledge and information exchange. In *Proceedings of the 13th International Distributed Artificial Intelligence Workshop*, pages 127–136, Seattle, WA, USA, 1994.
8. FIPA. *AgenTalk Reference Manual*. NTT Communication Science Laboratories and Ishida Laboratory, Department of Information Science, Kyoto University., 1996.
9. Gerard J. Holzmann. *Design and Validation of Computer Protocols*. Prentice Hall, 1991.
10. M. Kolb. A cooperation language. In *Proceedings of the First International Conference on Multi-Agent Systems (ICMAS'95)*, pages 233–238, June 1995.
11. Jean-Luc Koning, Marc-Philippe Huget, Jun Wei, and Xu Wang. Extended Modeling Languages for Interaction Protocol Design. In *Proceeedings of the Second International Workshop on Agent-Oriented Software Engineering (AOSE-2001)*, Montreal, Canada, 2001.

12. Jürgen Lind. *Iterative Software Engineering for Multiagent Systems - The* MASSIVE *Method*, volume 1994 of *Lecture Notes in Computer Science*. Springer, May 2001.
13. Hyacinth S. Nwana, Divine T. Ndumu, Lyndon C. Lee, and Jaron C. Collins. ZEUS: A tool-kit for building distributed multi-agent systems. *Applied Artificial Intelligence Journal*, 13(1):129–186, 1999.
14. H. V. D. Parunak and James Odell. Representing Social Structures in UML. In *Proceeedings of the Second International Workshop on Agent-Oriented Software Engineering (AOSE-2001)*, Montreal, Canada, 2001.
15. Stefan Philipps and Jürgen Lind. Ein System zur Definition und Ausführung von Protokollen für Multi-Agentensystemen. Technical Report RR-99-01, DFKI, 1999.
16. Programming Systems Lab. The mozart programming system. University of the Saarland, 1999. http://www.mozart-oz.org.
17. J. Rumbaugh, I. Jacobson, and G. Booch. *The Unified Modeling Language Reference Manual*. Addision-Wesley, 1999.
18. The International Organization for Standardization. IS-9074 (Information processing systems/Open systems interconnection): Estelle — a formal description technique based on an extended state transition model, 1997.
19. J. Wei, S.-C. Cheung, and X. Wang. Towards a Methodology for Formal Design and Analysis of Agent Interaction Protocols. In *Proceeedings of the International Software Engineering Symposium*, Wuhan, Hubei, China, 2001.

Agents and the UML: A Unified Notation for Agents and Multi-agent Systems?

Bernhard Bauer[1], Federico Bergenti[2], Philippe Massonet[3], and James J. Odell[4]

[1] Siemens, CT IC 6
D-81730 München, Germany
Bernhard.Bauer@mchp.siemens.de

[2] Università degli Studi di Parma, Parco Area delle Scienze 181A
43100 Parma, Italy
Bergenti@CE.UniPR.IT

[3] CEDITI, Av. Georges Lemaître, 21
B-6041 Charleroi, Belgium
Philippe.Massonet@cediti.be

[4] James Odell Associates, 3646 W. Huron River Drive
Ann Arbor, MI 48103-9489 USA
jodell@compuserve.com

Over the last few years, agent-oriented software engineering has promoted the adoption of agents as a first-class paradigm for software engineering in research and industrial development. Agents have been used in research development for more than twenty years, while they still do not find complete acceptance in industrial settings. We believe that basically three characteristics of industrial development prevent the adoption of agents: *(i)* The scope of industrial projects is much larger than typical research efforts, *(ii)* The skills of developers are focused on established technologies, *(iii)* The use of advanced technologies is not part of the success criteria of a project. In order to establish a solid ground for giving agent technologies these characteristics, we recognize that accepted methods for industrial development depend on standard representations of artifacts supporting all phases of the software lifecycle. Standard representations are needed by tool developers to provide commercial quality tools that mainstream software engineering departments need for industrial agent systems development.

Nowadays, many agent-oriented methodologies and tools are available, and the agent community is facing the problem of identifying a common vocabulary to support them. The idea of using UML as a common ground for building such a vocabulary has led to a remarkable work that is summarized in papers presented at various workshops and conferences. Just to mention papers that appeared in 2001, we find a great interest in this topic in AOSE-2001 [1, 2, 3, 4, 5, 6, 7, 8] and OAS-2001 [13, 14] workshops and in Autonomous Agents conference [9, 10, 11, 12]. Two practical reasons for using UML as a common ground are that many agent systems can be implemented in terms of distributed object-oriented technologies, and many mainstream software engineering departments already know and use UML.

M.J. Wooldridge, G. Weiß, and P. Ciancarini (Eds.): AOSE 2001, LNCS 2222, pp. 148-150, 2002.

The panel discussion at AOSE-2001 workshop focused on the idea of using the UML to model agents and multi-agent systems and it showed some agreement of the audience on this topic. The critiques to this idea were only technical and they concerned basically the first attempts to use the UML to model agent concepts, i.e., AUML interaction-protocol diagrams. The question that the audience raised periodically was: *"Do we really need to extend the UML or shall we go with what we have now?"* One of the original proposers suggested that the current UML language should provide a base from which we can reuse notations found useful to model agents; in this way we could minimize inventing yet-another notation, while extending and adding notation where appropriate. Two of the original proposers of such diagrams agreed that the extension of the UML was not the main point of their proposal. They decided to extend the notation only to model concepts, such as interaction protocols and roles within interaction protocols, that were not expressible with the current UML at the time of writing. Moreover, the UML community accepted some of their ideas and integrated them in next the release of the notation.

Some members of the audience expressed the fear that using UML as a basis for an agent notation would not emphasize the fact that the agent paradigm is radically different from the object-oriented paradigm. They referred to the transition from the structured to the object-oriented paradigm in the last decade and the difficulties that programmers had when making the transition from C to C++ (basically writing C++ programs in the structured programming style as if they were C programs).

Panelists agree that the discussion showed the interest of the community in finding a common vocabulary for agent technologies and, besides some technical issues, they find the idea of defining the AUML a good starting point to achieve this purpose. For the current status of the AUML please refer to the official website:
http://www.auml.org.

Papers in Proceedings of AOSE-2001

1. Bauer, B.: "UML Class Diagrams: Revisited in the Context of Agent-Based Systems," pp.1-8.
2. Parunak, V., Odell, J.: "Representing Social Structures in UML," pp. 17-31.
3. Gervais, M.P., Muscutariu, F.: "Towards an ADL for Designing Agent-Based Systems," pp.49-56.
4. Bresciani, P., Perini, A., Giorgini, P., Giunchiglia, F., Mylopoulos, J.: "Modeling early requirements in Tropos: A Transformation-based Approach," pp. 67-75.
5. Sparkman, C.H., DeLoach, S.A., Athie, L.: "Self Automated Derivation of Complex Agent Architectures from Analysis Specifications," pp.77-84.
6. Flores, R.A., Kremer, R.C.: "Bringing Coherence to Agent Conversations," pp. 85-92.
7. Koning, J.L., Huget, M.P., Wei, J., Wang, X.: "Extended Modeling Languages for Interaction Protocol Design," pp. 93-100.
8. Caire G., Leal, F., Chainho, P., Evans, R., Garijo, F., Gomez, J., Pavon, J., Kearney, P., Stark, J., Massonet, P.: "Agent Oriented Analysis using MESSAGE/UML," pp. 101-108.

Papers in Proceedings of Autonomous Agents 2001

9. Karacapilidis, N., Pavlos, M.: "Intelligent Agents for an Artificial Market System," pp. 592-599.
10. Bergenti, F., Poggi, A.: "A Development Toolkit to Realize Autonomous and Inter-operable Agents," pp. 632-639.
11. Depke, R., Heckel, R., Küster, J.M.: "Improving the Agent-Oriented Modeling Process by Roles," pp. 640-647.
12. Bresciani, P., Perini, A., Giorgini, P., Giunchiglia, F., Mylopoulos, J.: "A Knowledge Level Software Engineering Methodology for Agent Oriented Programming," pp. 648-655.

Papers in Proceedings of OAS-2001

13. Cranefield, S., Hausteiny, S., Purvis, M.: "UML-Based Ontology Modelling for Software Agents," pp. 21-28.
14. Cranefield, S., Purvis, M.: "Generating Ontology-Specific Content Languages," pp. 29-35.

Modeling Early Requirements in Tropos: A Transformation Based Approach

Paolo Bresciani[1], Anna Perini[1], Paolo Giorgini[2], Fausto Giunchiglia[2], and
John Mylopoulos[3]

[1] ITC-irst, via Sommarive, 18, I-38050 Trento-Povo, Italy
{bresciani,perini}@itc.it
[2] Department of Information and Communication Technology, University of Trento,
via Sommarive, 14, I-38050 Trento-Povo, Italy
{pgiorgini,fausto}@cs.unitn.it
[3] Department of Computer Science, University of Toronto,
M5S 3H5, Toronto, Ontario, Canada
jm@cs.toronto.edu

Abstract. We are developing an agent-oriented software development methodology, called Tropos, which integrates ideas from multi-agent system technologies and Requirements Engineering research. A distinguishing feature of Tropos is that it covers software development from early requirements analysis to detailed design, allowing for a deeper understanding of the operational environment of the new software system. This paper proposes a characterization of the process of early requirements analysis, defined in terms of transformation applications. Different categories of transformations are presented and illustrated by means of a running example. These transformations are then mapped onto a set of primitive transformations. The paper concludes with observations on the form and the role of the proposed transformations.

1 Introduction

We are working on an agent-oriented software development methodology called Tropos[1], that integrates ideas from multi-agent system technologies, mostly to define the implementation phase for the software development process [2], and ideas from Requirements Engineering, where actors and goals have been used heavily for early requirements analysis [6,13]. In a recent state of the art survey on agent-oriented software engineering [5] several principled but informal methodologies (see also [10,3]) have been considered together with approaches based on the use of formal methods (see also [16,8]) for engineering multi-agent systems. Tropos shares with these approaches several methodological principles. In addition, it also features both diagrammatic and formal specification techniques, allowing for application of formal analysis techniques, such as model checking [7] and formal verification [14].

---

[1] Tropos (from the Greek "τροπη", "tropé", which means "easily changeable", also "easily adaptable").

M.J. Wooldridge, G. Weiß, and P. Ciancarini (Eds.): AOSE 2001, LNCS 2222, pp. 151–168, 2002.
© Springer-Verlag Berlin Heidelberg 2002

More concretely, Tropos is based on two key ideas. First, the notion of agent and all the related mentalistic notions (for instance: beliefs, goals, actions and plans) are used in all phases of software development, from the early analysis down to the actual implementation. Second, Tropos covers also the very early phases of requirements analysis, thus allowing for a deeper understanding of both the environment where the software must operate and the kind of interactions that should occur between software and human agents. In particular, Tropos rests on five main phases for agent based systems development: the early requirements analysis, the late requirements analysis, the architectural design, the detailed design, and the implementation. A complete example of the application of the Tropos methodology to a realistic case-study is presented in [11].

Following current approaches in software development, Tropos rests on the use of a conceptual model of the system-to-be. The conceptual model is specified by a modeling language resting on Eric Yu's i^* paradigm [15], which offers actors, goals, and actor dependencies as primitive concepts for modeling an application during the requirements analysis. We are currently working on the specification of the Tropos modeling language. A preliminary definition can be found in [12], where a meta-model of the language is given. At present, the graphical notation is largely borrowed from i^*. Using this notation, different ways for visualizing the structural properties of the models can be introduced, as e.g., the actor diagram, that mainly shows actor dependencies, and the rational diagram, that provides a rationale of actor dependencies, through, for instance, a goal analysis conducted from the point of view of a specific actor [11].

In the present paper we focus on the definition of the transformations that can be applied for refining an initial Tropos model to a final one, working incrementally. This is, in general, a very basic issue, when defining a new methodology, as reported in works on Entity-Relationship schema design [1], goal oriented requirements analysis [6], and functional and non-functional requirements analysis [9]. Here, we describe the model transformation process that corresponds to the first phase in Tropos methodology —the early requirements analysis. This phase concerns with the understanding of the problem by studying an existing organizational setting: the requirement engineer models and analyzes the desires and the intentions of the stakeholders, and states their intentional dependencies. Desires, intentions, and dependencies are modeled as goals and as softgoals which, through a goal-oriented analysis, provide the rationale for the specification of the functional and non-functional requirements of the system-to-be, that will be defined during the subsequent late requirement analysis.

In section 2, a running example is introduced, for being used in successive sections. Section 3 discusses how the conceptual model definition and refinement process can be described in term of transformation applications. Different categories of transformations are introduced in sections 4, 5, and 6. Finally, in section 7, we provide a minimal set of *primitive* transformations which can be used as a base for describing compound transformations, as those used in the running example. In section 8, we discuss some open points and future research directions.

2   A Running Example

The example considered refers to a web-based broker of cultural information and services (the *eCulture System* [11]), developed for the government of Trentino (Provincia Autonoma di Trento, or PAT). The system is aimed at presenting integrated information obtained from museums, exhibitions, and other cultural organizations and events, to the users, that are both citizens and tourists looking for things to do.

During the development process, the requirements engineer begins the analysis identifying the main stakeholders, and their desires and intentions. In Tropos, stakeholders are modeled as actors who may depend on other ones for goals to be achieved, tasks to be performed, and resources to be provided. Desires and intentions are modeled as goals and softgoals.[2]

The list of relevant actors for the eCulture project includes, among others, the following stakeholders:

- Provincia Autonoma di Trento (PAT) is the government agency funding the project; their objectives include improving public information services, increasing tourism through new information services, also encouraging Internet use within the province.
- Museums are major cultural information providers for their respective collections.
- Tourists want to access cultural information before or during their visit to Trentino.
- (Trentino's) citizens want easily accessible information, of any sort, and (of course) good administration of public resources.

Figure 1 shows the initial early requirements model in form of actor diagram. An actor diagram is a graph where each node represents an *actor*, and each link between two actors indicates that one actor depends on the other for something in order that the former may attain some goal. We call the depending actor the *depender* and the actor who is depended upon the *dependee*. The object around which the dependency centers is called the *dependum*. By depending on another actor for a dependum, an actor is able to achieve goals that it is otherwise unable to achieve on its own, or not as easily, or not as well. At the same time, the depender becomes vulnerable. If the dependee fails to deliver the dependum, the depender would be adversely affected in its ability to achieve its goals. So, for instance, in Figure 1 the actor `Citizen` is associated with a single relevant goal: `get cultural information`, while the actor `Visitor` has an associated softgoal `enjoy visit`. Softgoals are distinguished from goals because they don't have a precise definition, and are amenable to a different (more qualitative) kind of analysis (see [4] for a detailed description of softgoals). Along similar lines, `PAT` wants to `increase internet use` while `Museum` wants to `provide cultural services`. Finally, the diagram includes one softgoal dependency where `Citizen` depends on `PAT` to fulfill (or *satisfice*, see [4]) the `taxes well spent` softgoal.

---

[2] Softgoals are mainly used for specifying additional qualities or vague requirements.

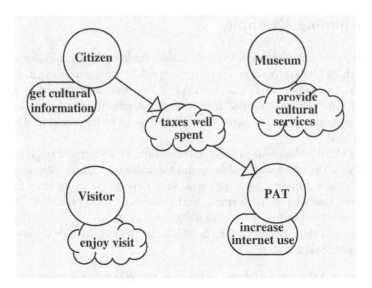

Fig. 1. Actor diagram: the stakeholders of the eCultural project.

3   Conceptual Model Transformations

As introduced in section 2, during the early requirement analysis, the engineer models the set of desires and intentions, informally expressed by the stakeholders, in terms of goals and dependencies between actors. This is an iterative process, at each step of which details are incrementally added and rearranged starting from a rough version of the model, containing only few actors, goals, softgoals, and dependencies, as, for example, shown in Figure 1. The details added at each step are aimed at representing increasing knowledge and insight on the problem and its environment, and their introduction corresponds to a deeper and more precise understanding of the requirements. Of course, to accomplish this task, the engineer might need to acquire new information or interact with the stakeholders. In the present paper, these aspects are not dealt with, and we assume that the relevant knowledge is somehow available to the engineer.

The process of conceptual modeling, that is the core part of the early requirement analysis phase, can be described in terms of simple transformations of subsequent versions of the model. Each of these transformations allows the progressive introduction of more structure and details in the model. In other words, by iterating the application of transformations, the engineer can move from a very sketchy first version to the final complete model, going through subsequent, more and more precise and detailed, versions. At each step of the process several transformations are, in general, applicable. It is up to the engineer deciding which transformation to apply: different choices result in different strategies for the modeling activity. The analysis of possible different strategies is, indeed, a topic that would deserve its own space for discussion. In the present paper, due to lack of room, we do not tackle this argument.

In the following sections, the most relevant transformations are introduced, under the form of generic rules transforming patterns in the model into more complex configurations.[3] The transformations are illustrated through their application to the already mentioned case study. Moreover, they are grouped accordingly to the fact that they are used for actor, goal, or softgoal analysis. Another orthogonal classification is represented by the *role* that the transformation application plays in the actual process: we distinguish between *top-down* (TD) and *bottom-up* (BU) applications. Applying transformations in a top-down way allows the engineer to analyze high level conceptual elements (actors, goals, softgoals) by adding details in terms of relationships (specialization, decomposition, softgoal contribution, etc.) or dependencies with respect to other conceptual elements. Vice versa, bottom-up applications allow us to aggregate finer grain conceptual elements in order to express their contribution —compositional, hierarchical, functional or non-functional— to other, somehow more generic, conceptual elements. This notion of top-down and bottom-up partially differs from that given by other authors in different modeling contexts (see [1]). In fact, they mainly mean top-down as "adding more elements" in the schema vs. "linking existing elements" (bottom-up), with the only exception for the only generalization relationship (ISA between entities). In our context, instead, other kinds of *abstraction* are possible, e.g., of the kind of *aggregation* and *composition*, and, in some sense, also *softgoal contribution*, allowing for a wider range of *genuine* ways of applying transformations in top-down or bottom-up directions.

Indeed, strictly speaking, each transformation application should be considered as a symmetric operation that introduces a new conceptual relationship between two (sets of) elements, and no distinction between top-down and bottom-up should be meaningful. Nevertheless, it must be noted that, during the modeling process, the engineer focuses, in turn, on different (sets of) conceptual elements of the model. If we consider whether the (set of) element(s) currently under analysis is the most generic or the most specific among those involved in the transformation, a *direction* —top-down or bottom-up, respectively— emerges. Focusing in turn on the different elements is an essential aspect of the methodology. For this reason, it is important distinguishing between the two directions as relevant features for the strategy of the process. This distinction is explicit in Table 1, Table 2, and Table 3, as well as in the running example that illustrates the transformations in the following sections.

Finally, a deeper analysis of the transformations allows us to note that, although they correspond in a natural way to the steps made by the engineer in

---

[3] The transformations listed in the tables of the present paper are given in the form of graph transformation rules. A *graph transformation rule* $L \rightarrow R$ may be applied to a graph G when the *left-hand* side L is matched by a sub-graph of G; the matching sub-graph is replaced in the resulting graph by (an instance of) the *right-hand* side R of the rule. In the tables we provide, thicker borders are used to denote nodes that are the same in the right-hand side and in the left-hand side of the rule.

order to build the model, they cannot be considered as atomic. A smaller set of simpler, although less operable, transformations may be introduced: we call them *primitive transformations* (see section 7). At this level of granularity, the distinction between top-down and bottom-up is, of course, meaningless.

4   Goal Transformations

Goal transformations (see Table 1) allow us to perform goal analysis by introducing relationships between goals, or actors and goals. Of course, relationships between conceptual elements already present in the model can be introduced, but the process can also lead to the introduction of previously unconsidered conceptual elements. In this case, the diagram is enriched not only with new structure (in terms of links between items), but also with new items. In a Tropos model, each goal must always be associated to at least one actor.[4] Thus, it is necessary to define a *default* actor dependency for the introduced goals. Our assumption is that the new goals initially belong and depend on the same dependee of the goal(s) under analysis. This implies that, if we have more goals under analysis (as in some bottom-up cases), they must share the same dependee.

4.1   Goal Decomposition

Goal decomposition transformations allow for the decomposition of a goal in and/or subgoals such that the subgoal achievements "automatically" implies the goal achievement. In other terms, the achievement of one (for the *OR-decomposition*) or all (for the *AND-decomposition*) subgoals, corresponds to the achievement of the top (decomposed) goal.

For example, consider Figure 2, where, starting from the situation depicted in Figure 1, some goal analysis on Citizen's goals is carried on. An instance of goal decomposition is here applied to the goal get cultural info (step **(1)**) in order to OR-decompose it into the two possible subgoals visit institution and visit web site.

In parallel with both OR-decomposition and AND-decomposition transformations, that are classified as top-down, also the corresponding bottom-up transformations can be given, namely *OR-composition* and *AND-composition* (see Table 1). An example is given in Figure 3, subsection 5.1.

4.2   Precondition Goals

Precondition goal transformations substantially differ from goal decomposition transformations. They allow us to list a set of necessary (but not sufficient) preconditions in terms of other goals; precondition goals *enable* the achievement of the higher level goal. Typically, goal analysis obtained by the application of

---

[4] That is, the depender of a goal must always be defined. Unless it is otherwise stated, the dependee is assumed to be the same actor as the depender.

Table 1. Goal Transformations: different kinds of arrow are used to denote different kinds of relationship.

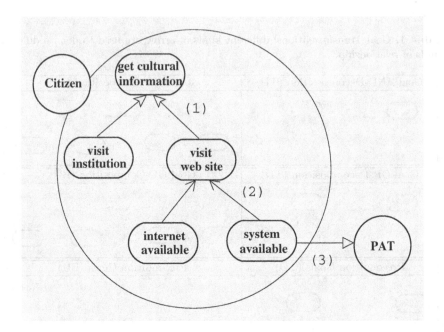

Fig. 2. Citizen's goals analysis.

a precondition goals transformation has to be somehow completed, with more elements provided by further goals analysis and/or task analysis, that are part of later Tropos phases like the late requirement analysis.[5]

Proceeding with our example, we can think of providing some preconditions for goal visit web site, introducing the precondition dependencies marked with **(2)** in Figure 2. This step corresponds to recognizing that the fulfillment of goals internet available and system available are necessary, although non sufficient, preconditions for the fulfillment of the goal visit web site.

4.3   Goal Delegation

Goal delegation transformations are aimed at allowing to express the assignment or a change of responsibility in goal fulfillment. In Tropos methodology, when initially defined, each goal is either expressed as a dependum between two actors or it is associated with an actor, who *desires* its fulfillment. As already mentioned, in the first case the dependee is assumed to be committed for the fulfillment of the goal. In the second case, instead, further analysis is required to the engineer in order to define which actor (possibly the same one) is committed to the fulfillment of the goal on behalf of the first. After this level of detail is reached, the goal is considered as an *intention* of the committed actor. This step

---

[5] Late requirement analysis and the role of task analysis is briefly introduced in [11].

in the process is called goal delegation transformation (including the *goal self-delegation transformation* as a special case). The goal delegation transformation can be applied to a goal and the actor it is initially assigned to (that is, the actor that desires the goal), as shown in Table 1, but also to a goal and the delegated actor, in order to obtain a *cascade* of delegations: in this case the *intention* is transferred (delegated) to another actor.[6]

Using our running example, we can see an example of goal delegation in Figure 2, where the responsibility for the goal `system available` is delegated to `PAT` (transformation number **(3)** applied to `Citizen` and its goal `system available`).

Summarizing, after the application of goal decomposition, precondition goal and goal delegation transformations to the model containing only `Citizen` and `get cultural info`, that is, namely, after steps **(1)**, **(2)** and **(3)**, our model is evolved as depicted in Figure 2.[7]

4.4   Goal Generalization

In some situations it can be useful to apply *goal specialization* or *goal generalization* transformations. In these cases, goal depender and dependee are, by default, inherited both for the top-down and the bottom-up transformations. When, instead, they are already defined, the ISA hierarchy introduced for the two goals must also hold between their respective dependers and dependees.

5   Softgoal Transformations

For softgoal analysis, transformations similar to some of those listed for goal analysis are available. Also the default actor assignment follows the rules already stated for goal analysis.

Moreover, for softgoals, during early requirement analysis, also a contribution analysis is performed (see [9,11]). It is therefore necessary to foresee some specific transformations.

The transformations for softgoal analysis are listed in Table 2. Below, only few remarks and examples are given.

5.1   Softgoal Contribution

Contribution transformations allow us to specify whether a goal or soft-goal contributes to some other softgoal (BU) or, starting from the other side, whether there is some goal or soft-goal that contributes (TD) positively or negatively to the softgoal satisficement.

---

[6] It can be noted that, also in this case, the transformation could require the introduction of new elements in the model, as well as just introducing the dependency between existing elements.

[7] The numbers in bold and parenthesis "**(1)**", "**(2)**" and "**(3)**" are not part of the diagram, but are here used only for describing the process.

Table 2. SoftGoal Transformations: different kinds of arrow are used to denote different kinds of relationship.

SoftGoal-Goal Contribution (TD)	Goal-SoftGoal Contribution (BU)
SoftGoal-SoftGoal Contribution (TD)	SoftGoal-SoftGoal Contribution (BU)
SoftGoal-AND Decomposition (TD)	SoftGoal-AND Composition (BU)
SoftGoal-OR Decomposition (TD)	SoftGoal-OR Composition (BU)
SoftGoal Specialization (TD)	SoftGoal Generalization (BU)
SoftGoal Delegation	

Two examples of application of contribution transformations are shown in Figure 3, namely, steps **(6)** (bottom-up) and **(7)** (top-down). It is also worth noticing that new instances of goal decomposition have been applied, once in a top-down way (step **(4)**) and once in bottom-up direction (step **(5)**).

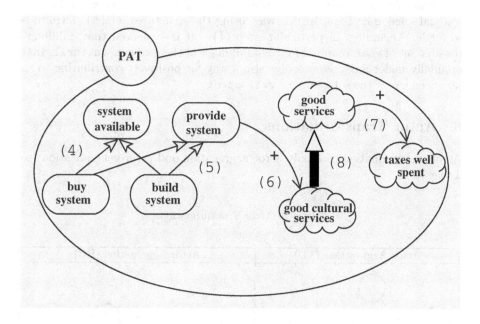

Fig. 3. PAT's goals analysis.

5.2   Softgoal Decomposition

Softgoal decomposition transformations allow us to perform softgoal – sub-soft-goals (or super-softgoals) analysis. Also in this case we distinguish between *softgoal decomposition* (TD) and *softgoal composition* (BU) (see Table 2).

While for goal analysis the decomposition gives a set of necessary subgoals (AND decomposition), or alternatives subgoals (OR decomposition), the fulfillment of which has to be considered as necessary and sufficient condition for the fulfillment of the higher level goal, for softgoal analysis the satisficement of the decomposition can never be considered as a sufficient condition, but only as a (positive) contribution.

5.3   Softgoal Delegation

We list *softgoal delegation transformations* here for completeness, but nothing different from what already written for goal delegation transformations has to be added.

5.4   Softgoal Generalization

The same observations made for goal generalization transformations could be repeated here. Moreover, an example of application of a *softgoal generalization transformation* can be shown. Consider Figure 3: step **(8)** introduces a softgoal generalization between the softgoal `good cultural services` and the the softgoal `good services`. In this way, using the structured analysis introduced so forth —including, in particular, step **(7)**— it is evidenced that, fulfilling a possible set of goals required for the fulfillment of the goal `get cultural info`, originally under analysis, provides also a way for positively contributing to the satisficement of the softgoal `tax well spent`.

6   Actor Transformations

Actor transformations are only actor aggregation and actor generalization (see Table 3).

Table 3. Actor Transformations.

6.1   Actor Aggregation

Aggregating actors means recognizing that different actors are part of an organization or a system. This way of grouping can be helpful in order to more precisely delegate goals and softgoal responsibilities that are initially assigned to the aggregate. Thus, goal/softgoal delegation from an aggregate to its inside components or among components of the same aggregate should be preferred to other kinds of delegations. Of course, this preference can be recognized only once the components have been defined as such. For example, as further step in our running example, PAT could be *decomposed* in departments, and responsibility for each subgoal delegated to the appropriate department.

In the drawings, the set of aggregated actors is enclosed in a rectangle *attached* to the actor representing the whole aggregate.

6.2 Actor Generalization

Actor generalization transformations can be used to introduce taxonomic structure among actor types. The engineer must be advised that the ISA relationship is meaningful as far as actor types are concerned as more generic elements. If the actor under analysis is instead an instance, only a bottom-up generalization transformation can be applied, or aggregation transformations have probably to be considered.

As for goal generalization transformations, it is worth noticing that possibly existing goal dependencies with the involved actors must involve goals that respect the actor ISA hierarchy.

In our example, although not reported in the figures, consider the case in which the engineer wants to classify PAT as a Government institution. In this case, all the goals (or specialized versions of them) possibly deriving from previously made analysis on Government institution, can automatically be inherited by PAT.

7 Primitive Transformations

As mentioned in section 3, the set of transformations presented in the previous sections is largely redundant. The reason why they have been presented here is that, from a practical point of view, they reflect the approaches the engineer may locally adopt for analyzing, in turn, the different conceptual elements of the model. By applying top-down transformations, the engineer breaks the problem into more manageable sub-elements: the analysis has to be carried on until a sufficient level of details is reached for each necessary goal (originally present or later introduced) and the most specific components are likely to be easily operationalized, in terms of tasks analysis, by means of the successive *late requirement* phase.[8] For softgoals, a *reasonable* level of satisficeability has to be reached. Of course, top-down steps can be interleaved with bottom-up transformation applications. They are used, e.g., for structuring scattered models and for taking advantage of analyses made for parts of the model, with respect to different, but interacting, elements of the model.

---

[8] Of course, also inadequate evaluations can be expected to be done in this transition step, but it must also be said that the two phases are permeable, and backward jumps are always possible.

Here, it can be useful to briefly show that a smaller set of transformations can be provided, that is enough, although in a less compact way, to perform any kind of analysis provided by the more structured transformations introduced before. Moreover, each of these transformations must be such that it cannot be expressed as the composition of other transformations. For this reason we call these transformations *primitive.*

The set contains a primitive transformation for each kind of relationship that can be introduced between the conceptual elements. In addition, *initial* transformations for introducing the different conceptual elements in the model are needed. Of course, as already noted, the distinction between top-down and bottom-up is not applicable for primitive transformations.

The set of primitive transformations is give in Table 4, Table 5, and Table 6, for primitive transformations that focus on goals, softgoals, and actors, respectively. It must be remembered that, accordingly with Tropos methodology, a goal or a softgoal in the model is always associated with an actor (or two, when delegated). This justifies for the form of the **G-I** and **SG-I** primitive transformations. Thus, the only primitive transformation available for starting populating an empty model is the **A-I** transformation.

Using the listed primitives, assuming as syntactic convention that they can be applied to conceptual elements, and for the introduction primitives, to names of the elements to be introduced, the example of model development process described in the previous sections can be rewritten as shown in Figure 4. It must be noted that almost each step corresponds to the composition of some primitive applications.

---

1. **G-DEC-OR**(`Get-Cultural-info`,**G-I**(`Citizen`,"visit institution"),
  G-I(`Citizen`,"visit web site"))
2. **G-P**(`visit web site`,**G-I**(`Citizen`,"internet available"),
  G-I(`Citizen`,"system available"))
3. **G-DEL**(`system available`,`PAT`)
4. **G-DEC-OR**(`system available`,**G-I**(`PAT`,"buy system"),
  G-I(`PAT`,"build system"))
5. **G-DEC-OR**(**G-I**(`PAT`,"provide system"),`buy system`,`build system`)
6. **SG-C-G**(**SG-I**(`PAT`,"good cultural services"),`provide system`,+)
7. **SG-C-SG**(`tax well spent`,**SG-I**(`PAT`,"good services"),+)
8. **SG-G**(`good services`,**G-I**(`good cultural services`))

Fig. 4. The example described with primitive transformations.

8   Conclusion

In this paper we have presented one aspect of our research aimed at defining a comprehensive methodology, called Tropos, for agent oriented software engi-

Table 4. Goal Primitive Transformations.

neering. In particular, we dealt with the early requirement analysis phase, that, in Tropos, is used for defining the environment of the system-to-be. The activity of the requirement engineer has been described as an iterative process based on successive transformations that allow her to progressively define and refine the model of the social environment of the system-to-be. A set of transformations has been described, and illustrated through a running example. Finally, this set of practically usable transformations has shown to be reduceable to a more limited, but less usable, set of primitive transformations.

From our analysis, two main issues arise. First, the proposed transformation can be considered as the building block for guiding the engineer's activity. Moreover, the way they are used must be analyzed not only locally, but also with

Table 5. SoftGoal Primitive Transformations.

SoftGoal Primitive Transformations	
Softgoal Introduction (**SG-I**)	
Goal-Softgoal Contribution (**SG-C-G**)	Softgoal-Softgoal Contribution (**SG-C-SG**)
Softgoal AND decomp. (**SG-DEC-&**)	Softgoal OR decomp. (**SG-DEC-OR**)
Softgoal Delegation (**SG-DEL**)	Softgoal Generalization (**SG-G**)

Table 6. Actor Primitive Transformations.

Actor Primitive Transformations	
Actor Introduction (**A-I**)	
Actor Aggregation (**A-A**)	Actor Generalization (**A-G**)

respect to the strategic role they play in the process. The distinction between top-down and bottom-up applications is only a first attempt in this direction. More in general, different uses of the transformations correspond to different developments of the activity of the engineer. If we consider the activity of the engineer as a problem solving activity,[9] the problem solution can be seen as the result of the execution of a plan that the engineer elaborate in response to a precise goal. Of course, many details may be not clearly stated within the problem —engineering activity often include a considerable informal and human contribution— but it is essential the fact that the solution can be found after the application of a sequence of elementary steps. Using different sequences can lead both to different solutions and to the same solution, but with different performances in finding it. Tackling the analysis of the process as a planning activity is one of the next development of our research; in the present paper we have only defined the single actions that can be used in a plan.

A second aspect that emerged from our analysis is that there is a difference between transformations that can be proposed as practically usable by the engineer, and primitive transformations, that, from a more formal point of view can be considered as the essential basis for defining any process. How primitive transformations can be combined in order to obtain *usable* transformation, and the role they may have in the process seen as a planning activity, is also a topic that has to be further investigated, possible with more case studies.

Of course, another natural development of the present work is its extension to other phases of the Tropos methodology, in particular to the late requirement analysis, that includes the development of more details on the system-to-be, as its decomposition into components and their task analysis.

References

1. C. Batini, S. Ceri, and S. Navathe. *Conceptual Database Design. An Entity-Relationship Approach.* Benjamin-Cummings Redwood City, Calif., 1992.
2. P. Busetta, R. Rönnquist, A. Hodgson, and A. Lucas. JACK Intelligent Agents - Components for Intelligent Agents in Java. AOS TR9901, Jan. 1999. http://www.jackagents.com/pdf/tr9901.pdf.
3. G. Caire, F. Garijo, J. Gomez, J. Pavon, F. Leal, P. Chainho, P. Kearney, J. Stark, R. Evans, and P. Massonet. Agent Oriented Analysis Using MESSAGE/UML. In *this book*.
4. L. K. Chung, B. A. Nixon, E. Yu, and J. Mylopoulos. *Non-Functional Requirements in Software Engineering.* Kluwer Publishing, 2000.
5. P. Ciancarini and M. Wooldridge. *Agent-Oriented Software Engineering.* Springer-Verlag Lecture Notes in Computer Science (LNCS) Vol. 1957, 2001.
6. A. Dardenne, A. van Lamsweerde, and S. Fickas. "Goal" directed Requirements Acquisition. *Science of Computer Programming*, (20), 1993.

---

[9] An informal way in which we can define the engineer's problem is: "Define, using appropriate knowledge (the acquisition of which is left out of the problem setting), the environment for the system-to-be, with a sufficient level of details".

7. A. Fuxman, M. Pistore, J. Mylopoulos, and P. Traverso. Model Checking Early Requirements Specifications in Tropos. In *Proceedings of the Fifth IEEE International Symposium on Requirements Engineering (RE01)*, Toronto, Canada, August 2001.
8. C. Jonker, I. A. Letia, and J. Treur. Diagnosis of the Dynamics Within an Organization by Trace Checking of Behavioral Requirements. In *this book*.
9. J. Mylopoulos, L. Chung, S. S. Y. Liao, H. Wang, and E. Yu. Exploring Alternatives During Requirements Analysis. *IEEE Software*, 2001.
10. S. A. O'Malley and S. A. DeLoach. Determining When to Use an Agent-Oriented Software Engineering Paradigm. In *this book*.
11. A. Perini, P. Bresciani, F. Giunchiglia, P. Giorgini, and J. Mylopoulos. A Knowledge Level Software Engineering Methodology for Agent Oriented Programming. In *Proceedings of the Fifth International Conference on Autonomous Agents*, Montral CA, May 2001.
12. A. Perini, F. Sannicolo, and F. Giunchiglia. The Tropos Modelling Language Specification. Version 1.0. Technical Report, IRST, Feb. 2001. http://www.science.unitn.it/~pgiorgio/aose.
13. A. van Lamsweerde. Requirements Engineering in the Year 00: A Research Perspective. In *Proceedings of the 22nd International Conference on Software Engineering, Invited Paper*, ACM Press, June 2000.
14. X. Wang and Y. Lesperance. Agent-Oriented Requirements Engineering Using ConGolog and i*. In *Proceedings of the Third International Bi-Conference Workshop on Agent-Oriented Information Systems (AOIS-2001), at Agents 2001*, Montreal, Canada, May 28, 2001.
15. E. Yu. *Modeling Strategic Relationships for Process Reengineering*. PhD thesis, University of Toronto, Department of Computer Science, University of Toronto, 1995.
16. H. Zhu. A Formal Specification Lanaguage for MAS Engineering. In *this book*.

A Requirement Specification Language for Configuration Dynamics of Multi-agent Systems

Mehdi Dastani, Catholijn Jonker, and Jan Treur

Vrije Universiteit Amsterdam, Department of Artificial Intelligence, De Boelelaan 1081a,
1081 HV Amsterdam, The Netherlands
{mehdi, jonker, treur }@cs.vu.nl

Abstract. In agent-mediated applications, the configuration of the multi-agent system often changes due to the creation and the deletion of agents. The behaviour of such systems on the one hand depends on the structural dynamics of the system configuration, but on the other hand consists of the informational dynamics of the configuration. To specify and verify the properties of the system, including its configuration dynamics, a requirement language is needed that is capable to express those properties. In this paper, we discuss configuration dynamics properties of multi-agent systems and define a language by means of which those properties can be specified. A prototypical scenario for an agent-mediated system is discussed and some important requirements for this system are specified.

1 Introduction

Requirements Engineering is today a well-studied field of research within Software Engineering; e.g., [2], [13], [11]. Requirements describe the required properties of a system (this may include the functions of the system, structure of the system, static and dynamic properties). In recent years requirements engineering for distributed and agent systems has been studied in some depth, e.g., in [3], [5], [8]. In applications to agent-based systems, the dynamics or behaviour of the system plays an important role in description of the successful operation of the system. To be able to express requirements unambiguously, and to support verification by automated tools, formal requirements specification languages for dynamics are important.

Dynamics of agent-based systems can take different forms. Depending on the type of dynamics, different demands are imposed on the expressivity of a requirements specification language. A simple form of requirements for dynamics (close to functional requirements) expresses reactive types of behaviour. However, combinations of pro-active and reactive behaviour can require more complicated requirements expressions. Most types of behaviour of this type can be expressed using rather standard forms of temporal logic; e.g., [12], [6], [7]. Further complications arise if the evolution of a system over time is taken into account; then temporal logics of the more standard types do not suffice. Examples of behaviour of this type are relative adaptive behavi-

M.J. Wooldridge, G. Weiß, and P. Ciancarini (Eds.): AOSE 2001, LNCS 2222, pp. 169–187, 2002.

our (e.g., 'exercise improves skill'), in which two different possible histories have to be compared, and self-modifying behaviour: for example, the behaviour of one of the agents (e.g., a creation action) leads to a different system structure (e.g., with an additional agent). This paper addresses specifications of requirements for the latter type of dynamics.

In order to illustrate this type of dynamics, consider multi-agent mediating systems such as brokering systems, match making systems, and search engines, which are important electronic commerce applications. In such applications, a user that interacts with the system may receive its personal assistant, which in turn interacts with available intermediate and task specific agents to perform the user task. Note that in these types of systems agents (personal assistant and task specific agents) are created and removed from the system. In this paper, we use an abstract multi-agent architecture for such mediating systems as an application. According to this architecture, which is illustrated in Figure 1, mediating systems consist of a central maintenance agent, which is responsible for system configuration, an environment component, which represents the system including all components of the system except itself and is responsible for the realization of system modifications, and zero or more agents that can be distinguished in two types: personal assistant agents (P-agents), which assists their users to achieve their tasks, and intermediate task specific agents (I-agents such as negotiator, matchmakers, and auctioneer), which are responsible for the actual performance of the user tasks.

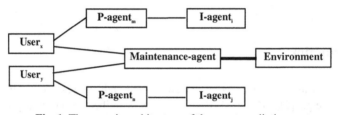

Fig. 1. The generic architecture of the agent mediating systems

Initially, the maintenance agent interacts with users (through dashed links) and determines the required modification of system configuration. The maintenance agent then interacts with the environment (through the bold link) to modify the system configuration. The environment implements how the system configuration is modified. Its role is limited to this: if it receives a modification action at its input, then it takes care that the results of this action are incorporated in the system configuration. The users can then delegate their tasks to their configured personal assistants, which in turn achieve the tasks by interacting with the configured task specific intermediate agents (through the remaining links). For example, a user who is willing to buy a car communicates with the maintenance agent and requires a car brokering system. The maintenance agent specifies a car brokering system consisting of a car broker agent (which may already exist) and a personal assistant agent for the user (other personal assistant agents may exist already since the buyer has been registered) in such a way that the car broker agent and personal assistant agents can interact. The specified system configuration is then communicated to the environment component, which realizes the required configuration. The user can now delegates its car-buying task to its assigned personal assistant agent, which in turn can interact with the car broker agent to achieve the delegated task. The user can decide to terminate the broking system in which case the personal assistant agent can be either deleted from the system or set idle. The car broker agent may also be either deleted or set idle if there are no other car related personal assistant agents.

One essential property of these agent-based mediating systems is their dynamic configurations: new agents are created and removed from the system. A correctly behaving system depends therefore on its configuration during its execution. For this reason, it is important to specify configuration properties of such systems during their executions. This is the focus of the paper. In particular, we will develop a trace requirement language that can express, beside functional and informational requirements, those requirements that are concerned with the system configuration during its execution traces. Based on this language, we will then identify a number of requirement types concerning the configuration of agent-mediated systems. A scenario for an agent-mediating system will motivate these requirements.

2 Requirement Language

In this section, we first define an ordered-sorted language, called Design Language (*DL*), the expressions of which specify the configurations of agent-mediating system. These expressions will be used to specify the required system configuration. Then, based on the *DL* expressions we define another ordered-sorted language, called Design Action Language (*DAL*), the expressions of which modify system configuration, i.e. the expressions indicate actions that change one system configuration to another. For example, the maintenance agent in our example generates such expressions. In order to modify the system configuration, the modification actions need to be communicated. In our example, the maintenance agent communicates such modification actions with the environment component. In order to specify these communication expressions, we define a third ordered-sorted language, called Communication Action Language (*CAL*) that uses the *DAL* expressions and generates such communication expressions. Finally, the expressions of these languages will be used to define the Trace Requirement Language (*TRL*) the expressions of which formalize properties of not only the functional behaviour of the system, but also the configuration of the system during execution traces.

Note that the first three languages are object languages in the sense that they are used by the components in the agent-mediating systems to specify and modify the configuration of the system, while the trace requirement language is a meta-language in the sense that it is used (by an external observer) to specify the (information and configuration) properties of the system behaviour. Consequently, the first three object languages presuppose certain type of multi-agent system architecture since their expressions are about system ingredients. In this paper, we concentrate on systems specified according to some form of compositional architecture, e.g. , [1]. These systems consist of a number of components that interact with each other through certain types of connections. Components may or may not be composed of other components. Components that are not composed are sometimes called primitive components. These components are defined in terms of certain ingredients such as input and output interfaces, control loop, signatures, embedded components (for non-primitive components), and knowledge bases (for primitive components). The to be formalized configuration properties are about these ingredients and their structural relations. Although we will not give an exhaustive list of all ingredients that may be used in these types of systems, we mention and use the most important ingredients. Thus we formalize systems on the basis of some form of component-based or compositional architecture, as for example (but certainly not exclusively) is possible within DESIRE, (DEsign and Specification of Interacting REasoning components; cf. [1]). The reader should note that the proposed object languages could be easily reformulated for different types of systems.

2.1 Design Language (*DL*)

The sorts in *DL* identify the ingredients in such systems. Although an exhaustive enumeration of all sorts is out of scope of this paper, some important sorts are mentioned in table 1.

Table 1. Examples of sorts in *DL*

Sort	Description
SP	sort for system components; part names identify a specific system component in the hierarchical system structure
SP_{prim}	sort for primitive system components
$SP_{Interface}$	sort for component interfaces (i.e. input or output)
SCON	sort for connections between system components
SSIG	sort for signatures used by components
SKB	sort for knowledge bases of primitive system components

These sorts can be ordered, like for example $SP_{prim} < SP$. For all sorts S a set of constants (i.e. $\{c \mid c$ is a constant of sort S $\}$) and a set of variables (i.e. $\{x:S \mid x$ is a variable of sort S$\}$) are assumed. Also, a set of n-ary functions (i.e. $\{f^n \mid f^n$ is an n-ary function for any n$\}$) is assumed. Given the above ingredients, the terms of the design language can be defined as follows:

1. If c is a constant of sort S, then c is a term of sort S.
2. If x:S is a variable of sort S, then x:S is a term of sort S.
3. If $f:S_1 \times \ldots \times S_n \rightarrow S$ is a n-ary function and t_i is a term of sort S_i (i=1,...,n), then $f(t_1,\ldots,t_n)$ is a term of sort S.

These terms refer to ingredients of the system, which can be related to each other according to some certain relations. These relations are denoted by sorted predicate symbols. Some important predicates are mentioned in table 2.

Table 2. Examples of predicates in *DL*

Predicate	Description
exists_comp:SP	component exists
sub:SP×SP	subcomponent relation between system components
connected_to:SP×SP×SCON	components connected by connection
has_input_sign:SP×SSIG	component uses input signature
has_private_sign:SP×SSIG	component uses private signature
has_KnowBase:SP$_{\text{prim}}$×SKB	primitive component has knowledge base

Based on these sorted predicates, the formulae of the design language *DL* can be defined as follows:

1. If $P:S_1 \times \ldots \times S_n$ is a n-ary predicate and t_i (i=1,...,n) is a term of sort S_i, then $P(t_1,\ldots,t_n)$ is a formula of *DL*.
2. If E_1 and E_2 are formulae of *DL*, then $E_1 \wedge E_2$ and $\neg E_1$ are formulae of *DL*.

Let sig_Σ be a signature such as ACL. "$Connected\_to(agent_{PA}, agent_{IA}, from\_to_3) \wedge has\_Input\_Signature(agent_{PA}, sig_\Sigma)$" is a design formula saying "the personal assistance $agent_{PA}$ is connected to the maintenance agent $agent_{IA}$ by connection $from\_to_3$ and agent $agent_{PA}$ uses input signature sig_Σ".

2.2 Design Action Language (DAL)

DAL imports all terms and formulae from *DL* as *terms* and generates new terms (no formulae) denoting plans to modify a system configuration. Note that importing *DL* formulae as terms implies that these terms refer to the structural configurations of agent-mediated system. The sorts in *DAL* are given in table 3.

Table 3. Sorts of *DAL*

Sort	Description
DEAT	imported design atoms from *DL*
DEFOR	imported formula from *DL*
DEFOR$^+$	imported positive design formulae (design atoms or conjunction of positive design formulae)
ACTION	actions
SIGN	truth values
S$_i$ i=1,...,n	imported sorts from *DL*

Note the following subsort relation: *DEAT< DEFOR$^+$ < DEFOR*. Similar to *DL*, for all sorts a set of constants and a set of variables are assumed. In order to import terms and formula from *DL* as terms in *DAL*, we introduce functions corresponding to both the imported functions and predicates. Given *sort(DL), func(DL),* and *pred(DL)* be respectively the sets of sorts, functions, and predicates from *DL*, the functions in *DAL* are defined as follows:

1. For all n-ary function $f \in func(DL)$ and all sorts $S, S_1, ..., S_n \in sort(DL)$ where $f: S_1 \times ... \times S_n \to S$, $\underline{f}: S_1 \times ... \times S_n \to S$ is an imported function in *DAL* (functions f from *DL* are imported as functions $\underline{f}$ in *DAL*).
2. For all n-ary predicates $p \in pred(DL)$ and all sorts $S_1, ..., S_n \in sort(DL)$ where $p: S_1 \times ... \times S_n$, predicate p is reformulated as a function $\underline{p}: S_1 \times ... \times S_n \to DEAT$ and imported in *DAL* (predicates are imported as functions).

Also, logical connectives that operate on *DL* formula are imported as functions.

1. $\underline{\land} : DEFOR^+ \times DEFOR^+ \to DEFOR^+$
2. $\underline{\land} : DEFOR \times DEFOR \to DEFOR$
3. $\underline{\lor} : DEFOR \times DEFOR \to DEFOR$
4. $\underline{\neg} : DEFOR \to DEFOR$

Two specific (action related) functions that are used in *DAL* but not imported from *DL* are as follows:

1. *Add* : $DEFOR^+ \to ACTION$
2. *Delete* : $DEAT \to ACTION$

Note that the imported functions in *DAL* are marked (by being underlined) in order to distinguish them from their corresponding functions or predicates from *DL*. Whenever there is no confusion, we will leave out these underlying marks. Given the above functions, the terms of *DAL* can be defined in usual way.

"*Add(Connected_to(agent$_{PA}$, agent$_{IA}$, from_to$_3$)* $\land$ *Has_Input_Signature(agent$_{PA}$, sig$_\Sigma$))*" is a *DAL* term, which denotes a plan to create a system consisting of *agent$_{PA}$* and *agent$_{IA}$* that are connected by connection *from_to$_3$* and, moreover, *agent$_{PA}$* uses the input signature *sig$_\Sigma$*. The function *add* should be interpreted as adding all system elements that occur in the design formula but not yet included in the system, in the given relation.

2.3 Design Communication Language (*DCL*)

DCL imports terms from *DAL* and generates expressions by means of which system components can communicate about system configuration and its modification. Any sort from *DAL* is also a sort in *DCL*. For all sorts a set of constants and a set of variables are assumed. Also, any function from *DAL* is imported as a function in *DCL*. Note that there is a one-to-one correspondence between terms from *DCL* and *DAL*. Moreover, a set of predicates is assumed that determines the communication between components about system configuration and its modification. These predicates are like those that are used in DESIRE, though we will not enumerate them exhaustively. Some important predicates are given in table 4.

Table 4. Sorts of *DAL*

Predicate	Description
to_be_performed:ACTION	design action to be performed
to_be_observed:DEFOR	observe if design formula holds
observation_result:DEFOR×SIGN	design formula has truth value

Based on the defined terms and predicates, the formulae of DCL can be defined as follows:

1. If $P:S_1\times\ldots\times S_n$ is a n-ary predicate and t_i is a term of sort S_i $(i=1,\ldots,n)$, then $P(t_1,\ldots,t_n)$ is an atomic formula of the design command language *DCL*.
2. All atomic *DCL* formulae are *DCL* formulae.
3. If E is an atomic *DCL* formula, then $\neg$E is a *DCL* formula.
4. If E_1 and E_2 are *DCL* formulae, then $E_1\wedge E_2$ is a *DCL* formula.

"$to\_be\_performed(Add(Connected\_to(agent_{PA},\ agent_{IA}\ from\_to_3)\wedge has\_Input\_Signature(agent_{PA},\ sig_\Sigma))$)" is a design communication formula, which states that the add-action should be performed.

2.4   Trace Requirement Language (*TRL*)

Trace Requirement Language (*TRL*) is defined to specify properties or requirements concerning either the configuration behaviour (e.g. what will be the system configuration if the maintenance agent sends a *DCL* expression to the environment component) or the information behaviour (e.g. what will be the system information state if a component sends an expression to another component) of agent-mediated systems. A trace is a sequence of system states (models) through the time. Thus, *TRL* generates expressions that specify the configuration and information behaviour of a system through time. For this reason, we define terms that denote system states, system traces, information content of system states, and structural configurations of system states. Moreover, we introduce predicates to represent relations between above entries.

Given a domain specific ordered-sorted signature Σ (like those used in DESIRE), we denote sorts, functions and predicates from Σ by *sort(Σ)*, *func(Σ)* and *pred(Σ)*, respectively. Also, we denote sorts, functions and predicates from DCL by *sort(DCL)*, *func(DCL)* and *pred(DCL)*, respectively. The sorts in *TRL* are mentioned in table 5.

Table 5. Sorts of *TRL*

Sort	Description
IFOR	information formulae from Σ
DCFOR	formulae from *DCL*
M_R	restricted states or models
M_C	complete states or models
T	time
Γ	trace
S_i i=1,...,n	imported sorts from Σ and *DCL*

We define a new sort *FOR* such that *IFOR<FOR* and *DCFOR<FOR*. Note that *DCFOR* formulae express communication about design formulae while *IFOR* formulae express communication about information formulae, $SP_{Comp}< SP$, $SP_{Interface}< SP_{Comp}$, $SP_{Input}< SP_{Interface}$, $SP_{Output}< SP_{Interface}$. Moreover, for all sorts a set of constants and a set of variables are assumed. For all n-ary function $f \in func(\Sigma) \cup func(DCL)$ and all sorts $S, S_1,...,S_n \in sort(\Sigma) \cup sort(DCL)$ where $f:S_1 \times ... \times S_n \rightarrow S$, $\underline{f}:S_1 \times ... \times S_n \rightarrow S$ is an imported function in the trace-requirement language (functions f from Σ or *DCL* are imported as functions $\underline{f}$ in the *TRL*). Also, for all n-ary predicates $p \in pred(\Sigma)$ and all sorts $S_1,...,S_n \in sort(\Sigma)$ where $p:S_1 \times ... \times S_n$, predicate p is reformulated as a function $\underline{p}:S_1 \times ... \times S_n \rightarrow FOR$ and imported in *TRL* (predicates from Σ are imported as functions). Similarly, for all n-ary predicates $p \in pred(DCL)$ and all sorts $S_1,...,S_n \in sort(DCL)$ where $p:S_1 \times ... \times S_n$, predicate p is reformulated as a function $\underline{p}:S_1 \times ... \times S_n \rightarrow DCFOR$ and imported in *TRL* (predicates from *DCL* are imported as functions). Finally, logical connectives that operate on Σ and *DCL* are imported as functions, i.e.

1. $\underline{\wedge}$: FOR $\times$ FOR $\rightarrow$ FOR
2. $\underline{\vee}$: FOR $\times$ FOR $\rightarrow$ FOR
3. $\underline{\neg}$: FOR $\rightarrow$ FOR

Some specific functions for the trace-requirement language that are not imported from Σ or *DCL* are as follows:

1.   input : $SP_{Comp} \rightarrow SP_{Input}$
2.   output : $SP_{Comp} \rightarrow SP_{Output}$
3.   state_r : $\Gamma \times T \times SP_{Interface} \rightarrow M_R$
4.   state_c : $\Gamma \times T \rightarrow M_C$

Given the functions as defined above, the terms of *TRL* are defined in usual way. The predicates mentioned in table 6 represent relations between system states and their information contents (*holds_info*), and system states and their design configurations (*holds_struct*).

Table 6. Predicates of *TRL*

Predicate	Description
$< : T \times T$	time ordering relation
holds_info_r : $M_R \times$ FOR $\times$ SIGN	formula holds in state
holds_info_c : $M_c \times$ FOR $\times$ SP$_{Interface} \times$ SIGN	formula holds in state of component
holds_struct_r : $M_R \times$ DEFOR $\times$ SIGN	design formula holds in state
holds_struct_c : $M_c \times$ DEFOR $\times$ SP $\times$ SIGN	design formula holds in state of component

Formulae of *TRL* can now be defined as follows:

1. If $P : S_1 \times ... \times S_n$ is a n-ary predicate and t_i is a term of sort S_i (i=1,...,n), then $P(t_1,...,t_n)$ is an expression of the requirement language.
2. If E_1 and E_2 are expressions and x:S is a variable of sort S, then $E_1 \wedge E_2$, $E_1 \Rightarrow E_2$, $\neg E_1, \forall x:S\ E_1$, $\exists x:S\ E_1$ are formulae of the requirement language.

Let δ be a design formula of sort *DEFOR*, agent$_{MA}$ be the Maintenance agent having sort SP$_{Comp}$, SYS be the system itself, then the following *TRL* formula states that in all system traces and at any time point if the output of the maintenance agent is a communication formula expressing a creation action (i.e. *to_be_performed(add(δ))*), then at some time later the system is modified according to the creation action:

$\forall \mathcal{M}:\Gamma\ \exists t:T$
[holds_info_c(state_c($\mathcal{M}: \Gamma$,t:T) , to_be_performed(add(δ)) , output(agent$_{MA}$) , true) $\Rightarrow$
$\exists t':T$ [t':T >t:$T \wedge$ holds_struct_c(state_c($\mathcal{M}: \Gamma$, t':T) , δ,SYS, true)]]

In the following, we will abbreviate the quantified expression "$\exists t':T$ t':T > t:$T \wedge$ ... " and write "$\exists t':T$ > t:$T \wedge$ ..." instead. Note that there is an ordering relation between defined languages (*DL, DAL, DCL, TRL*, and a domain specific signature Σ) according to which one language imports terms and formulae from another language. This import ordering relation is illustrated in Figure 2.

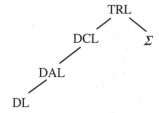

Fig. 2. The import relation between languages

2.5 On Semantics

The semantical relation between language expressions, models with respect to that language and the real world containing computer systems is twofold. The part of a model (at a certain time point) representing the information state of the system corresponds to the actual information state of the computer system at that time point. Also, the part of the model at a certain time point that represents the structure of the system corresponds to the actual structure of that system at that time point.

3   Requirements for an Example Scenario

In this section, we use the trace requirement language *TRL* to express a number of requirements that specify relevant properties concerning both configuration as well as information behaviour of agent-mediated systems. In order to motivate these requirements, we introduce a scenario where system configuration is modified.

3.1   Example Scenario

Consider a scenario for a system consisting of three components named UA (User Agent), MA (Maintenance Agent), and EW (Environment). At a certain time point, the User Agent may need a Personal Assistant agent and requests that to the Maintenance Agent. The Maintenance Agent generates an action (to be executed in the environment) to create a Personal Assistant agent for the User Agent. After the Personal Assistant agent is created (now the system consists of four components), the User Agent can communicate with its Personal Assistant agent and require certain information to be provided by the Personal Assistant agent. This scenario can be described as the following sequence of pairs indicating the system configuration and the system information states, respectively:

1.   System structure consists of UA, MA and EW,
      UA (internally) identifies the need for a personal assistance.
2.   System structure consists of UA, MA and EW,
      UA generates a request on its output for personal assistance.
3.   System structure consists of UA, MA and EW,
      MA has the user service-request for personal assistance on its input.
4.   System structure consists of UA, MA and EW,
      MA generates to_be_performed(add(PA)) on its output.
5.   System structure consists of UA, MA and EW
      EW has to_be_performed(add(PA)) on its input
6.   System structure consists of UA, MA, EW and PA
      EW has E (the effect of add(PA)) on its output
7.   System structure consists of UA, MA, EW and PA
      UA has information-request on its output
8.   System structure consists of UA, MA, EW and PA
      PA has the information request on its input
9.   System structure consists of UA, MA, EW and PA
      PA has an answer to the information-request on its output
10. System structure consists of UA, MA, EW and PA
      UA has the answer on its input

Given the above sequence of system states, we distinguish the following types of operations that transfer one system state into another:

a.   Communication initiation by UA (for MA, for PA)
b.   Communication event between UA and MA
c.   Action initiation by MA
d.   (World) interaction event between MA and EW
e.   Action execution by EW (resulting in creation of PA and generating E on its output)
f.   Answer generation by PA
g.   Event communication between UA and PA
h.   Event communication between PA and UA

3.2   Relevant Properties

In this section, the trace requirement language is used to specify and express some important properties of the system in the scenario mentioned above. These properties are distinguished into three classes called *global, basic* and *semantic properties*. The global properties concern the behaviour of the system as a whole, the basic properties concern the behaviour of the system parts, and the semantic properties are the assumed generic properties for the type of system.

3.2.1   Global Properties

Two important global properties for the example mentioned above are specified as the following requirements.

GR1 (UA-EW Impact): If at time point t the agent UA generates a service request Q to MA on its output, and there exists a design description E such that E would realize Q, then a time point t'>t exists such that EW has E on its output.

$\forall \, \mathcal{M}{:}\Gamma, \, t{:}T, \, Q{:}\text{SLTERM}, \, E{:}\text{DEFOR}$
[holds_info_r(state_r($\mathcal{M}{:}\Gamma$, t:T,output(UA)) , communiction_from_to(Q:SLTERM,UA,MA) , true)
$\wedge$ structure_realises_service(E:DEFOR , Q:SLTERM) $\Rightarrow$
$\exists$t':T>t:T holds_info_r(state_r($\mathcal{M}{:}\Gamma$, t':T , output(EW)) , E:DEFOR,true)]

Note that SLTERM is an assumed sort that refers to the service language terms by which the user denotes the kind of service (s)he is interested in. Examples that illustrate SLTERM expressions are "request(personal-assistant)" and "request(car-brokering-system)".

GR2 (Creation Successfulness): If at time point t the agent UA generates a service request Q (e.g., for having personal assistance) to MA on its output, and R is the behaviour required for service request Q, then a time point t'>t exists such that the system configuration contains the necessary structure (e.g., pers_ass) and the system shows behaviour R.

∀ 𝒪𝒞:Γ, t:T, Q:SLTERM

[holds_info_r(state_r(𝒪𝒞:Γ,t:T,output(UA)),communication_from_to(Q:SLTERM, UA, MA), true)

  ∧ ∃ E:DEFOR, d1:T, d2:T

    [structure_realises_service(E:DEFOR,Q:SLTERM) ∧ SB1$_R$ (E: DEFOR, d1: T, d2: T)] ⇒

∃ t':T>t:T, E': DEFOR, d1:T, d2:T

[structure_realises_service(E':DEFOR, Q:SLTERM)

  ∧   holds_info_r(state_r(𝒪𝒞:Γ, t':T, output(EW)), E':DEFOR,true)

  ∧   SB1$_R$ (E': DEFOR, d1: T, d2: T)

  ∧   ∀ t1: T, t2: T, t3: T, t4: T

      [t2:T − t1:T ≥ d1: T ∧ t1:T ≤ t3:T ≤ t2:T − d2: T ∧ t4:T − t3:T ≥ d2: T ⇒

      R(𝒪𝒞:Γ, t3: T, t4: T , pers_ass)]]

]

The terms SB1$_R$ and R occurring in this property are explained in Section 3.2.3.3. The term SB1$_R$ is a scheme of properties that relate a structure E: DEFOR to behaviour R. The occurrence of R makes it a scheme.

3.2.2 Global Properties

The basic properties are divided in three subclasses as follows.

3.2.2.1 Agent Properties

An agent property refers to the behaviour of a specific agent. An important agent property for the example mentioned above is specified by the following requirement.

AR1 (MA Action Initiation Successfulness): If at time point t the agent MA has a service request Q (e.g. a request for a personal assistance) on its input, then a time point t'>t exists such that MA has to_be_performed(add(E)) on its output where E is a system configuration that can satisfy the service request Q.

∀ 𝒪𝒞:Γ, t:T, Q:SLTERM , E: DEFOR

[holds_info_r(state_r(𝒪𝒞:Γ, t: T, input(MA)), communication_from_to(Q:SLTERM, UA, MA), true)

  ∧ structure_realises_service(E: DEFOR , Q:SLTERM)

  ∧ ¬∃ E': DEFOR

    [holds_info_r(state_r(𝒪𝒞:Γ,t:T,input(MA)),observation_result(E':DEFOR,pos), true)

      ∧ structure_realises_service(E': DEFOR , Q:SLTERM)]   ⇒

∃t':T>t:T [holds_info_r(state_r(𝒪𝒞:Γ, t':T,output(MA)), to_be_performed(add(E:DEFOR)), true)

    ∧ ∀ E'': DEFOR [structure_realises_service(E'':DEFOR , Q:SLTERM)

                ∧ holds_info_r(state_r(𝒪𝒞:Γ, t':T , output(MA)) ,

                         to_be_performed(add(E'':DEFOR)) , true)]

      ∧ equal(E: DEFOR , E'' : DEFOR)]]

]

3.2.2.2 World Properties

The required properties of the behaviour of the environment component are specified as follows.

ER1 (EW Action Execution Successfulness): If at time point t the world component EW has to_be_performed(α) on its input, and β is the effect of performing α, then a time point t'>t exists such that EW has β on its output.

$\forall \, \mathcal{M}:\Gamma, \, t:T, \, \alpha:\text{ACTION}, \, \beta:\text{DEFOR},$
[holds_info_r(state_r($\mathcal{M}:\Gamma$, t:T, input(EW)), to_be_performed(α:ACTION), true) $\Rightarrow$
$\exists t':T > t:T$ [holds_info_r(state_r($\mathcal{M}:\Gamma$, t':T, output(EW)), β:DEFOR, true)
         $\wedge$ is_effect_of(β:DEFOR , α:ACTION)]
]

Where the predicate is_effect_of(β,α) is defined as follows:
$\forall x:\text{DEFOR}^+$ is_effect_of(x , add(x))
$\forall x:\text{DEAT}$ is_effect_of($\neg$x , delete(x))

3.2.2.3 World Properties

The transfer properties specify that information transfer between agents that takes place in a proper manner. Two important transfer properties are specified as the following requirements.

TR1 (Transfer UA-MA): If at time point t the agent UA generates a request for MA on its output, then a time point t'>t exists such that MA has this request on its input.

$\forall \, \mathcal{M}:\Gamma, \, t:T, \, \varphi:\text{FOR}$
[holds_info_r(state_r($\mathcal{M}:\Gamma$,t:T,output(UA)),communication_from_to(φ:FOR,UA,MA),true) $\Rightarrow$
$\exists t':T > t:T$
  holds_info_r(state_r($\mathcal{M}:\Gamma$,t':T,input(MA)), communication_from_to(φ:FOR, UA, MA) , true)
]

TR2 (Transfer MA-EW): If at time point t the agent MA generates to_be_performed(α) for EW on its output (Note that α is of type ACTION such that it is either add(E) or delete(E)), then a time point t'>t exists such that EW has to_be_performed(α) on its input.

$\forall \, \mathcal{M}:\Gamma, \, t:T, \, \alpha:\text{ACTION}$
[holds_info_r(state_r($\mathcal{M}:\Gamma$,t:T,output(MA)), to_be_performed(α:ACTION) , true) $\Rightarrow$
  $\exists t':T > t:T$ holds_info_r(state_r($\mathcal{M}:\Gamma$, t':T , input(EW)), to_be_performed(α:ACTION), true)
]

3.2.3 Semantic and Coherence Properties

The semantic properties specify the assumed generic properties of the system. The following semantic properties are distinguished.

3.2.3.1 Semantic Properties

This property guarantees that if a system description holds in (the informational state of) the environment, then the actual system configuration (its structural state) is indeed described by that description.

RA1: If at time point t in trace $\mathcal{M}$ the world component EW has description E on its output, then at time point t in trace $\mathcal{M}$ the system has structure E (i.e. the system description Y is true).

∀ M :Γ, t:T, E: DEFOR
[holds_info_r(state_r(M :Γ, t:T, ouput(EW)), E:DEFOR , true) $\Rightarrow$
  holds_struct_c(state_c(M :Γ, t:T), E:DEFOR , true)]

3.2.3.2 Coherence Property

The coherence properties specify a relation between the informational and structural states of the actual system at any point in time. Two important properties that guarantee the coherency of the system are as follows.

CA1: At any time t in any trace $\mathcal{M}$ if a formula has a truth-value in the informational state for a specific system part, then this system part actually is part of the system structure (in the structural state).

∀ M :Γ, t:T, C:SP, F: IFOR , E: DEFOR, tv:TV
[holds_info_r(state_r($\mathcal{M}$:Γ, t:T, interface(C:SP)),F:IFOR , tv:TV) $\Rightarrow$
∃Σ:SIG
  [holds_struct_r(state_r($\mathcal{M}$:Γ, t:T,system), exists_comp(C:SP),true)
  $\wedge$ holds_struct_r(state_r($\mathcal{M}$:Γ, t:T,system), has_interface_signature(Σ:SIG,C:SP), true)
  $\wedge$ holds_struct_r(state_r($\mathcal{M}$:Γ , t:T, system) , is_formula_of(F:IFOR, Σ:SIG), true)]
]

CA2: At any time t in any trace $\mathcal{M}$ if the system has a certain structure (in its structural state), then the formulae that can be evaluated in this system structure have truth-values (in the system's informational state).

∀ $\mathcal{M}$:Γ, t:T, C:SP, F: IFOR , E: DEFOR, ∃ Σ:SIG
[[holds_struct_r(state_r($\mathcal{M}$:Γ, t:T,system),exists_comp(C:SP),true)
  $\wedge$ holds_struct_r(state_r($\mathcal{M}$:Γ, t:T,system), has_interface_signature(Σ:SIG,C:SP), true)
  $\wedge$ holds_struct_r(state_r($\mathcal{M}$:Γ, t:T, system) , is_formula_of(F:IFOR, Σ:SIG), true)] $\Rightarrow$
∃ tv:TV   holds_info_r(state_r ($\mathcal{M}$:Γ, t:T, interface(C:SP)), F:IFOR , tv:TV)]

3.2.3.3 Structure-Behaviour Properties

In this section (required) behaviour is related to structure properties and service requests. In the following $R(\mathcal{M}:\Gamma,\ t1:\ T,\ t2:\ T,\ C:\ SP)$ stands for a certain behavioural requirement. As an example, pers_ass_req($\mathcal{M}:\Gamma,\ t1:\ T,\ t2:\ T,\ C:\ SP$) denotes the following requirement; here INFO is a sort for the content of requests and answers:

$\forall$ A: INFO
[holds_info_r(state_r($\mathcal{M}:\Gamma$,t1:T,input(C: SP)), request(A: INFO), true) $\Rightarrow$
$\exists$ t:T, $\exists$B: INFO [t1:$T \le$ t:$T \le$ t1:T+t2:T
        $\wedge$ holds_info_r(state_r($\mathcal{M}:\Gamma$, t:T, output(C: SP)), answer_for(B: INFO, A: INFO) , true)]
]

By defining such abbreviations for the requirements of interest for the system in question a powerful scheme of structure-behaviour properties can be formulated: SB1$_R$ and SB2$_R$.

Let SB1$_R$ (E: DEFOR, d1:T, d2:T) denote the following scheme of structure-behaviour properties: If between time points t1 and t2 the system has structure E: DEFOR, then R is true between t1 and t2 – d2 for all periods of sufficient length (d1 minimum):

$\forall\mathcal{M}:\Gamma$, $\forall$ t1:T, t2:T, t3:T, t4: T
[[t2:T – t1:T $\ge$ d1: T
     $\wedge$ $\forall$ t$\in$[t1:T, t2:T] holds_struct_c(state_c($\mathcal{M}:\Gamma$, t:T) , E:DEFOR , true)
     $\wedge$ t1:T $\le$ t3:T $\le$ t2:T – d2: T $\wedge$ t4:T – t3:T $\ge$ d2: T] $\Rightarrow$
R($\mathcal{M}:\Gamma$, t3:T, t4:T, pers_ass)
]

In the next structure-behaviour scheme of properties SB2$_R$, the link is made between a service request Q, the behaviour R that satisfies Q, and the possible structures E: DEFOR that can realise R. SB2$_R$ denotes the following scheme of structure-behaviour properties:

$\forall$Q: SLTERM
[implied_service$_R$ (Q: SLTERM) $\Rightarrow$
     $\exists$ E: DEFOR, d1: T, d2: T
     [SB1$_R$(E: DEFOR, d1: T, d2: T) $\wedge$ structure_realises_service(E: DEFOR, Q: SLTERM)]
]

4 System Evaluation

In order to evaluate the system behaviour, we need to verify that the system has the required properties. In Section 3, we have introduced certain properties for the proposed scenario. However, verifying such properties may be quite complex. Therefore, we may define some intermediate properties by means of which global properties can be proved easily and more efficiently, and which, by themselves, can be derived from basic properties.

4.1 Intermediate Properties

Intermediate properties can be derived from basic properties. However, it is useful to formulate them explicitly. These properties specify the output/output relations between different system components. Two important intermediate properties are as follows.

IR1 (UA-MA Interaction): If at time point t the agent UA generates a service request Q for MA on its output, then a time point t'>t exists such that MA has to_be_performed(add(E)) related to this request on its output.

$\forall \mathcal{M}{:}\Gamma$, t:$T$, Q: SLTERM , E: DEFOR
[[holds_info_r(state_r($\mathcal{M}{:}\Gamma$,t:T,output(UA)), communication_from_to(Q: SLTERM,UA, MA),true)
   $\wedge$ structure_realises_service(E: DEFOR , Q: SLTERM)
   $\wedge \neg\exists$E':DEFOR
     [holds_info_r(state_r($\mathcal{M}{:}\Gamma$,t:T,output(EW)),observation_result(E':DEFOR,pos), true)
      $\wedge$ structure_realises_service(E': DEFOR , Q: SLTERM)]] $\Rightarrow$
$\exists$t':T > t:T
  [holds_info_r(state_r($\mathcal{M}{:}\Gamma$, t':T, output(MA)), to_be_performed(add(E: DEFOR)), true)
   $\wedge \forall$ E": DEFOR
    [structure_realises_service(E": DEFOR , Q: SLTERM)
    $\wedge$ holds_info_r(state_r($\mathcal{M}{:}\Gamma$,t':T, output(MA)),to_be_performed(add(E":DEFOR)), true)
    $\wedge$ equal(E: DEFOR , E": DEFOR)
    ]
  ]
]

IR2 (MA-EW Interaction): If at time point t MA has an action (e.g., to_be_performed(add(E)) or to_be_performed(delete(E))) on its output, then a time point t'>t exists such that EW has the effect of the action (e.g., E resp. not E) on its output.

$\forall \mathcal{M}{:}\Gamma$, t:$T$, α: ACTION , β: DEFOR
[[holds_info_r(state_r($\mathcal{M}{:}\Gamma$, t:T, output(MA)) , to_be_performed(α: ACTION) , true)
  $\wedge$ is_effect_of(β: DEFOR, α: ACTION)] $\Rightarrow$
$\exists$t':T > t:T
  holds_info_r(state_r($\mathcal{M}{:}\Gamma$, t':T, output(EW)), β: DEFOR , true)]

4.2 The Use of Proof Patterns

The following logical relationships hold between the different properties.

1.   Intermediate properties are implied by transfer properties and agent or world properties:
    TR1 & AR1 $\Rightarrow$ IR1
    TR2 & ER1 $\Rightarrow$ IR2
2.   Intermediate properties can be chained to indirect interaction properties expressing indirect impact of one component on another one:
    IR1 & IR2 $\Rightarrow$ GR1
3.   Indirect intermediate properties imply the global properties, assuming Representation and Coherence properties and Structure-Behaviour relationships:
    GR1 & RA1 & CA1 & SB2 $\Rightarrow$ GR2

4.3 Checking Properties

Given a trace or set of traces, all of the above properties can be checked automatically. To this end a software environment has been developed in Prolog. If the property GR2 is checked, the outcome can be one of the following:
1.   Indeed GR2 satisfied, or
2.   GR2 is dissatisfied; in this case, given the logical relationships defined by the proof patterns, at least some of the basic properties are also dissatisfied; which one(s) can also be found by running the checking software for all of the basic properties; the outcome of this check points to where the problem originates.
For more details of this model checking environment and its use in diagnosis, see [9].

5   Discussion

The requirements specification language introduced in this paper can be used in a number of ways. First, it allows for specification of requirements on the system structure over time. Most other requirement languages (e.g., [7], [4]) only allow for specification of informational system states, for a given, fixed system structure. In our language it is possible both to refer to the structural state of the system and the informational state of it.

A second use is that a broad class of behavioural properties can be specified of the system or of specific parts of the system, for example agents. Not only can, e.g., reactiveness and pro-activeness properties be specified, but also properties expressing adaptive behaviour, such as 'exercise improves skill', which are relative to (comparing two alternatives for) the history can be expressed in this language (in standard forms of temporal logic different alternative histories cannot be compared).

A third and more sophisticated use is to specify requirements on the dynamics of the process of modification of the system structure over time, for example, as initiated and performed by the system (e.g., one of its agents) itself. Here requirements on, for example, agent behaviour and the dynamics of the system structure and their relationships can be specified. For example it can be expressed whether a system modification initiation by one of the agents occurs and whether it is successful.

Requirements can be specified at different levels of aggregation. For example, a requirement for the overall system can be refined into requirements of different parts of the system, i.e., requirements on specific agents and on specific interactions between agents, which, together, logically imply the global requirement. For more details of refinement in the context of compositional verification of multi-agent systems, see [10].

For all different types of requirements discussed, for a given set of traces the requirements can be verified automatically. By specifying the refinement of a requirement for the overall system, it is possible to perform diagnosis of malfunctioning of the system. If the overall requirement fails on a given trace, then subsequently, all refined requirements for the parts of the system can be verified against that trace: the cause of the malfunctioning can be attributed to the part(s) of the system for which the refined requirement(s) fail(s) (see [9]).

References

1. Brazier, F.M.T., Jonker, C.M., and Treur, J., Principles of Compositional Multi-agent System Development. In: J. Cuena (ed.), *Proc. of the 15th IFIP World Computer Congress, WCC'98, Conference on Information Technology and Knowledge Systems, IT&KNOWS'98*, 1998, pp. 347-360. To be published by IOS Press.
2. Davis, A. M. (1993). *Software requirements: Objects, Functions, and States*, Prentice Hall, New Jersey.
3. Dardenne, A., Lamsweerde, A. van, and Fickas, S. (1993). Goal-directed Requirements Acquisition. *Science in Computer Programming*, vol. 20, pp. 3-50.
4. Darimont, R., and Lamsweerde, A. van (1996). Formal Refinement Patterns for Goal-Driven Requirements Elaboration. *Proc. of the Fourth ACM Symposium on the Foundation of Software Engineering (FSE4)*, pp. 179-190.
5. Dubois, E., Du Bois, P., and Zeippen, J.M. (1995). A Formal Requirements Engineering Method for Real-Time, Concurrent, and Distributed Systems. *In: Proceedings of the Real-Time Systems Conference, RTS'95*.
6. Engelfriet, J., Jonker, C.M. and Treur, J., (1999). Compositional Verification of Multi-Agent Systems in Temporal Multi-Epistemic Logic. In: J.P. Mueller, M.P. Singh, A.S. Rao (eds.), *Intelligent Agents V, Proc. of the Fifth International Workshop on Agent Theories, Architectures and Languages, ATAL'98*. Lecture Notes in AI, vol. 1555, Springer Verlag, 1999, pp. 177-194. Extended version in: *Journal of Logic, Language and Information*, in press.
7. Fisher, M., Wooldridge, M. (1997) On the Formal Specification and Verification of Multi-Agent Systems. *International Journal of Cooperative Information Systems*, M. Huhns, M. Singh, (eds.), special issue on Formal Methods in Cooperative Information Systems: Multi-Agent Systems, vol. 6, pp. 67-94.

8. Herlea, D.E., Jonker, C.M., Treur, J., and Wijngaards, N.J.E., (1999). Specification of Behavioural Requirements within Compositional Multi-Agent System Design. In: F.J. Garijo, M. Boman (eds.), *Multi-Agent System Engineering, Proceedings of the 9th European Workshop on Modelling Autonomous Agents in a Multi-Agent World, MAAMAW'99.* Lecture Notes in AI, vol.1647, Springer Verlag, Berlin, 1999, pp. 8-27.

9. Catholijn Jonker, Ioan Alfred Letia, and Jan Treur (2001). Diagnosis of the Dynamics Within an Organization By Trace Checking of Behavioral Requirements. In: Wooldridge, M., Ciancarini, P., and Weiss, G. (eds.), *Proc. of the 2nd International Workshop on Agent-Oriented Software Engineering, AOSE'01.* Lecture Notes in Computer Science, Springer Verlag, This Volume.

10. Jonker, C.M. and Treur, J. (1998). Compositional Verification of Multi-Agent Systems: a Formal Analysis of Pro-activeness and Reactiveness. In: W.P. de Roever, H. Langmaack, A. Pnueli (eds.), *Proceedings of the International Workshop on Compositionality, COMPOS'97.* Lecture Notes in Computer Science, **1536**, Springer Verlag, 1998, pp. 350-380. Extended version in: *International Journal of Cooperative Information Systems*, in press.

11. Kontonya, G., and Sommerville, I. (1998). *Requirements Engineering: Processes and Techniques.* John Wiley and Sons, New York.

12. Manna, Z., and Pnueli, A.. *Temporal Verification of Reactive Systems: Safety.* Springer-Verlag, 1995.

13. Sommerville, I., and Sawyer P. (1997). *Requirements Engineering: a good practice guide.* John Wiley & Sons, Chicester, England.

Determining When to Use an Agent-Oriented Software Engineering Paradigm

Scott A. O'Malley[1] and Scott A. DeLoach[2]

[1]Department of Electrical and Computer Engineering, Air Force Institute of Technology
Wright-Patterson Air Force Base, Ohio 45433-7765
omalleys@stratcom.mil

[2]Department of Computing and Information Sciences, Kansas State University
212 Nichols Hall, Manhattan, KS 66506
sdeloach@cis.ksu.edu

Abstract. With the emergence of agent-oriented software engineering techniques, software engineers have a new way of conceptualizing complex distributed software requirements. To help determine the most appropriate software engineering methodology, a set of defining criteria is required. In this paper, we describe out approach to determining these criteria, as well as a technique to assist software engineers with the selection of a software engineering methodology based on those criteria.

1 Introduction

Software engineers have a number of options when it comes to developing solutions for complex, distributed software requirements. One emerging technique is the development of multiagent systems. There are a number of reasons a software developer may consider a multiagent system. In particular, multiagent systems can provide benefits such as processing speed-up, reduced communication bandwidth, and increased reliability [10]. However, academia as well as industry are still trying to determine which problems require a multiagent approach [8, 11].

Once a designer has made the decision to use a multiagent design, a number of methodologies exist for building multiagent systems [2, 3, 4, 7, 14, 15, 19]. The methodologies range from extensions of existing object-oriented methodologies to new *agent-oriented techniques*, which offer a new perspective to developing multiagent systems by increasing the level of abstraction the developer uses to analyze and design the system. As agent-oriented software engineering techniques are becoming more popular, software engineers must select the particular approach that is best suited for the problem they are solving.

Our research at the Air Force Institute of Technology has focused on providing software engineers and managers with a decision-making framework to determine an appropriate methodology when faced with a set of viable software engineering methodology alternatives [12]. This paper focuses on the method we applied for developing this framework. The primary challenge in developing this framework was selecting a valid set of criteria upon which to base the decision.

M.J. Wooldridge, G. Weiß, and P. Ciancarini (Eds.): AOSE 2001, LNCS 2222, pp. 188-205, 2002.

The remainder of this section addresses other approaches to determining when an agent-oriented approach is appropriate as well as techniques for classifying software engineering methodologies. Section 2 describes how we defined our decision-making criteria while Section 3 describes a survey that we conducted in November and December 2000 to validate that criteria. Section 4 presents an example of using the framework and Section 6 discusses our results and conclusions.

1.1   Related Techniques

The strategy taken by Jennings and Wooldridge was to provide "intellectual justification" [8] for the validity of the agent-oriented techniques. Their justification, however, comes from a qualitative analysis of how well the technique addresses the principles that allow software engineering techniques to deal with complex problems proposed by Booch: abstraction, decomposition, and hierarchy [1, 8]. They leave "understanding of the situations in which agent solutions are appropriate" as an outstanding issue [8].

The European Institute for Research and Strategic Studies in Telecommunications (EURESCOM) used a different strategy in 1999 when they began a project to explore the use of agent technologies within the European telecommunications industry. One of the project's three objectives is to "define guidance for the identification of application areas where an agent-based approach is better suited than other approaches" [11]. The consortium produced the following five guidelines to help a developer decide whether an agent-oriented approach is appropriate [11]:

1. An agent-oriented approach is beneficial in situations where complex/diverse types of communication are required.
2. An agent-oriented approach is beneficial when the system must perform well in situations where it is not practical/possible to specify its behavior on a case-by-case basis.
3. An agent-oriented approach is beneficial in situations involving negotiation, co-operation and competition among different entities.
4. An agent-oriented approach is beneficial when the system must act autonomously.
5. An agent-oriented approach is beneficial when it is anticipated that the system will be expanded, modified or when the system purpose is expected to change.

These guidelines are a good beginning in determining whether or not an agent-oriented approach is well suited to a particular problem. However, based on these guidelines alone, there is still no clear answer.

1.2   Software Engineering Methodology Classification

In 1988, the Software Engineering Institute (SEI) presented a set of guidelines for assessing software development methods for real-time systems [17]. The guidelines define a five-step process for evaluating different methodologies. These five steps are:

1. Needs Analysis – Determine the important characteristics of the system to be developed and how individual methods help developers deal with those characteristics.
2. Constraint Identification – Identify the constraints imposed on the permitted solutions and determine how individual methods help developers deal with those constraints.
3. User Requirements – Determine the general usage characteristics of the individual methods.
4. Management Issues – Determine the support provided by the method to those who must manage the development process as well as the costs and benefits of adopting and using the method.
5. Introduction Plan – Develop an understanding of the issues that the method does not address and a plan to augment the method in those areas where it is deficient.

Based on these steps, the consortium developed questions to help analyze prospective methodologies. Some of the questions are meant to be rhetorical, while others require an in-depth knowledge of the methodology and its representations. The purpose of the questions is to make the assessor form an opinion regarding the methodology; however, this process does not over-simplify the problem of selecting a methodology. The questions do provide a framework to present a systematic evaluation process.

We based our assessment process on SEI's existing work in classifying software methods, which includes three major areas of characterization [6]. The SEI process involves determining what a method is, what a method does, and what issues the method addresses. SEI's three areas of characterization are:

- Technical Characteristics
- Management Characteristics
- Usage Characteristics

The *Technical Characteristics* look at classifying the technical characteristics of the software development through the three stages of development (specification, design, and implementation). The characteristics of the software problem dealt with during the specification—or analysis—phase relate to the behavioral and functional views of the problem. These views are carried through to the other stages of the system development. During the design phase, the behavioral and functional views are mapped into the behavioral and functional characteristics of the function. Effective methods allow for smooth transition across these stages and allow the ability to trace functional and behavioral characteristics through all stages of development.

The next set of characteristics, *Management,* is important for considering the support that a method provides to management when evaluating different methods. The characterization should consider how well the method deals with typical management and project issues such as estimating, planning and reviewing. The characterization should also look at how the method is related to the needs and processes that exist within the organization. Management practices are often a difficult thing to change and identifying potential changes is an important factor in adopting a new methodology [6].

The third set, *Usage Characteristics*, captures and describes the characteristics of the methodology that will affect its use by an organization. These characteristics include the basis for the methodology, the availability of training, and the availability of tool support. This characterization is important in understanding the magnitude of change involved with selection of a methodology.

2   Defining Decision Criteria

The challenge of selecting an appropriate methodology for a software development project is in understanding the differences between the methodologies. The ability to classify these methodologies is crucial to the understanding.

With the characteristics developed in [6] in mind, a set of criteria was developed. For the framework defined in [12], we combined the management and usage characteristics into one category, called *Management Issues*. The technical characteristics of the methodology are captured in the *Program Requirements category*. Each of these categories is discussed in detail below.

2.1   Management Issues

As indicated above, this category is closely related to the management and usage characteristics as defined by [6]. Because of their universal applicability, many of the issues addressed that pertain to this category are taken from the [17], as the management and usage issues for selecting a software development method for real-time systems are practical for any type of system. Below is the initial set of issues selected for this category.

- Cost of Acquiring the Methodology (Meth)
- Cost of Acquiring Support Tools (Tool)
- Availability of Reusable Components (Reuse)
- Effects on Organizational Business Practices (Org)
- Compliance with Standards (Stan)
- Traceability of Changes (Chan)

The first two issues deal with costs involved with selecting the methodology. Specifically, *Cost of Acquiring the Methodology* involves the costs associated with adopting the methodology for use. Factors that influence this issue include the costs incurred by sending personnel to available training, the purchase of reference material, etc. Additionally, *Cost of Acquiring Support Tools* deals with the costs incurred by purchasing tools that support the methodology. The tools include CASE tools as well as programming development tools. Further, the cost of factors such as additional hardware/software to operate the tools, maintenance costs for the tools, and training, should be included.

Another issue that indirectly deals with cost is *Availability of Reusable Components*. The incorporation of previously developed software into a new system reduces the overall design, implementation, and testing phases for software development. This category is used to measure the methodology's ability to incorporate predefined components into the system.

The final three issues reflect usage issues. First, *Effects on Organizational Business Practices* measures the impact the adoption of a methodology will have on the existing business practices of the organization. The business practice includes ideas such as tracking development progress through milestones, reports, and customer interactions. Next, *Compliance with Standards* is proposed to determine how well an alternative is able to meet standards, whether local to the organization or outside the organization such as national or international. Finally, the last issue in this category, *Traceability of Changes*, measures the methodology's support to trace changes throughout the development lifecycle.

2.2   Project Requirements

The second category of criteria, Project Requirements, is related to the technical characteristics. For this category, the criteria for real-time systems are not directly relevant. In order to derive a set of criteria, we turned to current research and identified a number of technical issues that relate to complex software systems [10, 16]. The issues selected are:

- Legacy System Integration (Leg)
- Distribution (Dis)
- Environment (Env)
- Dynamic System Structure (Struc)
- Interaction (Int)
- Scalability (Scal)
- Agility and Robustness (Agi)

The first three issues in this category relate to constraints of the problem. First, *Legacy System Integration* is a measurement of the methodology's ability to support for the incorporation of previously developed systems, commonly called legacy systems, with the new project requirement. Next, *Distribution* focuses on the ability to support the modeling of distributed aspects of the problem. Distribution can occur in the form of processors, resources, or information. Then, *Environment* measures the methodology's support of developing software systems for environments that have heterogeneous hardware or software.

The next three issues in the category are *Dynamic System Structure*, *Scalability*, and *Agility and Robustness*. *Dynamic System Structure* represents the methodology's ability to develop software capable of handling the introduction and removal of system components in a manner that is not detrimental to the users of the system is considered in this category. *Scalability*, similar to *Dynamic System Structure*, measures the methodology's ability to develop software capable of handling the introduction and removal of system-level resources while minimizing the impact on users. Last, *Agility and Robustness* focuses on the methodology's ability to create flexible software systems that will be resilient to dynamic changes in the environment.

The final issue in the Project Requirements category is *Interaction*. This category determines the methodology's ability to handle the interaction between system-level components as well as entities outside the system such as human users and other systems.

3   Survey

After we selected the criteria above based on a number of literature sources [11, 16], the compiled list was presented to software engineering professionals in academia, industry, and government through a survey questionnaire on the Internet for validation [12]. The purpose of the survey was to collect the opinions of software engineering practitioners with regard to the importance of each of the evaluation considerations to the overall decision.

In order to increase survey participation, an announcement was distributed to software engineering professionals through electronic mail lists maintained by the Object Management Group (OMG), University of Maryland Agent Web, and the Software Engineering Research Network at the University of Calgary. In addition to these broadcast mailings, announcements requesting participation were placed on related, moderated newsgroups—comp.ai and comp.software-eng. Finally, requests were sent directly to a number of respected academics, researchers, and industry leaders.

3.1   Survey Analysis

The period for response collection was set at three weeks. Over that period, thirty-three valid responses were collected.   The survey began with some basic demographic questions in order to develop a profile of the responders. Of the thirty-three responders, twenty-two people indicated that they were associated with the academic community, three responders were associated with government organizations, and eight were associated with the industrial/commercial sector. As for experience, seventeen indicated 1-5 years of experience in their field.   Nine responders categorized themselves as having 5-10 years of experience, and seven responders indicated over 10 years of experience.

The survey also collected the opinions of the responders on the importance of the evaluation consideration that were proposed for the decision as well as their thoughts on the suggested factors, the relative weighting of the management and technical categories, and additional possible factors.   As for the criteria proposed, the responders were asked to rate each on a scale of zero to four.   Additionally, responders could leave considerations "not rated".

The set of scores each factor received indicates that the responders believed the technical issues are more important that the management issues. Fig. 1 shows the average scores each of the considerations received.   Again, the responders felt more emphasis should be placed on technical issues versus management issues.

The survey asked whether basing the weights for the evaluation considerations relative to only the other considerations in the same category was more appropriate than determining weights relative to all of the considerations.   The majority of responses were to determine weights relative to all of the considerations. Most responders did provide an opinion on the total weight each of the major issues. Like the trend seen in Fig. 1, fourteen responders felt that the technical issues should influence the decision more than the management issues. On the other hand, five responders felt that the management issues should weigh more on the decision. Three responders indicated that both sets of issues should have an equal weight. The remaining responders did not specify a particular partitioning. Table 1 shows the data gathered from this particular question.

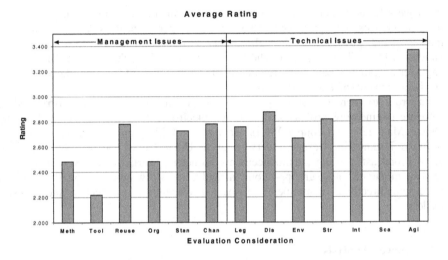

Fig. 1. Average rating for proposed evaluation considerations

Table 1. Partition weightings

Management Issues	Technical Issues	Number of Responses
10%	90%	2
25%	75%	1
30%	70%	2
33%	66%	1
35%	65%	3
40%	60%	3
45%	55%	2
50%	50%	3
60%	40%	2
75%	25%	3
No Partition		11

Finally, the survey posed the question: what important factors are missing? Several alternatives were suggested for the cost category. Responders indicated that other factors would have more significance to the problem such as a cost/benefit ratio, cost savings, and productivity gains, because the benefit of the new methodology, if it were great enough, would mitigate any impact that the initial cost would have. Other management factors suggested —availability of tools and experience base—would be appropriate to evaluate the maturity of the methodology. Considerations in this area included the availability of tools as opposed to just the cost, and the experience base of the methodology. No suggestions for technical issues were submitted.

Based on the research and the survey results, several changes were made to the list of proposed evaluation considerations. Similar categories, like *Dynamic System Structure* and *Scalability*, were combined to form a single category, as were *Organizational Business Practices*, *Compliance with Standards*, and *Traceability of Change*; and the *Cost of Acquiring the Methodology* and *Cost of Acquiring Support Tools*. *Methodology Maturity* was added to the list in order to capture that aspect in the decision. The final list of issues is:

- Management Issues
  - Cost of Acquiring Methodology and Tools
  - Organizational Business Practices
  - Availability of Reusable Components
  - Methodology Maturity
- Project Requirements
  - Legacy System Integration
  - Distribution
  - Environment
  - Dynamic Structure and Scalability
  - Agility and Robustness
  - Interaction

4   Application of Criteria

Our research included the development of a decision-making process built upon a decision analysis framework [12]. This section describes how the criteria specified above are incorporated into the selected strategic decision-making technique.

The strategic decision-making technique selected for the problem of methodology selection is Multiobjective Decision Analysis [9]. Multiobjective Decision Analysis was selected as the underlying framework because (1) of its ability to handle multiple criteria, (2) it is based on a mathematical framework, (3) it is a flexible technique, and (4) it is a mature technique.

4.1   The Decision Analysis Tool

The first step in decision-making based on the Multiobjective Decision Analysis is the development of a value hierarchy. A *value hierarchy* is tree-like structure used for capturing evaluation considerations, objectives, and evaluation measures relevant to the decision. *Evaluation considerations* are criteria that need to be taken into account when evaluating alternatives. An *objective* is the preferred movement with respect to an evaluation consideration. An *evaluation measure* is a scale for measuring the degree of attainment of an objective.

For the methodology selection problem, the issues, described in Section 4, map directly to evaluation considerations in the decision problem's value hierarchy shown in Fig. 2. The objectives of the evaluation considerations, with the exception of *Cost of Acquiring Methodology and Tools*, are to maximize the rating of the methodology's ability to represent the issues. For *Cost of Acquiring Methodology and Tools*, the objective is to minimize the real dollar cost involved with acquiring the methodology and supporting tools.

In order to measure the evaluation considerations, a set of questions has been developed for each. Like the questions developed for the selection of a methodology for developing real-time systems, the questions are designed to measure the methodology's ability to represent the relevant issues [17]. Unlike the system of questions in [17], the decision-maker is asked to rate each question on a scale of zero to four. In order to capture the information, a series of worksheets have been created in [12] that collect the data, as well as provide the decision-maker with guidelines for rating each question. The purpose of the guidelines is to provide a standard for decision-makers to use while evaluating a set of subjective questions.

The Multiobjective Decision Analysis technique provides the decision-maker with a normalized score representing the fitness of an alternative with regard to the problem. This score, called the multiobjective fitness value is the additive combination of the product of the weight, *w*, and rating for each evaluation consideration, *v*. Equation 1 is the multiobjective fitness function for the decision analysis tool.

$$V(X) = \sum_{\forall i} w_i v_i(X_i) \tag{1}$$

where i = cost, bus, mat, reuse, ent, dis, env, ar, dss, int

Weights are used to capture the level of importance the decision-maker places on a particular evaluation consideration. The weights make this technique flexible. The weights of evaluation considerations that are not important to the decision can be set to zero, effectively taking the evaluation consideration out of the decision.

4.2   Application of Decision Analysis Tool

The process of making the decision is captured in a decision analysis tool. This tool is the encapsulation of several data gathering steps and algebraic calculations. The process, itself, is defined by four steps:

1. Weight the Evaluation Considerations
2. Rate the Relevant Evaluation Considerations
3. Calculate the Multiobjective Fitness Value
4. Determine the Best Alternative

Weighting the Evaluation Considerations involves determining which of the evaluation considerations are important to the particular software requirements problem that the decision-maker is trying to select a methodology. After determining the relevant considerations, the decision-maker determines a raw weighting for each consideration based on the relative importance each consideration has with regard to the least important evaluation consideration. The raw weights are then normalized for use in the decision analysis.

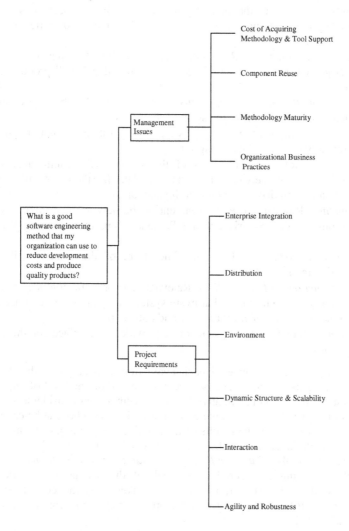

Fig. 2. Methodology selection value hierarchy

For example, one of the case studies evaluated in [12] was based on the system requirements for a content search system [13]. The content search system is a distributed software application in which the users of the system are able to search data files throughout the users' network for key words or phrases. Based on the evaluation consideration in Fig. 2, each of the categories and the analysis decision made as to whether or not the consideration is relevant is shown below.

- *Cost of Acquiring Methodology and Support Tools* – Relevant. The approach to this problem is that the software engineer is part of an organization that is looking to adopt the methodology and supporting tools.
- *Organizational Business Practices* – Relevant. Although the software engineer is the only employee in the fledgling department, the engineer does have the responsibility of providing project updates to other interested parties outside of the department.
- *Methodology Maturity* – Relevant. The decision to change to a new methodology will require some degree of evidence that it will produce quality software.
- *Integration of Reusable Components* – Irrelevant. A library of reusable components is not available to the software engineer.
- *Legacy System Integration* – Irrelevant. The system is not required to incorporate any existing software systems.
- *Distribution* – Relevant. The users of the system will require access from different nodes on the network. Likewise, the data that the users will require is stored on many hard drives throughout the network.
- *Environment* – Relevant. The environment of the network is a mixture of Sun Workstations running Solaris OS and Personal Computers running Windows NT.
- *Agility and Robustness* – Relevant. The users of the system will expect predictability and reliability.
- *Dynamic Structure and Scalability* – Relevant. The organization is growing and as new employees are hired, the hardware systems they are given will need to be linked to the software system for access and data storage.
- *Interaction* – Relevant. The system must provide an interface for the user to submit requests.

After determining the relevance of each evaluation consideration, the decision-maker specifies weights for each. The raw weight is based on the level of importance each evaluation consideration has relative to the least important consideration. After the raw, or relative, weighting is complete, the normalized weights can be calculated. For this particular case study, the results of the relative weighting and normalization are shown in Table 2, the details for the calculation can be found in [12].

Next, the decision-maker *Rates the Relevant Evaluation Considerations* for each of the methodologies being considered. For each of the evaluation considerations considered relevant in the Step 1, the decision-maker rates the consideration by answering the respective set of questions developed during the research with respect to each alternative [12].

This research evaluated an object-oriented software engineering methodology developed by Booch [1] and an agent-oriented software engineering methodology, called Multiagent System Engineering (MaSE), developed at the Air Force Institute of Technology [5] as alternatives for developing solutions to the content search problem. The documentation of the ratings can be found in [12]. For each relevant evaluation consideration, a single-dimensional value function gives the rating based on the input from the user. Table 3 summarizes the ratings of each evaluation consideration for the respective methodologies.

Table 2. Content search weighting summary

Rank	Evaluation Consideration	Relative Weight	Normalized Weight
1	Cost	1	0.172
.1	Dis	1	0.172
1	Env	1	0.172
1	Int	2	0.172
2	AR	1	0.086
2	DSS	1.25	0.086
3	Mat	1	0.069
3	Org		0.069

Table 3. Content search rating summary

Evaluation Consideration	SDVF Fitness – MaSE	SDVF Fitness – Booch
Cost	0.937	0.591
Dis	0.750	0.500
Env	0.833	0.833
Int	0.500	0.833
AR	0.417	0.250
DSS	0.750	0.625
Mat	0.333	1.000
Org	0.679	0.714

After rating each set of questions, the decision-maker has the last information needed to *Calculate the Multiobjective Fitness Values*. Using Equation 1, the weights and ratings are combined to form a single fitness value for each alternative. In the case of the evaluation considerations that were determined to be irrelevant, the term can be dropped or a zero can be entered. An example of the calculation is shown below for the MaSE alternative.

$$
\begin{aligned}
\mathbf{V_{MaSE}(X)} = {} & w_{cost} V_{cost}(x_{cost}) + w_{org} V_{org}(x_{org}) + w_{mat} V_{mat}(x_{mat}) + w_{dis} V_{dis}(x_{dis}) \\
& + w_{env} V_{env}(x_{env}) + w_{ar} V_{ar}(x_{ar}) + w_{dss} V_{dss}(x_{dss}) + w_{int} V_{int}(x_{int}) \\
= {} & 0.172 \; vcost(1690) + 0.069 \; vorg(19) + 0.069 \; vmat(4) + 0.172 \; vdis(9) \\
& + 0.172 \; venv(10) + 0.086 \; var(5) + 0.086 \; vdss(6) + 0.172 \; vint(6) \\
= {} & 0.161 + 0.047 + 0.023 + 0.129 + 0.143 + 0.036 + 0.065 + 0.086 \\
= {} & \mathbf{0.689}
\end{aligned}
$$

The summary of multiobjective fitness values (MFV) is shown below in Table 4.

Table 4. Content search MFV summary

Case Study	MaSE MFV	Booch MFV
Content Search System	0.689	0.668

With the multiobjective fitness values for each alternative, the decision-maker has a quantified value to base the decision. For this example, the decision analysis tool recommends MaSE over Booch. In cases where the results are close, there are a number of techniques for evaluating the sensitivity of the decision based on the weights assigned in step 1.

4.3   Sensitivity Analysis

The two factors that determine the value of the multiobjective are the weights assigned to each evaluation consideration and the score the alternatives receive for each evaluation consideration. Though the ratings of each of the focus points are subjective, each rating is based on the assessor's experience and we assume it is accurate. However, because the weights are defined strictly on a perceived importance of one evaluation consideration over another, we are wary of their accuracy and subject them to sensitivity analysis. To give the assessor a feeling for the definitiveness of the decision, we can perform sensitivity analyses on the weightings of each evaluation consideration. We focus this analysis on the areas where a slight change in an evaluation consideration's weight could significantly change the overall fitness score.

Using the Data Analyzer tool that we developed to work with the output of the decision analysis tool, a full sensitivity analysis can be performed on the weights of all of evaluation considerations. The analysis focuses on the most sensitive of the considerations with regard to the original normalized weight by evaluating the fitness of each methodology over a range of weights for a particular methodology. For our case study, we calculated the entire range of possible weight, from 0 to 1. To ensure that the total normalized weight remains 1, the other considerations (those not currently being analyzed) are adjusted to be proportional to the total weight minus the weight of the consideration being analyzed. We consider the final decision *sensitive* if a small change to the weight – a change of 5% to 7% [9] – produces a change in the final decision. We consider a recommendation is *definitive* when the percentage of sensitive considerations is less than 33% [9].

Detecting sensitivity relies on the identification of critical points. A *critical point* is where the weight for the particular consideration changes the decision analysis tool's preference. The sensitivity analysis chart for *Methodology Maturity* of our case study is shown in Fig. 3. The analysis chart is annotated to highlight the critical points. For example, this figure has three critical points. The first is when the weight for *Methodology Maturity* is 0.098. When the weight is within the range 0 to 0.098, the MaSE methodology has the highest multiobjective fitness value. The second critical point, at 0.382, is the weight that the Yourdin methodology rates begins to rate higher than MaSE, however, it is still less than the Booch methodology. The third critical point, 1.000, is where the Booch and Yourdin methodologies intersect. However, by setting the weight of *Methodology Maturity* to 1.000, it is the only factor being taken into account.

The critical points and original weights for our case study are shown in Table 5. For the considerations where there is no critical point, "-" is entered as the critical point. Additionally, the amount of the change in weight needed to alter the final decision is noted with changes less than and equal to 7% highlighted in bold font.

Our case study was sensitive to three criteria out of six making the answer produced non-definitive. While our decision analysis recommended MaSE, our the sensitivity analysis indicates that if the user's weighting preferences were slightly different, the Booch methodology could easily win. In all likelihood, either methodology would satisfy the user's needs.

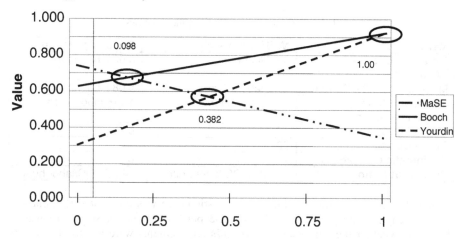

Fig. 3. Methodology maturity sensitivity analysis chart

Table 5. Case study weights and critical point summary

Evaluation Consideration	MaSE – Booch Critical Point	MaSE – Yourdin Critical Point	Booch – Yourdin Critical Point	Original Weight	Change (+/-)
Cost	0.117	-	-	0.172	**0.056**
Org	0.419	1.000	-	0.069	0.350
Dis	0.094	-	-	0.172	0.078
Env	1.000	-	-	0.172	0.828
AR	-	-	-	0.086	-
DSS	-	-	-	0.086	-
Int	0.223	1.000	-	0.172	**0.051**
Mat	0.098	0.382	1.000	0.069	**0.029**

4.4   Validation of Decisions

The decision analysis tool was demonstrated on a number of example software requirements in [12]. The challenge with validating the decision the tool returns is that the decision is being made based on subjective criteria. As an example, the software requirement for the content search was developed via the two rated methodologies—MaSE and Booch.

During the development process, a set of metrics was collected. The metrics collected focused on the productivity of the developer. They included labor hours spent developing the analysis and design models and the implementation, the size of the programs measured in lines of code and number of components, and the complexity of the developed code. The time spent analyzing and designing the systems were similar, but more time was spent on the object-oriented implementation.

The size of the agent-oriented code was roughly twice as large as the object-oriented code. The data collected is shown in Table 6.

Table 6. Content search development metrics

Metric	MaSE Approach	Booch Approach
Modeling Effort – Analysis	4.83 labor hours	4.53 labor hours
Modeling Effort – Design	2.17 labor hours	4.08 labor hours
Modeling Effort – Implementation	8.17 labor hours	11.75 labor hours
Size – SLOC	1252	638
Size – Classes	20	11
Cyclomatic Complexity	74	6
Size/Effort Ratio	153.2 SLOC/labor hour	54.3 SLOC/labor hour

In addition to collecting the metrics, a questionnaire was distributed to a class of software engineering graduate students. The purpose of the questionnaire was to determine whether the details of the system's requirements were identifiable within the analysis and design models of the respective methodologies. The students reviewing the agent-oriented analysis and design models scored higher than those reviewing the object-oriented did. This corresponds with the decision analysis tool's determination that the agent-oriented methodology was more appropriate the requirement [12].

The first set of questions the respondents answered was to their familiarity with methodologies they were evaluating. Eight of the nine students reviewing the Booch models indicated that they were familiar with the methodology, and five of those indicated that they had developed systems using the methodology in the past. Only six of ten students indicated that they were familiar with the MaSE methodology, and of those, only five students had actually used the methodology for system development. These results were expected since MaSE is a recently defined agent-oriented methodology while the Booch methodology is much more mature. Asked to identify other methodologies with which they are familiar, the students indicated object-oriented techniques, functional decomposition techniques, and ad hoc methods for developing software.

The next question was a general question about the respondents' confidence that they understood the models. Each was asked to rate his confidence on a scale of zero to four, with four indicating the greatest confidence in understanding the system. On the average, the understanding rating for the students evaluating the MaSE methodology was 3.2. The rating was 3.125 for the students evaluating the Booch methodology. Seven of the eight students reviewing the Booch methodology were able to identify the correct statement of description for the system. Only two of the ten students reviewing the MaSE methodology were able to select the correct statement; the other eight students selected the "nearly" correct answer.

The next set of questions looked at a number of details in the models, including the identification of legacy systems, reusable components, the network environment, and interface issues. The students reviewing the Booch methodology were divided equally with regard to identifying a legacy system. Because there was not a legacy system incorporated in this system and the responses as to what the legacy system could possibly be, the naming convention was likely the reason for the misidentification. Only one student misidentified the legacy system in the set of MaSE models.

Determining the network environment was the intention of several questions. Identifying the configuration of the network the system was being designed for is important information that needs to be communicated to the developers. These questions measured the respondents' ability to discover this environment information. The group evaluating the MaSE example was able to more completely identify the hardware and software system components in the models. With regard to the user interface, both groups were able to identify the input and output of the systems as well as the options.

Based on the scoring included next to each question on the questionnaire in [12], the average scores are 25.5 for the MaSE group and 25.4 for the Booch group. Furthermore, by considering the results for the students who were familiar and experienced with the respective methodology, the average score for the MaSE group was 27.2 and for the Booch group was 25.1.

The student responses pointed out positives and negatives associated with each approach. However, the results of this experiment are consistent with the results produced by our decision analysis tool.

5   Conclusions

The reasons for software engineering methodologies are clear: develop a high quality software product at the least cost. When faced with the challenge of creating one of these high quality/low cost products, it is necessary to use the methodology that best fits the problem. The challenge is to discover the answer to the question, "how do you decide what the best method is?"

The challenge becomes even greater as methodologies are developed that specifically address new technologies, such as the development of multiagent systems. Agent-oriented software engineering provides a different way of looking at the same problem by raising the level of abstraction. The solution for this is to be able to classify different software engineering methodologies quantitatively based on the software requirement at hand.

The challenge in this is developing a set of criteria that represents the problem space. To generalize this problem space, we developed a set of criteria from current software engineering literature. To ensure that others agree with our criteria, we invited various members of the software engineering community to participate in a survey. Based on the results of this survey, we adjusted the criteria to include additional factors that we missed as well as to remove criteria the community did not find important.

The method provides the user with the ability to determine the best methodology for a particular problem. There is still an outstanding question of when to use multiagent systems. The challenge with this is that there does not exist a large body of evidence to support the hypotheses that multiagent systems are superior to traditional systems. Because there is currently so much research focused on developing new methodologies, more multiagent systems will inevitably be created, which, in turn, will create a larger body of data to compare with traditional systems.

Acknowledgements. This work was performed while both authors were at the Air Force Institute of Technology and was supported by the Air Force Office of Scientific Research. The views expressed in this article are those of the authors and do not reflect the official policy or position of the United States Air Force, Department of Defense, or the US Government.

References

[1]   Booch, G.: Object-Oriented Analysis and Design with Applications. The Benjamin/Cummings Publishing Company, Redwood City, CA (1994)

[2]   Brauer, W., Nickles, M., Robatsos, M., Weiss, G., Lorentzen, K.: Expectation-Oriented Analysis and Design. In this volume (2001)

[3]   Bresciani, P., Perini, A., Giorgini, P., Giunchiglia, F., Mylopoulos, J.: Modeling Early Requirements in Tropos; a Transformation Based Approach. In this volume (2001)

[4]   Caire, G., Garigo, F. Gomez, J., Pavon, J., Leal, F., Chainho, P., Kearney, P., Stark, J., Evans, R., Massonet, P.: Agent Oriented Analysis Using MESSAGE/UML. In this volume (2001)

[5]   DeLoach, S. A., Wood, M., Sparkman, C.: Multiagent Systems Engineering. To appear in the Intl. J. on Software Engineering and Knowledge Engineering (2001)

[6]   Firth, R., et al.: A Classification Scheme for Software Development Methods. Software Engineering Institute Technical Report 87-TR-41. Software Engineering Institute, Carnegie-Mellon University, Pittsburgh, PA (1987)

[7]   Iglesias, C.A., Garijo, M., Gonzalez, J.C.: A Survey of Agent-Oriented Methodologies in Intelligent Agents V – Proceedings of the Fifth International Workshop on Agent Theories, Architectures, and Languages (ATAL-98), Lecture Notes in Artificial Intelligence, Vol. 1555. Springer-Verlag, Berlin Heidelberg New York (1998)

[8]   Jennings, N.R., and Wooldridge, M.J.: Agent-Oriented Software Engineering. To appear in Bradshaw, J. (ed.): Handbook of Agent Technology. AAI/MIT Press (2001)

[9]   Kirkwood, C. W.: Strategic Decision Making: Multiobjective Decision Analysis with Spreadsheets. Wadsworth Publishing, Belmont, California (1997)

[10] Lesser, V.R.: Cooperative Multiagent Systems: A Personal View of the State of the Art. IEEE Trans. on Knowledge and Data Engineering. **11** (1) (1999) 133-142

[11] MESSAGE: Methodology for Engineering Systems of Software Agents – Initial Methodology. EURESCOM Participants in Project P907-GI (2000)

[12] O'Malley, S.A.: Selecting a Software Engineering Methodology Using Multiobjective Decision Analysis, AFIT/GCS/ENG/01M-08. School of Engineering and Management, Air Force Institute of Technology (AU), Wright-Patterson AFB OH (2001)

[13] O'Malley, S.A., Self A., and DeLoach, S.A.: Comparing Performance of Static versus Mobile Multiagent Systems. Proceedings of the National Aerospace and Electronics Conference. IEEE (2000) 282-289

[14] Omicini, A.: SODA: Societies and Infrastructures in the Analysis and Design of Agent-Based Systems. In Ciancarini, P., Wooldridge, M. (eds.): Agent-Oriented Software Engineering: First International Workshop, AOSE 2000. Lecture Notes in Artificial Intelligence, Vol. 1957. Springer-Verlag, Berlin Heidelberg (2001) 185-194

[15] Rana, O.: A Modelling Approach for Agent Based Systems Design. In Ciancarini, P., Wooldridge, M. (eds.): Agent-Oriented Software Engineering: First International Workshop, AOSE 2000. Lecture Notes in Artificial Intelligence, Vol. 1957. Springer-Verlag, Berlin Heidelberg (2001) 195-206

[16] Shen, W. and Norrie, D.: Agent-Based Systems for Intelligent Manufacturing: A State-of-the-Art Survey. Intl. J. Knowledge and Information Systems. 1 (2) (1999) 129-156

[17] Wood, B., Pethia, R., Gold, L.R., and Firth, R.: A Guide to the Assessment of Software Development Methods. Software Engineering Institute Technical Report 88-TR-8. Software Engineering Institute, Carnegie-Mellon University, Pittsburgh, PA (1988)

[18] Wooldridge, M.J.: Intelligent Agents. In Gerhard Weiss (ed.): Multiagent Systems: A Modern Approach to Distributed Artificial Intelligence. MIT Press, Cambridge, Massachusetts (1999)

[19] Zhu, H.: A Formal Specification Language for MAS Engineering. In this volume (2002)

Agent-Oriented Modelling: Software versus the World

Eric Yu

Faculty of Information Studies
University of Toronto, Toronto, Canada M5S 3G6
yu@fis.utoronto.ca

Abstract. Agent orientation is currently pursued primarily as a software paradigm. Software with characteristics such as autonomy, sociality, reactivity and pro-activity, and communicative and cooperative abilities are expected to offer greater functionality and higher quality, in comparison to earlier paradigms such as object orientation. Agent models and languages are thus intended as abstractions of computational behaviour, eventually to be realized in software programs. However, for the successful application of any software technology, the software system must be understood and analyzed in the context of its environment in the world. This paper argues for a notion of agent suitable for modelling the strategic relationships among agents in the world, so that users and stakeholders can reason about the implications of alternate technology solutions and social structures, thus to better decide on solutions that address their strategic interests and needs. The discussion draws on recent work in requirements engineering and agent-oriented methodologies. A small example from telemedicine is used to illustrate.

1 Introduction

Agent orientation is emerging as a powerful new paradigm for computing. It offers a higher-level abstraction than the earlier paradigm of object orientation. Software agents have autonomy and are social; they communicate, coordinate, and cooperate with each other to achieve goals [3, 26, 50]. As agent software technology is maturing and entering into the mainstream, methods and techniques are urgently needed to guide system development in a production setting. Agent-oriented software engineering has thus become one of the most active areas in agents research (see, e.g., [9, 48]). For each application system, one needs to address the full range of software engineering issues – requirements, design, construction, validation and verification, deployment, maintenance, evolution, legacy, reuse, etc. – over its entire product life cycle.

Requirements engineering is an especially demanding, yet critical, task for a new technology such as agent-based software technology. Some adopters will have high expectations of the new capabilities, while others may be wary of potential pitfalls. Yet, most users will be unfamiliar with the new technology and unclear about its implications and consequences. Consider the healthcare domain. The potentials for applying agent technology, along with other kinds of information technology, are far-reaching. One can easily envisage software agents enhancing the information and communication infrastructure by offering better semantic interoperability, local autonomy, dynamic management of resources, flexible and robust exception handling, etc. Yet, it is by no means straightforward to go from idealized visions to viable systems in actual contexts. In real-life application settings, there are many competing

M.J. Wooldridge, G. Weiß, and P. Ciancarini (Eds.): AOSE 2001, LNCS 2222, pp. 206-225, 2002.

requirements, and different interests and concerns from many stakeholders. As with any software technology, each stakeholder may be asking:

- What do I want the software to do for me? What can it do for me? Would I be better off to do the job myself, or to delegate to another human, or to another (type of) system?
- Can the software be trusted? Is it reliable? Will I have privacy?
- How do I know it will work? What if some function fails – what aspects of my work will be jeopardized? How do I mitigate those risks?
- What knowledge and information does it depend on? Where do they come from? How do I know they will be accurate and up-to-date, and effective? Will my skills and expertise continue to be valued?
- Will my job be easier? tougher? Will my position be threatened? How will my relationships with other people (and systems) change?

With agent technology, these issues and questions are accentuated by its greater reliance on codified knowledge, by its supposed flexibility and adaptivity, and by its autonomy (and thus possibly reduced perspicuity). Given their "intelligence" capabilities, agent systems can be expected to do more decision-making and problem solving. How does one decide what responsibilities to turn over to agent systems? Agent technology (including multi-agent systems) opens up many more opportunities and choices. At the same time, the task of exploring and analyzing the space of possibilities and their consequences has become much more complex.

The Requirements Engineering (RE) area in Software Engineering has been developing techniques for dealing with these issues. It has been recognized that poor requirements had led to many system failures and discontinued projects (see, e.g., [43]). Requirements engineering focuses on clarifying and defining the relationship between intended systems and the world. The introduction of a new system (or modification of an existing one) amounts to a redistribution of tasks and responsibilities among agents in the world – humans, hardware, software, organizational units, etc. Requirements engineering is therefore more than the specification of behaviour, because the ultimate criteria for system success is that stakeholders' goals are achieved and their concerns addressed.

Recent work in requirements engineering has thus adopted an agent-oriented perspective. The notion of agent in Requirements Engineering, however, is about agents in the world, most of which the software developer has no control over. The purpose of introducing an agent abstraction (or any other abstraction) for requirements modelling is to support elicitation, exploration, and analysis of the systems-in-the-world, possible alternatives in how they relate to each other, and the pros and cons of the alternatives. The requirements engineer needs to help users and stakeholders articulate their needs and concerns, explore alternatives, and understand implications. Thus, while agents-as-software and agents-in-the-world may share conceptual features, their respective abstractions are introduced for different reasons and serve different purposes. Characteristics such as intentionality, autonomy, and sociality have different connotations and consequences when treated as attributes of software than as attributes of agents in the world. In proposing or choosing an agent abstraction, different criteria and tradeoffs need to be considered.

In this paper, we examine the notion of agent as applied to the modelling of agents-in-the-world. In Section 3, we offer an outline of the *i** framework as an example of an agent-oriented modelling framework.   Section 4 reviews the main contrasts between the notion of strategic agent-in-the-world, versus that of agent-as-software. In section 5, we discuss recent related work in requirements engineering and agent-oriented methodologies. In Section 6, we suggest a broader conception of AOSE not exclusive to agent-oriented software, and argue that the strategic view of agents-in-the-world should guide the entire software engineering process.

2   From Modelling Software to Modelling the World

Most agent models and languages are intended as abstractions of computational behaviour, eventually to be realized as software programs.   Such models are needed for specifying and for constructing the software.   Different kinds of models are needed for different stages and aspects of software engineering.   As agent technology is maturing, attention is turning to the development of a full set of complementary models, notations, and methods to cover the entire software lifecycle [9, 48].

In Requirements Engineering, the need to model the world has long been recognized, as requirements are about defining the relationship between a software system and its environment. The major activities in requirements engineering include domain analysis, elicitation, negotiation & agreement, specification, communication, documentation, and evolution [47, 34]. Modelling and analysis techniques have been devised to assist in these tasks.

The Structured Analysis techniques first popularized the use of systematic approaches for expressing and analyzing requirements.   The Structured Analysis and Design Technique (SADT) focused on the modelling of activities and data (inputs, outputs, and control flows among activities), and their hierarchical decomposition [40].   Dataflow diagrams include information stores, as well as external sources and sinks, thus demarcating a system's interfaces with its environment [12].   Complex descriptions were reduced into structured sets of diagrams based on a small number of ontological concepts, thus allowing for some basic analysis. For example, one could check completeness and consistency by matching input and output flows.   Later on, these tasks were supported by CASE tools, although support is limited by the degree of formality in the models. These techniques continue to be widely used.

As the size of the models grew, and the need for reuse became recognized, structuring mechanisms were introduced to manage the knowledge in the models and to deal with complexity.   For example, RML [21] provided for classification, generalization, aggregation, and time. To strengthen analysis, various approaches to formalization   were   introduced,   accompanied   by   appropriate   ontological enhancements.   For example, RML offered assertions in addition to activities and entities, and provided semantics based on translation to first-order logic. Temporal, dynamic, deontic and other logics have also been introduced for requirements modelling [34].   Many of these features subsequently found their way into object-oriented modelling (e.g., UML [41]), which packages static and dynamic ontologies together into one behavioural unit. However, the analysis done with these models continue to be about the behaviour and interactions. There are no intentional concepts or considerations of strategic alternatives.

The Composite Systems Design approach [16, 15] first identified the need to view systems and their embedding environments in terms of agents that have choice. An agent's decisions and actions can place limits on other agent's freedom of action. In the KAOS framework [10], global goals are reduced through and/or refinement until they can be assigned as responsibilities to agents. These become requirements for systems to be built, or assumptions about agents existing in the environment. Goal modelling has been incorporated into a number of RE frameworks [57]. They provide incremental elicitation of requirements (e.g., [38]). They support the repeated use of "why, how, and how else" questions in the constructions of means-ends hierarchies, to understand motivations, intents, and rationales [52]. They reveal conflicts and help identify potential resolutions [39]. Quality goals constrain choices in a design space and can be used to guide the design process [8].

The introduction of goals into the ontology of requirements models represented a significant shift. Previously, the world to be modelled consisted of entities and activities and their variants. The newer ontologies attributed goals to agents in the world. In other words, to do requirements engineering, it is not enough to attend to the static and dynamic aspects, one also need to acknowledge intentionality in the world.

While recent research in requirements has given considerable attention to goals, the concept of agent has not been developed to the same extent. In particular, few RE frameworks have elaborated on or exploited concepts of agent autonomy, sociality, etc. The logical next step for RE is to go from goal-oriented requirements engineering to full-fledged agent-oriented requirements engineering, to acknowledge the social as well as the intentional [54, 33]. The need for this step is apparent as one considers the changing nature of systems and their environments. In the past, systems and their environments were much more stable and well delineated. Systems tended to be developed in isolation in relation to other systems. So the simplifying assumptions were that global goals could be identified, and that differences could be resolved to achieve agreement across the system.

Today, most systems are extensively networked and distributed, operating under multiple jurisdictions each with their own mandates and prerogatives. Stakeholders want local autonomy but cooperate on specific ventures. They depend on each other, and on each other's systems in multiply-connected ways. They have limited knowledge about each other, and have limited influence and control over each other. The traditional mechanistic worldview needs to give way to a more sophisticated social worldview [55].

In the next section, we outline a modelling framework in which agents play a central ontological role. The framework begins to address the more complex relationships and issues that arise in Requirements Engineering. Agents-in-the-world are taken to be intentional and semi-autonomous. They associate with each other in complex social relationships. Their identities and boundaries are contingent. They reflect upon their relationships in the world and strategize about alternate relationships in order to further their interests.

It must be recognized that the framework represents only one possible approach. In adopting a richer ontology, one gains in expressiveness and analytical power. On the other hand, it places greater demands on elicitation and validation. So there are significant trade-offs that need to be considered in the context of an overall development methodology.

3   A Framework for Modelling Agents-in-the-World

Consider a home care scenario in which a patient receives remote monitoring and telemedicine services from one or more healthcare service providers – hospitals, physicians, nurses, pharmacies, laboratories, clinics, emergency centres, consultants, etc., allied to varying degrees but sometimes also in competition.[1] Such arrangements can potentially improve quality of care and reduce overall healthcare costs, while allowing patients to lead more normal lives at home. Agent technology can be used to achieve greater functionality, robustness, and flexibility in such systems, for example, by incorporating knowledge-based decision support and knowledge discovery, by offering context-aware initiatives and failure recovery, by enabling dynamic resource discovery, negotiation, and mediation, or by facilitating collaboration among individuals and groups through multimedia and logistics support, and cooperation among disparate systems. Patients get more customized care while healthcare professionals are relieved of the more mundane aspects of their tasks.

But how does one decide what functionalities the systems should have? Who should these systems be accountable to? How should responsibilities be divided among them, and why? Do the stakeholders have common goals? Can the systems function despite ongoing differences and competing interests? Clearly these questions would results in different answers for each setting, depending on the context. In each setting, there could be numerous options to consider. Some may appear workable initially, but may turn out to be, upon further analysis, technical infeasible, or unacceptable to certain stakeholders. During requirements engineering, it is important for all stakeholders, customers, users, system developers, and analysts to understand each other's interests and concerns, to jointly explore options, and to appreciate the implications of alternative decisions about the systems to be constructed.

In the past, notations and methods in software development have focused more on the specification of systems after these decisions have been made. Few of the commonly used notations, e.g., UML, provide explicit support for expressing, analyzing, and supporting decisions about these issues.

Today, systems and their surrounding context in the world are constantly changing. Aside from rapid technological innovations, systems need to respond to frequent changes in organizational structures, business models, market dynamics, legal and regulatory structures, public sentiments and cultural shifts. We need systematic frameworks – models, methods, and tools – to support the discovery of requirements, analysis of their implications, and the exploration of alternatives.

The *i** framework [53, 52] is used to model and analyze relationships among strategic actors in a social network, such as human organizations and other forms of social structures. Actors are semi-autonomous units whose behaviours are not fully

---

[1] This home care setting is loosely based on [23].

controllable or predictable, but are regulated by social relationships. Most crucially, actors depend on each other for goals to be achieved, tasks to be performed, and resources to be furnished. By depending on someone else, an actor may achieve goals that would otherwise be unachievable. However, a dependency may bring along vulnerabilities since it can fail despite social conventions such as commitments. The explicit representation of goals allows the exploration of alternatives through means-ends reasoning. A concept of softgoal based on the notion of satisficing is used to provide a flexible interactive style of reasoning.

Note that in the context of modelling the world, unlike the modelling of software agents for the purpose of construction, qualities such as autonomy and sociality are being externally ascribed to some elements in the world for the purpose of description and analysis. Some selected elements depicted in the models may end up being implemented as software agents, others may materialize as more conventional software, while many of them are, and will remain mostly human wetware. The implementational construction of the actors is irrelevant to this level of modelling of the world. These considerations will be further discussed in Section 4.

The *i** modelling framework consists of two types of models – the Strategic Dependency (SD) model and the Strategic Rationale (SR) model.

3.1   Modelling Intentional Relationships among Strategic Actors – The Strategic Dependency Model

The Strategic Dependency (SD) model is a graph, where each node represents an actor, and each link between two actors indicates that one actor depends on the other for something in order that the former may attain some goal. We call the depending actor the depender, and the actor who is depended upon the dependee. The object around which the dependency relationship centres is called the dependum. An actor is an active entity that carries out actions to achieve goals by exercising its knowhow. In the SD model, the internal goals, knowhow, and resources of an actor are not explicitly modelled. The focus is on external relationships among actors.

Figure 1 shows a Strategic Dependency model of a (much simplified) telemedicine setting. A Patient depends on a Healthcare Provider to have Sickness Treated. The latter in turn depends on the patient to Follow a Treatment Plan. As the patient would like to integrate the treatment into other activities, she wants the treatment plan to be Flexible. The healthcare provider partly addresses this by monitoring vital signs remotely, with the help of equipment on the patient site (Monitoring Agent), and a host system (Monitoring System) that oversees a number of patients.

The SD model expresses what actors want from each other, thus identifying a network of dependencies. The intentional dependencies, in terms of wants and abilities to meet those wants, are expressed at a high level, so that details about information and control flows and protocols are deferred. Even at this high level, many issues are already apparent. Healthcare Provider enables Patient to achieve the Sickness Treated goal that the latter may not be able to achieve on her own. In taking advantage of this opportunity, the depender becomes vulnerable to the dependency. The model assists them in deciding whether their dependencies are acceptable, or that they should seek alternate arrangements.

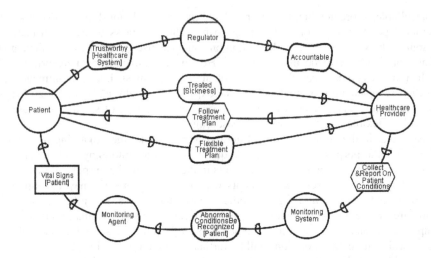

Fig. 1. A Strategic Dependency model

Four types of dependencies are distinguished for indicating the nature of the freedom and control in the relationship between two actors regarding a dependum. In a *goal dependency*, the depender depends on the dependee to bring about a certain state of affairs in the world. The dependum is expressed as an assertional statement. The dependee is free to, and is expected to, make whatever decisions are necessary to achieve the goal (the dependum). The depender does not care how the dependee goes about achieving the goal. For example, Patient depends on Healthcare Provider to have Sickness Be Treated. It is up to the Provider to choose how to treat the sickness, as long as the goal is achieved.

In a *task dependency*, the depender depends on the dependee to carry out an activity. The dependum names a task which specifies how the task is to be performed, but not why. The depender has already made decisions about how the task is to be performed. Physician depends on Patient to Follow Treatment Plan, described in terms of activities and sub-activities, possibly with constraints among them, such as temporal precedence. Note that a task description in *i** is not meant to be a complete specification of the steps required to execute the task. It is a constraint imposed by the depender on the dependee. The dependee still has freedom of action within those constraints.

In a *resource dependency*, the depender depends on the dependee for the availability of an entity (physical or informational). By establishing this dependency, the depender gains the ability to use this entity as a resource. A resource is the finished product of some deliberation-action process. In a resource dependency, it is assumed that there are no open issues to be addressed or decisions to be made. For example, Vital Signs from the patient is treated as a resource, as it is not considered problematic to obtain.

In a *softgoal dependency*, a depender depends on the dependee to perform some task that meets a softgoal. A softgoal is similar to a goal except that the criteria of success are not sharply defined a priori. The meaning of the softgoal is elaborated in terms of the methods that are chosen in the course of pursuing the goal. The depender decides what constitutes satisfactory attainment ("satisficing" [42]) of the goal, but does so with the benefit of the dependee's knowhow. Whether a treatment plan is considered to be sufficiently Flexible is judged by the Patient, with the Healthcare Provider offering alternate methods for achieving flexibility. Similary, Trustworthiness of the healthcare system, and Accountability of the healthcare provider are treated as softgoals, since there are no clear-cut criteria for their satisfaction.

The model also provides for three degrees of strength of dependency: open (uncommitted), committed, and critical. These apply independently on each side of a dependency.

Actors can assess the desirability of alternate configurations of relationships with other actors according to what they consider to be significant to them. The viability of a dependency can be analyzed in terms of enforceability (Does the other actor depend in return on me for something, directly or indirectly?), assurance (Are there other dependencies on that actor that would reinforce my confidence in the success of that dependency?), and insurance (Do I have back-ups or second sources in case of failure?). Strategic dependencies can be analyzed in terms of loop and node patterns in the graph.

The generic concept of strategic *actor* outlined above can be further differentiated into the concepts of role, position, and agent [56]. A *role* is an abstract collection of coherent abilities and expectations. A *position* is a collection of roles that are typically occupied by one agent. An *agent* is an actor that has concrete manifestations such as human, hardware, or software, or combinations thereof. Agents, roles, and positions may also be composed into aggregate actors.

3.2   Modelling the Reasoning Behind Strategic Relationships – The Strategic Rationale Model

Whereas the Strategic Dependency model focuses on relationships between actors, the Strategic Rationale (SR) model provides support for modelling the reasoning of each actor about its intentional relationships. The SR model is a graph whose nodes are goals, tasks, resources, and softgoals. These may be connected by means-ends links or task-decomposition links. A goal may be associated, through means-ends links, with multiple, alternative ways for achieving it, usually represented as tasks. The means-ends links for softgoals, however, require more differentiation because there can be various types of contributions leading to a judgement of whether the softgoal is sufficiently met ("satisficing"). These include Make, Break, Help, Hurt, Positive, Negative, And, Or, Unknown, and Equal [8]. Task-decomposition links provide hierarchical decomposition of tasks into subtasks, subgoals, resources, and softgoals that make up the task.

Figure 2 is an SR model showing some of the reasoning behind one possible telemedicine arrangement. It has been argued that current healthcare systems are too provider-centred, in that patients have little control over the information collected about them, and cannot participate effectively in their own care.[2]

---

[2] The patient-centred scenarios draw on those of [45] and [30].

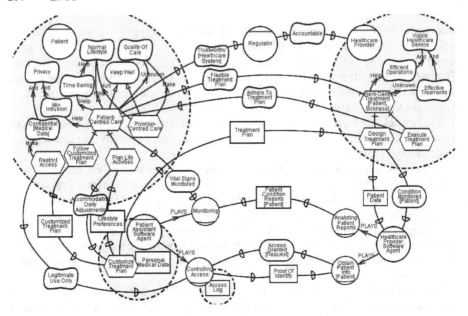

Fig. 2. A Strategic Rationale model showing some reasoning behind patient-centred care

One way to achieve patient-centred care is to have the full medical records and history of the patient controlled by the patient. A software agent acting in the interest of the patient would grant access to healthcare providers for legitimate use. This arrangement is in contrast to the current practice in which each provider generates and keeps their own records, resulting in fragmented, partial views, delays and duplication (e.g., the same lab tests repeated at multiple sites). The integrated personal medical data would also allow the intelligent assistant to customize treatment plans to suit the specific needs and the lifestyle of the patient. The healthcare provider monitors the progress of the patient through her own software agent assistants.

The SR model for the Patient in Figure 2 shows that the patient has the goal of Keeping Well, but is also concerned about Privacy, Quality Of Care, and maintaining a Normal Lifestyle. The SR modelling constructs allow the systematic refinement of these goals to explore ways for achieving them. According to the model, Privacy is achieved if the medical data is kept Confidential, and if Intrusion Is Minimized (And). Confidentiality is sufficiently addressed (Make) if Access Is Restricted. The goal of Keeping Well can be accomplished with Patient-Centred Care or with Provider-Centred Care (means-ends links). Patient-Centred Care involves the subtasks of Follow Customized Treatment Plan and Plan Life Activities. These subtasks have dependencies with the Patient Assistant Software Agent.

The example model is greatly simplified but provides some hints on the types of reasoning to be supported. These include the raising of issues, the identification and exploration of alternatives, recognition of correlated issues (good and bad side-effects), and the settling of issues. For example, while Patient-Centred Care contributes positively to Privacy and Normal Lifestyle, its contribution to Quality Of Care is Unknown. This suggests further elaboration and refinement of the Quality Of Care softgoal so that the nature of the contributions can be better assessed. Elaboration of this and other goals may help discover other kinds of provider-centred and patient-centred care, each of which may have different contributions to the various goals.

We have presented *i** in terms of a graphical representation. *i** modelling is implemented on top of the Telos conceptual modelling language [31], which offers knowledge structuring mechanisms (classification, generalization, aggregation, attribution, time). Generic knowledge codified in terms of methods and rules provide semi-automatic support from a knowledge base. A prototype tool has been developed to support *i** modelling. Further analysis support is being developed in the Tropos project [32].

4   Agents-in-the-World versus Agents-as-Software

Having reviewed *i** as an example framework for modelling agents-in-the-world, we now consider some of the key issues in designing such frameworks. These issues help clarify the distinctions between modelling agents in the world versus modelling agents as software entities. We consider the issues of autonomy, intentionality, sociality, identity and boundaries, strategic reflection, and rational self-interest. While most of these issues have their counterparts in agents-as-software, their significance for modelling agents-in-the-world are quite different.

4.1   Autonomy

Traditional requirements analysis techniques rely heavily on the modelling of processes or interactions. Through activity diagrams, event sequence charts, etc., one describes or prescribes what would or should happen under various known conditions. Real-life practice, however, often departs from these idealizations [44] and frequently require workarounds [19]. There are many aspects of the world over which one has little control or knowledge, so it is hard to anticipate all contingencies and be able to know in advance what responses are appropriate.

Thus, in introducing autonomy into a model of agents-in-the-world, we are adopting a less simplistic view of the world, so as to take uncertainties into account when judging the viability of proposed alternatives, such as different ways for achieving patient-centred care using software agents. Agents-in-the-world need to be aware of uncertainties around them. At the same time, they themselves are sources of uncertainty in the world.

In devising a modelling scheme that acknowledges agent autonomy, the challenge is to be able to describe or prescribe agent behaviour without precluding openness and uncertainties. In *i**, actors are assumed to be autonomous in the sense that the analyst should not rule out any behaviour. An actor's dependencies and strategic interests provide hints on the actor's behaviour, but do not provide guarantees. Thus, one would be well advised to adopt mechanisms for mitigating risks, based on an analysis of vulnerabilities, e.g., backup systems and procedures in case of failure in the patient monitoring system. The dependency types in *i** are used to differentiate among the types of freedoms that actors have with regard to some specific aspect of the world, as identified by the dependum.

For agents-as-software, autonomy refers to the ability of the software to act independently without direct intervention from humans or other agents. It is a desired property that must be consciously created in the software. It is a property only achievable with recent advances in software and artificial intelligence technology. For agents-in-the-world, autonomy is an inherent property, but it has been ignored in the past for simplicity of modelling. Now we want it back because we want to face up to these more challenging aspects of the world. For software agents, greater autonomy implies more powerful software, which are likely to be more challenging to design and implement. For modelling the world, allowing greater autonomy in the agent model means one would like to analyze the implications of greater uncertainties and variability in the world.

4.2   Intentionality

Conventional requirements analysis (e.g., as supported by UML) assumes complete knowledge and fully specifies behaviour, so there is little need for intentional concepts. To account for uncertainties and openness in the world, however, intentional concepts such as goals and beliefs can be very useful. In modelling agents-in-the-world, we ascribe intentionality to them so as to characterize alternate realities in the world. Some of these alternate realities are desirable, but an agent may not know how to get there, or may not want to fix the path for getting there to allow for flexibility. Intentional concepts thus allow agents to be described without detailing specific actions in terms of processes and steps. Explicit representation of goals allows motivations and rationales to be expressed. They allow "why" questions to be raised and answered. Beliefs provide for the possibility that an agent can be wrong in its assumptions about the world, and mechanisms to support revisions to those assumptions.

For agents-as-software, intentionality is a property that is used to generate the behaviour of the agent. For example, there may be data structures and internal states that represent goals and beliefs in the software. For agents-in-the-world, we do not need to presuppose intentionality in their internal mechanisms. Multi-agent modelling allows different goals, beliefs, abilities, etc., to be attributed to different agents. An agent can be thought of as a locality for intentionality. Instead of having a single global collection of goals, belief, etc., these are allocated to separate agents. The agent concept provides a local scope for reconciling and making tradeoffs among competing intentionality, such as conflicting goals and inconsistent beliefs.

4.3   Sociality

Traditional systems analysis views systems and their environments mechanistically. They produce outputs from inputs, either as pre-defined processes or as reactive responses to control signals or events. Complexity and scalability is primarily dealt with by composition or decomposition, with the behaviour of the whole being determined by the behaviour of the parts together with compositional rules. When systems and their environments have autonomy, these assumptions no longer hold. Active autonomous entities in the world have their own initiatives, and are not necessarily compliant with external demands or desires, such as those from a system designer. Autonomous agents can choose to cooperate, or not, to varying degrees, and on their own terms. A social paradigm is needed to cover the much richer kinds of relationships that exist in such settings.

Social agents have reciprocal dependencies and expectations on each other. They tend to have multi-lateral relationships, rather than one-way relationships. Agent A can expect agent B to deliver on a commitment because B has goals and interests that A can help fulfil or meet. Reciprocity can be indirect, mediated via other agents. In general, social relationships exist as networks and patterns of relationships that involve multi-lateral dependencies. In mechanistic artificial systems, where one designer oversees interaction among parts, it is more common to see master-slave relationships that go one-way.

Social agents typically participate in multiple relationships, with a number of other agents, at the same time or at different times. In mechanistic systems as portrayed in most traditional models, relationships are narrowly focused around intended functions.

Conflicts among many of the relationships that an agent participates in are not easily resolvable. There may be conflicts or potential conflicts arising from the multiple relationships that an agent engages in. In traditional approaches, competing demands need to be reconciled in order for requirements to be defined, then frozen for system development and implementation. In a more fluid and open environment, the demands of various agents may keep changing and may not be fully knowable. Agents may also build new relationships with other agents and dissolve existing ones. The management of conflicts is an ongoing one. Therefore it becomes necessary to maintain an explicit representation of the competing interests and their conflicts.

Agent relationships form an unbounded network. There are no inherent limits on how far the impact of dependencies may propagate in a network of agents. In considering the impact of changes, one may ask: Who else would be affected? Who will benefit, who will be hurt? Who can help me improve my position? These questions may lead to the discovery of agents not previously considered.

Cooperation among agents cannot be taken for granted. The potential for successful cooperation may be assessed through the analysis of agents' goals and beliefs. Techniques are needed to support the analysis of various aspects of cooperation, including synergy and conflict among goals, how to discover shared goals, and how goals may change.

For software agents, sociality refers to properties that must be created in the software to enable them to exhibit richer behavioural patterns. For agents-in-the-world, sociality refers to the acknowledgement of the complex realities in the world. Instead of abstracting them away as in earlier modelling paradigm, we try to device modelling constructs and analysis techniques that encompass them.

4.4   Identity and Boundary

In a social world, identities and boundaries are often contingent and contentious. Many social or organizational problems arise from uncertainties or disputes about boundaries and identities. For example, software agents working on behalf of or in cooperation with healthcare workers need to deal with a complex array of organizational roles, positions, and professions, often with sensitive relationships among them. Requirements analysis needs to be able to deal with these, to arrive at viable systems.

Boundaries and identities change, usually as a result of ongoing social processes such as socialization, negotiation, and power shifts. Technical systems often introduce abrupt changes in boundaries and identities, as they reallocate responsibilities and powers. Agents-in-the-world are concerned about their boundaries, and may attempt to change them to their advantage. Boundaries may be based on concrete physical material criteria, or abstract concepts such as responsibilities. In *i**, dependums serve as actor boundaries at an intentional level. The boundaries are movable as dependums can be brought "inside" an actor or moved "outside" along means-ends hierarchies in the Strategic Rationale model. The *i** constructs of role, position, and agent distinguish among abstract and concrete actors, and provide mappings across them.

In models for agents-as-software, issues of identity and boundary can be much simpler, if all the agents are within the control of a designer. They would be determined by design criteria such as functional specialty, coordination efficiency, robustness, flexibility, etc. However, if the agents in a multi-agent system are designed and controlled by different designers and operators, and are thus autonomous in the social (agents-in-the-world) sense, then the more complex social notions of identity could be applicable.

4.5   Strategic Reflectivity

Traditional requirements models are typically used to express one way – the intended way – in which the system will operate in the world. Even if a space of alternatives was explored in arriving at the requirements, there is little representational or reasoning support for navigating that space. With today's systems undergoing frequent changes, the need to support evolution and to avoid legacy problems is well recognized.

Reasoning about alternative arrangements of technical systems in the world is a reflective process. Agents need to refer to and compare alternate ways of performing tasks, rather than executing the tasks without question. The reflective process is strategic because agents want to determine which changes would better serve their strategic interests. For example, patients want healthcare technologies that improve the quality of care while protecting their privacy. Hospitals may want greater efficiency without increased dependence on high-cost professionals.

During requirements analysis, strategic reflection is carried out by the human stakeholders, assisted by requirements analysts. In software agents, this kind of strategic reflection can potentially be done at run-time by the software. This characteristic requires higher sophistication to be built into the software (see, e.g., [1]) and is not yet a common feature. Strategic reflection is, however, a fairly basic need at the requirements stage.

4.6   Rational Self-Interest

Most languages for modelling and requirements analysis (e.g., UML) do not provide explicit support for rationales. Since their ontologies do not include autonomous agents-in-the-world, the rationales, even if made explicit, would likely be a rationalization of the many contributions that led to the eventual requirements for a new system. In treating systems and environments as a multi-agent world, we try to explicate the preferences and decisions of each stakeholder in terms of rational self-interest. Each agent selects those options that best serve its interests. This assumption provides a convenient idealization for characterizing agents whose behaviour are otherwise unpredictable. Note that rational self-interest does not imply selfishness, as an agent can have altruistic goals.

The modeller attributes rationality and coherence to agents-in-the-world in order to draw inferences about their behaviour. However, the inferences are limited by incomplete and imperfect knowledge. The rationality is bounded and partial. The agent construct can be viewed as a scoping mechanism for delineating the exercising of rationality within a limited local scope.

In contrast, for software agents, rationality is a regime for governing the behaviour of the software according to internal states of goals and beliefs. Again, it is a characteristic that needs to be explicitly built into the construction of a software agent.

4.7   Summary

To summarize, agent concepts are useful both for software construction and for modelling the world. However, abstractions for agents-as-software and agents-in-the-world came about with different motivations, premises, and objectives, and thus can differ in ontology.

For software agents, the objective is to create a new software paradigm that would make software more powerful, more robust, and flexible. The realization of software agent characteristics requires greater sophistication in the implementation technology, which are ideally hidden under the agent abstraction.

In contrast, in devising some concept of agent for modelling the world, we recognize that the world already exists in its full complexity. Earlier modelling paradigms have adopted abstractions that removed too much of that complexity, resulting in ontologies that are too impoverished for dealing with today's problems. The agent abstraction is used to being back some of that complexity and richness to support appropriate kinds of modelling and analysis.

In either case, there is choice in what agent abstraction to adopt. For software agents, we want a concept of agent that fully embodies the behaviour to be generated. We need to consider the feasibility of implementation, and the difficulty of verifying implementation against the specification. For modelling agents-in-the-world, we want rich enough description of the world (expressiveness) to allow us to make the distinctions that we want, leading to analyses that matter in stakeholders' decision making. We do not want more detail than we can use, since there are costs in elicitation and validation, and potential for errors.

5   Related Work

Most of the current work in Agent-Oriented Software Engineering (AOSE) originated from the programming and AI/DAI systems construction perspective. As the technology infrastructure matures, attention is increasingly being paid to software engineering and application methodology issues. The focus therefore continues to have a strong systems construction flavour, with a gradual broadening to encompass contextual activities such as requirements engineering.

The predominant notion of agent in the current AOSE literature is therefore that of agent-as-software. Methodological frameworks have focused mostly on the "analysis and design" stages (e.g., [51, 2, 6, 27]). Requirements are assumed to be given, at least as informal descriptions. The analysis stage constructs a model of the intended behaviour of the software system.

The importance of requirements is beginning to be recognized, with attention being paid to the embedding environment. However, they are typically specified in terms of behavioural interactions, as in conventional requirements approaches. The notion of agent employed is still that of agent-as-software. For example, notions of autonomy, intentionality, etc., are those associated with the software, not with agents-in-the-world outlined in Section 4. Alternatives during requirements analysis, as viewed by strategic agents-in-the-world, are not explicitly addressed.

Social and organizational concepts are applied to software agents, not to agents in the world (e.g., [58, 36, 11, 13, 35]). Selective aspects of sociality are built into the agent software, with the purpose of enhancing the capabilities of the software, as opposed to the richer analysis of the environment for the purpose of defining the right technical system to build.

When reflection is used, it is as a computational mechanism in software agents (e.g., [1]), not used by stakeholders to reflect on strategic implications of alternative arrangements of technical systems in their environment.

In Requirements Engineering, agents have served as a modelling construct without assuming the use of agent software as the implementation technology. The concept of agent has been elaborated to varying degrees. For example, the EKD methodology [5] contains many of the concepts needed for agent-oriented modelling, but does not explicitly deal with issues of agent autonomy and sociality. Agents appear in one of six interconnected submodels: the Goal model, the Concepts model, the Business Rules model, the Business Process model, the Actors and Resources model, and the Technical Components and Requirements model. The KAOS approach [47] (also mentioned in Section 2) offers a detailed formal framework for eliciting and refining goals until they are reduced to operations that can be assigned to agents. The openness and autonomy of agent actions is not considered when generating or evaluating alternatives. Agents interact with each other non-intentionally, so they do not have rich social relationships. Both EKD and KAOS can be said to be more goal-oriented than agent-oriented.

Action-Workflow is a notation and method for modelling cooperative work [29]. The basic unit of modelling is a workflow between a customer and a performer. The customer-performer relationship is characterized in terms of a four-phased loop, representing the stages of proposing, agreeing, performing, and accepting. Each phase involves different types of communication acts which can be analyzed using Speech Acts theory. This framework has a stronger orientation to deal with the social nature of agents, especially their reliance on commitments and the potential for breakdowns. Intentional structures such as goals or means-ends relationships are not explicitly represented, so there is no support for reflection or shifting boundaries of responsibilities.

Many other techniques in Requirements Engineering bear close relations to agent modelling, e.g., managing multiple viewpoints [17], dealing with inconsistencies [20], supporting traceability [25] and negotiation [39], and scenario analysis [24].

While the *i** framework arguably goes farthest in addressing agent modelling issues in the spirit of this paper, many open issues remain, both in theoretical and practical areas. Recent work that have built on or extended *i** include the incorporation of temporal constraints to support simulation and verification [18, 49], development methodologies [14, 46], and multi-perspective modelling [37, 28].

The Tropos project [32, 7, 4] aims to develop a software development methodology that would carry the requirements ontology (based on *i**) as far downstream as possible, to ensure that the resulting software would be requirements-driven. Agent orientation is assumed throughout all the development stages. Formal techniques are being developed to support analysis at various stages.

6   Engineering of Agent-Oriented Software vs. Agent-Oriented Engineering of Software

The predominant interpretation of the phrase "Agent-Oriented Software Engineering" is that of the engineering of software that uses the agent concept as the core computational abstraction. However, it is also possible to conceive of the use of agent concepts to support the software engineering process, without necessarily committing a priori to a software agent technology implementation. For the purpose of distinction, we could refer to the two conceptions of AOSE as EAOS and AOES respectively.

Agent-oriented techniques for requirements engineering, as exemplified by the *i** framework, suggests that agent concepts can be used profitably without prejudging the implementation technology. We have argued that issues of autonomy, intentionality, sociality, etc. are just as relevant in requirements engineering as in software construction, though in somewhat different senses.

A basic tenet in software engineering is to defer commitments on design and implementation decisions as much as possible, so as not to over-constrain those decisions unnecessarily. Conventional models and languages in software engineering – for requirements specification, architectural design, detailed design, programming, configuration, etc. – do not allow for the explicit representation of open decisions, freedoms and constraints, and argumentation about them. While each stage or activity in software engineering requires considerable deliberation and decision-making, the notations can only express and record the results of decision processes. Current notations provide hardly any support for the communication of intentional content among software engineers, e.g., design intents and rationales. Intermediate products in software engineering are passed on from one stage to another only after they are fully reduced to non-intentional representations, e.g., input/output relationships in architectural block diagrams.

Agent abstractions and models offer the expressiveness and flexibility that conventional notations lack. Today's increasingly fast-paced and fluid demands in software engineering suggests that agent abstractions could be useful for supporting software engineering processes in general. This is the premise behind the Tropos project [32, 7, 4]. Agent-based ontologies are used for representing requirements, architectures, and detailed designs. Intentional models involving goals and beliefs provide higher-level descriptions that allow suitable degrees of freedom. The ontologies that are appropriate are those for modelling agents-in-the-world. For the most part, the subject matter in software engineering activities are not (yet) software artefacts, but their precursors. While executable software would eventually emerge, many of the key engineering processes occur at the earlier stages where relationships among earlier design artefacts (e.g., architectural blocks or design modules) are worked out. The appropriate ontology is therefore not a computational ontology for machine execution, but a world ontology in which there are many human decision makers and stakeholders, exploiting opportunities, mitigating vulnerabilities, and choosing among alternatives according to strategic interests. The $i*$ framework is used as the starting point for the Tropos project.

Since software engineering work continues to rely heavily on human social processes, a full development of the AOES vision should include the many human players in a software engineering projects as full-fledged agents (or actors in $i*$ terminology). Human agents, roles, and positions would be interwoven with those representing the emerging artefacts. As the software development process unfolds, new actors and relationships would be created, existing ones evolve, others dissolve. The agents-in-the-world modelling paradigm allows a uniform representation of machine and human processes. This would support, for example, reasoning about whether an activity should be done at run-time or at development time, by human or by machine. These would be indicated as alternate boundaries among actors in $i*$. This conception of AOES is currently being explored [22].

Many software engineering challenges are not only technical, but social and organizational, e.g., reusability, maintainability, evolvability, comprehensibility, outsourcing, componentization, etc. A representation and engineering framework that provides full and equal treatment to technical artefacts as well as to human processes (including knowledge management and human capital considerations) can potentially offer a fuller account of software engineering, as well as more effective solutions.

While the general vision of AOES is independent of software implementation technology, the greatest benefit is obtained when the implementation does employ software agent technology. This would allow certain open decisions to be deferred to run-time to be executed by the agent software. Which ones to defer would be a frequent question that occurs throughout the development process. AOES modelling frameworks and tools should provide support for addressing such questions.

7   Conclusions

Agent orientation can contribute to software engineering in more ways than one. We have outlined a notion of agent from the viewpoint of requirements engineering, which focuses on the relationship between systems and their environments in the world. This notion of agent benefits from the development of the agent-as-software concept, but is distinct from it. We have outlined some major distinctions in terms of key agent properties such as autonomy and sociality. Because of the differences in context and objectives in different stages and aspects of software engineering, it is not surprising that differing agent abstractions have developed. However, as requirements engineering turns to face the new challenges raised by agent software technology, and as software agents acquire greater abilities to reason strategically about themselves and the world, one can expect closer links between conceptions of agents-as-software and agents-in-the-world. These are topics of ongoing research.

Acknowledgements. Financial support from the Natural Sciences and Engineering Research Council of Canada, Communications and Information Technology Ontario, and Mitel Corporation are gratefully acknowledged.

References

1. Barber, K.S., Han D.C., Liu, T.H.: Strategy Selection-based Meta-level Reasoning for of Multi-Agent Problem Solving.   In: Ciancarini, P., Wooldridge, M.J. (eds): Agent-Oriented Software Engineering: AOSE 2000. Lecture Notes in Computer Science, Vol. 1957. Springer-Verlag. (2001) 269-284
2. Bauer, B., Müller, J.P., Odell, J.: An Extension of UML by Protocols for Multiagent Interaction. Proc. 4th Int. Conf. on Multi-Agent Systems. IEEE Computer Society. (2000) 207-214
3. Bradshaw, J. (ed.): Software Agents. AAAI Press (1997)
4. Bresciani, P., Perini, A., Giunchiglia, F., Giorgini, P., Mylopoulos, J.: A Knowledge Level Software Engineering Methodology for Agent Oriented Programming. Proc. 5th Int. Conf. on Autonomous Agents, Montreal, Canada. (2001)
5. Bubenko, J., Brash, D., Stirna, J.: EKD User Guide. (1998). Available at ftp://ftp.dsv.su.se/users/js/ekd_user_guide.pdf
6. Caire, C., Garijo, F., Gomez, J., Pavon, J., Leal, F, Chainho, P, Kearney, P., Stark, J., Evans R., Massonet, P.: Agent Oriented Analysis Using MESSAGE/UML. In this volume.
7. Castro, J., Kolp, M., Mylopoulos, J.: A Requirements-Driven Development Methodology, 13th International Conference on Advanced Information Systems Engineering (CAiSE'01), Interlaken, Switzerland. LNCS Vol. 2068 Springer-Verlag (2001) 108-123
8. Chung, L., Nixon, B.A., Yu, E., Mylopoulos, J.: Non-Functional Requirements in Software Engineering. Kluwer Academic Publishers. (2000)
9. Ciancarini, P., Wooldridge, M.J. (eds): Agent-Oriented Software Engineering: First Int. Workshop, AOSE 2000. Limerick Ireland, June 10, 2000. Lecture Notes in Computer Science, Vol. 1957. Springer-Verlag. (2001)
10. Dardenne, A., van Lamsweerde, A., Fickas, S.: Goal-Directed Requirements Acquisition, Science of Computer Programming. 20 (1-2): (1993) 3-50
11. Dastani, M., Jonker, C., Treur, J.: A Requirement Specification Language For Configuration Dynamics Of Multi-Agent Systems. In this volume.
12. DeMarco, T.: Structured Analysis and System Specification. New York: Yourdon, (1978)
13. Dignum, V., Weigand, H., Xu, L.: Agent Societies: Towards Frameworks-Based Design. In this volume.
14. Dubois, E., Yu, E., Petit, M.: From Early to Late Formal Requirements: a Process Control Case Study. Proc. 9th Int. Workshop on Software Specification and Design, Ise-Shima, Japan. IEEE Computer Society (1998) 34-42
15. Feather, M.S., Fickas, S.F., Helm, B.R.: Composite System Design: The Good News And The Bad News, Proceedings of Fourth Annual KBSE Conference, Syracuse. (1991) 16-25
16. Feather, M.S.: Language Support For The Specification And Development Of Composite Systems. ACM Trans.on Programming Languages and Systems , 9(2): (1987) 198-234
17. Finkelstein, A., Sommerville, I.: The Viewpoints FAQ: Editorial - Viewpoints in Requirements Engineering. IEE Software Engineering Journal, 11(1): (1996) 2-4
18. Gans, G., Jarke, M., Kethers, S., Lakemeyer, G.,.Ellrich, L., Funken, C., Meister, M.: Requirements Modeling for Organization Networks: A (Dis-)Trust-Based Approach. 5th IEEE Int. Symp. on Requirements Eng., Toronto, Canada. (2001)
19. Gasser, L.: Social Conceptions of Knowledge and Action: DAI Foundations and Open Systems Semantics. Artificial Intelligence. 47(1-3): (1991) 107-138

20. Ghezzi, C., Nuseibeh, B.: Guest Editorial - Managing Inconsistency in Software Development. IEEE Transactions on Software Engineering 24(11): (1998) 906-907

21. Greenspan, S.: Requirements Modelling: The Use of Knowledge Representation Techniques for Requirements Specification, Ph. D. thesis, Dept. of Computer Science, Univ. of Toronto (1984)

22. Gross, D., Yu, E.: Evolving System Architecture to Meet Changing Business Goals: an Agent and Goal-Oriented Approach. ICSE-2001Workshop: From Software Requirements to Architectures (STRAW), Toronto, Canada. (2001) 13-21

23. Inverardi, P. et al.: The Teleservices and Remote Medical Care System (TRMCS): Case Study for the Tenth International Workshop on Software Specification and Design (IWSSD-10) (2000) http://www.ics.uci.edu/iwssd/case-study.pdf

24. Jarke, M., Kurki-Suonio, R.: Guest Editorial - Special Issue on Scenario Management. IEEE Transactions on Software Engineering, 24(12): (1998) 1033 -1035

25. Jarke, M.: Requirements Tracing - Introduction. Communications of the ACM, 41(12): (1998) 32-36

26. Jennings, N.R., Sycara, K., Wooldridge, M.: A Roadmap of Agent Research and Development. Autonomous Agents and Multi-Agent Systems, 1 (1998) 7-38

27. Kendall, E.A.: Agent Software Engineering with Role Modelling. In: Ciancarini, P., Wooldridge, M.J. (eds): Agent-Oriented Software Engineering: AOSE 2000. Lecture Notes in Computer Science, Vol. 1957. Springer-Verlag. (2001) 163-170

28. Kethers, S.: Multi-Perspective Modeling and Analysis of Cooperation Processes. Ph.D. thesis. Technical University of Aachen (RWTH), Germany. (2001)

29. Medina-Mora, R., Winograd, T., Flores, R., Flores, F.: The Action Workflow Approach to Workflow Management Technology. Proc. Computer-Supported Cooperative Work. ACM Press. (1992) 281-288

30. Miksch, S., Cheng, K., Hayes-Roth, B.: An Intelligent Assistant For Patient Health Care, Proc. of the First Int. Conf. on Autonomous Agents (Agents'97) ACM Press (1997) 458-465

31. Mylopoulos, J., Borgida, A., Jarke, M., Kourbarakis, M.: Telos: A Language for Representing Knowledge About Information Systems. ACM Trans. on Information Systems 8(4) (1990) 325-362

32. Mylopoulos, J., Castro, J.: Tropos: A Framework for Requirements-Driven Software Development In J. Brinkkemper, A. Solvberg (eds.), Information Systems Engineering: State of the Art and Research Themes, Lecture Notes in Computer Science, Springer-Verlag (2000) 261-273

33. Mylopoulos, J.: Information Modeling in the Time of the Revolution. Information Systems 23(3-4): (1998) 127-155

34. Nuseibeh, B.A., Easterbrook, S. M.: Requirements Engineering: A Roadmap. In: Finkelstein, A.C.W. (ed): The Future of Software Engineering. (Companion volume to the proceedings of the 22nd Int. Conf. on Software Engineering, ICSE'00. IEEE Computer Society Press. (2000)

35. Omicini A.: SODA: Societies And Infrastructures In The Analysis And Design of Agent-based Systems. In: Ciancarini, P., Wooldridge, M.J. (eds): Agent-Oriented Software Engineering: AOSE 2000. Lecture Notes in Computer Science, Vol. 1957. Springer-Verlag. (2001) 185-194

36. Parunak, H.V.D., Odell, J.: Representing social structures in UML. In this volume.

37. Petit, M.: A Multi-Formalism and Component-Based Approach to the Formal Modeling of Manufacturing Systems Requirements. Ph.D. thesis. University of Namur, Belgium. (2000)

38. Potts, C., Takahashi, K., Anton, A.: Inquiry-Based Requirements Analysis. IEEE Software, March (1994) 21-32

39. Robinson, W.N., & Volkov, S. Supporting the Negotiation Life-Cycle. Communications of the ACM, 41(5): (1998) 95-102
40. Ross, D.T.: Structured Analysis (SA): A Language for Communicating Ideas. IEEE Transactions on Software Engineering, SE-3(1) (1977) 16-34
41. Rumbaugh, J., Jacobson, I., Booch, G.: The Unified Modeling Language Reference Manual, Addison-Wesley (1998)
42. Simon, H.A.: The Sciences of the Artificial. MIT Press (1969).
43. Standish Group: Software Chaos (1995) http://www.standishgroup.com/chaos.html
44. Suchman, L.: Plans and Situated Actions: The Problem of Human-Machine Communication. Cambridge University Press (1987)
45. Szolovits, P., Doyle, J., Long, W.J., Kohane. I., Pauker, S.G.: Guardian Angel: Patient-Centered Health Information Systems. Technical Report MIT/LCS/TR-604 (1994)
46. Taveter, K.: From Descriptive to Prescriptive Models of Agent-Oriented Information Systems. 3rd Int. Workshop on Agent-Oriented Information Systems. Interlaken, Switzerland. (2001)
47. van Lamsweerde, A.: Requirements Engineering in the Year 2000: A Research Perspective. Proc. 22nd Int. Conf. on Software Engineering, June 2000, Limerick, Ireland (2000) 5-19
48. Wagner, G., Lespérance, Y., Yu, E., (eds): Agent-Oriented Information Systems 2000: Proceedings of the 2nd International Workshop. Stockholm, June 2000. iCue Publishing, Berlin (2000)
49. Wang, X., Lespérance, Y.: Agent-Oriented Requirements Engineering Using ConGolog and i*. 3rd Int. Workshop on Agent-Oriented Information Systems. Montreal, Canada. (2001)
50. Weiss, G. (ed.): Multiagent Systems. MIT Press (1999)
51. Wooldridge, M., Jennings, N.R., Kinny, D.: The Gaia Methodology for Agent-Oriented Analysis and Design. Journal of Autonomous Agents and Multi-Agent Systems 3 (3): (2000) 285-312
52. Yu, E.: Modelling Strategic Relationships for Business Process Reengineering. Ph.D. thesis. Dept. of Computer Science, University of Toronto. (1995)
53. Yu, E.: Towards Modelling and Reasoning Support for Early-Phase Requirements Engineering. Proc. of the 3rd IEEE Int. Symp. on Requirements Engineering (1997) 226-235.
54. Yu, E.: Why Agent-Oriented Requirements Engineering. In: Proc. of the 3rd Int. Workshop on Requirements Engineering: Foundations for Software Quality. Barcelona, Catalonia. E. Dubois, A.L. Opdahl, K. Pohl, eds. Presses Universitaires de Namur (1997)
55. Yu, E.: Agent Orientation as a Modelling Paradigm. Wirtschaftsinformatik 43(2) (2001) 123-132.
56. Yu, E., Mylopoulos, J.: Understanding "Why" in Software Process Modelling, Analysis, and Design, Proc. 16th Int. Conf. Software Engineering, Sorrento, Italy, (1994) 159-168
57. Yu, E., Mylopoulos, J.: Why Goal-Oriented Requirements Engineering, Proc. of the 4th Int. Workshop on Requirements Engineering: Foundations of Software Quality, Pisa, Italy. E. Dubois, A.L. Opdahl, K. Pohl, eds. Presses Universitaires de Namur (1998) 15-22
58. Zambonelli, F., Jennings, N.R., Wooldridge, M.: Organisational Abstractions for the Analysis and Design of Multi-Agent Systems. In: Ciancarini, P., Wooldridge, M.J. (eds): Agent-Oriented Software Engineering: AOSE 2000. Lecture Notes in Computer Science, Vol. 1957. Springer-Verlag. (2001) 235-251

Expectation-Oriented Analysis and Design*

Wilfried Brauer[1], Matthias Nickles[1], Michael Rovatsos[1], Gerhard Weiß[1], and
Kai F. Lorentzen[2]

[1] Department of Informatics, Technical University of Munich,
80290 München, Germany
{brauer,nickles,rovatsos,weissg}@cs.tum.edu
[2] Department of Technology Assessment, Technical University of Hamburg,
21071 Hamburg, Germany
lorentzen@tu-harburg.de

Abstract. A key challenge for agent-oriented software engineering is
to develop and implement *open* systems composed of interacting *autonomous* agents. On the one hand, there is a need for permitting autonomy in order to support desirable system properties such as decentralised
control. On the other hand, there is a need for restricting autonomy in
order to reduce undesirable system properties such as unpredictability.
This paper introduces a novel analysis and design method for open agent-
oriented software systems that aims at coming up to both of these two
contrary aspects. The characteristics of this method, called EXPAND,
are as follows: (i) it allows agents a maximum degree of autonomy and
restricts autonomous behaviour only if necessary (ii) it uses system-level
expectations as a key modelling abstraction and as the primary level of
analysis and design; and (iii) it is sociologically grounded in Luhmann's
systems theory. The application of EXPAND is illustrated in a "car-
trading platform" case study.

1 Introduction

As new requirements arise from the increasing complexity of modern software
systems and from the distributedness of today's information economies, it has
been recognised that the modularity and reusability provided by object-oriented
analysis and design is insufficient and that there is a need for encapsulation
of more functionality at the level of software components. Agent-oriented approaches [5] offer an interesting perspective with this respect, as they view *interaction* as the primary abstraction for future software engineering approaches
[10,15]. However, interaction among autonomous entities implies contingencies
in behaviour since, in the most general case, neither a peer agent nor a designer
can *know* what goes on inside a (semi-)autonomous agent. These contingencies
are a source of potential unpredictability and undesirable chaotic behaviour at
the system level. The designer is thus faced with an apparent dilemma – to apply methods for building systems for such open, heterogenous and unpredictable

---

* This work is supported by DFG (German National Science Foundation) under contracts no. Br609/11-1 and MA759/4-2.

M.J. Wooldridge, G. Weiß, and P. Ciancarini (Eds.): AOSE 2001, LNCS 2222, pp. 226–244, 2002.

domains as the Internet on the one hand (which offer new perspectives on computation and have already proven to yield more open, flexible and adaptive software) and to harness the potential dangers of openness on the other. In order to get rid of this aspect of agent-based systems, the usual design strategy is to restrict oneself to *closed* systems (see e.g. [17,18]). This obviously means losing the power of autonomous decentralised control in favour of a top-down imposition of social regulation to ensure predictable behaviour.

To build truly *open* systems [9] means constructing systems that may be entered by autonomous entities. Even if a developer of an open system would be willing to severely restrict autonomy (and thus to give up potential advantages induced by autonomy such as decentralised control and self-organisation), it is most unreasonable to assume that full control over autonomous entities being parts of the system (temporarily or permanently) can be guaranteed under all circumstances. Taking autonomy seriously means to accept that any "strictly *normative*" (in the sense of action-prescribing) system-level design of social activity must be abandoned – instead, desired or persistent interaction patterns can only be modelled as *descriptions* of possible or probable behaviour which might or might not occur in actual operation. Likewise, *agents* can only use models of interaction as *expected* courses of social action that are always hypothetical unless when actually enacted by them and their co-actors. A combination of *normative* and *deliberative* motives in agents' actions (the former resulting from previous system behaviour, the latter from agents' autonomy) [4] makes certainty about future interactions impossible.

Starting from these observations, this paper identifies a novel level of analysing and designing agent-based software: the *expectation level*. An analysis and design method called EXPAND ("EXPectation-oriented ANalysis and Design") is introduced that uses expectations as the primary modelling abstraction and that supports the evolutionary identification, evaluation and adaptation of system-level expectations. The core idea underlying EXPAND is to make expectation-level knowledge about the social behaviour of agents *explicit* and *available* to the system analyst and designer as well as to the agents contained in the system. From the point of view of an analyst and designer, this method offers the possibility of developing and influencing open systems that consist of black-box autonomous entities which can *not* be controlled completely; and from the point of view of the agents, it allows to retain a high degree of autonomy by using the system-level expectations as a valuable "system resource" for reducing contingency about each other's behaviour. To our knowledge, EXPAND is the first analysis and design method that aims at tackling the expectation level of agent-oriented software systems explicitly and systematically. In doing so, its main contributions lie in (i) separating social expectations (which, in the most general sense, can be seen as communication structures) from agents' mental processes, (ii) in viewing expectations as *systemic* (supra-individual) data structures that are subject to manipulation by system-level software components, and (iii) in focusing on principles and techniques for analysing and designing expectations in the process of developing open agent-based systems. Another characteristic of EXPAND is that it possesses a strong sociological background; more specifically, its underlying view of expectations and sociality follows the *systems theory* by the sociologist Niklas Luhmann [14].

The remainder of this paper is structured as follows. Section 2 presents the generic conceptualisation of expectations underlying EXPAND. Section 3 describes EXPAND, and shows how a feasible and adequate incremental analysis and design process can be derived that exploits the importance of the expectation level in open and autonomous agent-based software systems. This is followed by an exemplification of the usefulness of our approach in a case study based on a "car-trading platform" application scenario in Section 4. Finally, Section 5 provides more general considerations on the challenge of engineering agent-oriented software, shows relationships to other methods and approaches, and indicates directions for future research.

2   Expectations

A major consequence of the autonomous behaviour of agents is that a certain agent appears to other agents and observers more or less as a *black box* which cannot fully be predicted and controlled. Because only the actions of an agent in its environment can be observed, while its mental state remains obscure, *beliefs* and *demands* directed to the respective agent can basically be stylised only as mutable *action expectations* which are fulfilled or disappointed in future agent actions. This suggests that it is justified, and even inevitable, to integrate expectations as a modelling abstraction into the analysis and design process of open agent-oriented software. A theory that is particularly well suited for putting this suggestion into practice is Luhmann's systems theory [14]. This theory not only provides a strong notion of expectations and their role in societies, but also focuses on interaction and communication and thus on basic ingredients of agent-oriented systems. In the following, several aspects of this theory essential to EXPAND are described; this is done in more detail because these aspects are not "common knowledge" in the field of computational agency.

2.1   Sociality and Communication

Because we are focusing on systems with multiple inter-operating agents, we are primarily interested in expectations addressing agent interactions which constitute *sociality*: if it comes to an encounter of two or more agents, the described situation of mutual indeterminacy is called *double contingency* [14]. To overcome this situation, that is, to determine the internal state and future behaviour of the respective other agent and to achieve reasonable coordination (including "reasonable" conflicts), the agents need to *communicate*. A single communication is the whole of a message act as a certain way of telling (e.g., via speech or gesture), plus a communicated information, plus the understanding of the communication attempt. Communication is observable as a course of related agent interactions. Because communications are the only way to overcome the problem of double contingency (i.e. the isolation of single agents), they are the basic constituents of sociality and they form the *social system* in which the communicating agents are embedded. EXPAND adopts this view, and assigns communication a key role in analysing and designing systems composed of interacting software agents.

2.2 Expectation Structures and Structure Evolution

As action expectations are related to communications and thus to sociality, *social structures* can be modelled as *expectation structures*. Systems theory distinguishes four concepts that correspond to expectation structures: (i) *social agents* as sets of all current action expectations regarding single physical agents; (ii) *roles* as "variables" that are associated with certain kinds of expected behaviour and that can be instantiated by different physical agents; (iii) *social programs* as flexible interaction schemes for multiple interacting social agents and/or roles; and (iv) *social values* as ratings of expected generalised behaviour (e.g., "Conflictive behaviour is always bad"). The focus of EXPAND is on social programs, since they are particularly well-suited for describing processes that occur between agents.

By processing existing expectations, agents determine their own actions, which, then, influence the existing expectations in turn. So communication is not only **structured** by individual agent goals and intentions, but also by expectations, and the necessity to test, learn and adopt expectations for the use with future communications. The process of continuous **expectation** structure adaption by means of interaction (or communication, respectively) is called *structure evolution*. As described in Section 3, this kind of evolution also plays a key role in EXPAND.

2.3 System-Level Expectations and System Design

Expectations regarding agent behaviour can be formed not only by other agents (as an aspect of their mental state), but also by observers with a global view of the multiagent system. Such ***system-level expectations*** are called *emergent* if they are formed solely from the statistical evaluation of the observed communications.

As we will see in the next section, system-level expectation **structures** can be used as the target of a multiagent system design and analysis process, because they allow us to observe and structure the multiagent system at the *system level* (i.e. the level of sociality and thus of communication) itself, and not just at the level of single agents as usual. But despite their supra-agent nature, system-level expectations need to be *expected* themselves by the agents to be able to have any influence on the system. The establishment of such *"expectations of expectation"* can be achieved through the communication of the **system-level** expectations to the agents or through the publishing of the **expectations** via an appropriate agent-external instance within the multiagent system. Once achieved, agents can "expect" what "is expected by the social system". As described in Section 3, EXPAND technically realises this achievement through a so-called "social system mirror".

2.4   Four Key Attributes of Expectations

Systems theory reveals multiple attributes of expectations, and among them the following four are of particular relevance to EXPAND: strength, normativity, representation, and derivation.

Strength and Normativity. Expectations can be weighted in two complementary ways, namely, w.r.t. their *strength* and w.r.t. their *normativity* (or inversely, their *adaptability*). The strength of an expectation indicates its "degree of expectedness": the weaker (stronger) the strength of an an expectation is, the less (more) likely is its fulfilment (violation). Against that, the normativity of an expectation indicates its "degree of changeability": the more normative (adaptive) an expectation is, the smaller (greater) is the change in its strength when being contradicted by actual actions. With that, the strength of a lowly normative expectation tends to change faster, whereas the strength of a highly normative expectation is maintained in the longer term even if it is obviously inconsistent with reality (i.e. with the agents' actual activities). The idea of expectation weighting based on strengths and normativity is adopted by EXPAND, and in accordance with systems theory it is also assumed that there is a continuous transition from weak to strong strength and from low to high normativity. Here are some examples of examples of extreme combinations of strength and normativity: *rules that govern criminal law* (strong/non-adaptable: even hundreds of actual murders will not alter the respective laws, and most people think of murder as a rather exceptional event); *habits* (strong/adaptable: before the times of fast food, people took full service in restaurants for granted, but as fast food became popular, they were willing to abandon this expectation); *public parking regulations* (strong/hardly adaptable: almost everyone surpasses them even if they are, in principle, rigid); and *shop clerk friendliness* (weak/adaptable: most people expect bad service but are willing to change their view once encountering friendly staff).

Representation. To design multiagent systems at the expectation level, we need data structures for the representation of expectation structures and statistical methods to derive emergent expectation structures from observed communications. Settling on particular representation formalisms naturally affects the level of abstraction and with it the scope of designed expectation structures. Here, we focus on social programmes, for which a basic graphical notation is introduced as illustrated in the example shown in Fig. 1. The nodes correspond to message/speech acts that are uttered and addressed to/by instances of roles (r_i) (i.e. agents). The directed arcs represent the respective expectation that a communication is followed by a certain subsequent communication. Arcs are labeled by pairs $s{:}n$ of real values ranging between 0 and 1, where s denotes the strength of the expectation (in Fig. 1 additionally visualised through arrow thickness) and n denotes its normativity. Note that outgoing edges of a node always do have the same normativity, because the degree of change always uniformly applies to the entire distribution of their strength.

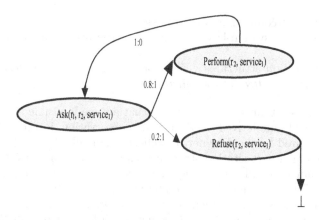

Fig. 1. A social program.

Derivation. The process by which expectation structures are derived must be able to calculate the expectations' strength and normativity values. This calculation can be done using standard statistics and probability theory. As expectations are extrapolations of observed communication processes into the future, their normativity can be quantified as the percentage of their change in the case of being contradicted by actually occurring events. For this reason it is reasonable (i) to derive the strength of an expectation by means of computing the *probability* of the communicative actions that fulfil or contradict this expectation given prior communication, and (ii) to capture the normativity of an expectation by *rules* for updating its strength.

3   EXPAND

Based on the description of EXPAND's sociologically founded view of expectations, this section presents EXPAND – its software-technical concept of a social system mirror and its analysis and design phases – in detail.

3.1   The Mirror Concept

The activities of identifying, evaluating and adapting system-level expectation structures are crucial to EXPAND. EXPAND supports these activities by means of a so-called *social system mirror*, henceforth briefly called *mirror*. (Details on the mirror concept are provided in [13].) Conceptually, a mirror is a software component (corresponding to an EXPAND-specific CASE tool) which models an agent-oriented software system as a social system. Technically, a mirror is a knowledge base which derives system-level expectation structures from communications and makes them available to both the participating agents and the designer of the software system. The mirror has three major purposes:

1. monitoring agent communication processes,
2. deriving emergent system-level expectation structures from these observations, and
3. making expectation structures visible for the agents and the designer (the so-called *reflection effect* of the mirror).

It is important to see that not all structures that are made visible to the agents need to be emergent and derived through system observation. Rather, the mirror can be pre-structured by the designer to "reflect" manually designed ("manipulated"), non-emergent expectation structures as well. In both cases, the agents can access the mirror's and actively use the expectation structures provided by it as "guidelines" influencing their reasoning and interactivity.

For example, agents can participate in social programs which seem to be useful to them, or refrain from a certain behaviour if the mirror tells them that participation would violate a norm. Social programs (or structures in general) in which agents continue to participate become stronger, otherwise weaker. (The degree of change in strength depends on the respective normativity.) Thus, the mirror reflects a model of a social system and makes it available to the agents. As a consequence, the mirror *influences* the agents – very much like mass media do in human society. Conversely, the mirror continually observes the actual interactions among the agents and adopts the announced expectation structures in its database accordingly. In doing so, the mirror never restricts the autonomy of the agents. Its influence is solely by means of providing information, and not through the exertion of control.

The mirror, and with it actually the entire EXPAND method, realise the principle of *evolutionary* software engineering [1,16]. More precisely, within the overall EXPAND process (i.e. within the EXPAND phases described below) two mirror-specific operations are continuously applied in a *cyclic* way:

1. it makes the system-level expectations derived by the designer from her design goals explicit and known to the agents; and
2. it monitors the system-level expectation structures which emerge from the communications among the software agents.

These two operations constitute the core of the overall analysis and design process, and together they allow a designer to control and to influence the agents' realisation and adoption of her specifications.

3.2 A Note on Scalability

Depending on the application, the number of agents within the multiagent system may be very large. Usually, CASE-tool supported software engineering methods like EXPAND are intended primarily for large-scale applications, and in particular in open, web-based multiagent systems (like the application described in our case study in section 4) it is undesirable to impose limitations regarding the number of participating agents. Given large numbers of interacting agents, there may be a vast amount of communication which has to be observed and evaluated by the social system mirror. Undoubtedly, the efficient achievement of this task constitutes a serious technical challenge, and a possible way to cope with this problem is to structure the mirror into – interacting – subsystems. (How such a structuring could look like in detail is an open issue that we are planning to investigate in a future work.)

On the other hand, a mirror (as an "information spreading medium") can provide for stronger coherence of the multiagent system because it makes global social structures (especially norms) known to the agents. Such structures would otherwise be invisible to the agents which usually perceive the interactions in their local social environments only. This consequence of the mirror's reflection effect is important particularly in large-scale, open and heterogenous systems where agents can tend to be isolated or to be contained disjoint social groups. In such systems, many communications are solely required to gather information about social facts, and communications can be inefficient or redundant due to ignorance of social structures. A mirror can reduce the amount of such avoidable communications and thus is expected to have a strong "ordering" influence on such multiagent systems.

Therefore, we expect the issue of efficiently observing and processing all communication reduce itself to a mere technical problem, while the actual *complexity* and *variety* of the ongoing communication will be effectively *reduced*.

3.3   The Engineering Phases

Phase I: Modelling the System Level. In the first phase, the software designer models the system level of the multiagent system according to her design goals in the form of design specifications which focus on "social behaviour" (i.e. desired courses of agent interaction) and "social functionality" (i.e. functionality which is achieved as a "product" of agent interaction, such as cooperative problem solving) in the widest sense (we don't take into account "second-order" design goals like high execution speed or low memory consumption). For this task, the usual specification methods and formalisms can be used, for instance, the specification of desired environment states, constraints, social plans etc. In addition or as a replacement, the specification can be done in terms of system-level expectation structures, like social programs.

Phase II: Deriving Appropriate Expectation Structures. In the second phase, the designer models and derives system-level expectation structures from the design specifications and stores them in the social system mirror. If the design specifications from phase I are not already expectation structures (e.g., they might be given as rules of the form "Agent X must never do Y"), they have to be transformed appropriately. While social behaviour specifications are expectation structures *per se*, social functionalities (for instance: "Agents in the system must work out a solution for problem X together") possibly need to be transformed, most likely into social programs. Sometimes a full equivalent transformation will not be feasible. In this case, the designer models expectation structures which cover as many design requirements as possible.

System-level specifications can be modelled as adaptable or normative expectations. The former can be used for establishing *hints* for the agents which are able to adapt during structure evolution, the latter for the transformation of *constraints* and other "hard" design requirements into expectations.

Figure 2 shows the spectrum of system-level specifications and expectation structures that result from this phase of the analysis and design process.

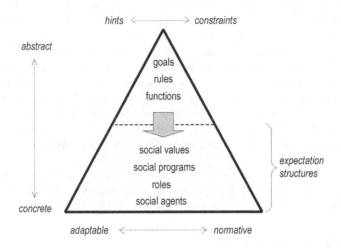

Fig. 2. System-level specification.

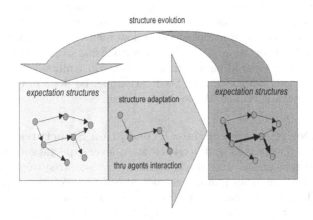

Fig. 3. Evolution of expectation structures.

Phase III: Monitoring Structure Evolution. After the designer has finished modelling expectations, she makes them visible for the agents via the social system mirror and puts the multiagent system into operation (if it is not already running). In the third phase of the design and analysis process, it is up to the designer to observe and analyse the evolution of expectation structures which becomes visible to her through the mirror (Fig. 3). In particular, she has to pay attention to the relationship of the continuously adapted system-level expectation structures and her design specifications from phase I, which means that she analyses the expectation structures with regard to the fulfilment of norms established by the designer and the achievement of the desired social functionality. Because the mirror is only intended to show expectation structures, it could be necessary to support the mirror with a software for the (semi-)automatical "re-translation" of expectation structures into more abstract design specifications like social goals.

As long as the expectations structures develop in a positive way (i.e. they match the design goals) or no emergent structures can be identified that deserve being made explicit to improve system performance, the designer does not intervene. Otherwise she proceeds with phase IV.

Phase IV: Refinement of Expectation Structures. In the last phase, the designer uses her knowledge about the positive or negative emergent properties of the multiagent system to improve the system-level expectation structures. Usually, this is achieved by removing "bad" expectation structures from the mirror database, and, if necessary, by introducing new expectation structures as described in phases I and II. In addition, expectation structures which have proven to be useful can be actively supported, e.g. by increasing their expectation strength and/or their normativity. The process proceeds with phase III until all design goals are achieved or no further improvement seems probable.

Having described how the EXPAND process is supposed to be carried out in theory, we next turn to a concrete case study that will illustrate what the process might look like in practice, what problems and questions it raises, and what perspectives it offers. The phases that our analysis and design method consists of can be integrated into a single process model that is summarised by the scheme shown in Table 1 which makes the individual actions taken in each phase more explicit.

4   Case Study: The Car Trading Platform

4.1   Scenario Overview

Imagine a website that brings together car dealers, private pre-owned car sellers and potential buyers who trade cars online (cf. www.imotors.com , www.auto-web.com, www.autointernet.com, www.autotradecenter.com). There is an "offers" section in which sellers can display images, technical details and prices of cars for sale. In the "requests" area, buyers can post requests for cars that they would be interested in. A forum is available, in which inquiries can be placed, discussions, bargaining and negotiations may take place publicly or privately (as forum users wish), etc.

Table 1. Detailed view of the EXPAND process.

	Action	Description	Output
I	**Model system level**	**Specify social-level requirements**	**Social-level requirements specification**
I.1	Model social be-haviour.	Identify behaviour requirements, i.e. desired/undesired courses of interaction.	Social behaviour specifica-tion.
I.2	Model social function-ality.	Identify functional requirements, i.e. desired outputs of system operation.	Social functionality specifi-cation.
II	**Derive expectation structures**	**Transform requirements from phase I into appropriate expec-tation structures**	**Mirror instantiation with expectation structures**
II.1	Derive expectation primitives.	Define what is expected of which agent(s) under what conditions.	Expectation structure prim-itives.
II.2	Specify expectation at-tributes.	For all derived structures, determine strength, normativity, representation and derivation.	Complete specification of expectation structure attributes.
II.3	Instantiate mirror.	Supply mirror with representations of the defined expectation structures.	Concrete mirror data struc-tures and processing rules.
III	**Monitor system op-eration**	**Observe structure evolution**	**Evaluation of emergent system behaviour**
III.1	Identify emergent structures.	Spot interesting/unexpected phe-nomena in unfolding communication processes and emergent system char-acteristics. Employ statistical meth-ods, interpret data.	Catalog of emergent struc-tures.
III.2	Evaluate emergent structures.	Categorise emergent structures ac-cording to their desirability wrt re-quirements identified in phase I.	Evaluation for emergent sys-tem behaviours identified in III.2.
III.3	Determine next action.	Assess risk of changes and urgency of changes. If changes seem necessary, continue with **IV**; else, go back to **III**.	
IV	**Refine expectation structures**	**Determine useful modifications to mirror structures**	**Modified mirror struc-tures**
IV.1	Identify structures re-sponsible for undesired behaviour.	Involves finding "misused" or "un-used" structures, structures that are too normative or too adaptable, and missing structures that lead to chaotic interaction.	Specification of appropriate modifications.
IV.2	Adjust mirror con-tents.	Insert/delete necessary/obsolete ex-pectation structures or adjust exist-ing ones according to IV.1	Updated mirror.
IV.3	Deploy changes.	Determine appropriate mode of up-dating the mirror without disrupting operation or causing distrust toward mirror.	Deployment of modified so-cial system mirror.
IV.4	Proceed to phase **III**.		

4.2   Making Top-Level Design Decisions

Having made a decision on taking an agent-based approach for the above ap-plication, the designer must develop a top-level description of the system which will, to the least, include decisions regarding infrastructure, interaction environ-ment and, above all, participating agents (or agent types).

Here, we will assume that the designer of the platform is designing a semi-open system: on the one hand, the system offers user interface agents that monitor the platform on behalf of users, profile users to derive interests/needs and draw their attention to interesting information on the platform. A second, pre-built type of agents are search agents that constantly re-organise the platform's database and can search it efficiently. These can be contacted by user interface agents as well as by humans for search purposes. We assume that all interactions with these search agents are benevolent, since they are not truly autonomous (they simply execute others' requests). On the other hand, there is a number of agent types that have not been designed by the designer of the platform. There can (and should) exist human and non-human agents representing individuals or organisations that interact with the platform in a "socially" unprescribed way (only restricted by implementation-level protocols and standards, e.g. FIPA compliance). Generally speaking, these agents are black-boxes for the system designer.

Further refinement of these initial design decisions will require looking at a multitude of issues, ranging from communication facilities and standards and capabilities of in-built profiling and search agents to database models etc. For our purposes, we can restrict this identification of requirements to social level characteristics of the platform since these are the subject of the EXPAND process.

4.3   Identifying Social Level Requirements

As system-level or "social level" goals, we consider the following motives of a car trading platform (CTP) provider:

1. Maximum quality of service should be provided: the range of offered and requested cars has to be broad and their specifications must relate to their prices; the reliability of transactions must be high; trust between buyers and sellers and between all users and the platform must be at a reasonable level.
2. Transaction turnover should be maximised, because it indicates (in our example) high return on investment for the CTP provider stakeholders.
3. Traffic on the platform must be maximised, to ensure high advertisement returns.

In the following, we sketch how the EXPAND process model can be applied in the analysis and design of such a system.

The dilemma in designing the social level of such a platform is obvious: system behaviour should meet the design goals and at the same time it shouldn't compromise participating external agents' private goals by being overtly restrictive. An expectation-level model of social structures is needed to cope with this situation. We next sketch the application of the suggested analysis and design process to the CTP.

4.4   Implementing the EXPAND Process

Phase I: Modelling the System Level. In the first step the social structures are modelled in the form of design specifications. They might include the following (we use natural language for convenience and concentrate only on a few design issues for lack of space):

1. Agents committing themselves to purchase/sell actions towards other must fulfil all resulting obligations (deliver, pay, invoice etc.).

2. Unreliable behaviour induces reluctance to enter business relationships on the side of others. Fraudulence leads to exclusion from the platform.
3. Interest in offers and requests must be shown by others in order to provide motivations to keep up the use of the platform.

The first specification is very important in order to foster trust among agents in such a platform. If communication were only inducing a bunch of loose pseudo-commitments that are never kept, the CTP risks becoming a playground instead of a serious, efficient marketplace. This principle is refined by item 2: the "must" in the first rule can obviously not be deontically enforced on autonomous agents, so it has to be replaced by a "softer" expression of obligation: by specifying that unreliable behaviour decreases the probability of others interacting with the unreliable individual in the future, we provide an interpretation of the former rule in terms of "consequences". Also, we distinguish "sloppy" from "illegal" behaviour and punish the latter with exclusion from the platform, a centralised sanction that the platform may impose. The third specification is somewhat more subtle: it is based on the assumption that agents will stop posting offers and requests, if they don't receive enough feedback. Since we have to ensure both a broad range of offers as well as reasonable traffic on the site, we want to make agents believe that their participation is honoured by others so that they keep on participating (for private buyers this might be irrelevant, since they buy a car once every 5 years, but it is surely important to have plenty of professional dealers frequent the site).

The process of specifying such possible societal behaviours should be iterated on the basis of "scenarios" for all courses of communication that are of interest and seem possible, so as to yield requirements for the social system that is to be implemented.

Phase II: Deriving Appropriate Expectation Structures. Clearly, the three requirements above can be analysed in terms of expectations, that is, as variedly normative, possibly volatile rules that are made known to agents and evolve with observed interaction.

The second phase of the EXPAND process consists of making these abstract requirements concrete in the form of expected communication structures. As mentioned before (see 2.4) we do not intend to restrict ourselves here to a single formalism and will only use the already introduced graph-like notation to present but a few sample structures for the above specifications. Two such expectation structures derived from the above requirements 1. and 3. are shown in Figs. 4 and 5. The first example depicts an expectation structure of an order-deliver-pay-procedure in the CTP. It encapsulates high delivery and payment expectations (i.e. high transaction reliability), but also a more specific expectation as concerns availability statements that are made by dealers: although it is equally probable that the requested car will be available upon a first order, it is highly unexpected that a car that had not been available is suddenly available upon a second, identical order (in our model, responses to communication are supposed to occur in time-spans that are much shorter than those needed to change stock). Thus, the first response is given much more weight, and a notion

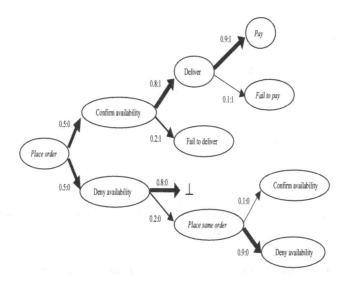

Fig. 4. Social program "order-deliver-pay" (buyer actions are shown in italic font, seller actions in plain face, as in all following figures, speech act arguments are omitted for lack of space): expectations about availability are balanced; in the "available" case, dealers are expected to deliver and customers are expected to pay. In the "not available" case, dealers are expected to confirm their prior statement if asked a second time (even though the probability of such a second request is low).

of "honesty" in responding to orders is assumed. The second example is closely related to design goal 3 introduced above. Here, the expectation structure is used to express that few posted offers go unanswered by interested customers, and that the enquiries of such customers are responded to with high probability. By using such a structure, the designer can reassure both dealers and customers that it is *worthwhile* posting orders and enquiries to orders. If followed by the users of the CTP, such a structure would imply that postings will be answered even if the other party is not *actually* interested in the offer/question, and is just replying out of a sense of "politeness", to the end of making everyone feel that their contributions are honoured. Associated with such conventions would be the designer's goal to keep the CTP frequented, by presenting the social structures as open and rich.

These simple examples given, we can return to our EXPAND design process model. We have shown how two social structure specifications were turned into concrete expectation structures (phases I and II). For lack of space, we have concentrated on *social programmes* and neglected roles, social agents and values. Preassuming that the CTP is implemented and observed during operation, we can now proceed to phase III.

Phase III: Monitoring Structure Evolution. Unlike phases I and II, this phase focuses on *observation* of the system in operation in order to further refine expectation structures and their processing. It is essential to keep in mind

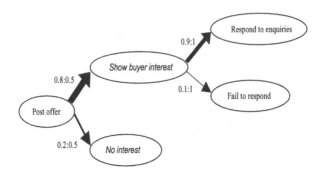

Fig. 5. "Initiatives are honoured" program: it is expected that dealers receive some response to their offers by potential customers, and that they react to enquiries themselves.

that the systemic expectation "mirror" (as a software component) leaves plenty of choices not only as concerns the *choice* of employed expectation structures, but also with respect to how these structures are *processed*, that is, how they *evolve* through monitored agent behaviour in system operation. To stress this second aspect, we concentrate on this processing of expectations in the following examples.

Suppose, first, that we observe that actual behaviour largely deviates from that assumed in Fig. 4 in that there are many fraudulent customers who do not comply with their obligation to pay once the car has been delivered unless the dealer threatens with legal consequences several times. Obviously, identifying such a problem preassumes that interaction is tracked and that interaction patterns are statistically analysed and evaluated with respect to existing system goals. Therefore, the software engineer's primary duty is, at this stage, to spot interesting behaviours (both desirable and undesirable ones). Once realised, we are faced with a problem. By default, even though payment was designed as a norm, the "expectation mirror" would simply "truthfully" decrease the normativity in the longer term and adapt the expectation strengths subsequently so that the strength of "fail to pay" increases. This would mean that an emergent, hidden structure would be made explicit in the system, but, unfortunately, this would be a structure that embodies a functionality which does not serve the system goals (even though it has been "selected" through actual interaction) because it would make future dealers doubt the reliability of the system.

As a second example, suppose that the expectation structure in Fig. 5 corresponds to the actual system behaviour, but not because of some "polite" policy of customers to show interest in *any* dealer posting – instead, demand in cars is simply (temporarily) so high (and maybe the CTP is for some other reasons very attractive for customers) that almost no offer posting goes unanswered. Assume, further, that our initial design was to enforce "politeness" by insinuating that it was a convention of the platform, even if customers would not have been polite at all, that is, we had implemented this expectation structure as rather immutable (normativity of 0.5/1) regardless of the agents' behaviour.

In both cases, we have identified emergent (positive and negative) properties of the system that must be dealt with in phase IV.

Phase IV: Refinement of Expectation Structures. As designers of the platform, we can react to such emergent properties in different ways. To give a flavour for the kind of decisions designers have to make when refining expectation models, we discuss the two examples mentioned above.

In the case of the "spreading fraudulent customers", the most straightforward solution would be to impose sanctions on the fraudulent behaviour observed (i.e. to add new expectation structures). Let us assume, however, that an analysis has shown that it is too costly to verify customers' solvency and payment reserves (e.g., by inquiring other E-commerce platforms about them). On the other hand, ignoring the changes by keeping the old expectation structure (and asserting a high payment reliability in a "propaganda" way) might result in future inconsistencies: if too many individuals realise that it does not correspond to the actual social structure, they will use it less, and the "social design" level will provide lesser possibilities to influence system behaviour for the designer.

Obviously, a trade-off has to be found. One possible solution would be to extend the structure in the way suggested by Fig. 6, such that failure to pay results in reluctance of dealers to accept future orders from the unreliable customer. So, in phase IV we can specify a new functionality that feeds into the system in the next cycle.

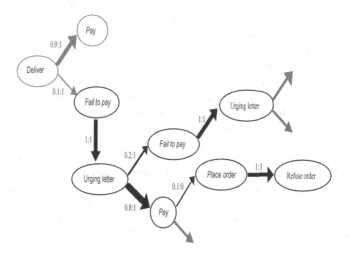

Fig. 6. Specifying a new functionality.

As concerns the second, "positive" emergent property, we might consider lifting the constraint of presenting an "immutable" politeness convention, in order to allow for optimisation on the agents' side: making the rule normative implies that it wouldn't change, even if, for example, dealers' offers changed over time – hence, there is little pressure for dealers to actively try to meet customer demand. Thus, if we allowed this expectation to *adapt* to the actual interest shown in offers (e.g., by updating expectation strengths as *real* probabilities, which can be achieved by decreasing the normativity value shown in Fig. 5), dealer agents would start noticing which of their postings are good (ones which increase the rate of customer inquiry) and which aren't. (After all, maximising market efficiency in this way might help maximising CTP profits, which also depend on gross trade turnover.) We therefore decide to increase the adaptivity of this expectation structure.

Performing such modifications to the expectation level design of a system nicely illustrates how rather restrictive social structures can give way to more emergent phenomena in "safe" non-risky situations as the one depicted here when optimisation is the prominent issue, and not the reduction of chaos.

These simple examples underpin the usefulness of explicit modelling of social structures in the proposed EXPAND process model. In particular, they show how both designing social *structures* and designing the *processing* of such structures plays an important role in the open systems we envisage. Also, they illustrate the evolutionary intuition behind our design process: agents select social structures through their interaction, and designers select them through design.

5   Conclusions

Engineering agent-oriented software while at the same time taking autonomy as a key feature of agency seriously is a great challenge. On the one hand, it is (among other things) autonomy that makes the concept of an agent powerful and particularly useful, and that makes agent orientation significantly distinct from standard object orientation. There is an obvious and rapidly growing need for autonomous software systems capable of running in open application environments, given the increasing interoperability and interconnectivity among computers and computing platforms. On the other hand, autonomy in behaviour may result in "chaotic" overall system properties such as unpredictability and uncontrollability that are most undesirable from the point of view of software engineering and industrial application. In fact, it is one of the major driving forces of standard software engineering to avoid exactly such properties. To come up to each of these two contradictory aspects – the urgent need for autonomous software systems on the one hand and the problem of undesirable system properties induced by autonomous behaviour on the other – must be a core concern of agent-oriented software engineering, and is the basic motivation underlying the work described here.

A number of agent-oriented software engineering methods are now available (see [11] for a good survey). EXPAND is most closely related to those among these methods which also focus on the analysis and design of the system level (e.g., Gaia [18], Aalaadin [8], Cassiopeia [7], and MESSAGE [2]). All available methods as well as EXPAND aim at supporting a structured development of "non-chaotic" agent software. However, they do so in a fundamentally different way. EXPAND admits agents a maximum degree of autonomy and restricts autonomous behaviour only if this turns out to be necessary during the evolutionary analysis and design process. Against that, most other methods show a clear tendency toward seriously restricting or even excluding the agents' autonomy a priori. Different mechanisms for achieving autonomy restrictions have been proposed, including e.g. the hardwiring of organisational structures[1], the rigid predefinition of when and how an agent has to interact with whom, and the minimisation of the individual agents' range of alternative actions. As a consequence, methods based on such mechanisms run the risk to design software agents that eventually are not very distinct from ordinary objects as considered in standard object oriented software engineering since many years. EXPAND aims at avoiding this risk by accepting autonomy as a necessary characteristic of agency that must not be ruled out headily (and sometimes even can not be ruled out at all, as is typically the case for truly open systems). With that, EXPAND is in full accordance with Jennings' claim to search for other solutions than the above mentioned restrictive mechanisms [12, p. 290]. Moreover, EXPAND with its grounding on Luhmann's theory of social systems precisely is in the line of Castelfranchi's view according to which a socially oriented perspective of engineering social order in agent systems is needed and most effective [3]. In addition to that, and more generally, this thorough sociological grounding also makes EXPAND different from other approaches that apply sociological concepts and terminology in a comparatively superficial and ad hoc manner.

Taking expectations as a level of analysis and design opens a qualitatively new perspective of agent-oriented software and its engineering. To explore and to work out such a new perspective constitutes a *long-term* scientific and practical endeavour of considerable complexity. This also is why it is not surprising that EXPAND in its current version does not yet answer all relevant issues, but necessarily includes aspects that are tentative in flavour and so leaves room for improvement. Our current work focuses on the improvement of three of these aspects that we consider as particularly important; these are a more formal treatment of system-level expectations, the technical refinement of the mirror concept, and a more systematic transition from the expectation level down to the group and agent levels and further down to the standard object level. EXPAND should be considered as a first, pioneering step toward a better understanding of the benefits and the limitations of expectation-oriented analysis and design. Faced with the challenge to build "autonomous non-chaotic agent software", we think it is important to further investigate the expectation level in general and EXPAND in particular.

References

[1] L. J. Arthur. *Rapid Evolutionary Development: Requirements, Prototyping & Software Creation.* John Wiley & Sons, 1991.
[2] G. Caire et al. Agent oriented analysis using MESSAGE/UML. In this volume.

---

[1] In [6] three organisational frameworks – markets, networks, and hierarchies – are considered, differing from each other in the degree of autonomy they concede the individual agents.

[3] C. Castelfranchi. Engineering social order. In *Working Notes of the First International Workshop on Engineering Societies in the Agents' World (ESAW-00)*, 2000.

[4] C. Castelfranchi, F. Dignum, C. M. Jonker, and J. Treur. Deliberate normative agents: Principles and architecture. In *Proceedings of the Sixth International Workshop on Agent Theories, Architectures, and Languages (ATAL-99)*, Orlando, FL, 1999.

[5] P. Ciancarini and M. J. Wooldridge. *Agent-oriented Software Engineering: first international workshop (AOSE-2000)*. Springer-Verlag, Berlin et al., 2001.

[6] V. Dignum, H. Weigand, and L. Xu. Agent societies: towards frameworks-based design. In this volume.

[7] A. Drogoul and A. Collinot. Applying an agent-oriented methodology to the design of artificial organizations: a case study in robotic soccer. *Autonomous Agents and Multi-Agent Systems*, 1(1):113–129, 1998.

[8] J. Ferber and O. Gutknecht. A meta-model for the analysis and design of organizations in multi-agent systems. In *Proceedings of the 3nd International Conference on Multi-Agent Systems (ICMAS-98)*, pages 128–135, 1998.

[9] C. Hewitt. Offices are open systems. *ACM Transactions on Office Information Systems*, 4(3):271–287, July 1986.

[10] M. N. Huhns. Interaction-oriented programming. In *Agent-Oriented Software Engineering: first international workshop (AOSE-2000)*, Lecture Notes in Artificial Intelligence Vol. 1957. Springer-Verlag, 2000.

[11] C. Iglesias, M. Garijo, and J.C. Gonzales. A survey of agent-oriented methodologies. In J.P. Müller, M.P. Singh, and A. Rao, editors, *Intelligent Agents V. Proceedings of the Fifth International Workshop on Agent Theories, Architectures, and Languages (ATAL-98)*, Lecture Notes in Artificial Intelligence Vol. 1555, pages 317–330. Springer-Verlag, 1999.

[12] N.R. Jennings. On agent-based software engineering. *Artificial Intelligence*, 117:277–296, 2000.

[13] K. F. Lorentzen and M. Nickles. Ordnung aus Chaos – Prolegomena zu einer Luhmann'schen Modellierung deentropisierender Strukturbildung in Multiagentensystemen. In T. Kron, K. Junge, and S. Papendick, editors, *Luhmann modelliert. Ansätze zur Simulation von Kommunikationssystemen*. Leske & Budrich, 2001. To appear.

[14] N. Luhmann. *Social Systems*. Stanford University Press, Palo Alto, CA, 1995 (orignally published in 1984). translated by J. Bednarz, Jr. and D. Baecker.

[15] M.P. Singh. Toward interaction-oriented programming. Technical Report TR-96-15, Department of Computer Science, North Carolina State University, 1996.

[16] I. Sommerville, editor. *Software Engineering*. Addison-Wesley, 1998.

[17] M. J. Wooldridge, N.R. Jennings, and D. Kinny. A methodology for agent-oriented analysis and design. In *Proceedings of the Third International Conference on Autonomous Agents (Agents'99)*, pages 69–76, 1999.

[18] M. J. Wooldridge, N.R. Jennings, and D. Kinny. The Gaia methodology for agent-oriented analysis and design. *Autonomous Agents and Multi-Agent Systems*, 3(3):285–312, 2000.

Abstractions and Infrastructures for the Design and Development of Mobile Agent Organizations

Franco Zambonelli

Dipartimento di Scienze dell'Ingegneria
Università di Modena e Reggio Emilia
Via Vignolese, 905 – 41100 Modena – ITALY
franco.zambonelli@unimo.it

Abstract. Internet applications can take advantage of a paradigm based on autonomous and mobile agents. However, suitable abstractions and infrastructures are required for the effective engineering of such applications. In this paper, we argue that a conceptual framework for context-dependent coordination, supported by an infrastructure based on programmable media, can promote a modular and easy to manage approach to the design and development of mobile agent applications in terms of computational organizations. The MARS coordination infrastructure is presented as an implementation of a coordination infrastructure promoting context-dependent coordination. A case study in the area of workflow management is introduced to clarify the concepts presented.

1   Introduction

Agent-based computing is being widely recognized as a useful paradigm for the design and development of complex software systems. Among the others, Internet applications such as E-commerce, information retrieval, distributed project-management, can effectively take advantage of the new paradigm.

As a rather young paradigm, agents and related features are still being analyzed and studied along several dimensions, one of which, *mobility*, is one of the most debated ones in the context of Internet applications. In most of the literature [13,28], agent mobility refers only to the agents' capability of dynamically transferring their execution onto different Internet sites, with the goal of improving reliability and efficiency, and it is often highly criticized due to the technical problems it introduces. However, mobility is also a necessary abstraction to model the network-aware activities of Internet agents as well as the presence, in applications, of (software running on) mobile computing devices. In other words, mobility of agents is not only a useful feature, but it can be considered an intrinsic characteristic of Internet agents. As that, any methodology for the design and development of Internet-agent applications must exploit suitable abstractions, concepts, and infrastructures to deal with mobility.

One of the major problems introduced by mobility relates to the handling of the agents' coordination activities. First, when agents need to access data and services and to coordinate with other agents in a foreign Internet site, they are required to face all the typical problems of open systems and open organizations: heterogeneity of

M.J. Wooldridge, G. Weiß, and P. Ciancarini (Eds.): AOSE 2001, LNCS 2222, pp. 245–262, 2002.
© Springer-Verlag Berlin Heidelberg 2002

languages and protocols, and opportunistic behavior in interactions [16,30]. Second, each Internet site has its own specific characteristics and may be in need of constraining – for security or resource-control reasons – the behavior of an agent in accessing the local resources and in coordinating with other local agents (in other words, the environment can enact specific rules on the local organization and can bound agents to play a specific role in there [7,10]). Finally, agents that are part of a specific multi-agent application/organization may require their coordination activities to occur according to specific application needs, and/or to the specific role an agent is assigned in its original organization, despite the different characteristics of the Internet sites where they execute [30].

In this paper, we focus on the conceptual framework of *context-dependent coordination*, firstly introduced in [5], and show that it introduces suitable organizational abstractions to model the coordination activities of mobile application agents. The main idea is to abstract the "place" in which an agent execute and interact as a *local* and *active organizational context*. A local organizational context can actively enact specific rules on the agent's coordination activities, and different contexts may enact different, independent rules. Such a model promotes thinking mobile agents as organizational entities, moving across different organizational contexts, each enacting local organizational rules (or "social conventions") on local coordination activities. Moreover, by conceiving agents as capable of configuring (at least partially) the activities of interaction contexts, one can think at mobile agents as entities that belong to their original application/organization, and that can somehow enact application-specific organizational rules on their coordination activities, independently of their current position. Not only the organizational perspective of context-dependent coordination suits modern approach to agent-based computing, but it also promotes a clean separation of concern in the analysis and design of mobile agent application. In fact, the analysis and design of application can clearly separate the intra-agent issues, related to the internal computation activities of application agents, from the inter-agent ones, related to the management and control of the agents' coordination activities in an organization.

Of course, as is it the case of any model, the potentials of context-dependent coordination can be fully exploited in application development and execution only via the availability of proper infrastructures. In particular, context-dependent coordination can be effectively supported by a coordination infrastructure based on a multiplicity of independent programmable coordination media, each associated to an Internet site. By implementing the concept of active interaction contexts, programmable coordination media become the places where to embed the code implementing organizational rules, whether statically imposed by site administrators to rule activities in local organizations, or dynamically programmed by mobile application agents when arriving at a site. Such an infrastructure enables an easy translation of a context-dependent design into actual code, and promotes the writing of modular, easy to change and maintain, code.

In the following of this paper, we go into details about agent mobility, context-dependent coordination, and their impact on application analysis and design (Section 2). Then, we analyze the main issues underlying programmable coordination infrastructures, describing an actual implementation of such an infrastructure, i.e., MARS, and analyzing their impact on application development (Section 3). We introduce a simple case study to clarify the concepts expressed (Section 4). Finally, we discuss related work in the area (Section 5) and conclude the paper by outlining promising research directions (Section 6).

2 Context-Dependent Coordination

2.1 Types of Mobility

Mobility of agents may appear in different flavors in today's Internet computing environments:

- *Virtual agent mobility.* The wideness and the openness of the Internet scenario makes it suitable to develop applications in terms of *network-aware* agents, i.e., agents that are aware of the distributed nature of the target and explicitly locate and access resources, services, and agents. From a different perspective, agents "navigate" the Internet and virtually move across its resources [6,27].

- *Actual agent mobility.* This refer to the agents' capability of moving across Internet sites while executing by dynamically and autonomously transferring their code, data, and state, toward the resources they need to access [13].

- *Physical agent mobility.* Mobile devices accessing the Internet – such as palmtop, cellular phones, etc. – can be modeled in terms of autonomous agents whose position with respect the fixed network infrastructure (and thus the point from which to access it) changes accordingly to their geographical movements (that, from the point of view of the fixed infrastructure, are perceived as autonomous movements).

Virtual agent mobility is a useful abstraction to be exploited in the design of Internet-agent applications. Although it is possible to think at network-aware agents as autonomous components that have the possibility of globally interacting with a world-wide environment from a fixed perspective, minimization of conceptual complexity suggests conceiving network-aware agents as localized, situated, entities, that moves across a world-wide network of independent sites, no matter if their execution is tied to a fixed Internet node [27].

Actual agent mobility is a useful dimension of autonomy for the effective execution of application agents. In fact, despite the technological challenges (in terms of security and resource control) that agent mobility introduces, its wise exploitation can provide for saving network bandwidth, increasing both the reliability and the efficiency of the execution, handling mobility of users [18,28]. Moreover, even if similar advantages and functionality of actual agent mobility can be exploited by weaker forms of low-level mobility (e.g., code mobility [13]), only agent mobility can naturally map at the execution level the virtual mobility already exploited at the design level.

Physical mobility is likely to become an increasing issue to be taken into account in the design of Internet applications, as more and more there will be the need of mobility-enabled services and applications. Many applications and services that we currently design and develop for being exploited via non-mobile Internet-connected devices are likely to be exploited in the near future in a mobile setting. Devices will become mobile and will be in need of accessing the Internet from different – and dynamically changing – access points. Thus, all software agents that are currently non-mobile will become mobile agents simply for the fact of executing in a mobile device. Moreover, even if no agent-technology is exploited inside a mobile device, the observable behavior of a mobile-device w.r.t. the fixed infrastructure is actually those of an autonomous (in terms of mobility and proactivity) component, i.e., of a mobile agents, and will have to be modeled accordingly.

2.2   Local Interaction Contexts

To deal with all the above types of mobility in a uniform way, a suitable modeling of the scenario in which applications execute is required. In particular, it is suitable to model and develop Internet applications in terms of agents that can autonomously move across a multiplicity of different sites or environments, e.g., Internet nodes or administrative domains of nodes (see Figure 1). A site defines the *context* in which an agent executes and interacts. In other words, a site acts both as *execution context*, i.e., the place in which agents executes, whether virtually, actually, or physically, and as *interaction context*, i.e., the place in which agent coordination activities occur. Coordination activities may include accessing the local resources of a site and communicating and synchronizing with other locally executing agents, whether belonging to the same application or foreign Internet agents.

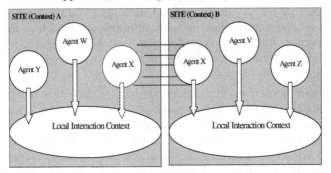

Fig. 1. Mobility across interaction context

What the interaction model to be actually exploited for modeling interaction is not of primary influence. Interaction in a context may occur via message passing (and, at a higher-level, via ACLs [11]), via event-channels [1], via meetings [28], or via shared information spaces [3]. The choice of a specific interaction model can be determined both by the specific application needs and by the available communication and coordination infrastructure. What really matters from the software engineering perspective is the locality model of interaction enforced by local interaction spaces, which naturally reflects – at the level of application modeling – a notion of context which is intrinsic in mobility. In fact, for the very fact of moving across the Internet, agents will access different data, services, and will interact with different agents, depending on their current position, i.e., of their current interaction context.

2.3   From Interaction Contexts to Organizational Contexts

The above form of *context-dependency*, intrinsic in agent mobility and made explicit by a modeling of the Internet as a multiplicity of interaction contexts, does not imply interaction contexts to play any active role in it. In fact, an interaction context may act as a simple data and service repository, or as an event and message forwarder. In other words, an interaction context is simply a *place* rather than an *organization*. However, more sophisticated forms of context-dependency may be needed in Internet applications suggesting an active role of interaction contexts and leading to an *organizational perspective*:

- each context has its own specific characteristics and security policies, and it may be somehow in need of enacting specific coordination laws to rule the coordination activities of the locally executing agents (*environment-dependent coordination*). These coordination laws may include security and resource control policies, as well as policy to rule inter-agent interactions and control the evolution of inter-agent coordination protocols.

- application agents belonging to a specific multi-agent application may require their coordination activities to occur according to specific application needs, e.g., agent may wish to each specific coordination laws on their coordination activities, independently of the interaction context in which they actually take place and on the coordination laws there enacted (*application-dependent coordination*).

With regard to the first point, as all coordination activities of mobile agents on a site occur via the local interaction context, it is conceptually wrong to think at local interaction policies and coordination laws as something unrelated to interaction contexts. Instead, by assuming an organizational (or social) perspective, one can consider the interaction context in terms of an organizational (or social) context. In other words, one must consider that an agent, by entering via migration an interaction context, it enters a foreign organization (society) in which specific organizational rules (or social conventions) are likely to be intrinsically enacted in the form of coordination laws. Thus, for the sake of conceptual simplicity, one must consider the interaction context as the locus in which the organizational rules ruling the activities of the local organization reside [31].

With regard to the second point, one must take into account that mobile agents executing within a distributed multi-agent applications, still logically belong to the organization (society) defined by the multi-agent application in itself, despite the fact that they may are currently executing in a foreign organization. In other words, the context in which an agent executes and interacts is not only the one identified by the local interaction context, but is also the one of its own organization. As that, a local interaction context should not only be though as the place in which local organizational rules reside, but also as a place in which application agents may enact their own, application-specific, organizational rules in the form of coordination laws.

Keeping all together, the introduced concepts lead to the scenario depicted in Figure 2, which represents a usable a modular conceptual framework for the analysis and design of mobile agent applications. On the one hand, interaction contexts associated to different sites may enact specific organizational rules and, thus, may exhibit different behaviors in response to the same interaction events. In an organization/site, agents are forced to play a specific role and their coordination activities occur accordingly to local, site-specific organizational rules. On the other hand, since agents also execute in the context of their original application/organization, coordination activities will be influenced not only by the local organizational rules, different from site to site. Instead, application-specific organizational rules can be enacted for all the agent of that application on any visited site, to act concurrently with the local organizational rules.

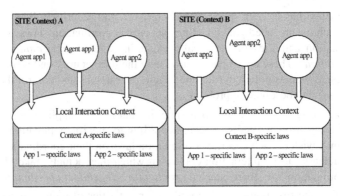

Fig. 2. Context-dependent coordination: The framework

2.4   Impact on Analysis and Design

From the point of view of application analysis and design, context-dependent coordination represents a useful conceptual framework. In fact, it naturally invites in analyzing and designing an application by clearly separating the *intra-agent* issues – related to the specific computational roles of the application agents – and the *inter-agent* ones – related to the interaction of the agents with the other agents of the same application and with the visited execution environments. In other words, context-dependent coordination promotes a clear separation of concerns, which is likely to reduce the complexity of application analysis and design.

Without the ambition of introducing a detailed methodology, we can sketch the general guidelines for the identification of intra-agent and inter-agent issues. These guidelines represent the adaptation to the area of mobile Internet agents of a previous study in the more general area of agent-oriented software engineering and methodologies [30,31].

From the point of view of application developers, the analysis phase can be organized as follow:

- at the intra-agent level, one has to analyze the global application goal and decompose it into sub-goals. This process should lead to the identification of the *roles* to be played in the application [29];
- at the inter-agent level, one should identify of how roles relate to each other, and of how interaction between roles must occur for the global application goal to be

correctly achieved. This process should lead to the identification of the organizational rules, driving the whole behavior of the agent organization [31].

The following design phase should build on the outcome of the analysis phase. One the one hand, accordingly with the guidelines of the Gaia methodology [29], the design phase should identify the agent classes that will form the application, and the agent instances that have to be instantiated from these classes. The agent of a class can play more roles, and more agents of a class can be instantiated to play the same roles. On the other hand, the identified application-specific organizational rules must be used to precisely define, in operative terms, the way coordination activities should be ruled [31]. This amount at defining the protocols to be used by agents to interact with each other as well as those to be used to access to the resources of the visited sites. In addition, this imply defining the constraints under which the protocols can be executed and the computational activity that must be issued in interaction contexts to properly mediate and support the execution of protocols.

Independent of the duty of application designers is the duty assigned by context-dependent coordination to *site administrators*. When new kinds of application agents are known to be going deployed on the Internet (or when sites are going to federate to share a common infrastructure) the administrator of one site can identify all the local organizational rules that he may find it necessary to enact. These rules can be used to facilitate the execution of the agents on the site, and/or to make the structure of the local organization homogeneous to agents' expectations (or to the requirements of the forming federation), and/or to protect the site from improper exploitation of the local interaction context. Again, the local organizational rules identified by the analysis phase are to be used in design to define protocols in operative terms and to define the associated computational activity to be performed in the local interaction context.

3   Programmable Coordination Infrastructures

Context-dependent coordination not only introduces a suitable, organization-oriented, framework for the analysis and design of mobile agent applications, but it also represent a reference model for an Internet coordination infrastructure suited to the needs of mobile agent applications.

3.1   Programmable Coordination Media

For a coordination infrastructure to enforce context-dependent coordination, it must somehow implement the abstraction of local programmable interaction contexts via an architecture based on local and *programmable coordination media*.

In general terms, a coordination medium is the software system enabling interaction and coordination, accordingly to a given interaction model, among a set of agent/processes executing within a locality. Whatever the interaction model defined, a coordination medium is characterized by: *(i)* a set of operations to be used by agents to access it and *(ii)* an internal behavior, intended as the computational activities performed inside the coordination medium in response to access events. For instance, with reference to the tuple space model, a coordination medium is characterized by *(i)* a limited set of primitive operations to store, read and consume tuples from the tuple space and *(ii)* an internal behavior based on a blocking pattern-matching access to tuples. In particular, an agent can request a tuple by providing a template; the tuple space returns to the agent one tuple matching the template, if available, blocks the requesting agent otherwise.

Most of the communication and coordination infrastructures (as well as most of available tuple space implementations) fix the internal behavior of coordination media once and for all. *Programmable coordination media* [4,8,19], instead, make it possible – without changing the set of primitive operations used by agents to access coordination media – to program the internal behavior of the coordination media in response to access events accordingly to the specific needs of the applications or of the local environments. For instance, let us consider the enhancement of the basic tuple-space model towards a *programmable tuple space model* [8]. In this case, one must enable, for each and every specific (class of) access events – i.e., requests for storing, reading, or extracting given tuple classes performed by a given classes of agents – a reaction different from the basic pattern-matching mechanism to be programmed and issued in response to it.

3.2   The MARS Infrastructure

MARS (*M*obile *A*gent *R*eactive *S*paces), developed at the University of Modena and Reggio Emilia and described in detail in [4], implements a programmable tuple-based coordination infrastructure for Java mobile agents. The characteristics of MARS and of its programmable tuple space model make it a suitable infrastructure for context-dependent coordination.

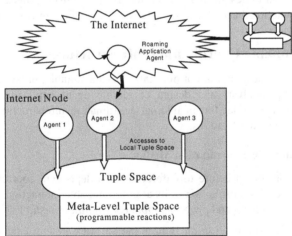

Fig. 3. The MARS Architecture

Globally, the MARS architecture is made up of a multiplicity of independent programmable tuple spaces. One tuple space is typically associated to a node and can be accessed only by the agents locally executing in that node (see Figure 3). Thus, MARS is explicitly conceived for actually mobile agents, in that to access a MARS tuple space agents have to actually execute on the corresponding node/domain. When an agent arrives on a node (or on a domain of nodes sharing a single MARS tuple space), it is automatically bound to the local MARS tuple space. To strictly enforce a context-dependent coordination model, the MARS tuple space on a node is intended as the only resource an agent can access on that node, and it should be therefore exploited for both inter-agent and agent-environment coordination.

The extension of MARS to support virtually mobile agents and physically mobile ones is under development.

The MARS interface to access a tuple space has been designed in compliance with the Sun's *JavaSpaces* one [12]. Tuples and template tuples (both usually called "Entries") are Java objects whose instance variables, possibly non-defined in the case of template tuples, represent the tuple fields. To access the tuple space, the write, read, and take operations are provided to store, read, and extract, respectively, a tuple. In addition, the readAll and takeAll operations are provided to read and extract, respectively, all matching tuples from the space. The default behavior of a MARS tuple space in response to access events is a quite traditional pattern-matching access to tuples of the tuple space model. A tuple T matches a template tuple U (which has to be provided as parameter of read, take readAll and takeAll operations) if the defined values of U are equal to the corresponding ones in T.

The programmable model of MARS enables the association of any needed reactions in response to access events performed by agents. This association occurs via *4-ples* stored in a *"meta-level"* tuple space. A meta-level 4-ple has the form of *(Rct, I, Op, T)*: it means that the reaction method (representing the reaction itself) of an instance of the class *Rct* has to be triggered when an agent with identity I invokes the operation Op on a tuple/template T. Putting and extracting tuples from the meta-level tuple space corresponds to installing and uninstalling, respectively, reactions associated to events at the base-level tuple space. The administrator can do that via special-purpose agents or via a simple GUI. Application agents can do that via event-handlers [18] that install the specified reactions automatically, without interfering with the agents' activities.

A meta-level 4-ple can have some non-defined values, in which case it associates the specified reaction to all the access events that match it. For example, the 4-ple (Reaction, null, read, null) in the meta-level tuple space associates the reaction of an object instantiated by the Reaction class to all read operations, whatever the tuple type and content and the identity of the agent performing the operation. When an access event to the base-level tuple space occurs, MARS issues the pattern-matching mechanism in the meta-level tuple space to look for reactions to be executed in response to the access event. If several 4-ples satisfy the meta-level matching mechanism, all the corresponding reactions are executed in a pipeline, accordingly to their installation order (or to a specific order determined by the administrator). When a reaction method executes, it is provided with the identity of the agents that has triggered the reaction, the operation it has performed, the tuple provided as parameter in the operation and the tuples returned in the reaction previously executed in the pipeline, if any.

The fact that a reaction can be associated to access events either when performed by agents with a specific identity or independently of the identity of the accessing agents enables for the embedding in the form of reactions in the tuple space of both local coordination laws and of application-specific coordination laws. On the one hand, depending on its own needs, the administrator can install reactions that apply to all the agents executing on the node, or to specific classes of agents. On the other hand, agents can install their own application-specific reactions on the visited nodes, and these reactions have to apply only to those agents belonging to the same application context. Since an agent must not be allowed to influence the coordination activities occurring in a different application contexts, specific security mechanism in MARS guarantee that agents, unless explicitly authorized, can influence only their local application context.

3.3   Impact on Development

Given the availability of a programmable coordination infrastructure, the separation of concerns between intra-agent issues and inter-agent, organizational, ones, enforced during analysis and design, can be preserved during the development and maintenance too.

If, as in MARS, the code of the agents can be clearly separated from the code implementing the coordination laws (representing local and/or application-specific organizational rules), agents and coordination laws can be coded, changed, and re-used, independently of each other. Thus, by avoiding to hardwire into agents the code related to the implementation of specific coordination laws, context-dependent coordination promotes the writing of more modular, manageable, and re-usable code.

The advantages of context-dependent coordination and of programmable coordination infrastructures make us strongly encourage their adoption. However, we also want to emphasize that, in the presence of an infrastructure based on programmable coordination media, neither the designer, nor the developers, nor the administrators of one site are obliged to commit to a context-dependent approach. They are fully free to neglect the programmability of the coordination media, develop applications in terms of agents interacting via non-programmed coordination media, and exploit applications already developed for such infrastructures.

4   A Case Study

As a simple case study in the area of workflow management, we consider the review process of a big international conference. The engineering problems related to the agent-mediated management of such a process has been analyzed in detail in [30,31]. Here, after having presented the case study in general terms, we focus on a few issues related to the management of the coordination activities of mobile agents.

The review process of a big international conference can be based on a partitioning of the submitted papers among PC members (or among the members of a steering committee). Each PC member is in charge of appropriately recruiting referees for its paper partition, of collecting the required number of reviews for each paper, and of sending them back to the PC chair. Referees, by their side, are in charge of retrieving papers to review and of filling the associated review form by the stated deadline.

Let us now consider the distributed scenario of a mobile-agent-mediated management of review process activities, by assuming the presence of the MARS infrastructure.

The PC chair is supposed to make available all submitted papers in the form of tuples in its local MARS tuple space. If the PC Chair gives to PC members the freedom of choosing which papers they should take care of, a PC member can exploit mobile agents to go to the PC Chair site and there select the required number of papers on the basis of personal preference criteria. PC member agents can copy these papers in the local PC member's MARS tuple space, which will also acts as a repository for both white and filled review forms, and will decide about the assignments of papers to referees. A referee, at its turn, will send a mobile agent to the site of the PC member that has recruited him, to retrieve the papers assigned to him (or to negotiate these assignments) and the associated review forms. Once the review is completed, the mobile agent of the referee is sent back to the PC member site to put in it the filled review forms, where PC member agents can eventually analyze the outcome of the review process.

4.1   Analysis

By relying on the conceptual framework of context-dependent coordination, and keeping into account the application developers' perspective, the analysis of the above case study introduces the issues of identifying the different roles to be played in the application and the organizational rules. In particular, after the analysis of the case study, one could have identified the different roles of "collector of papers for a PC member" and "referees recruiter", and the single role of "referee". Moreover, the analysis should have also identified organizational rules that must be respected in the review process activities. For instance, two of such rules may specify that *(r1)* the referee recruiter cannot assign more than N papers to the same referee, and that *(r2)* a referee cannot read a paper unless it is assigned to them. Further rules can be defined along the guidelines that traditionally rule the review process of a conference.

From the point of view of system administrators, the analysis should identify the possible "attacks" to the local system that can be performed by malicious application, and the problems that agents can encounter in accessing local resources. For example, the administrator of a PC member site can be required to store all local technical reports and documents, there included the submitted paper, in the "pdf" format. If papers have to be submitted to the conference in "ps" format, and application agents will accordingly look for "ps" files, a local organizational rule could then be the one that specify that *(r3)* requests for "ps" files must be considered as valid requests for "pdf" files.

4.2   Design

The outcome of the analysis phase should be used to drive the design of the application, aimed at identifying which agent classes should be defined and which agents should be instantiated from them. In the case study, a reasonable choice would be to collect in a single PC member agent class all the roles actually belonging to PC members, i.e., "collector of papers" and "referees recruiter". Instead, the role of "referee" would reasonably be implemented as a single agent class.

In addition to the identification of agents, the design phase in our approach also requires defining which behavior should be actually programmed by application agents in the interaction context so that all application protocols can execute in respect of the identified organizational rules. With regard to the organizational rule *(r1)*, it implies associating a behavior to interaction context, which avoids a PC member to involve a referee in a protocol/negotiation for the assignment of a paper more than *N* times. In a similar way, and from the point of view of system administrators, rule *(r3)* implies associating a behavior that is able to transform any protocol for the request of a "ps" file into a protocol for the request of a "pdf" file.

4.3   Development

The development phase simply reduce at separately coding agent classes and organizational rules (in the form of coordination laws). With reference to MARS and Java-based mobile agents, we sketch some code fragments for agents and coordination laws.

Figure 4 shows a fragment of the code of PC member and referee agents, and in particular the code associated with the protocol for assigning papers to referees. The PC member agent analyzes its paper, chooses a referee, and asks him for its willingness to review the paper. The referee agents goes to the site of the PC member, checks which papers the PC member has assigned to it, and decide if it want to review them or not. All this protocol occurs via exchanging of tuple in the MARS tuple space of the PC member. Although the figure shown agents implemented as simple Java thread, nothing in our approach and in the MARS infrastructure prevents from adopting any other suitable agent architecture. The only requirement is that agents interact with accordingly to the MARS interface.

Figure 5 shows the code of a Java class, in the format of MARS reactions, implementing the organizational rule *(r1)*. This simply amounts at avoiding the PC member writing more than N AssignmentTuples with the same referee ID as field. By writing the meta-level tuple:

(LimitNumber,PC-member-ID, write, AssignmentTuple(null,null))

in the tuple space, the reaction will be triggered whenever a PC member agent writes an AssignementTuple in the tuple space. Figure 6 shows the code implementing the organizational rule *(r2)*, to avoid a referee agent to read a paper unless that paper has been explicitly assigned to it. Figure 7 shows the code implementing the organizational rule *(r3)*, which transforms any request for a (tuple representing a) "ps" file info a request for a (tuple representing a) "pdf" file.

4.4   Discussion

Not only, as already stated, the code for agents and organizational rules can be changed, and re-used independently of each other, but also new organizational rules can be added and old can be dismissed by influencing neither the behavior of agents nor the one of organizational rules.

With reference to the protocol via which a referee access to papers, one can see that code of figure 6 naturally pipelines with the one of figure 7, leading to a composition of the local and application-specific organizational rules associated to the execution of that protocol. Once the local organizational rule select "pdf" papers on the basis of the "ps" request performed by agents, the application-specific rule can select, among all papers, only those that have been actually assigned to the requesting agents. Let us now suppose that the conference official decide that even those referee that are not in charge of the review of a paper can take a look at it. Then, the application can be simply updated by de-installing the code implementing the organizational rule *r2* (i.e., with reference to MARS, by simply deleting the associated meta-level tuple).

In a similar way, new organizational rules can be added and further pipelined with existing ones. For instance, let us suppose that the conference officials decide that a single referee cannot review more than one paper of the same author. This influences the protocol for assigning papers to referees, and should avoid a PC member to involve a referee in the paper assignment protocol if that referee has been previously involved in the same protocol for a paper of the same author. This new organizational rule can be coded by a MARS reaction that reacts to all insertions of AssignmentTuples performed by PC members, and checks them against the new organizational rule. Such a reaction can then be installed in the MARS meta-level tuple space to take effect, and it can be pipelined with the reaction of Figure 5, implementing rule *r1*.

```
// Excerpt of the class for the PC Member agents
class PCMemberAgent extends Agent {
private Space Local;
private PaperTuple PaperPattern, Paper; Identity ChosenRef;

public void run()
{ ...
// creation of template tuple - class PaperTuple representing papers
PaperPattern = new PaperTuple(null, null, null, null, null, "ps");
// retrieve from the space (via a read operation) a paper
Paper = Local.read(PaperPattern, null, NO_WAIT);
//analyse the paper on the basis of its characteristics
// and decide about a proper referee
// put in the space a tuple of class AssignmentTuple
// to specify the association paperID-refereeID
Local.write(new AssignTuple(Paper.Paper,ID,ChosenRef),null, 0);
// wait for a tuple of class AckTuple from the referee
Local.take(new AckTuple(Paper.PaperID,ChosenRef,null),...);
... // go on with the process
}

// Excerpt for the class for the referee agents
class RefereeAgent extends Agent {
private Space Local; ...

public void run()
{// the agent migrates to the PC member site
this.go_to("PCChair.site.com");
// note: that could also be a "virtual" migration
// creation of a template tuple – class AssignmentTuple
AssTupPattern = new AssignementTuple(null, MyID);
// retrieve from the space all AssignementTuples
AllAssigned = Local.readAll(AssTupPattern, null, NO_WAIT);
// checks, for each assigned paper, which it can referee,
// if the i-th paper assigned can be refereed it is read from the space
Local.read(new PaperTuple(AllAssigned[i].PaperID, null, null,..)...);
// the corresponding ack tuple is put in the space
Local.write(new AckTuple(AllAssigned[i].PaperID, MyID, YES);
...
}
```

Fig. 4. A Fragment of the code of the PC Member and the Referee agents

```
class LimitPapers implements Reactivity
{
  public Entry[] reaction(Space s, Identity Id, Operation Op, Entry Template, Entry
InputTuples[])
  { Identity CurrAssTo; AssignmentTuple PastAss[];
  CurrAssTo = (AssignmentTuple)Template.CurrentRef;
  // retrieve all tuple representing previous assignments
   // to the same referee
  PastAss = s.readAll(new AssignmentTuple(null,CurrAssTo, ..)..);
  // if there are less than N, also the current assignemment
  // can be written as a tuple
  if(PastAss.lenght()<N) s.write(Template, null, 0);
  return null;
}
```

Fig. 5. Reaction limiting the number of paper assignments to a referee

```
class PS2PDF implements Reactivity
{
  public Entry[ ] reaction(Space s, Identity Id, Operation Op, Entry Template, Entry
InputTuples [ ])
  // no match if the site stores the extension as "ps"
  { // thus modifies the extension of the required files
  ((PaperTuple)Template).Format = "pdf";
  // require matching with new extension
  Entry [ ] result = s.readAll(Template, null, NO_WAIT);
  // now the match can occurr with pdf files
  return result;
  } // end of method reaction
} // end of class PostScript2PS
```

Fig. 6. Reaction transforming request for "ps" files into requests for "pdf" files.

```
class ReadOnlyAssigned implements Reactivity
{
  public Entry[ ] reaction(Space s, Identity Id, Operation Op, Entry Template, Entry
InputTuples [ ])
  { // for each matching tuple (if any)
  for (int i = 0; (InputTuples != null) && (i < InputTuples.length); i++)
  // for each paper, checks if its is assigned to the agent
  // i.e., if a corresponding AssignmentTuples exists
  if (!s.read(new AssignmentTuple(InputTuple[i].PaperID, Identity)))
      // the paper tuple has not to be returned
      InputTuple[i]=null;
      // return only the updated tuples (null elements are purged)
  return compactArray(InputTuples);
  } // end of method reaction
} // end of class ModifiedOnly
```

Fig. 7. Reaction enabling a referee to read only those papers assigned to it

From the agent point of view, provided that the protocol interfaces remain unchanged from the agent point of view, one can change the code of the agents without necessarily changing the organizational rules. In the specific example, one can change the code that drive PC member agent toward the choice of a specific paper-referee assignment without influencing at all other the code of the coordination laws.

Clearly, the above considerations about re-use and maintenance of code also apply at the analysis and design level. In fact, due to the separation of concern enforced in the whole software development process, the analysis and design phases benefits from the possibility of separately modifying and updating the outcomes of inter-agent and intra-agent analysis/design.

5   Related Work

A few of the proposals in the area of Internet agents explicitly focus on models and coordination infrastructures suited to mobility. However, models and systems, in different areas, focus on problems (and propose solutions) strictly related to the ones discussed in this paper.

5.1   Coordination in Multi-agent Systems

Several works in the area of multi-agent systems and of agent-based software engineering are recently recognizing that modeling and engineering interactions in complex and open multi-agent systems cannot simply rely on the agent capability of communicating via agent communication languages and of acting accordingly to the need/expectations of each agent in the system. Instead, concepts such "organizational rules" [15,31], "social laws" [9,20], "social structures" [24], "social conventions" [2,21], "active environments" [23] are receiving more and more attention, and are leading to a variety of models and proposals. Under different terminology and techniques, the common idea is that, for the effective engineering of multi-agent systems, higher-level, inter-agent, concepts and abstractions must be defined to explicitly model the organization/society in which agents live and have to interact, and the associated organizational/societal laws.

As an example, several researches show that engineering a complex multi-agent organization does not simply require the identification of the roles to be played by agents, but it also requires the identification of the global constraints under which the interactions between roles in the organization have to occur. The identified global constraints can then be hardwired into the agents to limit their possible actions [20], or they can be used to select the most suitable organizational structure for the system [31]. As another example, in ant-based systems complex global behaviors can emerge from the interactions of very simple agents with the environment [23]. Agents put and sense pheromones in the environment, and act accordingly to the concentration of pheromones in given sections of the environment. The environment, by its side, makes pheromones vanish with time, according to specific laws. The global behavior that emerges depends strictly on the laws upon which pheromones vanish: in other words, the environment plays an active role by influencing the overall behavior of the system via an imposition of environment-specific rules.

The framework of context-dependent coordination is likely to facilitate the definition and the implementation of complex multi-agent systems. In fact, as we have shown, organizational rules can be easily mapped in terms of application-specific coordination laws and can be enforced by a proper programming of coordination media, without having to hardwire them into agents or into the organizational structure. Moreover, a programmable coordination medium represents the most natural implementation of an active environment upon which to rely for controlling the emergence of global behaviors.

5.2   Coordination Infrastructures

The *T Spaces* project at IBM [14] and the *JavaSpaces* project at Sun [12] define an infrastructure based on Linda-like tuple spaces to be used as both general-purpose network information repositories and coordination media. However, they do not define infrastructures conceived to meet the problem of mobility: agents can refer to multiple tuple spaces, whether local or remote, and access them in a location-unaware way. In addition, neither T Spaces nor JavaSpaces define a programmable coordination media, although T Spaces integrates a limited form of programmability, by enabling complex queries to be added as primitives to a tuple space.

The *TuCSoN* infrastructure [22], developed in the context of an affiliated research project, adopts an architectural model very similar to that of MARS, and enhances it by making it possible for agents to refer to remote tuple spaces via URLs, as an Internet service. This enforces network-awareness and virtual mobility without forcing actual agent mobility, although it requires agents to explicitly handle the URLs references to remote tuple space. With regard to the tuple space model, TuCSoN resembles MARS in its full programming capability of tuple spaces, but it defines logic tuple spaces where both tuples and tuple space behaviors are expressed in terms of untyped first-order logic terms, and where unification is the basic pattern-matching mechanism.

The LIME infrastructure faces the problem of handling interactions in the presence of any kind of active mobile entities [26]. Each "agent", whether a software agent, an Internet site, or a physical mobile device, owns and carries on in its movements a tuple space. Whenever the agent keeps in touch (i.e., gets connected) with another agent, the tuple spaces owned by each of the agents merge together, thus allowing to interact via the merged tuple space. A limited form of reactivity is provided to automatically move tuples across tuple spaces, and to notify agents about the events occurring in their tuple spaces. Thus, LIME naturally promotes a primitive form of context-dependent coordination: the effect of an agent accessing to its own-tuple space can be very different depending on whether the tuple space is currently merged with other tuple spaces and on which are the specified rules for tuple flowing across tuple spaces.

The model of Law-governed interactions, described in [19], addresses the problem of making peer-to-peer coordination within a group of non-mobile agents obey to a set of specified laws. These laws are typically security-oriented, and express which operations the agents are allowed to perform, and in which order. To enforce these laws, the model dynamically associates a controller process to each agent that joins the group. The controller process intercepts all messages to/from the agent and, by coordinating with other controllers, checks their compatibility with the enforced laws. A similar approach has been followed in the implementation of the Fishmarket system for agent-mediated auctions [21], with the goal of guaranteeing that auctions can proceed accordingly to specific auctions' conventions. Although not explicitly addressing agent mobility issues and application-dependent coordination issues, both the above approaches are suitable to enforce local coordination laws in systems of peer-to-peer interacting agents.

6   Conclusions and Future Work

In this paper, we have introduced context-dependent coordination as a conceptual framework for Internet applications based on mobile agents and have shown how it can promote a modular approach to application analysis and design. Moreover, we have shown how a programmable coordination infrastructure, by mapping at the infrastructure level the abstractions of context-dependent coordination, can lead to the development of easy to program and easy to maintain mobile agent applications.

In the future, we intend to develop a formal model of context-dependent coordination, possibly by exploiting already defined models for mobility and mobile agents [6,25]. In addition, we indent to better investigate and integrate in our model role modeling techniques [17,16] and agent communication languages [11].

References

1. J. Baumann, F. Hohl, K. Rothermel, M. Straßer, "Mole - Concepts of a Mobile Agent System", *The World Wide Web Journal*, 1(3):123-137, 1998.
2. W. Brauer, M. Nickles, M. Rovatsos, G. Weiss, K. F. Lorentzen, "Expectation-Oriented Analysis and Design", 2001, in this volume.
3. G. Cabri, L. Leonardi, F. Zambonelli, "Mobile-Agent Coordination Models for Internet Applications ", *IEEE Computer*, 33(2):82-89, Feb. 2000.
4. G. Cabri, L. Leonardi, F. Zambonelli, "MARS: a Programmable Coordination Architecture for Mobile Agents", *IEEE Internet Computing*, 4(4):26-35, July-Aug. 2000.
5. G. Cabri, L. Leonardi, F. Zambonelli, "Engineering Mobile Agent Applications via Context-Dependent Coordination", 23rd International Conference on Software Engineering, IEEE CS Press, May 2001.
6. L. Cardelli, A. D. Gordon, "Mobile Ambients", *Theoretical Computer Science*, 240(1), July 2000.
7. Y. Demazeau, A.C. Rocha Costa, "Populations and Organizations in Open Multi-Agent Systems", 1st National Symposium on Parallel and Distributed Artificial Intelligence, 1996.
8. E. Denti, A. Natali, A. Omicini, "On the Expressive Power of a Language for Programmable Coordination Media", Proceedings of the 10th ACM Symposium on Applied Computing, ACM, 1998.
9. V. Dignum, H. Weigand, L. Xu, "Agent Societies: Toward Framework-based Design", 2001, in this volume.
10. J. Ferber, O. Gutknecht, "A Meta-Model for the Analysis and Design of Organizations in Multi-Agent Systems", 3rd International Conference on Multi-Agent Systems, IEEE CS Press, pp. 128-135, July 1998.
11. T. Finin at al., "KQML as an Agent Communication Language", 3rd International Conference on Information Knowledge and Management", November 1994.
12. E. Freeman, S. Hupfer, K. Arnold, *JavaSpaces: Principles, Patterns, and Practice*, Addison-Wesley, 1999.
13. A. Fuggetta, G. Picco, G. Vigna, "Understanding Code Mobility", *IEEE Transactions on Software Engineering*, 24(5):352-361, May 1998.

14. "T Spaces: the Next Wave", *IBM System Journal*, 37(3):454-474, 1998.
15. N. R. Jennings, "On Agent-Based Software Engineering", *Artificial Intelligence*, 117(2):277-296, 2000.
16. N. R. Jennings, M. Wooldridge, "Agent-Oriented Software Engineering", in *Handbook of Agent Technology*, J. Bradshaw Ed., AAAI/MIT Press, 2000.
17. E. A. Kendall, "Role Modelling for Agent Systems Analysis, Design and Implementation", *IEEE Concurrency*, 8(2):34-41, April-June 2000.
18. D. B. Lange, M. Oshima, *Programming and Deploying Java™ Mobile Agents with Aglets™*, Addison-Wesley, August 1998.
19. N.H. Minsky, V. Ungureanu, "Law-Governed Interaction: A Coordination & Control Mechanism for Heterogeneous Distributed Systems", *ACM Transactions of Software Engineering and Methodology*, 9(3):273-305, July 2000.
20. Y. Moses, M. Tenneholtz, "Artificial Social Systems", *Computers and Artificial Intelligence*, 14(3):533-562, 1995.
21. P. Noriega, C. Sierra, J. A. Rodriguez, "The Fishmarket Project. Reflections on Agent-mediated institutions for trustworthy E-Commerce", Workshop on Agent Mediated Electronic Commerce (AMEC-98), 1998.
22. A. Omicini, F. Zambonelli, "Coordination for Internet Application Development", *Journal of Autonomous Agents and Multi-Agent Systems*, 2(3):251-269, Sept. 1999.
23. H. V. D. Parunak, S. Brueckner, J. Sauter, R. S. Matthews, "Distinguishing Environmental and Agent Dynamics ", 1st International Workshop on Engineering Societies in the Agents' World, Lecture Notes in Computer Science, No. 1972, Springer-Verlag, 2000.
24. H. V. D. Parunak, J. Odell, "Representing Social Structures in XML", 2001, in this volume.
25. G. P. Picco, A.M. Murphy, G.-C. Roman, "Software Engineering for Mobility: A Roadmap", in *The Future of Software Engineering*, A. Finkelstein (Ed.), ACM Press, pp. 241-258, 2000.
26. G. P. Picco, A.M. Murphy, G.-C. Roman, "LIME: Linda Meets Mobility", 21st International Conference on Software Engineering, ACM, pp. 368-377, May 1999.
27. J. Waldo, G. Wyant, A. Wollrath, S. Kendall, "A Note on Distributed Computing", Mobile Object Systems, Lecture Notes in Computer Science, No. 1222, pp. 49-64, Springer-Verlag, Berlin (D), 1997.
28. J. White, "Mobile Agents", in *Software Agents*, J. Bradshaw (Ed.), AAAI Press, pp. 437-472, 1997.
29. M. Wooldridge, N. R. Jennings, D. Kinny, "The Gaia Methodology for Agent-Oriented Analysis and Design", *Journal of Autonomous Agents and Multi-Agent Systems*, 3(3):285-312, 2000.
30. F. Zambonelli, N. R. Jennings, A. Omicini, M. J. Wooldridge, "Agent-Oriented Software Engineering for Internet Applications", in *Coordination of Internet Agents*, A. Omicini et al. (Eds.), Springer-Verlag, 2001.
31. F. Zambonelli, N. R. Jennings, M. J. Wooldridge, "Organizational Abstractions for the Analysis and Design of Multi-agent Systems", in *Agent-Oriented Software Engineering*, LNCS No. 1947, November 2000.

Towards an ADL for Designing Agent-Based Systems

Marie-Pierre Gervais[1,2] and Florin Muscutariu[1]

[1]Laboratoire d'Informatique de Paris 6, 8 rue du Capitaine Scott-F 75015 Paris
[2]University Paris 10
{ Marie-Pierre.Gervais, Florin.Muscutariu}@lip6.fr

Abstract. In this paper, we describe the Architecture Description Language (ADL) that we are defining for the design of agent-based systems. This aims at filing the gap between the analysis and design phases in agent-oriented methodologies. The analysis phase enables the description of the software architecture without any consideration of the execution environment while the design phase supplements the analysis output with descriptions related to the distributed environment in which the agents will run. The distributed environment we consider is an OMG MASIF compliant mobile agent platform. Our approach provides a UML profile concerning the distribution aspects related to the execution environment for the agent-based systems designers. This work is a part of the ODAC project dealing with the development of a methodology for the construction of agent-based systems. This is based on the ISO Open Distributed Processing standards that define an architectural framework for the construction of distributed systems.

1 Introduction

A multi-agent system is commonly considered as a distributed system in which the entities are agents. This characteristic requires that these agents are deployed in an environment that supports their execution. Constructing an agent-based system must then encompass all the steps from the analysis and design to the implementation of the system. As the terminology is not standardized, in order to avoid confusion, let us precise what we call analysis and design. The *analysis* relates to the development of a detailed solution that does not depend on achievement choices. It includes the description of all the processes composing the system operation, the information definition and the tasks' specification. The purpose of the *design* is to lead to the system implementation and to carry out choices to make the models operational for the system achievement. It relates to the operational specifications needed to ensure the achievement of the future system. It includes the taking into account of the means chosen for the adopted solution, namely a target environment that will support the execution of the system.

According to these definitions, it must be recognized that most of the current methodologies focus on the analysis phase in the sense that they define the organization, the architecture and the description of the system elements, namely the agents and their relations [5, 6, 12]. This corresponds to the functional definition of

M.J. Wooldridge, G. Weiß, and P. Ciancarini (Eds.): AOSE 2001, LNCS 2222, pp. 263-277, 2002.
© Springer-Verlag Berlin Heidelberg 2002

the system, i.e., its software architecture. On the other hand, some works deal with the development of platforms for the agents execution, either in conformance with standards such as MASIF or FIPA or not [7, 11,13]. However, no correlation is established between the software architecture resulting from the analysis phase and its mapping onto an operational environment. There is a breaking point between the two aspects.

We advocate that the construction of an agent-based system is a process that must take into account the definition of the system as well as its implementation into a target environment in which it will run. This process must be achieved in accordance with an AO methodology that encompasses all the steps including analysis, design and implementation. The methodology must reflect the specificity of the agent technology. The distinction between the agent technology and the other software technologies has been described in [28], based on a unique set of software characteristics. One of the characteristics is a required peer-to-peer protocol. In [33], the distribution of data and control is cited as a reason to consider the multi-agent systems as an important new direction in software engineering. Both the peer-to-peer protocol and the distribution of data and control assume the existence of a distributed infrastructure that provides transparent communication mechanisms (e.g., an agent naming service) or an eventual support for mobility, as identified in [30]. Concerns of *Compliance with Standards, Distributions and Environment* are highly rated by the agent community in a survey conducted in [24].

Based on these considerations, LIP6 started a project to develop such a methodology, named ODAC (Open Distributed Applications Construction), using its experience learned from the distributed systems development. For this, it makes use of an ISO standard related to the distributed processing that is the Open Distributed Processing standard (ODP) [14]. This defines a set of rigorous concepts for modeling distributed systems. It makes use of the object paradigm in such a general way that it is possible to deal with ODP objects in the same way as they would be agents. For example, ODP objects are autonomous entities able to act by themselves. In our view, an agent is an ODP object and agent-based systems are distributed in the ODP term sense, since they comply in a technical and organizational heterogeneous context. They consist of interacting entities, which can be agents and/or objects. The Reference Model of ODP (RM-ODP) can then be useful when building agent-based systems as it provides an architectural framework that encompasses all the needed aspects, i.e. the functional as well as the technical description of the system while providing some correspondence rules between them. However, ODP provides no prescriptive methodology that can be followed in developing a system. Furthermore, the standard supplies no support for this development. For example, it defines concepts and rules, but no notation or formalism is proposed to put in a concrete form the system specification. We then propose in ODAC the use of the UML standardized notation for specifying agent-based systems according to the ODP semantics. Thus, we are defining an Architecture Description Language (ADL) for modeling the system both in analysis and design phases. In a first step of the ODAC methodology development, we have defined the part of the ADL devoted to the analysis phase.

This paper focuses on the design phase of the ODAC methodology. More precisely, it illustrates the requirements for filing the gap between the analysis and the design phases and for achieving this design phase in order to get an operational description of the agent-based system to be implemented. As mentioned previously, the analysis output is the software architecture of the system related to its functional properties. The design activity adds to this description the non-functional properties according to the chosen execution environment. ODAC considers a specific kind of environment, namely a MASIF compliant mobile agent platform. We are then supplementing the ADL already defined in order to include the part devoted to the design phase. Our approach is to define a UML profile enabling the description of the distributed execution environment and the placement of the agents in this environment.

The paper is structured as follows. We first provide an overview of the ODAC methodology. Then we present our approach based on background coming from two fields related to the software design. We describe the UML profile we are defining for the design phase. At the end, we present a conclusion.

2 The ODAC Methodology Overview

A methodology must define a set of concepts, the usage rules of these concepts by organizing them into various steps, the process associated with these steps and a notation. ODAC makes use of RM-ODP concepts. The major one is the "viewpoint" concept, that is a structuring concept of the modeling activity and thereby of the agent-based system modeling. RM-ODP defines five viewpoints: Enterprise, Information, Computational, Engineering and Technology. Each of them focuses on a specific concern when modeling a system and enables to specify the system according to a set of relevant concepts for the preoccupations related to this viewpoint. Therefore this concept of "viewpoint" results from the separation of concerns approach in modeling activity. The complete system specification is then the set of each viewpoint specification with their correspondence rules.

In ODAC methodology, we make use of this concept by associating in an informal way the Enterprise, the Information and Computational viewpoints to the analysis and the Engineering viewpoint to the design [10]. The Technology viewpoint is out of our consideration as it refers to the implementation. ODAC then distinguishes in these two stages intended to define the system those that describe it independently of any target environment of those that describe it according to the environment in which it will be carried out. Two kinds of specifications are identified: the behavioral specification and the operational specification.

The *behavioral specification* results from the specifications established in the Enterprise, Information and Computational viewpoints. It describes the system according to its objective, its place in the company in which it is developed, information that it handles and the tasks that it carries out. For sake of simplicity, we do not mention the complete steps for writing a behavioral specification. Details can be found in [9]. Here, only the part devoted to the Enterprise specification is described. The basic concepts of the Enterprise viewpoint are ODP Enterprise object, role, community, objective, behavior and action [15]. An *ODP Enterprise object* is a model of an entity, either an entity of the system to be specified or an entity of the system environment. ODP Enterprise objects can be grouped to form a *community*. In that case, they exhibit the *behavior* needed to realize the *objective* of the community.

By doing this, they fulfill roles of the community since a *role* identifies a behavior. This is a set of *actions* with constraints on when they appear. Actions can be *interactions* between several objects or internal actions. ODAC prescribes the steps for elaborating an Enterprise specification as follows:

1)   Defining the objective of the system;
2)   Enumerating all the roles enabling to perform this objective;
3)   Among the roles of the system, identifying the possible interface roles, i.e. other communities. Assign then to these communities the roles that must be attached to them.

   For each community:

4)   Identifying the Enterprise objects fulfilling the roles of the community;
5)   Describing the behavior of the community;
6)   Describing the policies.

   To express these various descriptions, we provide the modeler with an ADL based on the UML standard notation. We then have mapped the RM-ODP Enterprise concepts onto the UML ones as illustrated in Table 1 [3].

Table 1. RM-ODP Enterprise and UML Concepts Mapping

RM-ODP Enterprise Concepts	UML Notation
Objective	Use Case
Role	Stereotype of Class "role"
Enterprise Object	UML Object
Community	Collaboration Diagram
Community Behavior	Sequence Diagram
Policy	Note

   The *operational specification* results from the design step corresponding to the projection of the behavioral specification on a target environment reflecting the real execution environment. It depends on the specification established in the Engineering viewpoint, which describes the execution environment. It constitutes the description from which code is generated and the implementation is carried out. We are then supplementing our ADL used in the analysis step in order to include the design concerns. For this, we make use of background coming from two areas related to the software design.

3 Related Works

We aim to fill the gap existing between the analysis phase and an agent execution environment. We want to provide the designer with a notation for describing the operational specification that is the mapping of the software architecture resulting from the analysis phase onto an operational environment. A similar mapping between two different levels of specification, part of the analysis phase in our approach, is done in [31].

The notation for the design step must include concepts related to the distribution aspects while enabling the description of the considered environment. The RM-ODP Engineering viewpoint provides such concepts as it focuses on required mechanisms and functions supporting distributed interactions among RM-ODP objects in the system. The definition of an ODP object as a model of an entity permits us to consider an ODP object as an agent. The agent execution environment we consider is in conformance with the MASIF standard. We have then mapped the MASIF standard concepts onto the RM-ODP Engineering concepts [20]. We refer them from now as the MASIF *platform elements* (e.g. region, agent system, place, agent, etc) [25]. In order to ensure continuity between analysis and design steps, the ADL we are defining for the design step must also be based on the UML notation.

We have investigated two fields that address issues relevant for our objective, namely the definition of an ADL for the description of an ODAC operational specification:

1. The *Object Engineering* field addresses the distribution aspects description through the use of UML. Moreover, some work has been done in considering object engineering on an RM-ODP base;

2. The *Architecture Engineering* field provides concepts to characterize the elements to be designed together with their relations. Since agent semantics is richer than the object semantics, Architecture Engineering represents a valuable work enabling the UML representation of different element semantics.

We detail hereafter some works related to these two fields.

3.1 Object Engineering

Object engineering has made some important progress since the appearance of UML. UML seems to be generally accepted as the language to describe object architectures. It is the result of a unified effort of other object languages (OMT, OOSE and OOADA). Basically, the notions that UML introduces can be grouped in three categories:

- Things;
- Relationships;
- Diagrams.

Although most of the efforts are devoted to the analysis phase of an object-oriented system, there are also possibilities to describe distribution issues (i.e. node, component, deployment diagram, etc). But UML lacks a methodology that defines the links between various elements.

Probably the most known methodology, which implicitly establishes a part of these links is the RUP (Rational Unified Process) developed by Rational Corporation [29].

This permits to describe some distribution concerns and is based on UML concepts as defined in UML Meta-Model.

Other projects consider their own object-oriented methodologies based on an RM-ODP approach.

a) The TRUMPET project consisted in modeling an RM-ODP system. This was done using a UML notation [16]. Most of the project was concerned with the analysis phase, although an extension of UML is presented for the RM-ODP engineering concepts dedicated to a chosen environment. This extension uses the UML subsystem considerations presented in [23]. In addition, the project is only concerned with UML deployment diagrams. Moreover, an RM-ODP object is considered to be an object in the usual meaning in object-oriented modeling, although its definition enables to map richer semantics on it.

b) Other efforts use an RM-ODP approach for UML object-oriented modeling but are only interested in the analysis phase [21]. More complete approaches never really passed the draft stage [22].

c) Lately, the DOT Profile project has proposed to consider an RM-ODP system on a component basis but for now it only addresses the analysis phase [4].

There are increasing efforts to adapt the UML notation to agent systems specification [1, 17,32].

3.2 Architecture Engineering

Architecture Engineering mainly consists of ADLs definitions enabling the description of architectures. Basically, ADLs have two main concepts: components and connectors. An architecture is then described as components connected by the connectors. The graphical representation for ADL is boxes for the components and lines for the connectors with specific semantics and properties. Few means are offered to describe the so-called non-functional properties of the components and connectors, i.e. properties that take into account an execution environment [18]. Most of the effort is dedicated to the analysis phase. Two main approaches are used in ADL-based methodologies for mapping the software architecture described in the analysis step onto the execution environment (Figure 1):

a) a *compilation* approach when the architecture is mapped directly onto a specific executing environment. An example of this approach could be seen in the OLAN project [2]. The compilation is done using an "OLAN configuration machine" which makes all the implementation choices.

b) the *construction* of a framework over the executing environment capable to match the ADL's semantics *(bottom-up construction)*. An example of this approach could be seen in C2 [19]. C2 constructs a class hierarchy that implements the component and the connector classes.

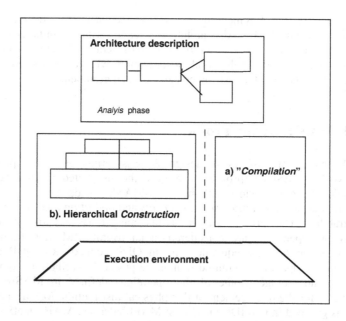

Fig. 1. Two approaches for implementing the architecture description.

Methodologies used for the architecture description based on particular ADLs representations have been supplemented lately with a UML approach. Instead of using specific ADL's boxes and lines, UML extensions are defined for capturing the ADL's semantics [8]. An example is the C2 ADL mapping to UML [19].

This trend of UML extension and adaptation for different purposes is encouraged by OMG and some *Profiles* are already made available [26].

3.3 Summary

We are defining a UML-based ADL for the *design* phase of a agent architecture system. RM-ODP offers the overall framework for that. The *object-oriented modeling* helps us to consider the *platform elements* representation using the existing UML concerns for distribution.

Since the *agent platform elements* have other semantics than the UML standard can offer, we have to choose:

- to create a different Meta-Model by operating modification at this level of abstraction,
- or to use the built-in mechanism of extension in order to obtain the required semantics.

Since the scope of UML is a "Unified Language", rather than modifying the Meta-Model, we propose to use the UML extension mechanism by introducing tagged values and semantics constraints expressed in OCL and grouped them in a UML profile.

The Architecture Engineering offers a feedback for different semantics representations with UML. Also architecture engineering permits us to situate our approach for the design phase as a *top-down construction*. The construction offers the possibility to refine the behavioral specification with the imposed choices and characteristics related to the distributed execution environment.

4 UML MASIF-Design Profile

The ADL that we propose for the design phase is defined as a UML profile. This is called "MASIF-DESIGN" profile, as for now, the distributed execution environment we consider is in conformance with the OMG-MASIF standard.

MASIF presents a minimum set of *concepts* and *operation* interfaces necessary for interoperability. The term *operation* in this context has a UML meaning. These concepts and operations are considered in an overall RM-ODP framework. The *operation* is the *function* equivalent in an ODP context. RM-ODP guide us in establishing the operations required to manage physical distribution, communication, processing and storage. Some of the operations defined in MASIF accomplish requirements for the management of this physical distribution. MASIF presents these operations grouped in two IDL interfaces: MAFFinder and MAFAgentSystem. These interfaces present the prototype of the methods that implement these operations.

The ADL for the design phase must enable the description of the considered environment. Thus we have first to model the MASIF platform elements with UML diagrams. As this model permits us further to locate agents in a distributed environment, two issues must be considered:

-   The placement of agents in the distributed infrastructure;
-   The representation of distribution transparencies.

A distribution transparency is the capacity of hiding the distribution aspects in the behavioral specification elaborated in the analysis phase. The platform elements cooperate to provide a transparency by bringing uniformity to some aspects of agents' distribution (e.g. uniformity of naming whatever the location of the agent). RM-ODP presents an inventory of assumed transparencies for a distributed system (e.g. access transparency or location transparency). MASIF presents a limited set of operations available to model the interactions between the platform elements needed for the transparency specification.

The transparencies have to be specified as analysis phase requirements. They enable to refine the existing behavioral specification with introducing additional behavior, including the use of one or more operations of the platform elements.

4.1 The Placement of Agents in the Distributed Infrastructure

The placement of agents in a distributed infrastructure is specified with UML deployment diagram. In order to do that, we have to model the infrastructure platform elements with UML diagrams. These platform elements are organized in a hierarchical configuration. First there is the *Region*, which makes the link among

Agent Systems. An *Agent System* includes *Places* where *Agents* reside and a *CoreAgency* as a management module.

This modeling process is not always straightforward. Each platform element can be represented at the *type level* and the *instance level*. An *instance* of a *type* is defined in ODP as a <X> (anything) that satisfies the *type*. A *type* is a predicate that characterizes collections of <X>s. The same approach of type and instance is referred in [8]. For simplicity, an analogy with object modeling concepts would be classes for *types* and instances of these classes.

We model the platform elements in the MASIF-DESIGN profile with stereotypes illustrated in Table 2.

Table 2. The stereotypes modeling the MASIF platform elements

MASIF platform elements	*Type* level UML Meta-model Class	*Instance* level	Stereotype Name
Region	Stereotyped Subsystem	Stereotyped Subsystem instance	Region
Agent System	Stereotyped Node	Stereotyped Node instance	Agent System
Core Agency	Stereotyped Subsystem	Stereotyped Subsystem instance	CoreAgency
Place	Stereotyped Package	Stereotyped Component instance	Place
Agent	Stereotyped Component	Stereotyped Component instance	Agent

a) The *Region* fully interconnects agent systems and enables the point-to-point transfer of information between them. The Region has a region registry with all the information about the places and agents. We represent Regions as stereotyped subsystems (Figure 2).

In UML, the subsystem is both package and classifier. A package is a grouping of model elements. A classifier is a *super-type* (abstraction) used to specify the common characteristics of the UML *Class*, *Interface* and *DataTypes*. A classifier describes behavioral and structural characteristics. The subsystem is instantiable.

A subsystem groups three elements: *operations*, *specification* elements and *realization* elements. The services provided by the subsystem are represented by interfaces and the corresponding operations. The specification and realization elements detail the internal behavior in order to assure these services and the elements that realize this behavior.

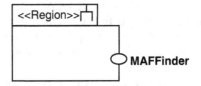

Fig. 2. The stereotyped subsystem "Region"

In MASIF, the region has an IDL interface named the MAFFinder. This is a set of operations needed to implement a "white pages" service. Thus graphical representation of the Stereotyped subsystem "Region" can be refined as illustrated in Figure 3. Only a few operations are listed here, the complete list can be found in the MASIF specification. It should be noted that the specification elements and realization elements of a Region are not addressed in MASIF. Thus each mobile agent platform that implements the MASIF standard has to make the desired choices.

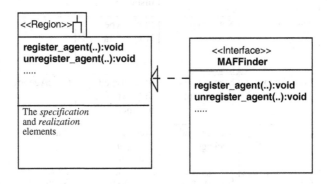

Fig. 3. Refinement of the stereotyped subsystem "Region"

b) The *AgentSystem* is the platform that can create, interpret, execute, transfer and terminate agents. We represent it as a stereotyped node. A node has an instance. The graphical representation is illustrated in Figure 4.

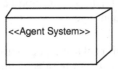

Fig. 4. The stereotyped Node "Agent System"

Each agent system has one CoreAgency, represented as a stereotyped subsystem.

c) The *CoreAgency* supports the management services provided to agents in an Agent System. The CoreAgency has an interface defined in MASIF as MAFAgentSystem.

Only a limited number of operations are described. The complete list of operations can be found in the MASIF specification. The specification elements and realization elements of the Core Agency Subsystem stereotype are not addressed in MASIF. The graphical representation and the implementation diagram are the same as the *Region* ones.

d) A *Place* is a context within an *Agent System* in which an agent can run. It can provide functions such as access control. We represent it as a stereotyped package (Figure 5).

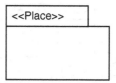

Fig. 5. The stereotyped package "Place"

Since a package has no instance, we represent the place instance as a component instance. The component *realizes* the place. Figure 6 illustrates the corresponding component diagram.

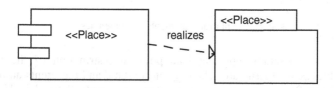

Fig. 6. The Place component diagram

e) We represent an *Agent* as a stereotyped component. The component *realizes* the stereotyped class that represents an agent in the analysis phase [27]. Additional information needed for the implementation can be included in the component diagram related to an agent implementation. For example, Grasshopper, which is a MASIF implementation platform, introduces an interface definition that specifies the agents' interaction points, i.e. the public operations (Figure 7).

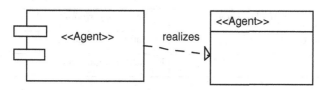

Fig. 7. The Agent component diagram

A component instance is defined in UML as a run-time implementation unit and may be used to show implementation units that have identity at run-time, including their location on nodes. The vast semantic of this definition permits us to consider the instance of a stereotyped package "Place" and of a stereotyped component "Agent" as components instances but with different semantics. The Place is a grouping unit of different agents. As for the Agents, they are the basic executable units. Components are things that participate in the execution of a system and nodes are things that execute components.

The dependency relations among the platform elements are represented in a component diagram (Figure 8).

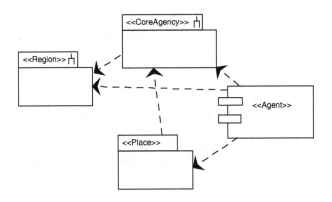

Fig. 8. The platform elements dependencies

The deployment diagram represents the physical distribution of the platform elements in a hierarchical structure. The diagram is static and represents an image of the system (Figure 9). We use transition stereotypes already defined in UML 1.3. These stereotypes permit us to specify all the locations that an agent visits during its lifetime and the eventual clones that it creates (Table 3).

As this representation could lead to an overloaded diagram, then we choose to multiply the deployment diagrams, one for small group of agents when it is necessary. This type of deployment diagram helps us to consider further some of the distribution transparencies.

Table 3. Transition stereotypes

UML Stereotype	Description
Become	Migration of an agent
Copy	Replication of an agent

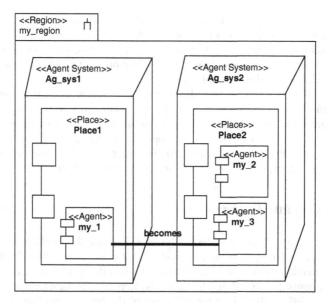

Fig. 9. The placement of agents in the hierarchical structure

4.2 Transparencies

The transparencies defined in RM-ODP are: access transparency, failure transparency, location transparency, migration transparency, relocation transparency, replication transparency, persistence transparency and transaction transparency. Our ongoing work only deals with location and access transparencies. The others are for further study.

a) Location transparency masks the use of information about location in space when identifying and binding interfaces of agents. Thus, agents can interact with other agents without using the location information.

There are two location issues, namely the location of an agent and the location of resources files for an agent.

In MASIF, the *location* is defined as the path to an agent system based on the agent system, the agent or the place. The operation named *MAFFinder.lookup_agent()* permits to connect two agents without knowing their location by requesting the region about the agents' location. The *location* descriptor in MASIF is either a URI containing a CORBA name or a URL containing an internet address.

We have also to consider the location of the agent definition file. An Agent System that executes an instance of an agent needs this agent definition. The operation *MAFFAgentSystem.fetch_class()* permits to retrieve this definition from the location of this file provided by the designer. In order that the designer can locate the source file with the agent definition, we introduce a tagged value named *FileDefinitionLocation.*

b) Access transparency masks differences in data representation and invocation mechanisms to enable interactions between agents. Here, there are also two issues, namely the link establishment of the communication and the security aspects in terms of access rights.

For the link establishment, MASIF refers existing mechanisms such as RMI, CORBA or RPC. However nothing is established in order that the designer makes the choice between these mechanisms. Some implementations, such as Grasshopper detail further the possibility to make these choices. We provide a tagged value *Link* so that the designer identifies the link he chooses.

As for the access rights, MASIF defines the notion of Agent's *authority*. An agent's *authority* identifies the person or organization for whom the agent acts. An authority must be authenticated. MASIF discusses the requirements for a secure mobile communication. The only operation related to access rights is *MAFFinder.list_all_agents_of_authority()*.In order that the designer identifies the authority of an agent, we introduce a tagged value named *Authority*.

5 Conclusion and Future Work

In order that designers of agent-based systems describe the model resulting from the analysis phase according to an execution environment, we provide them with an ADL. This enables the designers to describe the mobile agent platform they use and to locate the agents identified in the analysis step in this description. This ADL is defined as a UML profile since we make use of the built-in mechanism of extension. Thus it is based on UML notation.

Current work has identified the stereotypes needed to describe an OMG MASIF compliant mobile agent platform and its hierarchical structure and to locate the agents in such a structure. It also provides means in terms of tagged values enabling the designers to represent location and access transparencies. Further work is devoted to the refinement of our proposal by identifying attributes to characterize the platform elements and the transparencies not addressed in this paper. In addition, the approach described here in the definition of an ADL for the design of agent-based systems will be applied to another application domain, namely the active networks.

References

1.   Bauer, B.: UML Class Diagrams Revised in the Context of Agent-Based Systems, AOSE 2001
2.   Bellisard, L. and all., Distributed Application Configuration, In proceedings of the 16ᵗʰ International Conference on Distributed Computing Systems, IEEE Computer Society, Hong Kong, May 1996, pp579-585
3.   Blanc, X., Gervais, M.-P. and Le Delliou, R.: Using the UML language to express the ODP Enterprise Concepts, In proceeding s of the 3th International Enterprise Distributed Object Computing Conference (EDOC'99), IEEE Press, Mannheim, Germany, September 1999, pp50-59.
4.   Born, M., Holz, M. and Kath, M.: A Method for the Design and Development of Distributed Applications using UML, International Conference on Technology of of Object-Oriented Languages and Systems (TOOLS Pacific), Sydney Australia, November, 2000.
5.   Bresciani, P. and all: Modeling Early Requirements in Tropos: a Transformation Based Approach, AOSE 2001
6.   Caire, G.and all: Agent Oriented Analysis Using MESSAGE/UML, AOSE 2001
7.   FIPA-OS, http://fipa-os.sourceforge.net

8. Garlan D. and Kompanek A.J., Reconciling the Needs of Architectural Description with Object-Modeling Notations, UML'2000.
9. Gervais M.P., ODAC : une méthodologie de construction de systèmes à base d'agents fondée sur ODP, rapport LIP6 2000/28, November 2000 (in French)
10. Gervais M.P., ODAC: An Agent-Oriented Methodology Based on ODP, Submitted in Journal of Autonomous Agents and Multi-Agent Systems.
11. Glass G., Overview of Voyager : ObjectSpace's Product Family for State of the Art Distributed Computing, CTO Object Sapce, www.objectspace.com, 1999
12. Iglesias C. A., Garijo M. and Gonzalez J. C.: A survey of agent-oriented methodologies, In Proceedings of the 5th International Workshop on Agent Theories, Architectures and Languages (ATAL'98), LNAI n°1555 - Springer Verlag, Paris, France, July 1998, pp317-330
13. IKV++ GmbH, Grasshopper: A platform for mobile software agents, www.ikv.de/products/grasshopper
14. ISO/IEC IS 10746-x — ITU-T Rec. X90x, ODP Reference Model Part x, 1995
15. ISO/IEC CD 15414, ODP Reference Model : Enterprise Viewpoint, January 2000
16. Kandé M.M, Mazaher S., Prnjat O., Sacks L., Witting M., Applying UML to Design an Inter-Domain Service Management Application, OOPSLA'2000
17. Koning, J.-L., Huget, M.-P.,Wei, J. and Wang, X.: Extending Modeling Languages for Interaction Protocol Design, AOSE 2001
18. Medvidovic N. and Taylor R.N.: A Classification and Comparison Framework for Software Architecture Description Languages, IEEE Transactions on Software Engineering, 26(1), January 2000
19. Medvidovic N., Egyed A., Rosenblum D.S.: Round Trip Software Engineering Using UML: From Architecture to Design and Back, Proceedings of the Second International Workshop on Object-Oriented Reengineering (WOOR'99), Toulouse, France, September 6, 1999.
20. Muscutariu F. and Gervais M.-P.: Modeling an OMG-MASIF Compliant Mobile Agent Platform with the RM-ODP Engineering Language, in Proceedings of the 2nd International Workshop on Mobile Agents for Telecommunication Applications (MATA'00), Lecture Notes in Computer Science n°1931, Springer Verlag (Ed), Paris, France, September 2000, pp133-141
21. Milosevic Z., ODP viewpoint languages and UML: a case of study, ftp.dstc.edu.au/AU/staff/zoran-milosevic.html
22. Miller J., Relationships of the Unified Modeling Language to the Reference Model of Open Distributed Computing version 1.1.2, 21 September 1997.
23. Miller J. and Wirfs-Brock R., How can subsystems be both a package and a Classifier, (www.omg.org)
24. O'Malley, S.A. and DeLoach, S.A.: Determining When to Use an Agent-Oriented Software Engineering Paradigm, AOSE 2001
25. OMG MASIF Standard (orbos/98-03-09) http://www.omg.org
26. OMG Unified Modeling Language Specification, Version 1.3, Mars 2000, http://www.omg.org
27. Odell J., Van Dyke Parunak J. and Bauer B., Extending UML for Agents, AOIS Worshop at AAAI 2000.
28. Petrie C., Agent-Based Software Engineering, AOSE 2000.
29. RationalRose (www.rational.com)
30. Shehory, On. Software Architecture of Multi-Agent Systems, AOSE 2000
31. Sparkman, C.H., DeLoach, S.A.,Self, A.L.: Automated Derivation of Complex Agent Architectures from Analysis Specification, AOSE 2001
32. Parunak, H.v.D. and Odell, J.: Representing Social Structures in UML, AOSE 2001
33. Wooldrige, M., and Ciancarini P. Agent-Oriented Software Engineering: The State of the Art, AOSE 2000.

Automated Derivation of Complex Agent Architectures from Analysis Specifications

Clint H. Sparkman[1], Scott A. DeLoach[2], and Athie L. Self[1]

[1]Department of Electrical and Computer Engineering, Air Force Institute of Technology
Wright-Patterson Air Force Base, Ohio 45433-7765
clint.sparkman@lackland.af.mil,
athie.self@afpc.randolph.af.mil

[2]Department of Computing and Information Sciences, Kansas State University
212 Nichols Hall, Manhattan, KS 66506
sdeloach@cis.ksu.edu

Abstract. Multiagent systems have been touted as a way to meet the need for distributed software systems that must operate in dynamic and complex environments. However, in order for multiagent systems to be effective, they must be reliable and robust. Engineering multiagent systems is a non-trivial task, providing ample opportunity for even experts to make mistakes. Formal transformation systems can provide automated support for synthesizing multiagent systems, which can greatly improve their correctness and reliability. This paper describes a semi-automated transformation system that generates an agent's internal architecture from an analysis specification in the MaSE methodology.

1   Introduction

In the last few years, agent technology has come to the forefront in the software industry because of advantages that multiagent systems have in complex, distributed environments. As agent technology has matured and become more accepted, agent-oriented software engineering (AOSE) has become an important topic for software developers who wish to develop reliable and robust agent-based systems [10, 11, 19]. Methodologies for AOSE attempt to provide a method for engineering practical multiagent systems. However, there are currently only a few AOSE methodologies for multiagent systems, and many of those are still under development [1, 12, 13, 18, 20]. Additionally, most existing methodologies lack specific guidance on how to transform the specification of a system into the corresponding design and implementation. This lack of guidance is not unique to engineering multiagent systems and plagues most software engineering methodologies. Unfortunately, it leaves the designer questioning if the resulting design correctly fulfills the initial system requirements.

The Agent Research Group at the Air Force Institute of Technology (AFIT), and now Kansas State University, has developed and continues to mature an AOSE methodology, called Multiagent Systems Engineering (MaSE) [4, 17], which covers

M.J. Wooldridge, G. Weiß, and P. Ciancarini (Eds.): AOSE 2001, LNCS 2222, pp. 278-296, 2002.

the complete life cycle of a multiagent system. Recent work has focused on applying formal methods to develop a transformation system to support agent system synthesis. Formal transformation systems [8, 9] provide automated support to system development, giving the designer increased confidence that the resulting system will operate correctly, despite its complexity. While formal transformation systems, and formal methods in general, cannot *a priori* guarantee correctness [2], if each transform preserves correctness, then the designer can be sure that the resulting design is at least correct with respect to the initial system specification.

Given a sufficient level of automated support, a transformation approach allows the designer to make only high-level design decisions, while the low-level details of the transformations are carried out automatically by the system. Transformation systems also provide traceability from the system requirements through the development process to the final executable code. Furthermore, if the system engineer is able to adequately decompose the problem and capture the system behavior in the analysis phase, then there is hope that the undesirable system behavior, to which multiagent systems are prone, can be avoided.

This level of automation will be required if such a system is to ever be truly useful. As we all know, initial system specifications are rarely, if ever, complete and consistent. Therefore, the ability to change the system specification and re-derive the design and implementation is a necessity. In effect, the long-term goal of this research to move the maintenance of software from the implementation level to the specification level. While there has been much work on general-purpose software specification languages, there has also been considerable work in specifying agent systems as well [3, 21].

In this paper, we present a semi-automated formal transformation system that generates MaSE design models based on the analysis models [16], which is the first step in formal agent system synthesis. Specifically, we explain how our transformation system generates an agent's internal design based on an initial analysis specification.

2 Background – Multiagent Systems Engineering

The MaSE methodology consists of the seven steps depicted in Fig. 1. The boxes represent the different models used in the steps, and arrows indicate the flow of information between the models. While similar to the waterfall approach, we have designed MaSE to be applied iteratively. The first three steps represent the Analysis phase of the methodology, while the last four steps represent the Design phase.

2.1 Analysis Models

The Role Model is the end result of the MaSE analysis phase. Role Models graphically depict the roles in the system, the goals they are responsible for, the tasks that each role uses to accomplish its goals, and the communication paths between the roles necessary to complete their tasks. Roles are the abstract entities that exist in the system, and are defined much like an actor in a play, or a position in an organization (President, Vice President, Manager, etc.). Each role is responsible for accomplishing one or more system level goal, and there must be at least one role responsible for each goal. In this way, the analyst is able to ensure that all of the initial system requirements have been captured.

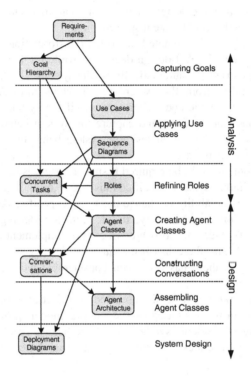

Fig. 1. MaSE Methodology

One example of a Role Model is shown in Fig. 2. The roles in the system are depicted as rectangles, and the goals that a role is responsible for are listed under the role. Each task that a role has is denoted by an oval attached to the role. The lines between the tasks denote communication protocols that occur between the tasks. The arrows indicate the initiator and responder tasks in the protocol, with the arrow pointing from the initiator to responder. Solid lines indicate peer-to-peer communication, which is external communication either between two tasks of different roles, or between two different instances of the same role. Conversely, dashed lines denote communication between two tasks of the same role instance.

As part of defining the Role Model, the analyst must define the tasks that each role has. Tasks describe the behavior that a role must exhibit in order to accomplish its goals, and are specified graphically using a finite state automaton, as shown in Fig. 3. A single role may have multiple concurrent tasks that define the complete behavior of the role. Each task is assumed to operate under its own thread of control, thus each task has its own state diagram that executes independently of the other tasks. An important aspect of multiagent systems is the ability of agents to interact to accomplish their goals. Concurrent tasks capture this interaction and can be used to specify complex communication protocols such as Contract Net, Dutch Auction, etc. [6].   Concurrent tasks also lay the foundation for conversations between the agent classes in the design phase of MaSE.

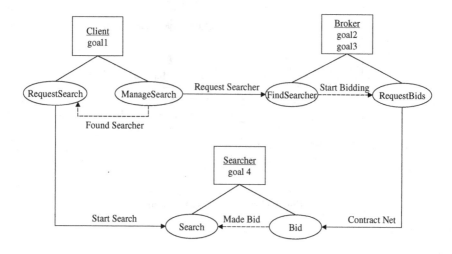

Fig. 2. Role Model

An important property of concurrent tasks is that they are able to capture communication with multiple tasks in order to accomplish their goals. In other words, Concurrent Task Diagrams naturally intertwine events belonging to different protocols. The other tasks being communicated with can belong to the same role, or they may belong to a different role. Tasks that belong to the same role can coordinate with each other through internal events. In Fig. 3, the *^backup(file)* event on the transition from the Wait_For_File state to the Wait_For_Backup state is an example of an internal send event, and the *done* event on the transition from the Wait_For_Backup state to the Process_File state is an example of an internal receive event. In order for a task to communicate with a task of another role, events that represent external communication are specified using *SendEvents* and *ReceiveEvents*. These events are defined to send and retrieve messages from an implied massage-handling component of the agent. The *^send(request(filename), server)* event on the transition from the Get_File_Name state to the Wait_For_File state is an example of an external *SendEvent*, and the *receive(inform(file), server)* event on the transition from the Wait_For_File state to the Wait_For_Backup state is an example of an external *ReceiveEvent*.

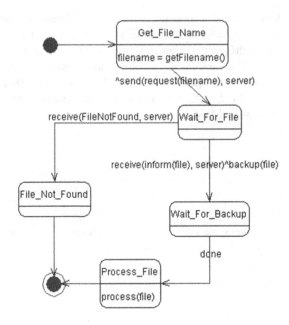

Fig. 3. Concurrent Task Diagram

2.2   Design Models

In the design phase of MaSE, the designer takes the Role Model in the analysis phase, and produces an Agent Class Diagram, as shown in Fig. 4. Each rectangle represents an agent class, with the roles played by each agent listed under the agent's name. The directed lines between the agents represent conversations between the agents, with the arrow pointing from the initiator to the responder. In order to ensure that all system goals are being met, each role must be played by at least one agent class, providing a traceable link from the goals in the analysis phase to the agents in the design phase.

Conversations define detailed coordination protocols between exactly two agents, and consist of a pair of Communication Class Diagrams, one each for the initiator and responder. Conversations are at the heart of any multiagent system as they detail how the agents communicate with each other. Like tasks, conversations are described using finite state automata that define each half of the conversation. Since conversations are point-to-point communication between two agents, every event within a Communication Class Diagram is represents a message to or from the other agent in the conversation. Conversations do not allow for communication with multiple agents simultaneously or for internal events to be exchanged with components internal to the agent. An example of a Communication Class Diagram is shown in Fig. 5.

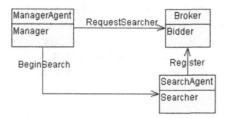

Fig. 4. Agent Class Diagram

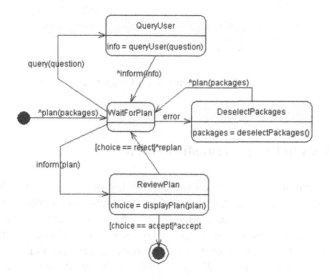

Fig. 5. Communication Class Diagram

In addition to the conversations that agents participate in, agents have internal components defined using an architectural modeling language combined with the Object Constraint Language (see Fig. 6). Components allow users to logically decompose the agents and define attributes and functions that are needed for the agent to carry out its tasks. The dynamic characteristics of the components are defined using a state diagram. The events passed within a component's state diagram are limited to internal events with other components that belong to that agent.

2.3   agentTool

In addition to the MaSE methodology, AFIT has developed a CASE tool named agentTool that serves as a validation platform and a proof of concept for MaSE. agentTool has a graphical user interface that allows a user to develop a multiagent system using the MaSE analysis and design models. agentTool is also able to generate Java code for a system based on the design models. Currently, the code generator is able to generate code for two different frameworks, agentMom [7] and Carolina [14], but work is being done to integrate agentTool with the AFIT Wide Spectrum Object Modeling Environment that is looking at the more general code generation problem [9].

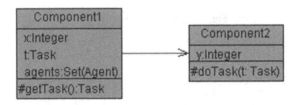

Fig. 6. Internal Agent Components

3   Analysis to Design Transformations

Before defining the specific transformations, this section first describes how the analysis models map to the design models. The MaSE methodology makes it clear that an agent class' roles, in conjunction with the protocols between the tasks, determine the conversations each agent class will have. However, if the external events are simply removed from the tasks to create the conversations, the problem we are faced with is that there will be nothing left in the design to capture how to coordinate the conversations and there will be no guarantee that the agent will behave consistently with the initial concurrent tasks. We must also capture the internal events in the design as well.

To solve this problem, we create a separate component for every task in each role that an agent is assigned to play. We then copy the concurrent task definition to the associated component state diagram. Next, we extract the states and transitions belonging to conversations and replace them with actions that represent the execution of the conversation. Using this approach, the component's state diagram retains the coordination and internal events necessary to ensure the behavior of the component matches the task from which it was derived.

Prior to this segment of our research, we had defined conversations as belonging directly to agents. However, based on the approach discussed above, we have redefined the generic architecture to have conversations belong to components. Fig. 7 illustrates how the models in the analysis phase translate to the models in the design phase as well as the relationship between the design models. Ultimately, the roles that the designer chooses for an agent to play determine that agent's components, as well as the set conversations in which the agent participates. To accurately capture the behavior as defined in concurrent tasks, we assume each component also executes as an independent thread.

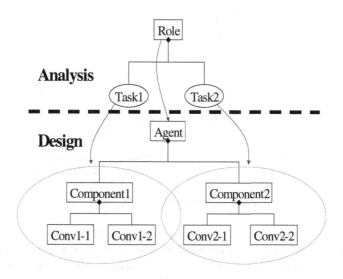

Fig. 7. Model Influences

Besides components derived from concurrent tasks, our transformations also create a special *Agent Component* for each agent [15]. This *Agent Component* captures how the agent coordinates its different components. Fig. 8 shows the basic state diagram for the *Agent Component*, which is designed to handle both transient[1] and persistent[2] components. The *Agent Component* can also be transformed to account for special agent characteristics like mobility, where the agent must halt all of its active components, move to a new location, and then resume the components where they were interrupted.

The transformation system created in this research is actually a series of small steps that incrementally change the roles and tasks in the analysis phase into agent classes, components, and conversations in the design phase. The process logically decomposes into three stages. Before the transformations can take place, the developer must analyze the system and develop a Role Model, which defines the roles that are present in the system, and a set of concurrent tasks, which the roles perform to accomplish their goals. The developer must also decide which agent classes will be in the system and the roles that each agent class will play.

---

[1] A transient component is started in response to the receipt of a specific event. There may be multiple transient components of the same type executing at any one time.

[2] A persistent component is started when the agent is instantiated and runs until its completion or the agent is terminated. There is only one instance of a persistent component running.

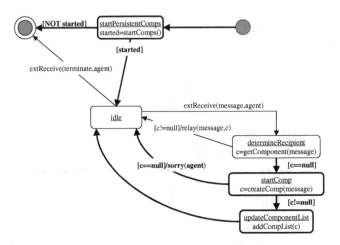

Fig. 8. Basic Agent Component State Diagram

During the first stage of the transformation process, the components for the agent classes are created based on the roles assigned by the developer. The set of protocols to which each external event belongs is also determined. The second stage centers on annotating the component state diagrams and matching external events in the different components that become the initial messages of a conversation. During the last stage the component state diagrams are prepared for removal of the states and transitions belonging to conversations. They are then removed and added to the state diagrams of the corresponding conversation halves. As they are removed from the components they are replaced with a single transition that has an action that starts the conversation.

Each transformation is defined by a predicate logic equation of the form: condition $\Rightarrow$ result, where the condition is the set of requirements that must be true for the transformation to take place, and the result describes what is guaranteed to be true after the transformation is performed. This notation is similar to defining functions with pre-conditions and post-conditions. These transformations describe *what* must take place, not *how* it must be done.

3.1   Creating Agent Components

Once the designer has developed the Role Model, defined the concurrent tasks, and assigned roles to agent classes, the transformation process can begin. The first transformations in stage one of the transformation process determine the protocols to which each external event belongs. This is important because the specific protocols that events belong to are used to determine where conversations begin and end in the component state diagrams. While the protocols for most events can be automatically determined, there are ambiguous cases where the designer must be asked to decide to which protocol specific events belongs.

Next, for every task of every role that an agent plays, a component is created for that task. Once again, the component's state diagram is initially identical to that of the task it was derived from. The rest of the transformation process is focused on moving the external events from these component state diagrams into conversations. The following predicate logic equation formally defines this transformation:

$\forall$ a : **Agent**, r : **Role**, t : **Task** • (r $\in$ a.roles $\wedge$ t $\in$ r.tasks)
   $\Rightarrow$ ($\exists$ c : **Component** • c $\in$ a'.components $\wedge$ c.stateTable = t.stateTable $\wedge$ c.name = t.name)

As an example of this transformation, consider the example Role Model shown in Fig. 9. If the developer decides in the design phase to create the agent classes with the roles shown in Fig. 10, then the transformation system creates the components shown for the agents. Since both agents play Role 2, there is a component created for each agent for Role 2's Task 2. Fig. 10 is not a MaSE diagram, but is presented to illustrate the internal agent components based on the initial Agent Class Diagram.

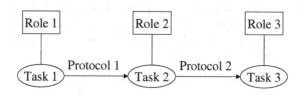

Fig. 9. Initial Role Model

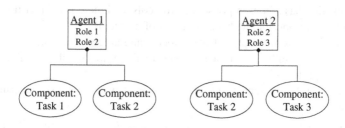

Fig. 10. Agent Components Created from Roles' Tasks

Once the agent components are created, for each pair of roles that are combined into an agent class, the designer must determine whether each protocol that exists between components of that agent is either internal or external. If a protocol is defined as internal, all events belonging to that protocol become internal events between components and not messages in a conversation.

3.2   Annotating Component State Diagrams

After the agent components are created, the next stage of the transformation process involves annotating the component state diagrams to prepare for conversation extraction. There are many different cases in which tasks are defined in the analysis phase that make removing conversations problematic. One such case occurs when multiple events not belonging to the same protocol reside on the same transition. To solve this (and other similar) problem, we defined a transformation that converts the component's state diagrams into a canonical form, which splits transitions having events belonging to different protocols. This canonical form simplifies conversation extraction while remaining consistent with the initial task specification.

Next, each transition is given a set of protocols that is based on the protocols for the external events on the transition. Then the state diagrams are annotated to indicate where each conversation begins and ends. Conversations are defined as point-to-point communication between two agent instances. Therefore, any time a component's state diagram has a transition with external communication to a different agent than one of the preceding transitions, a new conversation must begin, and that transition is labeled as the start of a conversation. The following six conditions indicate the start of a conversation by a change in who the agent is communicating with, which in most cases is due to a change in the protocols.

1. A transition has a protocol not found in at least one transition into its *from* state.
2. A transition has a non-empty set of protocols that is different than another transition leaving the same state.
3. A transition has a non-empty set of protocols, but lacks a protocol of another transition into its *from* state.
4. A transition has a non-empty set of protocols, and there is another transition into or out of its *from* state with an empty set of protocols.
5. A transition has an empty set of protocols and at least one SendEvent. In these cases, there is either a multicast event, or there are SendEvents that belong to different protocols.
6. A transition has a SendEvent whose recipient was previously determine by an action.

Similarly, when a component state diagram has a transition with external communication not guaranteed to continue on transitions leaving its *to* state, that transition is labeled as the end of a conversation. The following four conditions indicate that a transition is the end of a conversation

1. A transition has a protocol not found in a transition leaving its *to* state.
2. A transition has an empty set of protocols and at least one SendEvent.
3. A transition has a non-empty set of protocols and there is a start transition leaving its *to* state.
4. A transition to the end state has a non-empty set of protocols.

Once the start and end labels have been added to the component state diagrams, the initial messages of the conversations must be "matched up" (i.e., both sides of a conversation must start and end with the same message types). In most cases, this can be done automatically, but in some ambiguous cases the designer is required to decide how to match conversation halves.

3.3   Extracting Conversations

The last stage of the transformation process removes the conversations from the component state diagrams and places them in their appropriate conversation halves. To extract a conversation from a state diagram, each of its end transitions must exit to the same state. If different transitions of a conversation exit to different states, a transformation is applied to create a new "dummy" end state for the conversation. Then, the states and transitions that belong to the conversation are replaced with a single transition from the state where the transition originates to the state where the conversation ends. An action is added to the transition that represents the execution of the conversation.

Other transformations in this stage prepare variables in the states and transitions before they are removed from the components and placed in the conversations. If a variable is not exclusive to a single conversation, that variable must be stored in parent component to ensure any other conversations extracted from the component references the *same* variable. To annotate this, these variables are pre-pended with "parent.".

As the transitions are moved from the components into the conversations, the special "send" and "receive" parts of the events are removed from the events. They are used in the component state diagrams to distinguish between internal and external events, but are not needed in the conversations since conversations, by definition, define binary communication between exactly two agents.

4   Example

This section presents an example to demonstrate the results of the transformation system. The transformations were implemented in agentTool [5], and most of the figures are screen shots from the tool. Fig. 11 shows the initial Role Model for a simple multiagent system. There are three roles, each with a single task. The Manager role uses the ContractNet protocol to solicit bids for search tasks. The Bidder role bids on the tasks, and if awarded the contract requests a search from the Searcher role. The Bid task, shown in Fig. 12, demonstrates how the transformation system derives the agent components and conversations in the design phase from the roles and tasks in the analysis phase.

For the purposes of this example, we assume that the designer initially defines a SearchManager agent class, which plays the Manager role, and a MobileSearcher agent class, which plays both the Bidder and Searcher roles. During the first stage of the transformation process, the designer determines that the SearchRequest protocol is internal communication within the MobileSearcher agent. Therefore, every event in the MobileSearcher's Bid and Search components that belongs to the SearchRequest protocol is transformed into an internal event. The resulting architecture for the multiagent system is shown in Figure 13. Once again, this is not a MaSE model, but simply demonstrates the architecture created for the agents based on the roles they play. The external protocol, ContractNet, generates several conversations to carry out that communication.

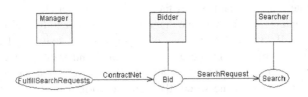

Fig. 11. Role Model

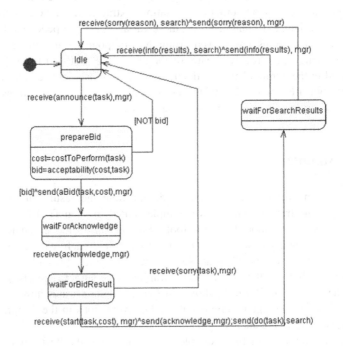

Fig. 12. Bid Task

Fig. 14 shows the Bid Component after being annotated in the second stage of the transformation process. The three events that belong to the SearchRequest protocol are now internal events, and three new null states have been added to split transitions that had both internal and external events. The letters "S" and "E" on the transitions denote where the conversations begin and end.

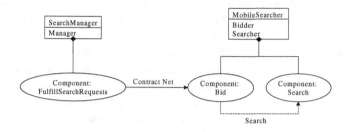

Fig. 13. Agent Architectures

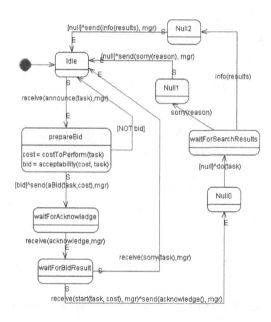

Fig. 14. Annotated Bid Component

A total of six different conversations were extracted from the events belonging to the ContractNet protocol. Some were due to the internal events passed with the Search component, while others were due to the way the SearchManager's FulfillSearchRequest component (not shown) was annotated.   For example, the reason the transition from the Idle state to the *prepareBid* state is both the start and end of a conversation is because the corresponding send event for the *receive(announce(task), mgr)* event in the FulfillSearchRequest component is a multicast. Similarly, the transitions leaving the waitForBidResults state are the start of different conversations because the corresponding send event for the *receive (sorry(task), mgr)* event in the FulfillSearchRequest is a multicast to all of the losers, and the corresponding send event for the receive*(start(task, cost), mgr)* event is only sent the winner agent, so they must be different conversations.

Fig. 15 shows the bid component after the third stage of the transformation process. The states and transitions that belong to the conversations were removed, and each conversation was replaced with a transition that has an action that instantiates it. When the conversation completes, the action is finished and the component enters the next state, thus preserving the original semantics of the state diagram.

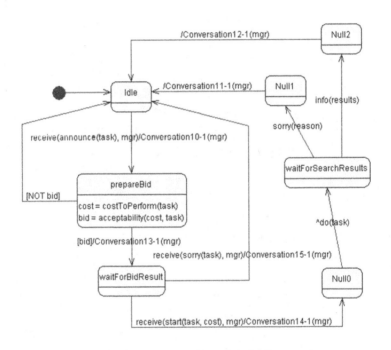

Fig. 15. Bid Component After Extracting the Conversations

Fig. 16 shows the initiator half of Conversation13-1, which was one conversation extracted from the MobileSearcher's Bid component. It is easy to see that the waitForAcknowledge state and the transitions to and from that state were taken directly from the Bid component. The *task* and *cost* variables were prepended with "parent." because they are both used either in the Bid component or in another conversation. Fig. 17 shows the Agent Class Diagram derived by our transformation system. Note that all external communication defined by the Contract Net protocol is captured in six conversations.

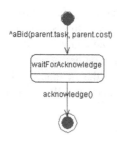

^aBid(parent.task, parent.cost)

waitForAcknowledge

acknowledge()

Fig. 16. Initiator Half of Conversation13-1

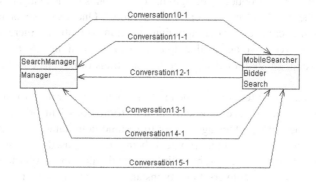

Fig. 17. Agent Class Diagram

4.1   Evaluation

The above example was analyzed and designed using the agentTool environment. The semi-automatic transformation system built into agentTool dramatically improved the time required to take the analysis specifications and create complete design specifications. The initial design was created in less than an hour, a task that would normally take several hours, or days, just to enter into agentTool.   The CPU time actually taken during this transformation was less than 10 minutes with the remainder of the time being spent by the designer looking at the "ambiguous cases" described in Section 3.2.   These cases required the designer to look at the analysis models to determine the correct action for the transformation to perform. Even more dramatic was the time required to re-design the system after analysis specification changes. As we discussed in the introduction, high-level specifications are rarely correct the first time. After making minor changes to the analysis specifications, the time required to re-design the system was just a few minutes since the ambiguous cases were already known.

Although the time saved in the analysis to design transformation was impressive, the fact that the design was correct with respect to the analysis specification was the key factor. We did not perform the analysis to design transformations manually and thus were not able to measure the number of errors or inconsistencies that might have been introduced. The only place that manual design could improve on the current transformation process is in efficiency. We will discuss this in detail in the next section.

5   Future Work

This research has opened the door to many areas of future work. Although transformation system produces a design that corresponds to the analysis specification, many times the result is not an optimal solution. One example is the way that conversations are created. After applying the transformations, there may be two conversations between two agents that do *exactly* the same thing. Although this is not necessarily wrong, an additional set of optimizing transformations could remedy these problems.

Another area of future work deals with what we refer to as embedded conversations. In many cases, the current transformations halt one conversation to carry out a dialog with another agent only to resume communication with the initial agent. This results in a single protocol being decomposed into several simple conversations that, by themselves, have little semantic meaning. Alternate approaches would be to allow one conversation to instantiate another conversation, or allow conversations to halt while a component carries out other communication, which would result in more robust and semantically intact conversations.

A final area of future research is in the area of transforming concurrent tasks to run in a single threaded execution environment. As described earlier, we assume that each component runs as its own thread; however, any many situations, we would rather have a single thread running. The challenge would be to capture a single threaded design that would behave consistently with a concurrent specification.

6   Conclusions

The multiagent paradigm provides a framework for developing increasingly complex and distributed software systems. However, better methods are needed to develop multiagent systems that can guarantee correctness, reliability, and robustness. Using formal transformation systems for multiagent system synthesis is one way to meet this growing need.

This paper presented a transformation system that generates design models from the analysis models, including the internal agent architectures and the specific conversations for the components. It is predominantly an automatic process, requiring only a few key design decisions from the system developer. Since each transformation preserves correctness from one model to the next, the developer has much more confidence that no inconsistencies or errors occurred during the design process. The transformation process also provides clear traceability between the analysis and design, simplifying the verification process.

Furthermore, when implemented in a development environment, such as agentTool, the transformations allow the developer to maintain the system in the more abstract analysis models and regenerate the design when any changes are made. How many times during a software development project are the models in the analysis phase forgotten once the project enters the design phase? In many cases, there is simply not enough time or manpower to maintain the consistency between the models in the two phases. The transformation system presented here can eliminate that problem for system engineers using the MaSE methodology.

Acknowledgements. This work was performed while the authors were at the Air Force Institute of Technology and was supported by the Air Force Office of Scientific Research. The views expressed in this article are those of the authors and do not reflect the official policy or position of the United States Air Force, Department of Defense, or the US Government.

References

[1] Brauer, W., Nickles, M., Robatsos, M., Weiss, G., Lorentzen, K.: Expectation-Oriented Analysis and Design. In this volume (2001)

[2] Clarke, E. Wing, J.: Formal Methods: State of the Art and Future Directions. ACM Computing Surveys. **28** (4) (1996)

[3] Dastani, M., Jonker, C., Truer, J.: A Requirement Specification Language for Configuration Dynamics of Multi-Agent System. In this volume (2001)

[4] DeLoach, S. A., Wood, M., Sparkman, C.: Multiagent Systems Engineering. To appear in the Intl. J. on Software Engineering and Knowledge Engineering (2001)

[5] DeLoach, S. A., Wood, M.: Developing Multiagent Systems with agentTool. In: Castelfranchi, C., Lesperance, Y. (eds.): Intelligent Agents VII: Agent Theories Architectures and Languages, Proceedings of the 7th International Workshop, ATAL 2000. Lecture Notes in Artificial Intelligence, Vol. 1986. Springer-Verlag, Berlin Heidelberg New York (2001)

[6] DeLoach, S. A.: Specifying Agent Behavior as Concurrent Tasks. Proceedings of the Fifth International Conference on Autonomous Agents. ACM Press, New York (2001) 102-103

[7] DeLoach, S. A.: Using agentMom. Air Force Institute of Technology, (2000)

[8]   Green, C., Luckham, D., Balzer, R., et al.: Report on a Knowledge-Based Software Assistant. In Rich, C., Waters, R. C. (eds.): Readings in Artificial Intelligence and Software Engineering. Morgan Kaufmann, San Mateo, California (1986) 377-428

[9]   Hartrum, T. C., Graham, R.: The AFIT Wide Spectrum Object Modeling Environment: An AWESOME Beginning. Proceedings of the National Aerospace and Electronics Conference. IEEE (2000) 35-42

[10] Jennings, N.: On Agent-based Software Engineering, Artificial Intelligence: **117** (2000) 277-296

[11] Lind, J.: Issues in Agent-Oriented Software Engineering. In Ciancarini, P., Wooldridge, M. (eds.): Agent-Oriented Software Engineering: First International Workshop, AOSE 2000. Lecture Notes in Artificial Intelligence, Vol. 1957. Springer-Verlag, Berlin Heidelberg (2001) 45-58

[12] Omicini, A.: SODA: Societies and Infrastructures in the Analysis and Design of Agent-Based Systems. In Ciancarini, P., Wooldridge, M. (eds.): Agent-Oriented Software Engineering: First International Workshop, AOSE 2000. Lecture Notes in Artificial Intelligence, Vol. 1957. Springer-Verlag, Berlin Heidelberg (2001) 185-194

[13] Rana, O.: A Modelling Approach for Agent Based Systems Design. In Ciancarini, P., Wooldridge, M. (eds.): Agent-Oriented Software Engineering: First International Workshop, AOSE 2000. Lecture Notes in Artificial Intelligence, Vol. 1957. Springer-Verlag, Berlin Heidelberg (2001) 195-206

[14] Saba, G. M., Santos, E.: The Multi-Agent Distributed Goal Satisfaction System. Proceedings of the International ICSC Symposium on Multi-Agents and Mobile Agents in Virtual Organizations and E-Commerce (MAMA '2000) (2000) 389-394

[15] Self, A.: Design & Specification of Dynamic, Mobile, and Reconfigurable Multiagent Systems. MS thesis, AFIT/GCS/ENG/01M-11. School of Engineering, Air Force Institute of Technology (AU), Wright-Patterson AFB, OH, (2001)

[16] Sparkman, C.: Transforming Analysis Models Into Design Models for the Multiagent Systems Engineering (MaSE) Methodology. MS thesis, AFIT/GCS/ENG/01M-12. School of Engineering, Air Force Institute of Technology (AU), Wright-Patterson AFB, OH (2001)

[17] Wood, M.: Multiagent Systems Engineering: A Methodology for Analysis and Design of Multiagent Systems. MS thesis, AFIT/GCS/ENG/00M-26. School of Engineering, Air Force Institute of Technology (AU), Wright-Patterson AFB, OH, 2000

[18] Wooldridge, M., Jennings, N., Kinny, D.: The Gaia Methodology for Agent-Oriented Analysis and Design. Intl. J. of Autonomous Agents and Multi-Agent Systems. **3** (3) (2000) 285-312

[19] Wooldridge, M., Ciancarini, P.: Agent-Oriented Software Engineering: the State of the Art In Ciancarini, P., Wooldridge, M. (eds.): Agent-Oriented Software Engineering: First International Workshop, AOSE 2000. Lecture Notes in Artificial Intelligence, Vol. 1957. Springer-Verlag, Berlin Heidelberg (2001) 1-28

[20] Zambonelli, F.: Abstractions and Infrastructures for the Design and Development of Mobile Agent Organizations. In this volume (2001)

[21] Zhu, H.: A Formal Specification Language for MAS Engineering. In this volume (2002)

A Lifecycle for Models of Large Multi-agent Systems[*]

Wamberto Vasconcelos[1,a], David Robertson[1,b], Jaume Agustí[2,c],
Carles Sierra[2,d], Michael Wooldridge[3,e], Simon Parsons[3,f],
Christopher Walton[1,g], and Jordi Sabater[2,h]

[1] Division of Informatics, University of Edinburgh, Edinburgh EH1 1HN, UK
{[a]wamb, [b]dr, [g]cdw}@dai.ed.ac.uk
[2] Institut d'Investigació en Intel·ligència Artificial (IIIA)
Campus UAB, 08193 Bellaterra, Catalonia, Spain
{[c]agusti, [d]sierra, [h]jsabater}@iiia.csic.es
[3] Department of Computer Science, University of Liverpool, Liverpool L69 7ZF, UK
{[e]M.J.Wooldridge, [f]S.D.Parsons}@csc.liv.ac.uk

Abstract. Two key issues in building multi-agent systems concern their *scalability* and engineering *open systems*. We offer solutions to these potential problems by introducing a lifecycle for models of large multi-agent systems. Our proposal connects a model for the collective analysis of agent systems with an individual-based model. This approach leads on to a virtuous cycle in which individual behaviours can be mapped on to global models and vice-versa. We illustrate our approach with a formal example but relatively easy for engineers to follow and adapt.

1 Introduction

A key issue in building multi-agent systems (MASs) is that of scalability. Large MASs are globally distributed intercommunicating collections of human, software and hardware systems each with hundreds or thousands of components. Such systems are becoming increasingly common and complex. Ensuring that these systems do not fall into unstable or chaotic behaviour is a main challenge designers face.

The wealth of knowledge about conventional information processing does not seem to scale up nor adapt easily to MASs [8,9]. It is important that we study and understand the dynamics of MASs, the forces that define these dynamics, and how these can benefit or impair a MAS. Hopefully this knowledge should cast light on issues of design, performance and reliability of components of MASs.

Another key issue concerns engineering open systems. A canonical example is the Internet: with the predicted increase in the number of personal agents (information filtering and shopping agents being two widely studied examples) and commercial agents (shopbots and pricebots, for example) the Internet seems likely to become an environment teeming with agents encountering situations for which they were not explicitly designed.

---

[*] Work sponsored by the European Union, contract IST-1999-10208, research grant **Sustainable Lifecycles in Information Ecosystems** (SLIE).

M.J. Wooldridge, G. Weiß, and P. Ciancarini (Eds.): AOSE 2001, LNCS 2222, pp. 297–317, 2002.
© Springer-Verlag Berlin Heidelberg 2002

At present we lack a theoretical understanding of how to design systems which can be guaranteed to exhibit good performance in such a free-for-all, and those empirical studies that have been carried out suggest that system behaviour is likely to be extremely complex (*e.g.* [10,11]). In contrast, as can be seen in other papers in this volume, we already have a range of tools and techniques for engineering closed agent systems.

We can model very large MASs at different levels of abstraction. At a very high level of abstraction we want to study the aggregate behaviour of agent populations. For this we suggest the use of equations of continuous change, abstracting away from the details of individual interaction. Such collective models can then be used to drive more detailed modelling of individual agent interactions: the global behaviour from our continuous models helps to map the behaviours we examine in more detail when we devise an agent-based modelling. The issue is then to build models of interaction at the level of individual agents which are as small and simple as possible while allowing us to prove or disprove hypotheses about the relation between agent structure (at the individual agent level) and MAS behaviour (at the population level). We demonstrate by example how this can be done using a method which is formal but is relatively easy for engineers to apply.

In the next section we describe the example problem we shall use to describe our approach. In Sections 3 and 4 we give more details of our proposed method for the study of MASs. In our approach, we employ established analysis techniques from dynamic systems, but we also use agent-based simulation. The two apparently conflicting views are, in fact, means to exploit different and complementing aspects of MASs. Section 5 presents a lifecycle embodying the two steps of our previous sections. In Section 6 we draw conclusions and give directions for future work.

Our interest in this topic stems from our involvement in the research grant **Sustainable Lifecycles in Information Ecosystems** (SLIE) [17]. The main goal of this project is to develop robust methodologies for the design, analysis, deployment and maintenance of successful components of MASs.

2   Example Problem

Our example concerns the distribution of resources in those supply systems for which it is important to ensure some uniform distribution of resources amongst a number of agents. If such a system has an uneven distribution of resources, we would like to know what sorts of behaviours this might engender and whether these behaviours are likely to differ as the size of our system increases.

To perform coherent sets of experiments we must limit the variability of the systems under study so we make the following idealisation assumptions in our modelling:

1. Resources are neither created nor destroyed by any agent so the only issue is transfer of resources from one agent to another. This rules out influences of internal resource generation or import of resources.
2. Transfer of resource is "frictionless". There is no loss of resource in transit; impediment to the amount of resource transferred; or disparity between the amount of resource one expects to have and the amount held.

3. All agents have the same decision procedure for choosing how much resource to offer or request when trading.
4. Every transfer of resource involves a balance between the needs of the donor and recipient so, for example, it is not possible for any agent to receive resource beyond what it calculates it needs.

These are strong assumptions which allow us to build models of an ideal case. This ideal case is valuable because it provides a baseline – a system which is unstable under the ideal assumptions is likely to be even more unstable if the assumptions are weakened. We do not expect the ideal case itself to occur in real systems but we expect real systems to have at least as many problems as we find in the ideal case.

3   Equation-Based Modelling (EBM)

Standard techniques and tools for dynamic systems analysis, modelling and simulation [4,6] are used in this first step. Dynamic systems have been successfully modelled and simulated by means of equations [6]. Standard techniques coupled with practical tools make dynamic systems modelling and simulation a straightforward engineering effort. We intend to build on this state-of-the-art, our initial model being equation-based.

We wish to relate behaviours hypothesised at the population level to features at the individual level. The first modelling step is therefore to develop our hypotheses about population behaviours. We do this by building a model which describes the essence of the dynamics, at a population level, of our idealised system. We hope that this model (although itself containing no agents) will generate interesting behaviours which we can then seek to understand in terms of agent structure using more detailed modelling. To be controllable and easily analysed, we require this early model to be as simple as possible while still generating insights into potential behaviours.

The model we use at this stage is expressed in a system dynamics modelling style [4,6]. We imagine the agent system to be composed of some number of sub-populations (the number of agents in each of these being immaterial) with the quantity of resource held by each sub-population being described by a single, integer state variable. Resource flow between each sub-population is controlled by a rate variable associated with that flow. Formally, this can be described by the following equations:

$$
\begin{aligned}
state_v(X, initial\_time) &= initial\_value(X) \\
state_v(X, T) &= state_v(X, previous(T))\ + \\
&\quad \sum \{rate_v(F_i, previous(T)) | \exists X_i.flow(F_i, X_i, X)\}\ - \\
&\quad \sum \{rate_v(F_o, previous(T)) | \exists X_o.flow(F_o, X, X_o)\}
\end{aligned}
$$

where $state_v(X, T)$ is the value for the state variable X at time point T; $rate_v(F, T)$ is the value for the rate variable of flow F at time point T; $initial\_time$ is the initial time point in the simulation; $initial\_value(X)$ is the initial value for state variable X; $previous(T)$ is the time point previous to T; and $flow(F, X_i, X_o)$ is true if there is a flow named F from state variable X_i to state variable X_o.

The definition above is generic for this sort of continuous flow model. We now decide on the specific model topology needed for our example. Many topologies are possible. For instance, we could have a fully connected distribution network in which all sub-populations are connected by flows to each other or we could select randomly which sub-populations are connected. One of the simplest topologies for our purposes is a distribution ring, in which we have a chain of sub-populations with the last link of the chain connecting back to the first. This topology allows a simple measure of size of system: the number of sub-populations in the ring, which we shall call the ring size and shall write as $\mathcal{R}$. It also allows a simple way of allocating an uneven distribution of resources to sub-populations at the start of the simulation: the total amount of resource for the population is distributed in proportion to its position in the ring. Some examples of distribution ring topologies generated in this way are shown in Fig. 1.

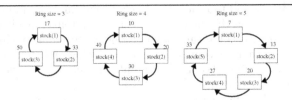

Fig. 1. Possible Distribution Ring Topologies

Our entire model is now a function of the ring size ($\mathcal{R}$). By setting $\mathcal{R}$ to different values we generate models of different sizes and resource distributions but with a uniform interaction between adjoining sub-populations in the ring. The formal definitions needed to achieve this sort of parameterisable model are shown in Fig. 2.

We are now in a position to run the model. We run a simulation for 1000 time steps for each value for $\mathcal{R}$ from 3 to 10. This simulation can be run with any system dynamics modelling package or it can (for uniformity with our other specifications) be run using a Prolog meta-interpreter. The meta-interpreter we used for this example can be obtained on-line in [17].

Fig. 3 shows a plot of the resource held by the first sub-population of the ring[1] for each value of $\mathcal{R}$. The lines for lowest ring sizes are those which start at the highest resource level. We can see from Fig. 3 that the time taken to obtain a stable distribution of resources increases, probably exponentially, with ring size (for $\mathcal{R} = 3$ stability is around time 180; for $\mathcal{R} = 4$ stability is around time 450; for $\mathcal{R} = 5$ stability is just beyond time 1000). Furthermore, at larger ring sizes

---

[1] Notice that we must focus on one of the sub-populations rather than taking a mean for the whole ring because the total resource for the ring remains constant throughout.

$flow(transfer(N1, N2), stock(N1), stock(N2)) \leftarrow ring(\mathcal{R}, N1, N2)$
where $ring(\mathcal{R}, N1, N2)$ is true when $N1$ and $N2$ are
adjoining ring elements.

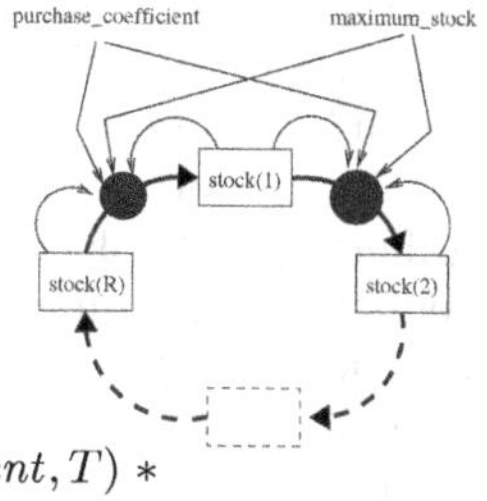

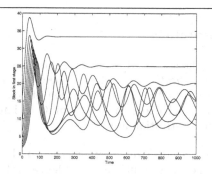

$initial\_time = 1$
$parameter(purchase\_coefficient) = 0.2$
$parameter(maximum\_stock) = 100$
$previous(T) = T - 1$
$initial\_value(stock(N)) = \mathcal{R} * \frac{parameter(maximum\_stock)}{\mathcal{R}!}$
$rate_v(transfer(N1, N2), T) = parameter(purchase\_coefficient, T) *$
$$state_v(stock(N2), T) *$$
$$1 - \frac{(parameter(maximum\_stock) - state_v(stock(N1), T)}{parameter(maximum\_stock)} *$$
$$1 - \frac{state_v(stock(N2), T)}{parameter(maximum\_stock)}$$

Fig. 2. Definitions of Continuous Change for Resource Ring of Size $\mathcal{R}$

Fig. 3. Behaviours of Continuous Change Model

we find sustained and pronounced oscillations which become more complex as
we increase the ring size.

These results show that we can quite rapidly obtain oscillatory behaviour in
resource distribution, even when we have a highly uniform distribution structure. This is the case for systems which are sufficiently large so that the transactions between agents can be viewed as continuous flows of resource between
sub-populations. Since the time taken for these oscillations to dampen to a steady
state grows very quickly with increased system size, it would be possible for the
oscillations in a large system to persist beyond its life span. The form of these oscillations may not be simple and easily predictable for large systems so it would
be possible to have this sort of behaviour within a system without being aware,
when looking at a sample of the time series, that a real oscillation was at work.

4   Agent-Based Modelling (ABM)

What features of individual agent structure could account for the increased delay in stabilisation with larger population sizes which we modelled in the previous section? As before, we want a parsimonious agent model (the simplest which will exhibit this sort of behaviour). However, parsimony must now be obtained with a different style of modelling in which the elements of the model are individual agents and communication between individuals is through (possibly concurrent) message passing.

When specifying our agent model we are not as constrained in our style of specification as we might be for specifications of agents which are to be deployed in real systems. In particular, we are free to specify in a straightforward way information about the global social structure of agents systems. For this we use a simplified form of the concept of *electronic institutions* [12,14,18], explained in Section 4.1 and put to use in Section 4.2. This gives us a way of expressing the agent system at the level of the potential interactions between agents, without specifying exactly how these interactions occur. The specification of potential interactions then gives us starting points for defining the decision procedures of types of individual agents, as we show in Section 4.3.

4.1   Electronic Institutions

The scenario in which the agents will perform should be formally described. For this we use *electronic institutions* [12,14,18]. These are formal structures based on process algebras that enable the specification of conventions and norms of individual and collective behaviour in a community of interacting agents. Some notions of an electronic institution are:

- *Agents and Roles* – agents are the players in an electronic institution, interacting by the exchange of illocutions, whereas roles are defined as standardised patterns of behaviour. The identification and regulation of roles is considered as part of the formalisation process of any organisation. Any agent within an electronic institution is required to adopt some role(s). As actions are associated to roles, an agent adopting a given role is allowed to perform the actions associated to that role. A major advantage of using roles is that they can be updated without having to update the actions for every agent on an individual basis.
- *Scene* – interactions between agents are articulated through agent group meetings, which we call scenes, with a communication protocol. We consider the protocol of a scene the possible dialogues agents may have.
- *Performative Structures* – scenes can be connected, composing a network of scenes (the so-called performative structure) which captures the existing relationships among scenes. The specification of a performative structure contains a description of how the different roles can legally move from scene to scene. A performative structure is to contain the multiple, simultaneous ongoing activities, represented by scenes. Agents in a performative structure may take part in different scenes at the same time with different roles.

- *Normative Rules* – agent actions in the context of an institution may have consequences that either limit or enlarge its subsequent acting possibilities. Such consequences will impose obligations to the agents and affect their possible paths within the performative structure.

Sophisticated interactions among agents can be elegantly expressed via institutions. These can be seen as finite-state machines describing all the possible message exchanges that may take place in a certain situation. We have employed an implementation of electronic institutions in our specification and simulation of MAS described below.

4.2 Specification at Agent Interaction Level

To specify potential agent interactions we use a notation similar to a simplified form of CCS (Calculus of Communicating Systems, [13]) but with a syntax adapted to agent modelling. In this section we describe the language and show how it is applied to our running example. An interaction specification is a set of clauses, each of the form A ::= D, where:

- A is an agent identifier of the form agent(S, R, A), where S is the scene to which the agent belongs; R is the agent's role in that scene; and A is the unique name of that agent.
- D can be of the form:
  - D_1 par D_2 denoting that D_1 and D_2 occur in parallel.
  - D_1 then D_2 denoting that D_1 must occur before D_2 (*i.e.* sequence).
  - D_1 or D_2 denoting that D_1 or D_2 can occur but not both (*i.e.* choice).
  - M => A_e where M is a message sent to an external agent A_e.
  - M <= A_e where M is a message received from an external agent A_e.
  - agent(S', R', A) where S' is a scene (possibly different from S) and R' is the agent's role in the scene (possibly different from R).

With this language we can describe a system of scenes for interaction between agents, stipulate the roles played by agents in these scenes, and define the ordering of interactions (through message passing) for different types of agent depending on which role and scene they inhabit. Our running example concerns resource distribution and it is common for this type of agent system to involve three sorts of scene: an agora in which agents with resource to buy or sell are put in touch with each other by a broker; a negotiation scene in which agents which were paired together in the agora interact to agree on a contract to transfer resource; and a delivery scene in which contracts to supply resource are either honoured or defaulted upon. Below we specify these in detail.

A broker agent in the agora can receive an offer of stock and request for stock (in parallel) from two traders in the agora; then may inform the trader offering stock of the name of a potential buyer; then may inform the trader requesting stock of the name of a potential supplier. Then it continues as a broker in the agora. Formally:

```
agent(agora,broker,B) ::=
    ( offer(stock,_) <= agent(agora,trader,A1) par
```

```
        request(stock,_) <= agent(agora,trader,A2) par
        (offer(buyer(A2),_) => agent(agora,trader,A1) then
          offer(seller(A1),_) => agent(agora,trader,A2) ) ) then
    agent(agora,broker,B).
```

A trader in the agora can offer stock to a broker and receive notice of a buyer from the same broker, then it becomes a supplier in the negotiation scene, or it can send a broker a request for stock and receive notice of a supplier, then it becomes a customer in the negotiation scene:

```
agent(agora,trader,X) ::=
    ( offer(stock,_) => agent(agora,broker,B1) then
      offer(buyer(_),_) <= agent(agora,broker,B1) then
      agent(negotiation,supplier,X) ) or
    ( request(stock,_) => agent(agora,broker,B2) then
      offer(seller(_),_) <= agent(agora,broker,B2) then
      agent(negotiation,customer,X) ).
```

The remaining cases are depicted in Appendix A. We now use this as a framework for introducing the definitions of individual agents.

4.3 Specification at Agent Decision Level

The decision procedures for agents are expressed using two types of clause. The first type defines the conditions under which a message can be sent and the second stipulates the reaction when a message is received. The syntax of these is, respectively, as follows:

$$A ::= M_r \texttt{<--} C_1 \text{ and } C_2 \text{ and } \ldots \text{ and } C_n$$
$$A ::= M_s \texttt{-->} R_1 \text{ and } R_2 \text{ and } \ldots \text{ and } R_n$$

where A is the identifier for an agent; M_s is a message sent to that agent; M_r is a message received by an agent; C_i are conditions which can be proved true in the agent and R_i are conditions which can be made true in the agent. In the remainder of this section we show how clauses of this form can be used to describe detailed decision procedures for the types of agent in our running example.

A trader in the agora can send an offer of stock to a broker if it knows the name of the broker and it has a surplus of stock above 50 units. A trader in the agora can send a request for stock to a broker if it knows the name of the broker and it has a deficit of stock below 50 units. More formally:

```
agent(agora,trader,_) ::=
  offer(stock,N) => agent(agora,broker,B) <--
    broker(B) and resource(stock,NS) and N is NS - 50 and N > 0.
agent(agora,trader,_) ::=
  request(stock,N) => agent(agora,broker,B) <--
    broker(B) and resource(stock,NS) and N is 50 - NS and N > 0.
```

The remaining cases are depicted in Appendix B.

4.4 Simulation Directly from Specification

We now have enough detail in the specification, both in possible interactions and in individual decision procedures, to run a simulation of the system. This could be done by translation to an execution language of choice or also by executing our specification directly, via a meta-interpreter.

Our specifications can be executed either sequentially or concurrently. In the former case, the meta-interpreter takes turns executing portions of each agent until it cannot progress due to an interaction (via message-passing) with another agent; the meta-interpreter then chooses another agent to execute portions of and so. In the concurrent execution, copies of the meta-interpreter are started up simultaneously each with the specification of the agent it should execute – the agents are independently executed by their meta-interpreter, provided adequate message-passing services are offered.

Ours is a sequential execution/simulation of our specification that can replicate runs – concurrent executions may be very difficult to re-enact when trying to debug or understand phenomena that took place. The sequential meta-interpreter, written in Prolog, we developed and employed can be obtained in [17]. It works as follows:

1. We supply the interpreter with a list of agents in our population and conditions for terminating the simulation.
2. Each agent in the list is replaced with a matching agent definition from the interaction clauses of Section 4.2.
3. The interpreter then attempts to expand appropriate subterms in the agent definitions according to the position of each subterm. For example if the definition is of the form A **then** B, the subterm A will be expanded before the subterm B.
4. Subterms corresponding to sending messages are expanded only when one of the decision procedure clauses of Section 4.3 permits it. The resulting message appears in the message queue.
5. Subterms corresponding to receiving messages are expanded only if a matching message is in the message queue. An appropriate reaction clause from Section 4.3 is matched and its consequences are made true in the agent.
6. This continues until no more rewrites of the current term are possible (in which case the interpreter may backtrack to search for alternatives) or the conditions for termination are satisfied.

The term constructed by this rewriting system represents the history of interaction in the simulation. An example of this sort of term is shown in Appendix C. This was produced for the simplest possible trading system, consisting of two traders ($a1$ and $a2$) and a broker. The appendix shows the formal structure of the constructed term and, in Fig. 4, we present the interactions which took place between agents. We can also analyse the interaction level of our specification for desirable/unwanted properties using standard model-checking techniques [1].

We now are in a position to return to the question with which we began Section 4: what features of individual agent structure could account for the increased delay in stabilisation with larger population sizes which we modelled in the previous section? Specifically, does the agent model we have just defined have

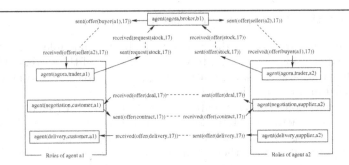

Fig. 4. Graphic Representation of Interactions in the 2-Agent Model

this sort of behaviour? To test this we run the model with increasing numbers of agents and measure the CPU time taken to obtain a uniform resource distribution (at a level of 50 units) and the number of rewrite steps contained in the final interaction term. The former is a measure of the amount of search needed to obtain a uniform distribution; the latter is a measure of the complexity of the distribution task. The table below shows results for models with 2, 4 and 6 trading agents:

Number of Traders	CPU Time	Rewrite Steps
2	70	19
4	220	40
6	6570	61

This shows that the number of rewrite steps needed to reach a stable resource distribution does not rise sharply with increasing numbers of trading agents but the CPU time taken to find the appropriate combination of rewrites rises very sharply. Most of the cost in CPU time for larger systems is in backtracking: when the simulator has to unravel a sequence of message passing which did not lead to a stable resource distribution. In other words, quite simple solutions to resource distribution problems may exist in this sort of agent model but simple negotiation strategies can take a very long time to discover them and are very likely to make local commitments which are sub-optimal for the global system.

5   A Lifecycle for Models of Large MASs

The basic idea grounding our methodology is that the two modelling views introduced in the previous sections, *i.e.* EBM and ABM, correspond to subsequent specification steps. We take the stance that in order to build a model for a society containing thousands or millions of agents, the general view provided by an EBM provides succint descriptions of population-level behaviours which we then attempt to replicate using models consisting of individual interacting agents, that is, the ABM. When dealing with a small number of interacting agents a different approach could be taken (*e.g.* [22]). Our proposed lifecycle is graphically depicted in Fig. 5. We note here that the focus of our attention is

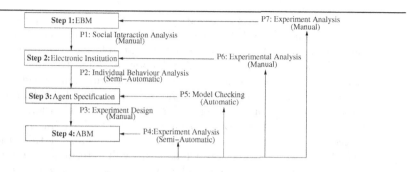

Fig. 5. A Lifecycle for Models of Large MASs

the *experimentation* of the interaction of groups of agents in a controlled environment with the general objective of giving insights for the design of MASs and not the *deployment* of stable agents.

An important characteristic of MASs from a software engineering perspective is the decoupling of two aspects: the interaction process between agents from the deliberative/reactive activity within each agent. This decoupling helps in simplifying the development of complex software systems and has guided methodological approaches [3,23]. We understand interaction as constrained by sets of norms that are enforced by an intermediation infrastructure [14,19,15,18]. The notion of *electronic institution,* as described in Section 4.1, plays this role in our methodology by establishing a framework that constraints and enforces the acceptable behaviour of agents. The different phases are:

Step 1 **EBM – Equation-Based Model**. In this first step, a set of state variables and equations relating them must be identified. These equations have to model the desired global behaviour of the agent society and will not contain references to individuals of that society. Typically these variables will refer to values in the environment and to averages of predictions for observable variables of the agents. Methodologically speaking, our approach has an essential difference with respect to the natural and social sciences that model their systems using EBMs. All other fields model *existing* systems: ecosystems, economies, physical systems, and so on. We, instead, are modelling yet-to-exist artificial systems. This distinction is crucial as the EBM is the starting point of the construction of a system that later on – once completely constructed – will be observed. Thus, a comparison between the EBM predicted behaviour and the actual ABM behaviour will be obtained.

Step 2 **EIM – Electronic Institution Model**. In this step the possible interactions among agents are the focus. It is a first "zoom in" of the methodology from the global view towards the individual models. The EBM obtained in the previous step determines different relations between environment variables and the agent society observables. These relations will now guide the building of an electronic institution permitting interactions between agents supported by the EBM. This step is not a refinement of the EBM but rather the design of a set of social interaction norms that are consistent with the relations established at Step 1. For instance, if in the EBM we model a global transfer of resources from a population of agents to another population of agents we will need to establish the means in the institution for the individual agents of these populations to interact for the individual transfers (aggregated in a variable in the EBM) to happen. Nonetheless, this is not enough since the designer will have to make new decisions at this stage, such as what type of interaction, what norms will determine each interaction and whether there are going to be contracts between agents, under which circumstances they will interact and so on. Additionally, constraints on the individual behaviours have to be established.

Step 3 **ABM – Agent-Based Model**. Here, we focus in the individual. We have to decide what decision models to use. This is the second "zoom in" of the methodology. Once the interaction conditions have been established, it is time in the methodology to design different agent models that will show an external behaviour that respects the interaction protocols and norms established in the EIM. For instance, when designing a "producer", the concrete strategy to interact – negotiate – with "consumer" agents, has to be decided. All admissible strategies could be explored at this stage – in principle, all strategies compatible with the EIM and EBM specified before. New elements of the requirement analysis (new variables) will be taken into account here. For instance, some rationality principles associated to agents (*e.g.* producers do not sell below production costs), or negotiation models to be used (*e.g.* as those proposed in [20]) have to be selected.

Step 4 **Multi-Agent System**. Finally, the last step of our methodology consists on the design of experiments for the interaction of very large numbers of agents designed in the previous step. For each type of agent the number of individuals and the concrete setting for the parameters will be the matter of decision here. The results of these experiments will determine whether the requirements of the artificial society so constructed have been consistently interpreted throughout the methodology and thus whether the expected results according to the EBM are confirmed or not. Moreover, our methodology permits the developer to establish at this step sets of formal and verifiable claims about the expected results and properties of the agents interaction in that particular experiment.

The different stages of the methodology are to be traversed from Step 1 to Step 4, that is, from the desired global behaviour down to the experiments. However, once the experiments designed at Step 4 are run and analysed, several redesigns are possible. Next, we enumerate the different feedback processes of the methodology:

P1 **Social Interaction Analysis**. Once the EBM has been constructed, the relations between the global variables and the analysis of the requirements of the society to model will determine what sort of agents exist (*i.e.* the roles), what sort of interactions the agents must have (*i.e.* the scenes), and what sort of transactions or dialogues they will have (*i.e.* ontology). This is an inherently manual process: there are many decisions to be made at this stage that have not been specified in the EBM. Experience in designing electronic institutions will help in deciding what scenes are most appropriate.

P2 **Individual Behaviour Analysis.** Once a complete picture of the institution is ready, the final aspect to consider is the modelling of the behaviour of the agents. Many aspects of this behaviour are already determined by the institution. The performative structure, the protocol of the scenes and the ontology definition enormously limit the repertoire of the decisions to be made by the agents [12,14,18], hence in many cases the behaviour is almost completely determined. For those aspects that are not completely determined the methodology strongly encourages the design of parametric decision models to fill in the gaps. These parameters will be used to set different experiments and will be the target of the agent design rules.

P3 **Experiment Design.** By choosing agents to participate with (possibly) different decision mechanisms, and by giving concrete values to the parameters of those decision mechanisms, different experiments can be constructed. The experiments should be set so as to explore all the possibilities and to see whether the EBM is making the right prognosis.

P4 **Experiment Analysis (ABM redesign).** The analysis of the experiments will be done by comparing the predicted values of the global variables by the EBM and the actual values of agent variables and their averages. Deviations on the values will be corrected at this stage by changes in the experiment design. That is, agent-based model parameter values will be changed. This phase will be semi-automatic, and we shall provide certain design rules that will determine what changes are to be made depending on the deviation detected, the current parameter value and the environment settings.

P5 **Model Checking.** The claims about the behaviour of a group of agents that the developer establishes when specifying an experiment will be model-checked [1] at this stage. The outcome of the model checking will help to change the agent-based models, *i.e.* change the decision-making models.

P6 **Experiment Analysis (EIM redesign).** Additionally, when the model checking determines that certain properties can never be guaranteed or that after several trials it is impossible to find parameter values that lead to the expected correct behaviour, different constraints over the agents interactions could be explored. This means that a redesign of the EIM may be in place. This is an intrinsically manual task.

P7 **Experiment Analysis (EBM redesign).** Finally, and if everything fails, it may happen that the part of the requirements that led to the initial EBM was misunderstood and that a variation in the initial EBM is necessary to explain why the experiments are showing a unexpected behaviours.

6   Conclusions and Directions of Research

Our proposal employs seemingly disparate approaches, equation-based (EBM) and agent-based modelling (ABM), to the task of modelling and analysing large MASs. System dynamics and EBM practitioners have a long-standing tradition with a successful record in modelling complex systems and analysing their results. By using EBMs as our initial step, we build on this success. ABM, on the other hand, has not been established as a rigorous practice and success may not be directly transferred from one experience to another because of the lack of standards and methodology.

The issue of scalability has been explicitly addressed by providing a means of modelling system behaviour "in the large", that is at a high level of abstraction at which instabilities in behaviour can be detected before the detailed design of the agents is carried out. This is in agreement with conventional wisdom in software engineering which advocates a top-down approach, on the grounds that it is easier/cheaper to identify/fix such problems before the detailed design of individual components has been carried out. The issue concerning the engineering of open systems has also been dealt with: we have made use of techniques for structuring the space of possible interactions within a MAS, creating areas in which interactions can be controlled, while leaving agents free to choose which areas they want to interact in. Since we can predict the interactions within the controlled areas, this allows us to ensure suitable system behaviour, while giving agents the freedom to choose where to interact ensures that the system is not closed.

EBM provides us with a technique for describing aspects of a MAS at a very abstract level, and then exploring its behaviour. This gives the designer of such a system a tool for ensuring that the overall shape of the system is within its design parameters. It provides a means of checking for stability, identifying if chaotic behaviour will occur, and ensuring that certain classes of agents can find a suitable niche to survive (or indeed will not find a niche if that is a desirable outcome). Thus equational modelling is a means of handling the scalability issue, by allowing some experimental guarantees that the MAS will behave as expected well in advance of its actual construction. When an EBM is built and tested, it provides a first, high level, specification of the system. However, EBMs concentrate on collective behaviour and interesting phenomena may only take place on an individual level. Negotiation [16] and argumentation [21], for instance, are two examples of interactions that are essentially and intrinsically performed among individuals. Agent-based modelling is called in as a means to address phenomena arising from the behaviour of individuals.

After the equational model has been developed, the next stage is to design the relevant electronic institutions. Once the institutions have been identified, the sets of actions they permit and the roles of the agents within them have been specified, they then place conditions on the agents which can use them. Thus, from the specification of an institution we can derive a partially-instantiated specification of an agent which can use that institution. This can then be fleshed out with what we might consider the "personality" of the agent, that is, the way that it operates within the rules of the institution. This refinement of the design of individual agents will be carried out in exactly the same way as for existing agent-oriented software engineering techniques.

We have devised a preliminary formalism and the underlying machinery for the specification of ABMs and their simulation. An appropriate interface for users to interact with experimental scenarios, that is, customising and changing parameters of agents, is under way. The specification of electronic institutions which will help define our experiments is a difficult and error-prone task. ISLANDER, a language to define institutions (and with which one can prove properties about it) has been defined with an associated visual tool to help the design (and test) of institutions [2,7].

Our experiments demonstrate fundamental limitations of size in multi-agent resource distribution systems. The basic structural problem is that negotiation strategies operate locally between agents, which seek individually to obtain resource stability. At a local level these choices may be rational. However, as we increase the size of the system the chances of a local decision being optimal with respect to global resource stability diminish. The time taken to reach stability tends to increase exponentially, as we saw in the agent model of Section 4. Furthermore, it may not be possible to know at any given point in the evolution of such a system whether or not we are converging on a stable distribution, since our experiments with a continuous flow model in Section 3 demonstrate that systems of very large size may produce complex patterns of oscillation. These oscillations, although repeating on a long time scale, may appear chaotic if observed only during a short segment of time.

There are two things to note here. The first is that these simulations are just another means of checking the design, one that operates at a lower level of abstraction than the equational model. We are not aiming to be able to directly execute the agents in a MAS. The entities in a simulation will be abstractions of the agents in the MAS itself. The second thing to note is that the simulations have an important complementary role to play alongside model checking. While model checking is to some extent a stronger way of verifying the behaviour of the system, in the sense that it is possible to prove that it behaves in a certain way, model checking itself is sufficiently computationally expensive that it is unlikely to be possible to model check an entire MAS at anything other than quite a high level of abstraction. But settling for the weaker guarantees offered by simulation, we can get results for a description of the MAS at a much lower level of abstraction.

Our proposed lifecycle for models of large MASs consists of constructive steps with connecting procedures/processes. Starting from an EBM, and following a sequence of well-defined processes, distinct stages/steps are reached with intermediate results that lead on to the final ABM. Some of the processes contemplate the analysis of such intermediate results with a view to correct or improve them (feedback). Ideally the activities of a lifecycle should be automatic, however in our proposal we have come across tasks that seem to be intrinsically manual, such as analysing the behaviours of an experimental electronic institution or the behaviours of an EBM.

The agents in our experimental framework have a clear distinction between their behaviour (as specified by the institutions they follow) and their decision procedures, that is, how agents decide on possible behaviours prescribed within an institution. This division is a profitable one: the behaviours of an institution can be proved/checked for desirable properties, and later run with different agents. The theoretical underpinning of institutions are finite state machines which enjoy desirable model-checking properties. Different languages can be used to define the decision procedures of agents. We have been experimenting with MABLE [24] a procedural language enriched with constructs from the agent-oriented programming paradigm. A MABLE system contains a number of *agents*, each of which has a *mental state* consisting of beliefs, desires and intentions; mental states may be nested, so that (for example), one agent is able have beliefs about another agent's intentions. MABLE agents are able to communicate with one-another using performatives in the style of the FIPA agent communication language [5].

Having developed a way of formally describing institutions in the language ISLANDER, we can do more than just identify the conditions that participation in an institution places upon agents. We can actually generate a partial specification of an agent automatically from the institution specification and the role (or roles) that the agent will play in the institution. Currently we translate the ISLANDER specifications into MABLE. The reason for doing this is that MABLE programs can be model checked. Thus we can take the specification of an institution and the conditions it imposes on agents that will use it and compile this into a partial MABLE program. It will be partial because the "personality" of the individual agents will be missing. Once these are added, it is possible to model check the resulting program, formally verifying the behaviour of the institution and the agents which will make use of it, allowing the system designer to check that undesirable conditions like deadlocks do not occur. If they do, then either the institution or the agent "personalities" need to be altered.

References

1. M. Benerecetti, F. Giunchiglia, and L. Serafini. Model Checking Multi-Agent Systems. *Journal of Logic and Computation*, 8(3):401–424, 1998.
2. M. Esteva and C. Sierra. ISLANDER1.0 Language definition. Technical report, IIIA-CSIC, 2001.
3. J. Ferber and O. Gutknecht. A Meta-Model for the Analisys of Organizations in Multi-Agent Systems. In *Proc. 3rd Int'l Conf. on Multi-Agent Systems (ICMAS-98)*, pages 128–135, Paris, France, 1998.
4. P. A. Fishwick. *Simulation Model Design and Execution: Building Digital Worlds*. Prentice-Hall, Englewood Cliffs, NJ, USA, 1995.
5. The Foundation for Intelligent Physical Agents. See http://www.fipa.org/.
6. A. Ford. *Modeling the Environment: An Introduction to System Dynamics Models of Environmental Systems*. Island Press, USA, 1999.
7. The ISLANDER Web-Page. http://www.iiia.csic.es/ISLANDER.html.
8. N. R. Jennings. On Agent-Based Software Engineering. *Artificial Intelligence*, 117:277–296, 2000.
9. N. R. Jennings and M. Wooldridge. Agent-Oriented Software Engineering. In *Handbook of Agent Technology*. AAAI/MIT Press, 2000.
10. J. O. Kephart and A. R. Greenwald. Shopbot Economics. In S. Parsons and M. J. Wooldridge, editors, *Proc. 1st. Workshop on Game Theoretic and Decision Theoretic Agents*, pages 43–55, 1999.
11. J. O. Kephart and A. R. Greenwald. Probabilistic Pricebots. In P. Gymtrasiewicz M. J. Wooldridge, editor, *Proc. 3rd. Workshop on Game Theoretic and Decision Theoretic Agents*, pages 37–44, 2001.
12. J. A. Rodríguez Aguilar, F. J. Martín, P. Noriega, P. Garcia, and C. Sierra. *Towards a Formal Specification of Complex Social Structures in Multi-Agent Systems*, pages 284–300. Number 1624 in LNAI. Springer-Verlag: Berlin, Germany, 2000.
13. R. Milner. *Communication and Concurrency*. Prentice Hall, 1989.

A Lifecycle for Models of Large Multi-agent Systems 313

14. P. Noriega and C. Sierra. Towards Layered Dialogical Agents. In J. P. Müller, M. Wooldridge, and N. R. Jennings, editors, *Intelligent Agents III (LNAI Volume 1193)*, pages 173–188. Springer-Verlag: Berlin, Germany, 1997.
15. P. Noriega and C. Sierra. *Auctions and Multi-Agent Systems*, pages 153–175. Springer-Verlag: Berlin, Germany, 1999.
16. S. Parsons, C. Sierra, and N. R. Jennings. Agents that Reason and Negotiate by Arguing. *Journal of Logic and Computation*, 8(3):261–292, 1998.
17. SLIE Project. Web-Pages of Research Grant **Sustainable Lifecycles in Information Ecosystems** (SLIE). http:// www.dai.ed.ac/groups/ssp/slie/, 2000.
18. J. A. Rodríguez, F. J. Martin, P. Noriega, P. Garcia, and C. Sierra. Towards a Test-Bed for Trading Agents in Electronic Auction Markets. *AI Communications*, 11(1):5–19, 1998.
19. J. A. Rodríguez, P. Noriega, C. Sierra, and J. Padget. A Java-based Electronic Auction House. In *2nd Int'l Conf. on Practical Applic. of Intell. Agents & Multi-Agent Technology (PAAM'97)*, pages 207–224, London, UK, 1997.
20. C. Sierra, P. Faratin, and N. R. Jennings. A Service-Oriented Negotiation Model between Autonomous Agents. In *MAAMAW'97*, number 1237 in LNAI, pages 17–35, Ronneby, Sweden, 1997. Springer-Verlag: Berlin, Germany.
21. C. Sierra, N. R. Jennings, P. Noriega, and S. Parsons. A Framework for Argumentation-Based Negotiation. In M. P. Singh, A. Rao, and M. J. Wooldridge, editors, *Intelligent Agents IV (LNAI Volume 1365)*, pages 177–192. Springer-Verlag: Berlin, Germany, 1998.
22. H. Van Parunak, R. Savit, and R. L. Riolo. Agent-Based Modeling vs. Equation-Based Modeling: a Case Study and Users' Guide. In *Proc. Workshop on Modeling Agent-Based Systems (MABS98)*, Paris, France, 1998.
23. M. Wooldridge, N. R. Jennings, and D. Kinny. The Gaia Methodology for Agent-Oriented Analysis and Design. *Journal of Autonomous Agents and Multi-Agent Systems*, 3(3):285–312, 2000.
24. M. J. Wooldridge and S. D. Parsons. MABLE: An Agent Programming Language and its BDI Semantics. Unpublished manuscript.

A Interaction Specification: Remaining Cases

A customer in a negotiation can receive an offer of a deal from a supplier; then offers a contract to that supplier and moves to the delivery scene; or refuses the deal and moves to the agora as a trader:

```
agent(negotiation,customer,X) ::=
    offer(deal,_) <= agent(negotiation,supplier,Y) then
    ( ( offer(contract,_) => agent(negotiation,supplier,Y) then
        agent(delivery,customer,X)) or
        ( refuse(deal,_) => agent(negotiation,supplier,Y) then
        agent(agora,trader,X) ) ).
```

A supplier in a negotiation scene sends an offer of a deal to a customer; then receives a contract from that customer and moves to the delivery scene; or receives a refusal from the customer and moves to the agora as a trader:

```
agent(negotiation,supplier,X) ::=
    offer(deal,_) => agent(negotiation,customer,Y) then
    ( ( offer(contract,_) <= agent(negotiation,customer,Y) then
        agent(delivery,supplier,X) ) or
```

```
(  refuse(deal,_) <= agent(negotiation,customer,Y) then
   agent(agora,trader,X) ) ).
```

A customer in a delivery scene receives notification of delivery or is informed of failure to deliver; then becomes a trader in the agora:

```
agent(delivery,customer,X) ::=
   ( offer(delivery,_) <= agent(delivery,supplier,Y) or
     inform(failure,_) <= agent(delivery,supplier,Y) ) then
   agent(agora,trader,X).
```

A supplier in a delivery scene sends notification of delivery or informs a customer of failure to deliver; then becomes a trader in the agora:

```
agent(delivery,supplier,X) ::=
   ( offer(delivery,_) => agent(delivery,customer,Y) or
     inform(failure,_) => agent(delivery,customer,Y) ) then
   agent(agora,trader,X).
```

This completes our specification of the potential interactions in the agent model.

B   Decision Procedures: Remaining Cases

A broker that receives a message offering stock or requesting stock from a trader notes that it received the message:

```
agent(agora,broker,_) ::
   offer(stock,N) <= agent(agora,trader,X) -->
     assert(made_offer(X,N)).
agent(agora,broker,_) ::
   request(stock,N) <= agent(agora,trader,X) -->
     assert(made_request(X,N)).
```

A broker in the agora sends an offer of a buyer, X, to a trader, Y, if Y has made an offer to the broker and X has made a request to the broker and the amount requested is at least as much as that offered. The broker forgets about the original offers and requests and notes that it has chosen a seller. A broker will offer a seller, Y, to a trader, X, if it has a note that it chose Y as a seller to X:

```
agent(agora,broker,_) ::
   offer(buyer(X),No) => agent(agora,trader,Y) <--
     made_offer(Y,No) and made_request(X,Nr) and Nr >= No and
     retract(made_offer(Y,No)) and
     retract(made_request(X,Nr)) and assert(chose_seller(X,Y,Nr)).
agent(agora,broker,_) ::
   offer(seller(Y),Nr) => agent(agora,trader,X) <--
     chose_seller(X,Y,Nr) and retract(chose_seller(X,Y,Nr)).
```

A trader in the agora that receives an offer of a buyer notes that it has a potential customer. A trader in the agora which receives an offer of a seller notes that it has a potential supplier:

```
agent(agora,trader,_) ::
  offer(buyer(X),N) <= agent(agora,broker,_) -->
    assert(customer(X,N)).
agent(agora,trader,_) ::
  offer(seller(Y),N) <= agent(agora,broker,_) -->
    assert(supplier(Y,N)).
```

A customer in a negotiation scene can offer a contract to a supplier if the amount of stock it would have if it accepts the amount on offer from the supplier would top up its stock to no more than 50 units. Otherwise, if the amount offered would increase its stock to more than 50, it sends a message refusing the deal:

```
agent(negotiation,customer,_) ::
  offer(contract,N) => agent(negotiation,supplier,Y) <--
    received_offer(Y,N) and resource(stock,NS) and
    NT is N + NS and NT =< 50 and retract(received_offer(Y,N)) and
    retract(supplier(Y,_)) and assert(contract_to_buy(Y,N)).
agent(negotiation,customer,_) ::
    refuse(deal,N) => agent(negotiation,supplier,Y) <--
        received_offer(Y,N) and resource(stock,NS) and
        NT is N + NS and NT > 50 and
        retract(received_offer(Y,N)) and retract(supplier(Y,_)).
```

A customer in a negotiation scene that receives an offer of a deal from a supplier notes that it received an offer:

```
agent(negotiation,customer,_) ::
  offer(deal,N) <= agent(negotiation,supplier,Y) -->
    assert(received_offer(Y,N)).
```

A supplier in a negotiation scene can send an offer of a deal to a customer if it has a surplus of stock above 50 units. It offers the whole surplus:

```
agent(negotiation,supplier,_) ::
  offer(deal,N) => agent(negotiation,customer,Y) <--
    customer(Y,NC) and resource(stock,NS) and
    NL is max(NS - 50,0) and N is min(NL,NC) and N > 0.
```

A supplier in a negotiation scene that receives an offer of a contract notes that it has a contract to deliver and deletes its note of a potential customer. If it receives a refusal of a deal it simply deletes its note of a potential customer:

```
agent(negotiation,supplier,_) ::
  offer(contract,N) <= agent(negotiation,customer,Y) -->
    assert(contract_to_deliver(Y,N)) and retract(customer(Y,_)).
agent(negotiation,supplier,_) ::
  refuse(deal,_) <= agent(negotiation,customer,Y) -->
    retract(customer(Y,_)).
```

A supplier in a delivery scene can send an offer of delivery to a customer if it has a contract to deliver to that supplier and it has a surplus of stock above 50 units which it can commit. Otherwise, it informs the customer of its failure to deliver:

```
agent(delivery,supplier,_) ::
  offer(delivery,N) => agent(delivery,customer,Y) <--
    contract_to_deliver(Y,NC) and resource(stock,NS) and
    NL is max(NS - 50,0) and N is min(NL,NC) and N > 0 and
    retract(contract_to_deliver(Y,N)) and decrement(stock,N).
agent(delivery,supplier,_) ::
  inform(failure,N) => agent(delivery,customer,Y) <--
    contract_to_deliver(Y,NC) and resource(stock,NS) and
    NL is max(NS - 50,0) and N is min(NL,NC) and N =< 0 and
    retract(contract_to_deliver(Y,N)).
```

A customer in a delivery scene that receives an offer of delivery deletes its note of a contract to buy and increments its stock by the amount committed. If it receives a message informing it of failure it deletes its contract note:

```
agent(delivery,customer,_) ::
  offer(delivery,N) <= agent(delivery,supplier,Y) -->
    retract(contract_to_buy(Y,_)) and increment(stock,N).
agent(delivery,customer,_) ::
  inform(failure,_) <= agent(delivery,supplier,Y) -->
    retract(contract_to_buy(Y,_)).
```

C   Formal Interactions in the 2-Agent Model

Given the specification above, we can simulate the interactions between agents for given sizes of rings. In the case of $\mathcal{R} = 2$, our interpreter obtains the term below, representing the sequence of message exchanges and changes in roles/scenes as the agents follow the electronic institution.

```
a(agent(agora,trader,a1),
  sent(request(stock,17)=>agent(agora,broker,b1)) then
  received(offer(seller(a2),17)<=agent(agora,broker,b1)) then
  a(agent(negotiation,customer,a1),
    received(offer(deal,17)<=agent(negotiation,supplier,a2)) then
    sent(offer(contract,17)=>agent(negotiation,supplier,a2)) then
    a(agent(delivery,customer,a1),
      received(offer(delivery,17)<=agent(delivery,supplier,a2)) then
      agent(agora,trader,a1)))),
  a(agent(agora,trader,a2),
    sent(offer(stock,17)=>agent(agora,broker,b1)) then
    received(offer(buyer(a1),17)<=agent(agora,broker,b1)) then
    a(agent(negotiation,supplier,a2),
      sent(offer(deal,17)=>agent(negotiation,customer,a1)) then
      received(offer(contract,17)<=agent(negotiation,customer,a1)) then
      a(agent(delivery,supplier,a2),
        sent(offer(delivery,17)=>agent(delivery,customer,a1)) then
        a(agent(agora,trader,a2),
        (offer(stock,_)=>agent(agora,broker,A) then
        offer(buyer(_),_)<=agent(agora,broker,A) then
        agent(negotiation,supplier,a2))or
        request(stock,_)=>agent(agora,broker,B) then
```

```
        offer(seller(_),_)<=agent(agora,broker,B) then
        agent(negotiation,customer,a2))))),
 a(agent(agora,broker,b1),
   (received(offer(stock,17)<=agent(agora,trader,a2)) par
    received(request(stock,17)<=agent(agora,trader,a1)) par
    sent(offer(buyer(a1),17)=>agent(agora,trader,a2)) then
    sent(offer(seller(a2),17)=>agent(agora,trader,a1))) then
    a(agent(agora,broker,b1),
      (offer(stock,_)<=agent(agora,trader,_) par
       request(stock,_)<=agent(agora,trader,_) par
       offer(buyer(_),_)=>agent(agora,trader,_) then
       offer(seller(_),_)=>agent(agora,trader,_)) then
       agent(agora,broker,b1)))
```

Author Index

Lecture Notes in Computer Science

For information about Vols. 1–2194
please contact your bookseller or Springer-Verlag